COMPLEX ORGANIZATIONS

COMPLEX ORGANIZATIONS:

A SOCIOLOGICAL PERSPECTIVE

J. Eugene Haas
Professor of Sociology
University of Colorado

Thomas E. Drabek
Associate Professor of Sociology
University of Denver

Macmillan Publishing Co., Inc.
NEW YORK
Collier Macmillan Publishers
LONDON

To Mary Helen and Ruth Ann

The Macmillan Company
866 Third Avenue, New York, New York 10022

Collier-Macmillan Canada, Ltd., Toronto, Ontario

Library of Congress catalog card number: 72–80179

Printing: 4 5 6 7 8   Year: 6 7 8 9

Material from *Organization and Environment: Managing Differentiation and Integration*, by Paul R. Lawrence and Jay W. Lorsch, has been quoted by permission of the Division of Research, Harvard Business School, Boston, the original publishers. Copyright 1967 by the President and Fellows of Harvard College.

Material from *Organizations in Action*, by James D. Thompson, copyright 1967 by McGraw-Hill Book Company, New York, has been used with permission of McGraw-Hill Book Company.

PREFACE

Throughout the past several years we have been involved in a variety of research projects focused on group and organizational functioning. Units selected for analysis have varied greatly in system complexity. They have ranged from large military installations and a major state university to small work groups of police officers and university students. Much of our work has been field research in communities that had just experienced large-scale natural disasters. In addition, we have investigated system stress in laboratory settings. Inter- and intra-organizational foci have been used depending upon the specific problem at hand.

Needless to say, many problems, both theoretical and methodological, have been confronted, examined, tentatively resolved, and then re-examined during these investigations. Through these studies and our efforts to learn from the work of others, a theoretical perspective for group and organizational analysis slowly has emerged. We believe that this perspective will be a significant aid to students of social organization. Although not yet a theory, it does provide a general orientation that can guide persons who are evaluating, designing, or conducting empirical research.

Preparation of this book has been guided by seven general objectives. First, we have attempted to provide a rigorous overview of the field for beginning students of complex organizations. Although this field has grown as an interdisciplinary one, we have strongly emphasized a sociological orientation. In doing so we have assumed the competence and background in sociology that are generally expected of advanced undergraduate students. But we have made every effort to minimize jargon in the hope that we can also communicate to students in related disciplines.

Second, we have viewed an integrated sociological conceptual framework for the analysis of groups and organizations as essential. In presenting this framework we have tried always to define concepts when introducing them and to use them consistently throughout. Some will find that our discussion of certain concepts commonly used in sociology, e.g., norm or role, is overly elementary at the outset. But these concepts form the foundation for much of what follows, and we have felt justified in this presentation because of the assumed diversity in audiences. The initiated may skim these sections rapidly.

Third, we have designed the conceptual framework to apply to systems with a variety of structural characteristics. The choice of such a framework reflects our belief that future comparative analysis will be most productive if analytical criteria are explicated and if miniature models are tested with systems that have common analytical characteristics. Students need to compare analyses of schools, prisons, business organizations, and the like, so as better to grasp the complexities of comparative analysis. There may be important differences among structures, but these differences remain submerged when specialists fail to compare notes. It is our conviction that future sociological theory will not reflect such simplistic "compartments" as are suggested by typical university curricula, e.g., crime, family, education, industry.

Fourth, we decided upon extensive coverage of what appeared to us to be significant variables and theoretical issues rather than intensive treatment of a selected few. This strategy would not be chosen by many, but it is in line with our initial objective of providing a broad introduction for the beginning student of organizations.

Fifth, we have placed much emphasis on organizational change, growth, stress, strain, and conflict. Too often, organizational analyses have been criticized for avoiding such topics and presenting a highly static image of organizational behavior. We agree that these criticisms are often legitimate, and we have tried to cope with them. Future empirical research will doubtless enhance our understanding of the more dynamic phenomena of organizations.

Sixth, we believe that beginning students should be introduced to the current dissensus about the relative utility of different theoretical strategies, basic presuppositional sets, psychological versus sociological perspectives, and the like. Although we have tried to present a coherent theoretical position, some discussion of alternative strategies and major points of dissensus was desired.

Seventh, and finally, we wish to give readers an introduction to several important research problems in group and organizational analysis. Discussion of some of the problems and procedures for the operational use of the framework proposed is necessary, we feel, to assist students to recognize the difficulties inherent in it and in other frameworks to which they might be exposed. Also, we believe that students should be introduced to several methodological innovations that have recently been applied to organizational analysis, innovations such as laboratory and simulation studies.

To accomplish these objectives, we emerged with a "plan of attack" that served as a general guide. As our work proceeded, some chapter titles were eliminated, e.g., socialization into organizations; a few were expanded, e.g., Chapter 9 on research strategies; and others were redesigned to reflect the imagery of our theoretical perspective as it became more crystallized in this writing process.

We begin the book with a brief statement about the nature of sociological theory. We believe (at least most of the time) that empirical research directed at the testing and clarification of theory can lead to a cumulative body of knowledge applicable under specified conditions. In the long run, theory that has been empirically verified through scientific research methods will prove more valuable to administrators and other practitioners than prescriptive statements about how organizations "ought" to behave under all conditions. Given this assumption, we propose that organizations be viewed as emergent phenomena comprised of the patterned interactions among participants. Such patterned interaction systems are defined as our objects of study. We discuss how interaction systems can be differentiated and why it is important to ask, "What analytical characteristics are posited to differentiate among systems?" "Why these characteristics, and not others?" Understanding the issues implicit in conceptualizations of types of systems, system boundaries, and system environments is essential if students are going to build on many of the perspectives currently in use. "What are organizations?" is a question we must take seriously. And in Chapter 1, we have tried to help students understand why this is so, as well as to provide one particular answer.

Students should be aware, however, that others have proceeded differently. Chapter 2 presents an extensive overview of eight "idea clusters" that have been pieced together with minimal forcing. Lumped together, these eight perspectives characterize the major orientations and assumption sets used by researchers today. Viewed singly, each suggests a contrasting image of organizations. Each presentation is organized uniformly with a brief historical sketch followed by a compact, and necessarily simplified, outline of the major themes. Illustrative propositions are stated, and difficulties inherent in each perspective are highlighted in a brief critique. Because of the breadth of the ideas selected, this chapter is somewhat lengthy. The eight "miniature snapshots" that comprise it are each reduced to the shortest discussion possible. However, footnote material can provide invaluable guidance for serious students.

In the next six chapters we present our own theoretical synthesis—a stress–strain perspective. Although structural variables like size, complexity, and formalization are important tools for organizational analysis, we prefer a more dynamic imagery right at the outset. For us, both order and change should be viewed as problematic. And excessive focus on structure too often blinds us to process. Thus, we posit at the outset that strains, tensions, and inconsistencies are found within all organizations—only the intensity, locations, and patterns vary. We also believe that organizational participants not only react to their environments, but also seek to act on them. And in this action–reaction process, strains within the organization and between it and various environmental sectors become altered.. Thus, strain is a critical concept for understanding internal organizational behavior, as well as that which occurs between the organization and key environmental sectors. Material presented in Chapters 3 through 8 outlines our exploration of this theme—one that permits a far more dynamic analysis than its alternatives.

Following Chapter 3, which presents an overview of the stress–strain perspective, we dig in. First, groups within organizations are discussed. We start here for two reasons. First, the conceptual framework we want to use to analyze organizations per se has parallels at the group level and is more easily presented initially with a simpler system as the unit of analysis. Second, we view organizations as phenomena that can be understood, in part, through analysis of the bargaining and negotiation struggles among participants within groups. Thus, starting with the internal dynamics of groups, we shift abstraction levels so as to focus next on organizations viewed as a network of groups. Then we shift once again and focus on relationships among organizations and key components of their environments. Finally, we look back at all of these referent systems with a specialized focus on strain, stress, and change.

Consistently, we have defined organizations as types of observable interaction systems. Others would not select this behavioral focus. But we are convinced that the correspondence between behavioral and normative systems must be viewed as problematic. Only in this way can we begin to devise research to ascertain analytical characteristics of types of normative systems that are accompanied by varying degrees of behavioral conformity.

In direct contrast to those who have posited an imagery of organizational participants as extreme conformists, which no doubt can be found in some instances, we emerged with more active creatures. We see normative, interpersonal, and resource structures constraining participant behavior. But there is "room for movement" within these structures—sometimes considerable room. And participants seek to enlarge their "living space" through a variety of strategies designed to increase the autonomy, security, and prestige of their respective groups. Thus, in contrast to those who posit organizations as phenomena that emerge from actors joining together to accomplish shared goals, we view organizations as reflections of continuing struggles among groups within and without. Through continual renegotiation efforts, participants within groups seek to redefine expectations held by others— expectations that often are vague and contradictory, and that are shifting constantly.

Projecting ourselves "above" the participants, in a helicopter, as it were, we find it is the patterns we see in these interactions that comprise the organization. And if we moved up a little "higher," in actuality shifting abstraction levels, we would "see" parallel processes occurring as organizational incumbents (our referent system) struggle with sectors of their environment. In all of these struggles, increases in autonomy, security, and prestige appear to be the desired aim, whatever the referent system. Whether or not this motivational mechanism and the strategies elicited will prove applicable to systems located in cultures other than ours remains a matter for future empirical inquiry.

But then, so does most of what we think we know about organizations in general. Certainly, it has been only in the past decade that American sociologists have outgrown their initial focus on pathology, social problems, and individual attitudes. Our knowledge base clearly lacks maturity. But simply more research, if poorly done, will not be of much help. How can the quality of organizational research be improved? Simple prescriptions may hinder more than they help. Thus, in the final chapter (9), we wrestle with this question. This chapter is intended as an introduction for students with minimal research experience and background. However, as in Chapter 2, wherein snapshots of various theoretical orientations are presented briefly, more serious students will find here that the footnotes can guide them into more detailed discussions of the issues raised.

Most would probably agree that our objectives were "noble." And at first glance the plan of attack might appear highly workable. But we are most aware of the limited degree to which the objectives were accomplished. However, if our efforts stimulate a few students to pursue some of the issues raised and to conduct more rigorous, theoretically significant research, then the efforts will have been worthwhile.

J. E. H.
T. E. D.

ACKNOWLEDG-
MENTS

Every author has a unique intellectual history that is dotted with persons to whom he is indebted for ideas, encouragement, and other forms of support. Because we have worked together throughout the past decade our histories overlap to a degree. But whereas there are persons to whom we are jointly indebted in a variety of ways, there are others whose influence was more direct on one or another of us.

As a beginning graduate student at UCLA, Haas worked with Philip Selznick, who made the study of organizations an exciting endeavor. Later, at the University of Minnesota, Henry W. Riecken, Roy G. Francis, and Marvin J. Taves provided the intellectual climate and assistance in securing financial support (National Institutes of Health) that made possible the study of hospital work groups. At The Ohio State University, Carroll Shartle and Raymond F. Sletto made available to Haas, as a new Assistant Professor, the time and facilities necessary to study a series of organizations. Frank Scarpetti, Norman J. Johnson, and Richard H. Hall made major contributions to that effort.

Through the guidance and encouragement of W. Arthur Shirey, longtime sociology chairman at the University of Denver, Drabek enrolled at The Ohio State University and enlisted Haas as his M.A. advisor. Haas's enthusiasm for organizational research proved contagious. Drabek joined his research team and greatly benefited from hours of dialogue with Johnson and Hall.

In 1963 the development of the Behavioral Sciences Laboratory and the Disaster Research Center at The Ohio State University made possible a series of both laboratory and field studies of organizations under simulated and actual disaster conditions. We worked together here and are both indebted to numerous DRC staff members, most especially E. L. Quarantelli, Russell R. Dynes,

Elaine S. Hobart, William A. Anderson, and Thomas Cree. Financial support and management for those studies came from Charles Hutchinson of the Air Force Office of Scientific Research and James Kerr of the Office of Civil Defense.

Upon leaving the Disaster Research Center in 1965, Drabek returned to the University of Denver where numerous students have provided continued stimulation that has been invaluable for his growth. William H. Key, a most effective administrator and perceptive organizational analyst, has been a major source of personal encouragement and has done much to create a climate wherein intellectual excellence is given top priority. Herman Sander, of the Air Force Office of Scientific Research, provided support that permitted exploration of many of the theoretical themes summarized in this book and an initial critique through a conference on organizational stress at which twelve persons offered numerous leads for alternative conceptualizations. Judy Chapman, Keith Boggs, and Boyd Littrell were most helpful during this phase. More recent empirical and theoretical continuity in the analysis of group and organizational responses to stress has been supported by Jack Weiner of the National Institutes of Mental Health.

Haas's research at the University of Colorado, where he has taught since 1967, has been focused on organization–environment interactions. This research has been supported by Peter Wyckoff and Fred White of the National Science Foundation, James Klaasse and Wilmot Hess of the National Oceanic and Atmospheric Administration, and W. R. John D. Kennedy of the National Center for Atmospheric Research.

As this book has gone through draft stages, several persons, with much patience and care, have typed and retyped that which finally emerged. We are most grateful to Deanna Nervig, Ruth Drabek, and Nancy Manzy for their efforts to make the manuscript as technically perfect as possible. Secretarial staff in the Department of Sociology at the University of Denver provided innumerable types of "backup" services for which we are appreciative.

In addition to numerous student critics who have been an invaluable source of help as we have tried to push ideas further and express them with greater clarity, detailed reviews were provided by James L. Price, James R. Wood, and Charles Perrow. As may be seen throughout the book, the work of James D. Thompson has left its imprint. We are grateful to the several authors and publishers who granted permission to reprint their work. Encouragement and technical assistance of Charles Smith, Kenneth Scott, and Frances Long of The Macmillan

Company brought the book to completion in fine order. Of course, remaining ambiguities, like errors of commission or omission, rest with us.

Finally, two persons loom most important for a type of support that only they can really understand. Without the continued encouragement of Mary Helen Haas and Ruth Ann Drabek, this book would have remained "a good idea we ought to talk over someday." And like other children who have had to live with parents while a book was being born, ours have been asked to make many sacrifices. However, Cindy, Mari, Debbie, and Russ have done so with more understanding than we had a right to ask.

J. E. H.
T. E. D.

CONTENTS

xiii

Chapter 8

ORGANIZATIONAL CHANGE

Types of System Change / Strain and the Change Process / Responses to Strain / Leadership for Self-renewal

Chapter 9

ORGANIZATIONAL RESEARCH STRATEGIES

What Do You Want to Know? / Where Can You Find the Phenomena You Want to Study? / What Do You Do When You Get There? / Toward a Science of Organizations

Chapter 1

WHAT ARE ORGANIZATIONS?

At first glance, the question raised by the Chapter title may appear unnecessary. Every American adult living during this period of history is aware of the complex networks of organizations that characterize our society.[1] Indeed, most of our time is spent in organizational settings. However, when organizations are analyzed in a rigorous and theoretical fashion, this question becomes highly important, for, as with any term used in a logical analysis, definitional variation at the outset will result in differences in conclusions. If organizations are to be our units of analysis, they must be defined. Criteria for membership and boundary identification also must be stipulated. Before attacking these problems, however, it would be advisable first to review a few notions about the scientific enterprise.

The Nature of Theory

The primary objective of sociological theory is to provide a basis for the prediction and explanation of social behavior. As an "article of faith," we proceed on the assumption that a theory of organizations is possible. By *theory* we mean "a set of inter-related constructs (concepts), definitions, and propositions that present

[1] See Presthus' book, and Boulding's, for excellent analyses of the emergence of large organizations in the United States.

Robert Presthus, *The Organizational Society* (New York: Vintage Books, 1962), pp. 59–92.

Kenneth E. Boulding, *The Organizational Revolution* (Chicago: Quadrangle Books, 1968), pp. 3–32 (original publication, 1953).

a systematic view of phenomena by specifying relations among variables, with the purpose of explaining and predicting the phenomena."[2]

It must be recognized at the outset that currently there is no generally accepted theory of organizations. There are many concepts that appear to be relevant. However, for the most part they are vague and often overlapping. Many prescriptive statements have been made as to how organizations ought to behave, but few of these have been rigorously tested. And propositions that have been tested are often at such a low level of abstraction that they usually appear to deal only with the obvious. Efforts to integrate these propositions into a coherent theory have met with little success.[3] Case studies have been written on single organizations and various subunits.[4] But it is not at all clear what comparative analyses, if any, can be made.[5]

The question then becomes, What is the best strategy to follow in attempting to develop a theory of organizations? There are almost as many answers to that question as there are writers in the field. These disagreements will be discussed in more detail in the next chapter. Because the present authors represent only one of the many theoretical positions that might be taken, it is desirable to explicate some of the major assumptions of our position.

Five assumptions are most critical. First, as already indicated, we have made the assumption that a theory of organizations is possible.[6]

[2] Fred N. Kerlinger, *Foundations of Behavioral Research* (New York: Holt, Rinehart, & Winston, Inc., 1964), p. 11.

[3] Among the better efforts at systematic inventorying of propositions are these:

Bernard Berelson and Gary A. Steiner, *Human Behavior, An Inventory of Scientific Findings* (New York: Harcourt, Brace, Jovanovich, Inc., 1964), pp. 325–382.

Joseph E. McGrath and Irwin Altman, *Small Group Research: A Synthesis and Critique of the Field* (New York: Holt, Rinehart, & Winston, Inc., 1966).

James L. Price, *Organizational Effectiveness: An Inventory of Propositions* (Homewood, Ill.: Richard D. Irwin, Inc., 1968).

[4] For example: Chris Argyris, *Organization of a Bank* (New Haven: Labor and Management Center, Yale University, 1954); William F. Whyte, *Human Relations in the Restaurant Industry* (New York: McGraw-Hill Book Co., 1948); Philip Selznick, *TVA and the Grass Roots* (Berkeley and Los Angeles: University of California Press, 1949); and Seymour M. Lipset et al., *Union Democracy* (New York: The Free Press, 1956).

[5] Scott reached a similar conclusion after completing his comprehensive review of organizational theory. W. Richard Scott, "Theory of Organizations," in *Handbook of Modern Sociology*, Robert E. L. Faris, ed. (Chicago: Rand-McNally, 1964), pp. 485–520.

[6] A complete presuppositional analysis is beyond our purposes here. But in making this assumption we are further assuming that reality exists, that reality can be known through sensory data, and that patterns and regularities characterize social phenomena. For extended discussion of the assumptions implicit in current social research, see Kerlinger, op. cit., pp. 3–50; and Abraham Kaplan, *The Conduct of Inquiry: Methodology for Behavioral Sciences* (San Francisco: Chandler Publishing Co., 1964).

Chapter 1. What Are Organizations?

Second, we assume that the components of such a theory will be constructs invented by scientists. Often these constructs may appear to conflict with "common sense," but that is not the criterion by which they are to be judged. Certainly, there was little common-sense basis for initially positing a multitude of constructs that are now commonplace to most grade school children—vitamins, atoms, gravity, energy, and the like. So it is with organizational theory. In contrast to agreement with "common sense," the utility of scientific constructs is to be judged on the basis of explanatory and predictive power.

Both of these assumptions are about methodology. We have also made three important assumptions pertaining to the substantive content of organizational theory. Thus, third, organizational behavior is assumed to be social in nature. And explanations of that behavior should remain at the social level rather than being "reduced" to psychological or biological levels.[7] Of course, a social psychological perspective is often useful for analyzing many of the types of questions that persons studying organizations wish to ask. For example, questions dealing with the interrelationships between individuals and social structures are very important. Such questions require a social psychological perspective. But when groups or organizations are used as units of analysis, a sociological perspective is required. Thus, we assume that each perspective is directed at different types of questions—each has its reason for existing.[8]

Fourth, theories of a "middle range" are assumed to be appropriate.[9] Rather than trying to develop a single comprehensive theory to explain all types of social behavior, a more productive strategy, it appears, for the present at least, is to focus on a general subtype of phenomena.

[7] A reductionistic position has been strongly advocated by Homans. George C. Homans, "Bringing Men Back In," *American Sociological Review*, 29: 809–18 (December 1964); and *Social Behavior: Its Elementary Forms* (New York: Harcourt, Brace, Jovanovich, Inc., 1961).

For rebuttals, see Guy E. Swanson, "On Explanations of Social Interaction," *Sociometry*, 28: 101–23 (June 1965); and W. Nevell Razak, "Razak on Homans," *American Sociological Review*, 31: 542–44 (August 1966).

[8] This is not to deny system interpenetration across levels. Thus, behavior systems at the social level affect and are affected by psychological, biological, and chemical systems. However, each level also is characterized by system independence. These ideas are elaborated in discussion of the "open system" perspective in the next chapter.

See also Marvin E. Olsen, *The Process of Social Organization* (New York: Holt, Rinehart, & Winston, Inc., 1968), pp. 4–7.

[9] Robert K. Merton, *Social Theory and Social Structure*, rev. ed. (New York: The Free Press, 1957), pp. 3–16.

Criticism and very helpful elaboration of Merton's concept have been provided by Willer. See David Willer, *Scientific Sociology: Theory and Method* (Englewood Cliffs, N.J.: Prentice-Hall, Inc., 1967), pp. xii–xvi.

Thus, although marriage, courtship, and crime are types of social behavior, these will not be our primary focus of concern.

Fifth, and finally, it has been assumed that groups and organizations are more meaningful analytical units than traditional "problem-oriented" approaches. It makes sense to us to compare prisons to religious organizations or clique formation in high schools to that found in industrial work groups. There are differences among organizations, but the differences are not that some are "good" and others "bad." By erecting barriers that impede comparison—e.g., typical university curricula—many significant commonalities remain submerged. Our preference is that analytical criteria be used as a basis for division, rather than historical accident. With these assumptions in mind, we can proceed to see what some of these analytical divisions might be.

Social Organization As an Approach to the Study of Human Behavior

Within sociology there are several general approaches that currently characterize the field. Some researchers prefer ecological or social psychological perspectives. The questions they ask and the techniques they use are very different from the perspective presented here. A social organizational perspective emphasizes that regularities and patterns characterize social behavior.[10] As a social creature, man is not entirely free to do as he wishes when he wishes. His behavior is continually being guided by the expectations that he perceives others hold for him. Social psychologists are interested in understanding how men perceive and internalize the expectations of others. Through what symbol manipulation processes do men decide on courses of action?[11] From a social organizational perspective, these questions are viewed as legitimate, but not exhaustive. Analysis of regularities in behavior patterns can also proceed at a higher level of abstraction. That is, patterned clusters of interaction such as groups and organizations may be selected as units of analysis instead of individuals. From a social psychological perspective, groups, organizations, and societies are viewed as constraint structures that define the limits of individual action. From a social organizational perspective, groups, organizations, and societies are viewed as interaction systems to be described and

[10] For excellent summaries of a social organizational perspective in sociology, see Scott Greer, *Social Organization* (New York: Random House, 1955); or W. Richard Scott, *Social Processes and Social Structure* (New York: Holt, Rinehart, & Winston, Inc., 1970).

[11] Current statements of the symbolic interactionist perspective include Arnold Rose, *Human Behavior and Social Processes* (Boston: Houghton Mifflin Co., 1962); and Jerome G. Manis and Bernard N. Meltzer, *Symbolic Interaction: A Reader in Social Psychology* (Boston: Allyn and Bacon, 1967).

explained as phenomena in themselves. However, there are many types of interaction systems that must be differentiated.

Some interaction systems are transitory and short-lived. For example, two strangers may interact for a couple of hours during a flight between Los Angeles and Chicago. Erving Goffman has aptly labeled this type of an interaction system an "encounter." [12] And whereas interaction systems vary in permanence, they also vary in structural complexity. A family group including a father, mother, and two children is different from a large organization such as Ford Motor Company or a major university. These two variables, permanence and complexity, can be used as the basis for constructing a typology of interaction systems.[13] Such a typology is outlined in Figure 1–1.

Several types of interaction systems are differentiated in the typology. However, each of the cells represents points on the continua rather than discrete categories. For example, Bales's research on group emergence illustrates this idea.[14] He analyzed the interactions among collections of students who were previously strangers as they met throughout the academic year in a classroom setting. There appeared to be definite phases that characterized the processes of group emergence.[15] Initially, much time was spent in "getting acquainted." As strangers became acquaintances, patterned sets of expectations emerged and each person found his own niche. A collection of persons who were initially strangers became a group.

When does a gathering become a group? Before this question can be

[12] Erving Goffman, *Encounters* (Indianapolis, Ind.: Bobbs-Merrill, 1961). Goffman used "degree of focus" as the basic variable here, but suggested that "focussed interaction occurs when people effectively agree to sustain for a time a single focus on cognitive and visual attention, as in a conversation, a board game, or a joint task sustained by a close face-to-face circle of contributors" (p. 8). "Degree of focus" and "degree of permanence" are not identical but appear to be related. It will undoubtedly prove necessary to make these and additional distinctions in the future.

[13] These two variables were selected because of their theoretical significance. But it is clear that a more elaborate typology is essential so that many types of social units can be differentiated. Certainly, social units vary in degree of task specificity, boundary rigidity, membership requirements, etc. Our objective then would be to differentiate among interaction systems with different analytical characteristics so as eventually to test hypotheses applicable to each cell of the typology. Willer's discussion of the derivation of "conditional universals" is especially helpful in describing this approach (Willer, op. cit., pp. 97–115). The implications are discussed further in Chap. 9.

[14] Robert F. Bales, "The Equilibrium Problem in Small Groups," in *Small Groups*, A. Paul Hare et al. (eds.), (New York: Alfred A. Knopf, Inc., 1961), pp. 424–56; and Robert F. Bales, *Interaction Process Analysis* (Reading, Mass.: Addison-Wesley Publishing Co., 1950).

[15] Theodore M. Mills, *The Sociology of Small Groups* (Englewood Cliffs, N.J.: Prentice-Hall, Inc., 1967), pp. 17–23; and Theodore M. Mills, *Group Transformation* (Englewood Cliffs, N.J.: Prentice-Hall, Inc., 1964).

FIGURE 1–1 A Typology of Interaction Systems

Degree of Permanence	Degree of Complexity			
	Low			High
Relatively Permanent	Groups	Organizations	Communities	Societies
Relatively Transitory	Gatherings	Emergent Organizations	Synthetic Organizations	Social Movements

answered, much more empirical work must be completed on processes by which each is characterized. Available evidence does suggest that important qualitative differences may exist between groups and gatherings.[16] As Goffman has stated, "a crucial attribute of focused gatherings—the participants' maintenance of continuous engrossment in the official focus of activity—is not a property of social groups in general, for most groups, unlike encounters, continue to exist apart from the occasions where members are physically together. A coming-together can be merely a phase of group life; a falling away, on the other hand is the end of a particular encounter."[17] Certainly, most gatherings never become groups. And when they do, the changes that occur are not altogether clear. By viewing gatherings and groups as polar extremes on a continuum, differences in processes can be investigated empirically. Also highlighted for empirical investigation are the processes involved in the states of transition when a particular gathering continues to persist over time and gradually takes on the characteristics of a group.

For lack of a better term, "emergent organizations" is the label used to specify transitory interaction systems that are structurally more complex than gatherings. Following crisis events such as community disasters, many interaction systems can be observed that fit the criteria of this category. Spontaneously emerging search and rescue collectivities and the like pervade in such areas.[18] They emerge, function for a while, and then disappear as community life returns to normality.

[16] Thomas E. Drabek and J. Eugene Haas, "Realism in Laboratory Simulation: Myth or Method?" *Social Forces*, **45**: 337–46 (March 1967).

See also Bartolomeo J. Palisi, "Some Suggestions about the Transitory–Permanence Dimension of Organizations," *British Journal of Sociology*, **21**: 200–206 (June 1970); and Charles K. Warriner, "Groups Are Real: A Reaffirmation," *American Sociological Review*, **21**: 594–54 (October 1956).

[17] Goffman, op. cit., p. 11.

[18] For detailed description of the emergence and functioning of such groups, see James B. Taylor, Louis A. Zurcher, and William H. Key, *Tornado* (Seattle: University of Washington Press, 1970), pp. 79–108. In addition, "ephemeral" institutions and government are discussed following the 1966 tornado in Topeka, Kansas.

Short-lived fund-raising efforts and transitory political action groups are other examples of this type of interaction system.

The permanence axis of the typology emphasizes system change. Hence, as in the instance of less complex interaction systems—i.e., groups and gatherings—two polar extremes on a continuum are identified. And the change processes through which some emergent organizations may survive their "liability of newness" become highlighted as a crucial problem to be empirically investigated. Stinchcombe suggests that new organizations are confronted with four major types of problems: (1) new roles must be learned for which there may not be any existing role models; (2) new roles must be defined and interrelated, and appropriate rewards and sanctions must be structured; (3) because strangers will most likely constitute much of the work force, a reasonable degree of trust must emerge among them; and (4) environmental relationships among suppliers, customers, and the like must be developed.[19] Thus, some emergent organizations will persist over time. However, we need to know much more about the processes of change involved. Equally important is knowledge about highly transitory systems, many of which are not intended to persist beyond a limited time. Thus, the typology highlights distinctions among highly transitory and more permanent organizations. Further, it emphasizes the need for empirical research on the change process by which some new organizations continue to persist.

At a more complex level, yet equally transitory, are synthetic organizations. Again, community responses to disaster provide excellent examples. Thompson and Hawkes have made an outstanding summary of several disaster case studies with this concept as their basic theme.[20] At the community level, new interorganizational alliances are required to cope with disaster demands. And coordination among emergency organizations and other types of organizations with needed resources, results in the emergence of a new "super structure" whereby the "mass assault" can take place more effectively. Thus, local personnel in police organizations, civil defense units, fire departments, the Red Cross, the Salvation Army, and the like discover that their efforts must be more highly coordinated than under nondisaster conditions. And a synthetic organization frequently emerges as coordination efforts become intensified. As the demands caused by the disaster are met, the synthetic organization dissipates but often not without argument as to allocation

---

[19] Arthur L. Stinchcombe, "Social Structure and Organizations," in *Handbook of Organizations*, James G. March, ed. (Chicago: Rand-McNally & Company, 1965), pp. 148–50.

[20] James D. Thompson and Robert W. Hawkes, "Disaster, Community Organization and Administrative Process," in *Man and Society in Disaster*, George W. Baker and Dwight Chapman, eds. (New York: Basic Books, Inc., 1962), pp. 268–300.

of responsibility. Most likely, the community will return to a structure nearly identical to that existing before the disaster with each separate emergency organization operating in a much more autonomous fashion than it did during the emergency period.[21]

Finally, at even a more complex level, social movements can be specified. A recent example is the network of interaction systems that comprised the civil rights movement throughout the 1960s. Thus, although each of these types of interaction systems varies in degree of structural complexity, they are all characterized by being relatively transitory.

Relatively permanent interaction systems that are less structurally complex than communities and societies will be the focus of our concern. But it is crucial to recognize clearly that there are other types of interaction systems that have different analytical properties from groups or organizations. Also, note that we conceptualize organizations as *interaction systems rather than collections of individuals*. Given these ideas, how might the term *organization* be defined?

Organizations: Definition of the Concept

An organization is defined as *a relatively permanent and relatively complex discernible interaction system*.[22] Organizations can be observed as a series of patterned interactions among actors. However, it is not the collection of actors that is our focus but, rather, the interaction among them. We posit that a reality exists that is something other than the sum of the individual parts.[23] Three components of the definition require further elaboration.

First, interaction systems designated as organizations are relatively permanent. Although this implies greater stability over time, the degree of stability required is relative. All interaction systems are in a constant state of flux. But for an interaction system to be labeled an organization, it must have a high enough degree of stability to be

---

[21] Disaster experience may precipitate important changes. For example, following a large explosion in Indianapolis in 1963, emergency organizations were severely hampered in their efforts to help by an inability to communicate directly with local hospitals. Following the event, an interhospital communication network was established whereby all hospitals and several emergency organizations can now communicate by means of a radiotelephone system. See Thomas E. Drabek, *Disaster in Aisle 13* (Columbus, Ohio: College of Administrative Science, Ohio State University, 1968).

[22] Groups are defined as relatively permanent and relatively simple discernible interaction systems.

[23] A classic elaboration of this position is Emile Durkheim, *Rules of the Sociological Method*, trans., Sarah A. Solovay and John Mueller (New York: The Free Press, 1964) original publication, 1895.

observable over time. Yet, how permanent is "relatively permanent"? The answer at present remains empirically unexplored. However, it does appear that qualitatively different processes operate in both organizations and groups when compared to more transitory systems such as gatherings and emergent organizations. The important point is to recognize the variable of permanence. As previously indicated, available empirical evidence indicates that different processes are found in highly transitory systems when compared to more stable and permanent interaction systems. But much additional empirical work is required before the implications of this continuum will be clearly understood. For the present, however, we may conclude that interaction systems that share a high degree of permanence appear to have other processes in common so as to permit comparative analysis regardless of other differences. Thus, if we disregard matters of purpose and consider only the way organizations function, we may more easily compare the functioning of the Roman Catholic Church with that of a long-standing crime syndicate than with the functioning of a newly emerging revivalist sect.[24] As more empirical research is completed, differences in organizational functioning due to degrees of permanence will be of much help in refining the typology. For the present, however, the distinction has much heuristic value as a crude classification device for this highly significant variable.

Second, organizations are distinct from groups and societies in terms of structural complexity. Again, the division points are somewhat arbitrary at present—i.e., should two, three, or four structural levels be used as the cut-off point? Structural complexity refers to both horizontal and vertical differentiation. Thus, as there is an increase in division of labor, organizations increase in horizontal complexity. As this occurs, new vertical levels may emerge to provide for regulation and control processes. Often, reference is made to "tall" or "flat"

[24] Degree of permanence has been implicitly included in several major previous typologies. For example, what Michels described as the "Iron Law of Oligarchy" is suggestive of the significance of this variable; Robert Michels, *Political Parties*, trans., Eden Paul and Cedar Paul (New York: The Free Press, 1949), original publication 1915.

More analytically, Trolesch, Weber, Becker, and others implied that the degree of permanence was a critical variable in church-sect analyses, e.g., Howard Becker, "Four Types of Religious Organizations," in *Complex Organizations: A Sociological Reader*, Amitai Etzioni, ed. (New York: Holt, Rinehart, & Winston, Inc., 1961).

Similarly, Zald and Ash have emphasized support for Michels' argument after analyzing emergent civil rights organizations. "As a social movement organization attains an economic and social base in society, as the original charismatic leadership is replaced, a bureaucratic structure emerges, and a general accommodation to the society occurs" (p. 327), Mayer N. Zald and Roberta Ash, "Social Movements of Organizations: Growth, Decay, and Change," *Social Forces*, 44: 327–39 (March 1966).

organizational structures when referring to variation in the number of vertical levels. And each of these aspects of complexity can be subdivided into several more specific indexes, e.g., number of departments, number of committees, and the like.

Some organizational theorists have tried to use absolute size (number of members) as a criterion to distinguish between groups and organizations.[25] Although somewhat similar to structural complexity, this criterion has proved less adequate. Empirical evidence strongly suggests that size is not always correlated with complexity.[26] Some organizations are very large in membership but have relatively simple structures, e.g., the Farm Bureau Federation or the Unitarian church. Others may be quite small in membership but highly complex in structure, e.g., small television stations or community hospitals.

A few theorists have proposed presence or absence of "face-to-face" or "one-to-one" interaction as a criterion with which to differentiate between groups and organizations.[27] Communications in organizations will frequently be directed through many positions before arriving at the intended recipient. However, this is but one of the many indicators of the structural complexity of the interaction system. As with permanence, the crucial point is to recognize the variable and the continuum. Rather than quibble about whether an interaction system is a group or an organization, it appears that a far better strategy is to recognize these two continua and to refrain from making hard distinctions by fiat. When sufficient empirical findings have been obtained in the future, then decisions as to one, two, three, or more discrete categories can be made. Clearly, groups appear to function in qualitatively different ways from gatherings. Similarly, organizations appear to be different from groups. But to move from the continua of permanence and complexity to discrete categories with hard lines will not prove productive at present—and may not even in the future.

Finally, organizations are viewed as interaction systems. There are several important ideas implied here. First, interaction refers to a process of mutual and reciprocal influencing by two or more persons. As our interest is limited to human organization, we focus especially on symbolic interaction. Whereas ants and bees may interact in one sense of the term, we assume that "man is a symbol manipulator, the only

[25] Theodore Caplow, *Principles of Organization* (New York: Harcourt, Brace, Jovanovich, Inc., 1964), pp. 25–28.

[26] Richard H. Hall, J. Eugene Haas, and Norman J. Johnson, "Organizational Size, Complexity, and Formalization," *American Sociological Review*, 32: 903–12 (December 1967); and J. Eugene Haas, Richard H. Hall, and Norman J. Johnson, "The Size of the Supportive Component in Organizations: A Multi-Organizational Analysis," *Social Forces*, 42: 9–17 (October 1963).

[27] For example, Presthus, op. cit., p. 11; and Harold Guetzkow, "Relations among Organizations," in *Studies on Behavior in Organizations*, Raymond V. Bowers, ed. (Athens, Ga.: University of Georgia Press, 1966), p. 14.

symbol-manipulating animal and the only animal whose social group-ings depend on and are pervaded by complex symbolic processes." [28] Such interaction, however, may be verbal, nonverbal, spoken, written, and so forth. And in highly technological systems, most interaction is indirect. Men on an assembly line, for example, may be viewed as an interaction system even though they might never speak to one another verbally. Thus, we view interaction as a broad term that includes such highly patterned sets of events. Behaviors by A influence B's behavior, which in turn influences C, and so on. When organizations are viewed as interaction systems, such patterened sets of behaviors are empha-sized.

Second, organizations are more than the simple additive sum of their parts. Although this appears to be a very simple idea, the implications are most complex. For example, if all of the parts of an automobile were laid on a large table in random array, one would not have an automobile. It is the unique series of *interdependent relationships* that exist between the parts that characterize the automobile. So it is with organizations. And the significant implication here is that one would gain little insight into either the automobile or the organization by measuring each of the parts independently.[29] Thus, both theoretical concepts and methodological strategies in organizational research must be directed at the interrelationships among the parts, characteristics of the functioning whole, and relationships between the whole and its environment.

Third, in all systems, be they social, technological, or astronomical, the criterion of greatest importance is that of interdependence. The components of systems are interrelated, so that a change in one will cause changes of various types in all others. However, neither the in-tensity nor type of changes caused are uniform throughout. And many of the changes may be indirect. The causal sequence that brings an automobile to stop as the brake pedal is pumped is a simple example.[30]

---

[28] Alfred R. Lindesmith and Anselm L. Strauss, *Social Psychology*, 3rd ed. (New York: Holt, Rinehart, & Winston, Inc., 1968), p. 7.

[29] This point has many implications for empirical research, which will be explored in chap. 9.

[30] Hans Zetterberg's analysis is most helpful in recognizing several varieties of causal linkages. He suggests that at least six types can be differentiated. A relation may be (1) *reversible* (if x, then y; and if y, then x) or irreversible (if x, then y; but if y, then no conclusion about x); (2) *deterministic* (if x, then always y) or *stochastic* (if x, then probably y); (3) *sequential* (if x, then later y) or *coextensive* (if x, then also y); (4) *sufficient* (if x, then y, regardless of anything else) or *con-tingent* (if x, then y, but only if z); (5) *necessary* (if x, and only if x, then y) or *substitutable* (if x, then y; but if z, then also y); and (6) *interdependent* (small in-crement in x results in a small increment in y, and the increment in y makes pos-sible a further increment in x, and so on). Hans L. Zetterberg, *On Theory and Ver-ification in Sociology*, 3rd ed. (Totowa, N.J.: The Bedminster Press, 1965), pp. 69–74.

FIGURE 1-2 Henderson's Diagram of a System

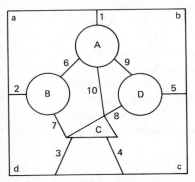

SOURCE: L. J. Henderson, *Pareto's General Sociology*, Cambridge, Mass.: Harvard University Press, 1937, pp. 13–14, as cited in *Sociological Research*, Matilda White Riley, New York: Harcourt, Brace, Jovanovich, Inc., 1963, p. 10.

Interdependence as it is found in social systems is far more complex. The imagery implied is perhaps best communicated in the following analogy discussed by Henderson (see Figure 1–2).

The four rigid bodies, A, B, C, and D are fastened to a framework . . . by the elastic bands 1, 2, 3, 4, and 5. A, B, C, and D are joined one to another by the elastic bands 6, 7, 8, 9, and 10. . . . Now imagine the point of attachment of 5 on the frame to be moving toward B, all other points of attachment remaining unchanged. What will happen? Consider A. There will be action on A by the path 5, 9, by the path 5, 8, 10, and by the path 5, 8, 7, 6. But in each case these actions do not cease at A, just as they do not previously cease at D. The first, for example, continues along the path 10, 8, and so back to 5.[31]

As is reflected in the recent works of Katz and Kahn, and also Thompson, organizations should be viewed as "open systems." [32] When so viewed, organizational boundaries lack the rigidity implicit in much research. Boundaries are not viewed as concrete realities but as abstractions to be deduced from many varieties of behavior. As open systems organizations are in constant interaction with aspects of their environment. When viewed in this way three central problems that have plagued organizational theorists become recast in an exciting

[31] Lawrence J. Henderson, *Pareto's General Sociology* (Cambridge, Mass.: Harvard University Press, 1937), pp. 13–14, as cited in *Sociological Research*, Matilda White Riley (New York: Harcourt, Brace, Jovanovich, Inc., 1963), p. 10.
[32] Donald Katz and Robert L. Kahn, *The Social Psychology of Organizations* (New York: John Wiley & Sons, Inc., 1966); and James D. Thompson, *Organizations in Action* (New York: McGraw-Hill Book Co., 1967).

way: (1) organizational membership; (2) organizational boundaries; and (3) organizational environments.

Organizational Membership

At first glance, the question of membership appears simple; either an individual is a member or is not a member. But there are several important points to be made. First, persons belong to several groups and organizations simultaneously. And at times this fact has significant consequences for all systems in which the individual has membership.[33] Strains emerge because of conflicting demands presented by the different systems. For example, the strain is apparent when a husband is required to work weekends, which his family may regard as "their" time. Similarly, friendships that emerge through Rotary, Lions, Kiwanis, and the like can affect many types of business decisions. Thus, it is important to recognize that individuals simultaneously occupy positions in several social systems.

Much organizational research has focused only on upper-echelon incumbents. As sociologists moved from business organizations to prisons, schools, and hospitals, it became clear that "lower participants," as Etzioni labeled them, were most influential in ordering the operations in these types of organizations.[34] This is revealed in the creative work of Gresham Sykes[35] in which he illustrates how, with the intent of rehabilitation, prison guards often lose their authority as they are hoodwinked and fooled by prisoners. Thus, patients, students, prisoners, among others, cannot be overlooked if many facets of organizational functioning are to be understood.

Homans, Merton, and others have wrestled with the problem of membership definition. Homans chose to emphasize frequency of interaction. That is, if A, B, C, and D interact far more frequently with one another than they do with E, then E can be considered as being outside the group.[36] Merton accepted this criterion, but suggested two additional requisites: (1) "that the interacting persons define themselves as

[33] Killian's analysis of the role conflict experienced by public officials in communities struck by disaster is an excellent illustration. Lack of knowledge about their families' safety created much personal stress, because they felt highly obligated to remain "at their posts." Lewis M. Killian, "The Significance of Multiple Group Membership in Disaster," *American Journal of Sociology*, **57**: 309–314 (January 1952).

[34] Amitai Etzioni, *A Comparative Analysis of Complex Organizations* (New York: The Free Press, 1961), pp. 17–19.

[35] Gresham Sykes, "The Corruption of Authority and Rehabilitation," *Social Forces*, 34: 257–62 (March 1956).

[36] George Homans, *The Human Group* (New York: Harcourt, Brace, Jovanovich, Inc., 1950), pp. 82–86.

'members,' i.e., that they have patterned expectations of forms of inter-action which are morally binding on them and on other 'members' but not on those regarded as 'outside' the group";[37] and (2) "that the persons in interaction be defined by others as 'belonging to the group,' these others including fellow-members and non-members." [38]

Merton's criticism of Homans is valid. Criteria in addition to "fre-quency of interaction" are required. But if Merton's suggestions are followed, one finds that these same concepts (i.e., "patterned expecta-tions"), used to define membership, are then used to account for the observed group behavior. Criteria proposed for the identification of the behavior patterns that one wishes to explain are built into the concep-tual apparatus, which is then used for explanation. Thus, the reasoning has become circular.

It is preferable to make a distinction between criteria that specify the object of study and those used to explain the behavior of that object. Interactions, not thoughts of actors, should serve as the basis for defin-ing membership. Two criteria seem appropriate: (1) frequency of in-teraction; and (2) content of interaction. Interaction among persons is observed over time. Those interaction units that are judged by the analyst as being high in frequency and similar in content constitute the interaction system.[39] Organizational membership is thereby defined using criteria based on the interaction itself without reference to ideas of actors as explanatory variables. And the degree to which normative expectations correspond to behavior can then be investigated; it be-comes problematic rather than definitional.[40]

The reader then is no longer concerned with the concept of member-ship as it is usually defined—i.e., specification of a biological entity (person) who is or is not a member of an organization. Rather, from this perspective, the "parts" of an organization are not persons but units of interaction. Let us now turn to the implications of this view for determination of organizational boundaries.

---

[37] Merton, *Social Theory and Social Structure*, op. cit., p. 286.

[38] Ibid.

[39] "Systems" connotes, as previously emphasized, the criterion of interdependence. Miller has put it less specifically, but similarly, by defining system as ". . . a set of units with relationships among them . . . the word 'set' implies that the units have common properties." James G. Miller, "Living Systems: Basic Concepts," *Behav-ioral Science*, 10 (July 1965), 200.

Thus, content of the interaction is used to determine not only "commonness" but also interdependence. Operationally, repetitive patterning of sequences of inter-action is used as an indicator of interdependence.

[40] Merton recognized this problem in later discussion of "degrees of membership," i.e., group expectations seem to be more binding for some members than others. Merton, op. cit., pp. 287–97.

Organizational Boundaries

If an organization is conceptualized as a relatively complex and relatively permanent interaction system, then to identify such a unit for analysis, we propose that interaction ought to be observed. Membership is decided on the basis of two criteria. (1) frequency of interaction; and (2) content of interaction. Boundaries of the interaction system are viewed as loose rather than rigid, open rather than closed.

To illustrate these ideas, assume that an analyst has observed a massive amount of interaction over a period of several weeks. This interaction has occurred through a variety of ways—i.e., face to face, telephone, telegraph, letter, memo, and so on. And each of these interaction units has been coded as to frequency and content and placed on a chart such as Figure 1–3. Using these criteria, the analyst might draw a dotted line around the collection of interaction units that he chose to designate as "the organization"—his unit of analysis. These recurring (frequency) patterns of interaction would comprise the system (content) toward which his analysis would be directed.

At first glance, the criterion of "common content" may appear to be so vague as to be of limited utility. But the flexibility is necessary. For we must recognize at the outset that analysts will need to specify organizational boundaries at very different places depending upon their research interests. At times, central organizational task might be used as the basis for content decisions. And, if interested, analysts could relate highly varied interaction sequences so as to include the entire gamut of organizational activity, ranging from top level policy decisions to routine procurement actions, to janitorial activity, and so forth. In descriptive case studies or when investigating the functioning of a total organization, boundary limits will be quite broad. Frequently, however, analysts have more focused interests. Desiring to compare major decision-making patterns among several organizations, an analyst might draw very narrow boundaries so as to include only upper-level personnel. And in the same study he might redraw his boundaries so as to compare communication channels in several different organizations. Thus, boundary decisions must be determined mainly by the questions being asked. And there is no simple, explicit set of procedures that will fit all, or even most, cases.

Specific procedures for combining the criteria of frequency and content must be explored and made more explicit. But it is clear that frequency is insufficient as a sole criterion. In Figure 1–3, for example, one frequently occurring interaction unit might be that of a man and his wife whom he telephones daily at noon. This interaction unit would not be defined as within the focal system despite high frequency, because of content. Discussion of family affairs, children's problems, and

FIGURE 1–3   Illustration of Organizational Boundaries

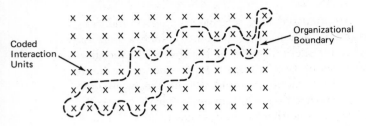

Coded Interaction Units

Organizational Boundary

so on, would be dissimilar from content of other interaction units that make up the organization.

However, the wife might be involved in the organization. She might advise her husband daily how to vote on policy decisions. Although seemingly difficult and perhaps exceptional at first, the example raises a generic problem—intersystem interaction. What is frequently discussed as interorganizational interaction is similar—that is, instances where one end of the interaction unit is in one system and the other lies in a different system. Sales personnel interacting with procurement or purchasing agents of other organizations are good examples. This "system overlap" is illustrated in Figure 1–4.

Thus, interaction among sales and procurement personnel of two different organizations is viewed as partially overlapping each of the systems. Similarly, the overlap may be among organizations and other types of social systems, such as families, bowling groups, and so on.

The boundary problem is a tough one, and many implications remain to be thought through more rigorously. Certainly the "overlap" idea is helpful. The basic criterion seems to be implicit in the following question: Does the continued occurrence of the interaction depend on one or more systems? That is, the analyst must decide whether or not the continuation of the interaction is *controlled* exclusively or principally by one system. If it is controlled by more than one system it is by definition intersystem interaction. Salesman–procurement agent interaction is clearly controlled by two systems. It may be terminated or altered by changes in other interaction units within either or both systems. Similarly, organizationally relevant interaction, such as might occur between a husband and his wife, is viewed as being within the system, i.e., the organization. Interaction with differing content between these same two persons—e.g., about children's music lessons—is viewed as being part of a different system, the family.

In summary, then, organizations as interaction systems can be identified. Boundaries can be established. But these interactions, defined as an organization on the basis of frequency and content, are patterned

FIGURE 1–4 Illustration of System Overlap

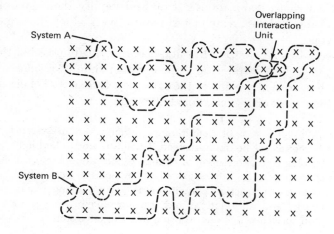

and recurring; they constitute a system. Interaction does not occur in a vacuum, however. And that which is not included in the organization comprises its environment—an important, complex, and little analyzed variable.

Organizational Environments

Few intensive analyses of organizational environments have been made to date.[41] But these analyses and our own research suggest that much organizational behavior cannot be understood except through analysis of the environment. While this topic will be explored in more detail in Chapter 6, several important points have a direct bearing on discussion of boundary specification. First, rather than continuing with the concept of one organizational environment, it is far more productive to structure the analysis in terms of environments, for there are many levels and types of interaction with a multitude of environments that must be differentiated. And in this way the complexity is recognized from the outset.[42] Clearly, organizations are affected by shifts in markets, general societal attitudes and values, and even weather conditions. And although most theorists conclude that organizations are

[41] Notable exceptions include Arthur L. Stinchcombe, op. cit.; Thompson, op. cit.; Paul R. Lawrence and Jay W. Lorsch, *Organization and Environment* (Homewood, Ill.: Richard D. Irwin, Inc., 1969).

[42] Barton's long-range work on college "climates" is most helpful on this point; see Allen H. Barton, *Organizational Measurement and Its Bearing on the Study of College Environments* (New York: College Entrance Examination Board, 1961).

affected by their environment (and then usually drop the point there), it is clear that organizations act on and modify their environments.[43] Such changes, then, create new situations with which the organizations must cope.

Once this is recognized, the significant implication is that the organization must be viewed as an "open" rather than as a "closed" system. Many have recently come to the same conclusion. As Schein suggested after his review of organizational literature,

I will not attempt to give a tight definition of organization in systems terms because this cannot as yet be done. Instead, I will attempt to highlight where a new definition has to enlarge upon or change the traditional one.

First, the organization must be conceived of as an open system which means that it is in constant interaction with its environment, taking in raw materials, people, energy and information, and transforming or converting these into products and service which are exported into the environment.[44]

Similarly, as was previously indicated, both of the recent statements by Thompson, and Katz and Kahn, suggest this open system perspective. The idea is stated very well in the following passage from Katz and Kahn:

Organizations by definition are specific arrangements of patterned behavior distinct from their social environment, but they differ in the degree to which they are so differentiated. The voluntary organization of firemen in a small community is often an open community activity. Any able-bodied man can join and the central office may be nothing more than the local telephone operator, who has been instructed to call the volunteers on word of a fire. The pattern of voluntary co-operation involving the members of the force, the local operator, and most of the members of the community, represents little differentiation from other community activities.[45]

In summary, when viewed from this perspective, the boundaries of the organization are based on the criteria of frequency and content of interaction. Depending upon the analyst's interest, boundaries may be drawn at different places for different analyses. And the organization may be viewed as a dependent and/or independent variable in different types of analyses.

Thus, the relationship between the organization and its environments is one of high interdependence. Environmental characteristics specify the "setting" within which the interaction system exists. As such, environments define the limits of the external constraint structure,

---

[43] Recent concern with air pollution is an obvious illustration.

[44] Edgar H. Schein, *Organizational Psychology* (Englewood Cliffs, N.J.: Prentice-Hall, Inc., 1965), p. 95.

[45] Katz and Kahn, op. cit., p. 122.

thus being a key variable in organizational autonomy. Krupp has described this interrelationship as follows:

> The range of behavior which the business firm's internal variables will have depends, among other things, on the structure of the market. Under conditions of oligopoly (let us assume the firm is large), phenomena that might appear external and compelling to the small competitive firm become themselves internal and susceptible of manipulation. Thus, the large firm in oligopoly is much more independent of external constraints than is the firm under competition. In a competitive market, on the other hand, the behavior of the firm is largely determined by environmental conditions. The firm in a world of oligopoly is a more self-contained empirical structure than the firm in competition. The independence of the firm from external factors is an empirical matter; empirical structure defines the bounded units of the world of observables.[46]

Environmental contact is not seen as being uniform throughout the organization. Thus, environments vary not only in terms of stability but also in terms of contact locations within organizations. Some facets of environmental contact may be highly stable and recurrent, whereas others may be much less so. And depending upon the nature of the environmental element, entry into the organization may be through a very specific point. Thus, communication exchanges across organizations may occur at similar vertical levels and/or through specialized entrance points. Salesmen for manufacturing firms represent one type of contact and will consistently interact with only one segment of a client organization. Similarly, citizen requests for police assistance are channeled into a specialized unit where they are transformed into a routine set of categories for organizational action. This entrance point is a crucial passage and, although the individuals contacting the police vary, they are all treated in a patterned fashion depending upon their particular social characteristics. Police contact with "the public" in this instance clearly illustrates the more general process that characterizes all organizations. The organization itself as a relatively patterned set of events can be distinguished from its environment. But many aspects of that environment are also sets of patterned behaviors that are linked to segments of the focal organization.

It must be emphasized, further, that boundaries may be specified at different places depending upon the interests of the investigator. For example, one might wish to study a metropolitan police organization. Boundary limits seem clear at first, but to understand the behavior of the organization it would be necessary to go far beyond police headquarters. Immediately, one would become aware that the police are but

---

[46] Sherman Krupp, *Pattern in Organizational Analysis* (New York: Holt, Rinehart, & Winston, Inc., 1961), p. 60.

one subsystem within a local governmental structure. Many limits on organizational autonomy are directly imposed through these channels. Major policy decisions, budget allocations, recruitment policies, and so on, all are linked to this segment of the environment. And although the police are structurally linked closely to the other local, nonpolice agencies, interaction with state police or county sheriff offices is far more significant in day-to-day task performance.

Similarly, requests from a vague, amorphous "general public" are encountered repeatedly by the police, who have established patterned response sets to them. Examples are formal and informal policies that specify when requests should be referred to an ambulance service or to another police agency. In an educational setting, such criteria were empirically explored by Aaron Cicourel and John Kitsuse.[47] And taking a cue from them, explanations of much organizational behavior may be derived from common-sense, normative ideas held by persons whose interactions compose the organization. Hence, common-sense items such as membership cards, uniforms, insignia rings, and the like are used by persons as guides in their interaction—that is, as ways of identifying organizational boundaries.

Thus, a series of important research problems are suggested: What are the "real" organizational boundaries perceived by the involved actors? What criteria do they use in identifying them? How diffuse, rigid, consistent, and accepted are these boundary criteria? How severe, important, and binding are the sanctions attached to such criteria? And comparatively, what differences in organizational functioning does variation on such variables produce? Such questions may identify specific normative ideas that can be used as explanations of organizational behavior. And further, if studied comparatively from several organizations, such data characterize a specific structural dimension that may be most important in accounting for variation in functioning among organizations.

However, a distinction needs to be emphasized at this point. First, organizational boundaries may be viewed as constructs invented by analysts who will draw them at different points, depending upon their theoretical interests. We might refer to these as "analytic boundaries." They are empirically based, but highly dependent upon the specific interests of the investigator, who may redraw them as he changes problems. Often, the criteria of frequency and content of interaction may be used in assessing such boundary limits. However, if he is interested in a single process or a particular type of interorganizational interaction, an investigator might now select a much more narrow focus.

---

[47] Aaron V. Cicourel and John I. Kitsuse, *The Educational Decision-Makers* (Indianapolis, Ind.: Bobbs-Merrill, 1963).

Still, the criteria that define which interaction comprises the system under study should be specified.

Second, "normative boundaries" are based on normative definitions of actors. And such definitions may be used to define organizational boundaries. For example, does an individual define himself as a member of a particular church organization? Is he defined as a member by several others? Do these others represent organizational insiders or outsiders? Although such normative criteria are often difficult to use in specifying boundaries, these norms can represent important explanatory variables. For example, organizations vary greatly in ease of boundary penetration. Some are open and absorb new members easily; others are more closed and require elaborate "rites of passage." Think of the boundaries around a prison or a secret revolutionary society. With more descriptive case studies in which such variables are included for assessment of their content, some major analytical dimensions can be derived that may prove to be highly significant in comparative analyses among organizations. However, the distinction between these two views of organizational boundaries should not become blurred.

Although this perspective may seem vague at first, and perhaps even unnecessarily complex, a moment's thought on the image of reality suggested by atomic physics reveals some helpful similarities. When viewed as a collection of atoms in patterned motion, where does one object stop and another begin? When does food eaten become a "part" of the human being? And because the organization is not a series of unchanging physical units but is, rather, an interaction system, any imposition of boundaries in the final analysis can be determined only by the theoretical interests of the analyst. And boundaries as they are thought of by organizational incumbents may not necessarily be the most logical boundaries for many types of analyses when explanation of various aspects of organizational behavior is the objective.

To summarize the discussion to this point, it is suggested that organizations should be viewed as relatively complex and relatively permanent interaction systems. Churches, manufacturing firms, governmental agencies, political parties, prisons, and girl scout units are all examples of such systems. Note that this definition is broader than those often used by others. It is proposed that these two criteria appear critical in differentiating organizations from other types of social systems such as groups or societies. However, as has been emphasized repeatedly, additional variables must be used to subdivide "types" of organizations into narrower analytic units. Others elect to "cut the pie" differently at the outset by selecting different criteria as initial points of differentiation. For example, Blau and Scott designate some organizations as "formal." "Since the distinctive characteristic of these organizations is that they have been formally established for the explicit purpose of achieving certain goals, the term 'formal organizations' is used to designate them. And this formal establishment for explicit purpose is the criterion that distinguishes our subject matter from the study of social organization in general." [48] We chose to make this variable problematic so that we can ask, Given several organizations that vary in the degree to which goals are made explicit, what differences in functioning might be observed? Others have focused on "voluntary associations" or "planned versus crescive" organizations. These distinctions are among many that may or may not prove useful in a future taxonomy of social systems—a point to be explored in more detail in Chapter 9.

Each organization constitutes an observable reality that can and must be explained by concepts at their own level. For individuals in organizations, the organization exists as a set of constraints, and resulting behavior is a significant area of study often labeled social psychology. What has been spoken of here, however, is at a different level of abstraction. For just as the organizational structure can be viewed as a set of constraints within which individuals interact, so too can organizational environments be viewed as structures within which organizational action occurs. And just as the properties of water cannot be explained by knowledge of its separate elements, oxygen and hydrogen, so too must our analysis proceed with the recognition that organizations and groups are emergent phenomena that cannot be explained by individual analysis of the involved actors. However, the analysis of organizations has proceeded in many different ways. It would be well to review briefly the major theoretical perspectives that have been proposed.

[48] Peter M. Blau and W. Richard Scott, *Formal Organizations* (San Francisco, Calif.: Chandler Publishing Co., 1962), p. 5.

Chapter 2

PERSPECTIVES
IN ORGANIZATIONAL
THEORY

A wide variety of theoretical formulations have been constructed to describe and explain organizational behavior. Beginning with the seminal work of Max Weber, we will review eight different clusters of ideas that currently characterize much organizational research: (1) a rational perspective; (2) a classical perspective; (3) a human relations perspective; (4) a natural system perspective; (5) a conflict perspective; (6) an exchange perspective; (7) a technological perspective; and (8) an open system perspective.

Presumably, each perspective represents the rudiments of a theoretical model. Each designates, to some degree, significant elements that are thought to approximate the patterning or order inherent in organizations.[1] A model is useful to the extent that it clearly specifies key variables and a "mechanism" by which the variables are related.[2] Thus, it serves as a crude map for researchers as it provides structure for analysis and calls attention to relationships that might otherwise go unnoticed. When a model has been tested repeatedly and found to be predictive of the phenomena for which it was designated, we then have a miniature

---

[1] Helpful discussion on theoretical models may be found in Black's essay, "Models and Archetypes," in Max Black, *Models and Metaphors* (Ithaca, N.Y.: Cornell University Press, 1962), pp. 219–243.

[2] Willer's discussion of the strategy of theory construction through conceptualization and testing of models is exceptionally helpful. See David Willer, *Scientific Sociology: Theory and Method* (Englewood Cliffs, N.J.: Prentice-Hall, Inc., 1967), pp. 15–21.

theory. Note, however, that such models are not intended to describe all facets of organizational life. Nevertheless models, like road maps and topographical maps, are useful for many purposes although they do not convey the same aspects of reality to us that a mountain hike does.[3]

The eight perspectives to be discussed are not models.[4] However, from these clusters of ideas, competing and complementary theoretical models may emerge as analysts continue to sharpen the concepts and specify the interrelationships among them. Each perspective presents a very different image of organizations. The images vary because of differential emphasis on what are considered to be "key" variables. Similarly, any analysis is deflected in different directions depending upon which perspective is selected. Although there are many similarities and points of overlap, important differences make synthesizing efforts difficult.

Even though none of these formulations provides us with an entirely adequate theoretical base, an understanding of the insights to be gained from each will greatly increase our ability to think conceptually about organizations. However, two cautions must be noted. First, although it is hoped that this classification scheme will prove useful, it must be recognized that many theorists have spanned one or more of these perspectives in their individual work. Only that portion of a particular theorist's work that fits into the perspective under consideration has been included. Second, there is nothing "ultimate" about this particular set of eight categories. Other writers might choose different labels and organize this material very differently. Therefore, we would discourage lengthy arguments as to whether or not a particular theorist "fits" into one category or another. Rather, these categories represent clusters of ideas that seem to us to fit together somewhat. And collectively they provide a mechanism with which to compare different concepts and points of emphasis that are reflected in much of the empirical research on organizations. Thus, despite these and many other dangers, this highly simplified set of eight categories has proved useful to us and our students in providing a broad and somewhat structured overview of major streams of thought regarding organizations.

A Rational Perspective

Writing in Germany during the late 1800s, Max Weber suggested that social conduct could be understood only if viewed from the subjective

---

[3] We are indebted to Richard Caldwell for this analogy.

[4] Gouldner and others have labeled some of these perspectives as "models." Surely, none of these formulations contains the rigor and precision that are associated with this term as used by Willer.

See Alvin Gouldner, "Organizational Analysis" in *Sociology Today*, Robert K. Merton et al., eds., (New York: Basic Books, Inc., 1959), pp. 400–28.

viewpoint of the actors involved.[5] Actors engage in social relationships in the sense that they each take account of the behavior and expectations of others. Persons have power over others to the extent that they can elicit from them desired behaviors. But why do the less powerful comply? Weber recognized that physical force, or the threat of it, could be used as a way of obtaining compliance. However, in most social relationships this does not seem to be the basis of compliance. "Conduct, especially social conduct, and more particularly a social relationship, can be oriented on the part of the individuals to what constitutes their 'idea' of the existence of a *legitimate authority.*" [6]

Weber thus argued that in order to understand a person's behavior, it was necessary to have insight into his feelings of obligation, his sense of duty.

> When a civil servant shows up at his office every day at the same time, it may be determined not only by custom or self-interest, since he can hold to that as he pleases, but it may be partly the result of his abiding by the office regulations which impose certain duties on him and which he may be loath to violate, since such conduct would not only be disadvantageous to him but may be also abhorrent to his "sense of duty," which, to a greater or lesser extent represents for him an absolute value.[7]

Person's comply, in part, out of a sense of duty, a feeling of obligation.

Weber suggested that three general types of authority could be differentiated. Each type of authority was dependent upon a different source of legitimation.[8] *Traditional* authority is legitimated by time. It rests "on an established belief in the sanctity of immemorial traditions and the legitimacy of the status of those exercising authority under them." [9] Parents as authority figures are an obvious example. In contrast, *charismatic* authority is legitimated by the overpowering personality of the leader. Such authority is legitimated by "devotion to the specific and exceptional sanctity, herosim or exemplary character of an individual person, and of the normative patterns or order revealed or ordained by him." [10] Spellbound by the oratorical skill of a religious

---

[5] Major translations of Weber's work include the following.

Max Weber, *The Theory of Social and Economic Organization*, trans. Alexander M. Henderson and Talcott Parsons (New York: The Free Press, 1947).

Hans Gerth and C. Wright Mills, eds., *From Max Weber: Essays in Sociology* (New York: Oxford University Press, 1946).

Max Weber, *Basic Concepts in Sociology*, trans. H. P. Secher (New York: The Citadel Press, 1962).

Guenther Roth and Claus Wittich, eds., *Economy and Society*, trans. Ephraim Fishchoff, et al. (New York: The Bedminster Press, 1968).

[6] Weber, *Basic Concepts in Sociology*, op. cit., p. 71.

[7] Ibid.

[8] Weber, *The Theory of Social and Economic Organization*, op. cit., pp. 328–36.

[9] Ibid., p. 328.

[10] Ibid.

evangelist, for example, persons do as he asks primarily because of the "magic" of his personality. Finally, Weber identified bureaucratic or *rational-legal* authority. Legitimacy is granted because it is in accordance with a larger set of rules that are designed to achieve valued ends. Thus, it rests "on a belief in the 'legality' of patterns of normative rules and the right of those elevated to authority under such rules to issue commands" [11] Weber viewed this type of legitimacy, which was based on "rational derivation," as the essential ingredient in the emerging organizations throughout Germany near the turn of the nineteenth century. And it was through his observations of some of these organizations, such as the Prussian army, that he formulated the notion of bureacratic authority and the "ideal type" of a bureaucracy.[12]

The General Image

Weber viewed organizations as instruments, "a system of continuous activity pursuing a goal of a specified kind." [13] A particular goal has been specified, and a collection of persons are engaged in a series of separate, interrelated, and rationally organized activities that presumably will result in goal attainment. The focus of attention is then on the legally prescribed structures and the mechanisms by which they are maintained. Persons comply with organizational rules mainly because the ends achieved by the total structure are valued and each must do his own part if the goal is to be attained.

In brief, Weber suggested that the purest type of legal authority was a bureucratic administrative staff to which individuals were appointed and where they functioned in accordance with the following ten criteria:

1. They are personally free and subject to authority only with respect to their impersonal official obligations.
2. They are organized in a clearly defined hierarchy of offices.
3. Each office has a clearly defined sphere of competence in the legal sense.
4. The office is filled by a free contractual relationship. Thus, in principle, there is free selection.
5. Candidates are selected on the basis of technical qualifications. In the most rational case, this is tested by examination or guaranteed by diploma certifying technical training, or both. They are *appointed*, not elected.

[11] Ibid.
[12] "The ideal type is thus the sum total of concepts which the specialist in the human sciences constructs purely for purposes of research." Julian Freund, *The Sociology of Max Weber*, trans. Mary Ilford (New York: Pantheon Books, 1968), p. 60. Freund's discussion of this methodology is most helpful; see pp. 59–79.
[13] Weber, *Basic Concepts in Sociology*, op. cit., p. 115.

6. They are remunerated by fixed salaries in money, for the most part with a right to pensions. Only under certain circumstances does the employing authority, especially in private organizations, have a right to terminate the appointment, but the official is always free to resign. The salary scale is primarily graded according to rank in the hierarchy; but in addition to this criterion, the responsibility of the position and the requirements of the incumbent's social status may be taken into account.
7. The office is treated as the sole, or at least the primary, occupation of the incumbent.
8. It constitutes a career. There is a system of promotion according to seniority or to achievement, or both. Promotion is dependent on the judgment of superiors.
9. The official works entirely separated from ownership of the means of administration and without appropriation of his position.
10. He is subject to strict and systematic discipline and control in the conduct of his office.[14]

Thus, existing organizations could be compared to this ideal type. And presumably the more closely they corresponded to it on the ten dimensions above, the more efficient they were.

This view of organizations as instruments focuses our attention on six central ideas.[15] First, organizations have explicit and reasonably well-defined goals. The entire organization in all of its component parts is viewed as a means for goal achievement. Second, policies, operational rules or procedures, space allocation, personnel recruitment and selection—indeed, all organizational behaviors—are seen as consciously and rationally administered with the goals in mind. Third, by following policies and rules, organizational members save time—they need not take time to make repeated choices—and their actions will be as efficient as it is possible for them to be in terms of cost and effort. Fourth, the organization is viewed as a collection of structures to be manipulated so as to increase the overall effectiveness of the total system. Fifth, "decisions are made on the basis of a rational survey of the situation, utilizing certified knowledge, with a deliberate orientation to an expressly codified legal apparatus."[16] Sixth, any departures from rationality are assumed to be random mistakes, due to ignorance or error in calculation.

Thus, there emerges an image of a highly efficient machine wherein a collection of actors are cooperatively engaged in a series of behaviors that all fit together into a grand scheme to accomplish a desired end.

---

[14] Weber, *The Theory of Social and Economic Organization*, op. cit., pp. 333–34.
[15] Many of these ideas were adapted from Gouldner, op. cit., pp. 404–405.
[16] Ibid., p. 404.

Given this image, what kinds of propositions about organizational functioning might emerge?

Illustrative Propositions

Upon completing an intensive analysis of fifty empirical studies on administrative organizations of various types, James Price presented thirty-one propositions that received at least some support from the studies reviewed.[17] Professor Price was interested in locating variables related to organizational effectiveness, i.e., the degree of goal achievement. Whereas Price's book is broader than the small portion of Weber's work just reviewed, many of the propositions he discussed clearly reflect this rational perspective, and as such they illustrate the type of propositions that can be derived from the Weberian perspective.

1. Organizations which have a single goal are more likely to have a high degree of effectiveness than organizations which have multiple goals.[18]
2. Organizations which have a high degree of goal specificity are more likely to have a high degree of effectiveness than organizations which have a low degree of goal specificity.[19]
3. Organizations which primarily have a rational-legal type of decision making are more likely to have a high degree of effectiveness than organizations which primarily have a charismatic type of decision making.[20]
4. Organizations which have a high degree of legitimacy are more likely to have a high degree of effectiveness than organizations which have a low degree of legitimacy.[21]
5. Organizations which have the maximum degree of centralization with respect to strategic decisions are more likely to have a high degree of effectiveness than organizations which do not have the maximum degree of centralization with respect to strategic decisions.[22]

Many other propositions could be stated, but these five illustrate some of the major points of emphasis of this view. However, it is not without shortcomings. What are some of the kinds of difficulties that

---

[17] James L. Price, *Organizational Effectiveness: An Inventory of Propositions* (Homewood, Ill.: Richard D. Irwin, Inc., 1968).

By "administrative organizations," Price refers to those ". . . composed primarily of full time members" (p. 8). Organizations included factories, schools, prisons, hospitals, restaurants, universities, and the like.

[18] Ibid., p. 44. Neither this nor the next proposition was included with the thirty-one central propositions proposed by Price, but both illustrate this rational perspective well. Proposed as "additional propositions," Price indicated that some of his data could be interpreted as supportive.

[19] Ibid. See previous footnote.

[20] Ibid., p. 55.

[21] Ibid., p. 49.

[22] Ibid., p. 60.

might be encountered if Weber's perspective is used as a basis for research?

Critique

Five major points of criticism can be raised with this rational perspective. First, the concept of organizational goal presents a variety of problems. Should researchers use only statements that are in official documents to determine an organization's goal? Or may they accept oral statements? But if so, oral statements by whom? Thus, implicit in the model is an assumption of goal consensus and clarity. But rather than make this assumption, would it not be far better to make the issue problematic? One might then ask to what degree is there goal consensus? What difference, if any does it make? What are the goal formulating processes that characterize the organization? In short, many important questions remain hidden when organizational goal is used as the central concept.

Equally important is the direction in which the researcher is guided. Too often he is left with a task that becomes increasingly difficult when he attempts to determine "the goals" of an organization.[23] As Etzioni and Perrow have indicated, distinctions might be made between *official goals*—i.e., those objectives or general purposes stated either orally or in writing by key members—and *operative goals*—i.e., designated objectives based on the actual operating policies of the organization.[24] According to Perrow, operative goals "tell us what the

[23] Among the discussions of problems and strategies in measuring and conceptualizing organizational goals, we have found the following to be most helpful:

Mayer N. Zald, "Comparative Analysis and Measurement of Organizational Goals: The Case of Correctional Institutions for Delinquents," *The Sociological Quarterly*, 4: 206–30 (Spring 1963).

Herbert A. Simon, "On the Concept of Organizational Goal," *Administrative Science Quarterly*, 9: 1–22 (June 1964).

Charles K. Warriner, "The Problem of Organizational Purpose," *The Sociological Quarterly*, 6: 139–46 (Spring 1965).

Ephraim Yuchtman and Stanley E. Seashore, "A System Resource Approach to Organizational Effectiveness," *American Sociological Review*, 32: 891–903 (December 1967).

Edward Gross, "Universities As Organizations: A Research Approach," *American Sociological Review*, 33: 518–44 (August 1968).

Charles Perrow, "Organizational Goals," in *International Encyclopedia of the Social Sciences*, David L. Sills (ed.) (New York: The Free Press, 1968), Vol. II.

Charles Perrow, *Organizational Analysis: A Sociological View* (Belmont, Calif.: Brooks/Cole Publishing Company, 1970), pp. 133–74.

Edward Gross, "The Definition of Organizational Goals," *British Journal of Sociology*, 20: 277–94 (September 1969).

Harry Perlstadt, "Goal Implementation and Outcome in Medical Schools," *American Sociological Review*, 37: 73–82 (February 1972).

James L. Price, "The Study of Organizational Effectiveness," *The Sociological Quarterly*, 13: 3–15 (Winter 1972).

organization actually is trying to do, regardless of what the official goals say are the aims." [25] Yet these distinctions are not of great help in making the concept operational because the criteria that specify "operative goals" remain vague. Finally, this goal perspective, "tends, though not invariably, to give organizational studies a tone of social criticism rather than scientific analysis." [26] It becomes too easy to focus on the relative lack of success of a single organization, rather than on conceptual analysis that might result in propositions of a comparative nature. In short, the perspective focuses our attention on the concept of organizational goal—a concept that tends to deflect our analysis so as to miss many significant questions that merit empirical investigation; a concept that is most difficult to operationalize; a concept that too easily directs us toward social criticism rather than scientific analysis.

Second, the view excludes any discussion of informal behavior in organizations.[27] Members are viewed as rule followers in a highly mechanistic sense rather than as social creatures interacting within a network of social relationships. And might not many unofficial group norms be highly significant in guiding behavior? Thus, both unofficial group norms and interpersonal relationships remained unmentioned.

Third, Weber's distinctions between authority types may have been exaggerated. As Etzioni has suggested, there are many "mixed" types, e.g., semitraditional, semibureaucratic organizations existed "in ancient Egypt, Imperial China and Medieval Byzantium in which hierarchical structures and adherence to rules and regulations were combined with a fairly diffuse, totalistic status structure, such as seems to characterize modern totalitarian regimes." [28] And organizations may shift from more bureaucratic to more charismatic and back to more bureaucratic struc-

---

[24] Charles Perrow, "The Analysis of Goals in Complex Organizations," *American Sociological Review*, 26: 854–66 (December 1961); and Amitai Etzioni, "Two Approaches to Organizational Analysis: A Critique and a Suggestion," *Administrative Science Quarterly*, 5: 257–78 (September 1960).

[25] Perrow, "The Analysis of Goals in Complex Organizations," op. cit., p. 855.

[26] Amitai Etzioni, *Modern Organizations* (Englewood Cliffs, N.J.: Prentice-Hall, Inc., 1964), p. 16.

[27] Weber did recognize the importance of the informal structure, but did not include it as an element in his ideal type of bureaucracy.

"It is generally not known that in some of his speeches and little known writings Weber himself described certain features of bureaucracy which were either not mentioned or in contradiction with his ideal type formulation." Anthony Oberschall, *Empirical Social Research in Germany, 1848–1914* (Paris: Monton et Cie., 1965), p. 134.

[28] Etzioni, *Modern Organizations*, op. cit., pp. 56–57.

Weber acknowledged this to some degree, however, when he discussed "combination of the different types of authorities," pp. 382–86, Weber, *The Theory of Social and Economic Organizations*, op. cit. Although Weber did discuss the long-term "transformation of pure charisma by the process of routinization," his analysis precluded the short-term shifting referred to here. See Weber, op. cit., pp. 362–86.

tures more rapidly than Weber acknowledged. In times of crisis or unusual demand loads, organizations often shift from bureaucratic routines, and authority may be legitimated for charismatic leaders until the crisis has passed.

Fourth, environmental changes and resulting repercussions for organizations are ignored. As already emphasized, environmental changes have both sudden and long-term consequences for organizations. Discussion of interrelationships between environmental changes and organizational functioning is absent from this perspective.

Fifth, although not discussed, internal conflict is clearly implied to be totally undesirable. In fact, given the image of a set of rationally integrated structures in which persons are following prescribed behaviors, conflict is assumed to be non-existent. Thus, another important dimension is ignored.

Despite these critical points, however, Weber's work remains of much value as a general perspective for organizational analysis. And the variables that are specified are certainly helpful in exploring many significant research questions.

A Classical Perspective

Although they were unaware of Weber's work in Germany, several American writers emerged with somewhat similar ideas. However, in contrast to Weber's theoretical and scientific focus, these men were primarily concerned with prescription. Thus, they attempted to formulate "laws of organizational efficiency." Among the most influential was Frederick W. Taylor—the "Father of Scientific Management." [29] Taylor obtained a journeyman machinist status in 1878, and then in eight years worked his way through the ranks of a steel company to emerge as chief engineer. Throughout this time he was consistently concerned with the failure of men under him to produce at the level at which he knew they were capable. Convinced that productivity could be increased through experimentation to find the best way of performing and the proper time of each operation, Taylor devised numerous experiments in an effort to locate "laws of least waste." So "time and motion study" was born.

Taylor first presented his ideas formally in 1895 in a paper entitled "A Piece Rate System." This was followed by "Shop Management" in

[29] The following material was adapted from Harlow S. Person's "foreword," pp. v–xvi in Frederick Winslow Taylor, *Scientific Management* (New York: Harper & Row, 1947).

For a perceptive biography of Taylor, see Sudhir Kakar, *Frederick Taylor: A Study in Personality and Innovation* (Cambridge, Mass.: M.I.T. Press, 1970).

1903, and "Principles of Scientific Management" in 1911. His ideas became more popular, and finally resulted in the often cited *Scientific Management,* published in 1947, which contained the last two writings and a lengthy set of transcripts of Taylor's testimony in 1912 before a Special Committee of the House of Representatives to "Investigate the Taylor and other Systems of Shop Management." Although many elaborations have been made on Taylor's basic formulations, writers such as Luther Gulick and Lyndall F. Urwick[30] relied heavily on Taylor's original assumptions.

More recently, a "neo-classical" view has received much attention through the work of such individuals as Herbert A. Simon.[31] Simon and others have selected the decision-making process as their focal concern. They have attempted to make more explicit the nature of the process and the design of optimal informational structures that will result in increased rationality in decision making. "A decision is rational from the standpoint of the individual (subjectively rational) if it is consistent with the values, the alternatives, and the information which he weighed in reaching it." [32]

Among the more interesting extensions of this neo-classical approach is PERT—Program Evaluation and Review Technique. Developed by the Navy Special Projects Office in cooperation with Booz, Allen, and Hamilton (a management consulting firm), PERT is credited with bringing the Polaris missile submarine into combat readiness about two years ahead of the original date scheduled.[33] PERT is an extension

[30] Luther Gulick and Lyndall F. Urwick, eds., *Papers on the Science of Administration* (New York: Institute of Public Administration, Columbia University, 1937). For a perceptive case study that describes how the introduction of the Taylor System into a U.S. Army Ordnance Arsenal resulted in increased productivity between 1908 and 1915, see Hugh G. J. Aitken, *Taylorism at Watertown Arsenal* (Cambridge, Mass.: Harvard University Press, 1960).

[31] Herbert A. Simon, *Administrative Behavior,* 2nd ed. (New York: The Macmillan Company, 1957).

[32] Ibid., p. 243.

Simon elaborated the relationship between rationality and administrative theory in the introduction to the second edition to incorporate related research published after the first edition (1947). *"The central concern of administrative theory is with the boundary between the rational and non-rational aspects of human social behavior.* Administrative theory is peculiarly the theory of intended and bonded rationality—of the behavior of human beings who *satisfice* because they have not the wits to *maximize"* (p. xxiv).

[33] Richard I. Levin and Charles A. Kirkpatrick, *Planning and Control with PERT/CPM* (New York: McGraw-Hill Book Co., 1966), pp. 2–8.

Equally popular, and somewhat similar in assumptions and objectives, is PPBS (Planning-Programming-Budget System); see Charles J. Hitch, *Decision-Making for Defense* (Berkeley and Los Angeles: University of California Press, 1965); and Virginia Held, "PPBS Comes to Washington," *The Public Interest,* 4: 102–15 (Summer 1966).

of Taylor's work and that of one of his contemporaries, H. L. Gantt. These men were primarily concerned with "rationalizing" work flows characterized by highly repetitious tasks, e.g., brick or steel manufacturing. In contrast, PERT was designed as a management tool to be used for complex nonrepetitive tasks. A Polaris submarine had never been built, and some mechanism was needed whereby the work of the 250 prime contractors and at least 9,000 subcontractors could be coordinated, for failure by any one subcontractor might have delayed the entire project.[34] And so an elaboration of Gantt's "milestone chart" was constructed, whereby a network of work units are ordered into a complex sequence culminating with the completed project.

Review Figure 2–1. Using the Gantt milestone chart as an orientation, organizational planners could divide the initial task into several central tasks (X, Y, and Z). Each of these in turn would be subdivided into more specialized tasks (1–7). These specialized subtasks could then be sequenced over time. In this way work would be phased so that as one aspect was completed another could begin. The lower diagram illustrates how this same job structure can be transformed through the PERT system by integrating specific time estimations. Highly complex networks of subtask "circuits" are possible, of course, and statistical probability theory can be incorporated to provide estimates of completion dates when there is uncertainty for each "leg" of the network. By viewing the project as an integrated whole, the interdependent nature of such "decision networks" is emphasized. This provides an important extension to the rationality of any individual decision, since presumably its impact on "the whole" can be more adequately assessed.[35]

Whereas much experimentation has been conducted in the past twenty years related to decision-making strategies used by subjects ranging from college students to generals,[36] other work has been addressed to the critical problem of establishing better techniques for locating and reporting input data. The theme of this argument is basically that the fewer data available, the greater the number of unknowns, and therefore the less rationality is possible in decision making. Beyer, for example, argues that new techniques in electronic data processing and operations research that emerged during the 1950s, have greatly expanded the scope of accounting so as to include (1) custodial accounting—"the financial accounting for the assets entrusted

[34] Levin and Kirkpatrick, op. cit., p. 8.

[35] Ibid., p. 7.

[36] David W. Miller and Martin K. Starr, *The Structure of Human Decisions* (Englewood Cliffs, N.J.: Prentice-Hall, Inc., 1967); and Howard R. Aiffa, *Decision Analysis* (Reading, Mass.: Addison-Wesley Publishing Co., 1968).

FIGURE 2–1   Illustrative Gantt and PERT Charts

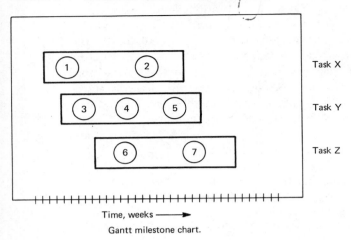

Task X

Task Y

Task Z

Time, weeks ———▶

Gantt milestone chart.

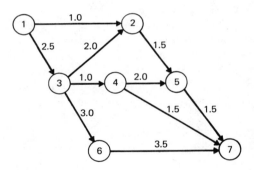

Gantt milestone chart completely transformed
into PERT network with arbitrary time units.

SOURCE: Adapted from *Planning and Control with PERT/CPM* by Richard I.
Levin and Charles A. Kirkpatrick (New York: McGraw-Hill Book Company,
1966), pp. 4 and 7. Used with permission of McGraw-Hill Book Company.

to the enterprise"; (2) performance accounting—"the quantitative
matching of performance against some plan by organizational responsibility"; and (3) decision accounting—"the quantitative evaluation of
alternative courses of action." [37] Thus, the organizational controller is
redefined to become "Director of Management Information." And so,

[37] Robert Beyer, *Profitability Accounting for Planning and Control* (New York:
Ronald Press, 1963), p. 17.

starting with Taylor's efforts with his small clipboard type of device that contained a writing pad and two or three stop watches, we now have massive information systems providing various types of data as men attempt to control and direct gigantic and enormously complex organizational structures. Yet the assumptions on which they often operate are not strikingly different from those made by Taylor, Gantt, and Gulick and Urwick.

The General Image

The problem remains as it was stated by Taylor—i.e., "What the workmen want from their employers beyond anything else is high wages, and what employers want from their workmen most of all is a low labor cost of manufacture." [38] He advocated that high wages and low labor cost were the foundations of ideal management. Work operations should be carefully analyzed and subdivided into minute components and a standard established as to the performance time required by a "first rate man," e.g., "S = time filling shovel and straightening up ready to throw; t = time returning one foot with empty shovel, L = load of a shovel in cubic feet; P = percentage of a day required for rest and necessary delays, and T = time for shoveling one cubic yard." [39] These values can then be used in a mathematical equation to determine a standard labor cost. In addition, it provides a scientific basis for planning work rather than forcing each employee to use a "rule of thumb" that is highly wasteful. "The work of every workman is fully planned out by the management at least one day in advance, and each man received in most cases complete written instructions, describing in detail the task which he is to accomplish, as well as the means to be used in doing the work." [40]

In this way, the greatest obstacle to organizational success—loafing—is overcome. Taylor suggested that loafing or "soldiering" proceeded from two causes: (1) natural soldiering, i.e., "the natural instinct and tendency of men to take it easy";[41] and (2) systematic soldiering, i.e., "from more intricate second thought and reasoning caused by their relations with other men." [42] Taylor argued that cooperative organizational structures, where all men are expected to share in the profits, were destined to failure since "personal ambition always has been and will remain a more powerful incentive to exertion than a desire for the general welfare. The few misplaced drones, who do the

[38] Taylor, "Shop Management," in *Scientific Management*, op. cit., p. 22.
[39] Ibid., p. 163.
[40] Taylor, "Principles of Scientific Management," in *Scientific Management*, op. cit., p. 40.
[41] Taylor, "Shop Management," op. cit., p. 30.
[42] Ibid.

loafing and share equally in the profits with the rest under cooperation are sure to drag the better men down toward their level." [43] Hence, the solution was to organize the work force so that each man had a highly specialized task and was rewarded in a direct ratio to his task accomplishment.

Taylor made a sharp distinction between "workers" and "managers." And his efforts at characterizing the responsibilities of "managers" was extended by such writers as Luther Gulick. " 'What is the work of the chief executive? What does he do?' The answer is POSDCORB." [44] The acronym stands for Planning, Organizing, Staffing, Directing, Coordinating, Reporting, and Budgeting. But among these, organizing and coordination are most critical. In this way the activities of many men are organized into specialized work units, with different tasks. But the units are arranged into a hierarchical structure so as to permit coordination. Thus a chain of authority is created in which the "span of control" of each manager is of a size adequate to permit close supervision. And the typical, widely used organizational chart was born (see Figure 2–2).

Following these leads, others have extended the analysis. For example, Harold Stieglitz has described the span of supervision model developed at Lockheed Missiles and Space Company. [45] Weights are assigned to the seven variables considered to be the most crucial in establishing the span of supervision: (1) similarity of functions; (2) geographic continuity of subordinates; (3) complexity of functions; (4) direction and control required by subordinates; (5) coordination of subordinates required; (6) planning importance, complexity, and time required; and (7) organizational assistance received by supervisor. These weights are then used to calculate a "supervisory index," which is in turn related to a "suggested standard span of control." For example, if the supervisory index (SI) is computed as forty to forty-two, using the seven variables, then the span of control (SC) for a supervisor should be four or five persons. If the SI ranges between thirty-one and thirty-three, then the SC may be as high as five to eight. An SI of twenty-two to twenty-four would permit a span of control ranging from eight to eleven persons for a single supervisor. [46] Following a similar line of reasoning, others have proposed strategies with which to select the span of supervision that maximizes organizational

[43] Ibid., p. 37.
[44] Luther Gulick, "Notes on the Theory of Organization," in Gulick and Urwick, op cit., p. 13.
[45] Harold Stieglitz, "Optimizing Span of Control," *Management Record*, 24: 25–29 (September 1962).
[46] Ibid., p. 29.

efficiency given the number of organizational levels, number of individuals, individual "efficiency levels," and the like.[47]

Thus, there emerges a theoretical perspective that emphasizes the formal structure. Individuals are viewed as economically motivated creatures who are placed within these structures. The key to success, defined as optimal organizational efficiency, lies in the arrangement of the "parts." The parts include men and machines. And the entire organization is viewed as one large machine. Machines, in this view, take on an image of being appendages to the members—or perhaps it is just opposite! As an analytical device to assist in understanding organizational behavior, numerous criticisms have been raised of this view. After reviewing a few illustrative hypotheses that reflect this perspective, we shall look at some of these criticisms.

Illustrative Propositions

1. Organizations with a high division of labor will be more efficient than those with a low division of labor.
2. Organizations with rigidly specified lines of authority will be more efficient than those with less rigidly specified lines of authority.
3. Organizations with a span of control that permits close supervision will be more efficient than organizations in which the span of control prohibits close supervision.
4. Organizations that reward members solely with reward systems based on performance output will be more efficient than organizations with reward systems based on other criteria.
5. Organizations that reward members over the shortest unit of time will be more efficient than organizations that reward members over a longer period of time.

Critique

Five major criticisms have been voiced about this cluster of ideas. First, the perspective is normative rather than analytical. The focus is on how organizations should or ought to function rather than an attempt to explain why existing organizational patterns are as they are. This, of course, is a clear reflection of the aims of the theorists, who were interested primarily in prescriptive advice rather than scientific analysis.

However, even as a prescriptive device, the model contains many deficiencies. Most glaring is the basic view of organizational members

---

[47] A brief summary and critique of the Fordham model of Span-of-Supervision is presented by Rocco Carzo, Jr. and John N. Yanouzas, *Formal Organization: A Systems Approach* (Homewood, Ill.: Richard D. Irwin, Inc., and The Dorsey Press, 1967), pp. 88–93.

FIGURE 2-2 Purpose and Process Subdivisions in Organizations

	Health Department	Education Department	Police Department	Park Department
	Director Assistant Directors	Superintendent Assistant Superintendents	Chief Assistant Chiefs	Commissioner Assistant Commissioners
Clerical and Secretarial Service — Director	Private secretaries Stenographers File clerks Clerks Messengers	Private secretaries Stenographers File clerks Clerks Messengers	Private secretaries Stenographers File clerks Clerks Messengers	Private secretaries Stenographers File clerks Clerks Messengers
Finance Department — Director	Budget officer Accountants Purchasing officer Statisticians	Budget officer Accountants Purchasing officer Statisticians	Budget officer Accountants Purchasing officer Statisticians	Budget officer Accountants Purchasing officer Statisticians
	Personnel manager Lawyer	Personnel manager Lawyer	Personnel manager Lawyer	Personnel manager Lawyer
Engineering Department — Director	Engineers Architects	Engineers Architects		Engineers Architects Landscape staff Repair force Janitors
	Repair force Janitors	Repair force Janitors	Repair force Janitors	

Physicians Dentists Nurses Psychologists	Physicians Dentists Nurses Psychologists	Physicians Psychologists	
Bacteriologists Inspectors	Laboratory assistants	Crime laboratory staff	Plant laboratory staff
	Gardeners Classroom teachers Special teachers Librarians Recreation leaders Playground supervisors	Police school staff	Gardeners
			Recreation leaders Playground supervisors
	Traffic supervisor	Uniformed force Detective force Traffic force Jail staff Mounted force	Traffic force
		Veterinarian Communications staff	Zoo staff Veterinarian Switchboard operator
Switchboard operator	Switchboard operator		
Mortorized service	Motorized service	Motorized service	Motorized service

Supt.

Motorized Service

Horizontal lines — Process Divisions;   Vertical lines — Purpose Divisions.

SOURCE: Adapted from Luther Gulick, "Notes on the Theory of Organization," in Luther Gulick and Lyndall F. Urwick (eds.), *Papers on the Science of Administration* (New York: Institute of Public Administration, Columbia University, 1937), p. 17.

as creatures motivated solely by economics. For example, whereas an extreme division of labor may make good sense in easing member training, low morale and alienation may result. This is especially true as the educational level of participants is increased. Thus, Taylor's assumptions may have been more appropriate for the United States at the time when he initially formulated them. Certainly, the rise of the leftist critique regarding bureaucratic death, loss of meaning in work, and hippies all suggest that many persons wish to be considered more than "cogs in an assembly line." [48] Failure to recognize this will result in many coping patterns all of which reduce overall efficiency, e.g., internal sabotage, apathy, and serious morale and recruitment problems.

Second, the model omits interactions among many critical structural variables. This is seen most easily when the perspective is applied to organizations with a large number of professionals, e.g., universities, hospitals, law firms, and so on. Thus, a professional orientation and commitment appear to be based on criteria quite distinct from those presented in this perspective. Many semi-professional groups such as nurses,[49] school teachers,[50] and public accountants[51] appear to develop strong commitment to a professional ideology that runs counter to Taylor's motivational assumptions. This form of conflict is but one type that the perspective fails to consider. Certainly, wages accepted as "fair compensation" by one generation may not be so defined by another. But Taylor assumed that if wages were based on "scientifically" determined standards, then harmony would prevail between managers and workers. Thus, such other fundamental bases for conflict were not assessed.

Third, rule violation is necessarily viewed as undesirable and remains unexplained in other than moralistic terms, e.g., lazy workers. Robert Merton's critique on this issue is especially illuminating.[52] He

[48] Many of Paul Goodman's writings are especially relevant, e.g., *People or Personnel* (New York: Random House, 1965).

[49] Ronald G. Corwin, "The Professional Employee: A Study of Conflict in Nursing Roles," *The American Journal of Sociology*, **66**: 604–15 (May 1961).

[50] Ronald G. Corwin, *A Sociology of Education* (New York: Appleton-Century-Crofts, 1965), pp. 229–63.

[51] James E. Sorensen, "Professional and Bureaucratic Organization in the Public Accounting Firm," *The Accounting Review*, **42**: 553–65 (July 1967); James E. Sorensen, "Professional and Organizational Profiles of the Migrating and Non-Migrating Large Public Accounting Firm CPA," *Decision Sciences*, **1**: 489–512 (July–October 1970).

[52] Robert K. Merton, *Social Theory and Social Structure*, rev. ed. (New York: The Free Press, 1957), pp. 195–206. Merton's thesis is modified and elaborated through an effort at empirical testing by Harry Cohen, "Bureaucratic Flexibility: Some Comments on Robert Merton's 'Bureaucratic Structure and Personality'," *British Journal of Sociology*, **21**: 390–99 (1970).

suggests an interesting chain of reasoning: "(1) An effective bureaucracy demands reliability of response and strict devotion to regulations. (2) Such devotion to the rules leads to their transformation into absolutes; they are no longer conceived as relative to a set of purposes. (3) This interferes with ready adaptation under special conditions not clearly envisaged by those who drew up the general rules. (4) Thus, the very elements which conduce toward efficiency in general produce inefficiency in specific instances." [53]

Rules cannot exist for every contingency. Frequently informal mechanisms emerge that greatly simplify task accomplishment. Because rules do not exist for every new situation, responses to them are also viewed as deviant. Thus, this highly oversimplified perspective prevents the analyst from seeing rule formulation as an ongoing process. The focus is exclusively on the formal policies that often have little to do with everyday organizational life. Further, as Merton indicates, when persons "live" in an organization administered under this perspective, they may become highly ritualistic; the rules become ends in themselves rather than means to ends. This is the characterization of the proverbial bureaucrat who lives a meaningless life guided by one major fear—that he may someday break a rule! Of course, such phenomena and the resulting rigidities both to person and structure are not suggested for analysis through Taylor's perspective.

Fourth, and somewhat implicit above, the view ignores the internal social life of organizational incumbents. Interpersonal disputes, extraorganizational interaction, friendship cliques, and the like are totally overlooked. Reflecting an economic image of men motivated exclusively by maximum wages, the perspective fails to include any dimensions of group life. Organizational members are viewed as isolated individuals to be arranged according to personal skills and task demands. Group identity or allegiance, as well as interpersonal likes and dislikes, are simply not considered except in negative terms—that is, that such variables can only reduce efficiency, not increase it.

Fifth, like the Weberian model, organizations are viewed as existing in a vacuum. External environments, as constraint systems, which might serve as sources of change, are not mentioned. Organizational change is viewed as originating with internal decision making given stated objectives. External pressures for change exerted at varied levels within the organization are excluded.

Despite these criticisms, this classical view of organization remains a widely used basis for both administrators and researchers. However, starting in the 1930s it was seriously contested by an alternative, now to be reviewed.

[53] Merton, op. cit., p. 200.

A Human Relations Perspective

During the late 1920s, a series of experiments was begun in the Cicero, Illinois, plant of the Western Electric Company. Under the leadership of Elton Mayo, Harvard University researchers attempted to discover new ways in which to increase plant productivity. As they had followed leads from the classical school theorists, at this time plant officials confronted two kinds of problems: (1) complaints of fatigue and monotony in factory work; and (2) design engineers well trained in engineering but with little sensitivity to possible reactions by the humans who would be required to work with newly designed machinery.[54] Thus the now classic Hawthorne studies were begun.

Data were collected on several types of experiments conducted between 1927 and 1932. Mayo and his colleagues drew many conclusions, but the central theme that emerged was that workers were social creatures, an idea that had little place in the classical organizational model.

Earlier (1923), Mayo had conducted research in a mule-spinning department of a textile mill near Philadelphia. Confronted with an annual turnover of 250 per cent, the company had tried several incentive schemes. Mayo first introduced a rest period, allowed workers in each alley to decide for themselves when the machines would be stopped, and hired a nurse. Rapidly, a sense of group life emerged, production rose, and turnover declined.[55] Although more successful than past consultants, Mayo still lacked precise scientific evidence. Hence, the Hawthorne plant offered a logical setting wherein these ideas might be tested more rigorously.

In *Management and the Worker*, Fritz J. Roethlisberger and William J. Dickson presented the analysis and conclusions drawn from the six years of work within the Hawthorne plant.[56] Because of the significance of the conclusions and the length of this book (over 600 pages, with 82 figures and charts), numerous summaries were prepared that further popularized the findings.[57] As would be suspected, the

---

[54] Lawrence J. Henderson, T. N. Whitehead, and Elton Mayo, "The Effects of Social Environment," in Gulick and Urwick, eds., op. cit., pp. 144–58. See also John Madge, *The Origins of Scientific Sociology* (New York: The Free Press, 1962), pp. 162–209.

[55] Elton Mayo, *The Human Problems of an Industrial Civilization* (New York: The Macmillan Company, 1933).

[56] Fritz J. Roethlisberger and William J. Dickson, *Management and the Worker* (Cambridge, Mass.: Harvard University Press, 1939).

[57] For example, George C. Homans, *The Human Group* (New York: Harcourt, Brace, Jovanovich, Inc., 1950), pp. 48–80; George C. Homans, "The Western Electric Researches" in Schuyler Dean Hoslett, ed., *Human Factors in Management* (New York: Harper & Row, 1951), pp. 210–41; Milton C. Blum, *Industrial Psy-*

---

book had its critics.[58] And the controversy over the validity of the conclusions continued as recently as 1967, nearly thirty years later.[59]

Although controversy regarding the Hawthorne studies may continue indefinitely, much additional research has been conducted and interpreted as supporting many of Mayo's original conclusions. Among the most influential in stimulating and synthesizing many of these empirical studies have been such theorists as Rensis Likert,[60] Douglas McGregor[61] and Chris Argyris.[62]

The General Image

Seven central ideas characterize a human relations perspective of organization. First, workers are viewed as complex social creatures with feelings, desires, and fears. Behavior on the job—like behavior elsewhere—is a consequence of many factors apart from economics. "Each of us wants appreciation, recognition, influence, a feeling of accomplishment, and a feeling that people who are important to us believe in us and respect us." [63] Hence, motivational forces are reconceptualized to include: (1) ego motives, i.e., the desire to achieve and maintain a sense of personal worth and importance; (2) security motives; (3) curiosity, creativity, and the desire for new experience; and (4) economic motives.[64] This is not to propose that workers are

---

chology and Its Social Foundations (New York: Harper & Row, 1956), pp. 11–47; and Delbert C. Miller and William H. Form, *Industrial Sociology* (New York: Harper & Row, 1951), pp. 35–83.

[58] For summaries and further analysis of the criticisms, see Henry A. Landsberger, *Hawthorne Revisited* (Ithaca, N.Y.: Cornell University Press, 1958).

[59] Alex Carey, "The Hawthorne Studies: A Radical Criticism," *American Sociological Review*, 32: 403–16 (June 1967).

[60] Rensis Likert, *New Patterns of Management* (New York: McGraw-Hill Book Co., 1961) and *The Human Organization* (New York: McGraw-Hill Book Co., 1967).

[61] Douglas McGregor, *The Human Side of Enterprise* (New York: McGraw-Hill Book Co., 1960) and *The Professional Manager*, Caroline McGregor and Warren G. Bennis, eds. (New York: McGraw-Hill Book Co., 1967).

[62] Chris Argyris, *Integrating the Individual and the Organization* (New York: John Wiley and Sons, Inc., 1964) and *Understanding Organizational Behavior* (Homewood, Ill.: The Dorsey Press, Inc., 1960).

[63] Likert, *New Patterns of Management*, op. cit., p. 102.

[64] Ibid., p. 98. Many writers reflecting a human relations perspective acknowledge such psychologists as Abraham Maslow and Carl Rogers as being especially influential in their thinking.

For examples, see Abraham H. Maslow, *Motivation and Personality* (New York: Harper & Row, 1954); Carl R. Rogers, *Client-Centered Therapy* (Boston: Houghton Mifflin, 1951); and Carl R. Rogers, "Toward a Theory of Creativity" in Sidney J. Parnes and Harold F. Harding, eds., *A Source Book for Creative Thinking* (New York: Charles Scribner's Sons, 1962), pp. 63–72.

unconcerned about wages, but rather that there are additional bases of incentive. When behavior settings limit or place these various motivational forces in conflict, less than optimal performance will result. This view of man represents a fundamental set of assumptions that differentiate these theorists from others, especially those with a classical perspective.[65]

Second, persons derive their primary satisfactions through the groups within which they interact. Failure to participate in satisfying group relationships will result in higher turnover, lower morale, more rapid fatigue, reduced performance levels, and the like. Work settings and flows should be designed to facilitate group emergence. Thus, coffee breaks, rest periods, and so on are important not only because they reduce individual physical fatigue, but also because they provide a mechanism whereby persons can interact—to get to know each other, to become a group.

Third, group formation and process can be manipulated. As implied above, various techniques can be used to encourage group formation. Most important, however, is the style of the supervisor. In contrast to the impersonal or harsh supervisory style implicit in the classical view, human relations researchers argue that their findings show "that those supervisors and managers whose pattern of leadership yields consistently favorable attitudes more often think of employees as 'human beings rather than just persons to get the work done.' Consistently, in study after study, the data show that treating people as 'human beings' rather than 'cogs in a machine' is a variable highly related to the attitudes and motivation of the subordinate at every level in the organization." [66] Thus, supervisors should be skilled in building peer-group loyalty through a leadership style that emphasizes "the principle of supportive relationships." [67] This principle states: "The leadership and other processes of the organization must be such as to ensure a maximum probability that in all interactions and all relationships with the organization each member will, in light of his background, values and expectations, view the experience as supportive and one which builds and maintains his sense of personal worth and importance." [68]

Fourth, group norms serve as major regulatory devices for member behavior. The discovery that production levels were being informally controlled by group norms was, of course, a major contribution of the

[65] McGregor emphasized this point to clarify discussion of his highly popular Theory X versus Theory Y. "Theory X and Theory Y are *not* managerial strategies: they are underlying beliefs about the nature of man that *influence* managers to adopt one strategy rather than another." McGregor and Bennis (eds.), *The Professional Manager*, op. cit., p. 79.

[66] Likert, *New Patterns of Management*, op. cit., p. 101.

[67] Likert, *The Human Organization*, op. cit., p. 64.

[68] Likert, *New Patterns of Management*, op. cit., p. 103.

Hawthorne studies. Social control was maintained through positive and negative sanctions. For example, persons who produce beyond the norm become labeled "rate busters" and those who do not meet the norm are "chiselers." Hence, social approval is given or withheld depending on the degree to which individual behavior conforms to group standards. As it is assumed that persons desire group acceptance, their behavior is thus regulated by group pressures. Individual conformity results in high or low performance levels, depending on the norm or level adopted by the group. Effective supervisors are characterized by an ability to manipulate members so as to precipitate high peer-group loyalty, high group performance standards, and high commitment to group and organizational goals. Thus, competition among group members is a less effective motivational strategy to increase group performance than cooperation.

> The best performance, lowest costs, and the highest levels of earnings and of employee satisfaction occur when the drive for a sense of personal worth is used to create strong motivational forces to *cooperate* rather than *compete* with one's peers and colleagues. The use of this motive in ways which yield cooperative rather than competitive relationships appears to yield stronger motivational forces oriented toward achieving the organization's objectives and is accompanied by positive rather than negative side effects. Subordinates aid each other and share leadership tasks rather than putting immediate self-interest ahead of long-range self-interest and organizational success.[69]

Fifth, effective organizations are viewed as sets of interlocked functioning groups. Pelz's research indicated that "subordinates expect their supervisors to be able to exercise an influence upward in dealing with problems on the job and in handling problems which affect them and their well being."[70] To be successful, supervisors must be able to exert such influence. The most effective way to accomplish this and to maintain necessary group coordination is to use the "linking pin" principle. As illustrated in Figure 2–3, Likert suggests that groups can be linked together to form a total functioning organization.

Sixth, the linking pin structure further increases an individual's motivation by maximizing his sense of participation in the entire organization. His ideas and desires can become expressed and felt beyond his single work group. He is aware of the organization's objectives and how he has helped, in part, to create and implement them. "Each member recognizes that the more adequately the organization's objectives are met, the greater is the extent to which his own goals and desires are fulfilled."[71]

[69] Likert, *The Human Organization*, op. cit., p. 75.
[70] Likert, *New Patterns of Management*, op. cit., p. 113.
[71] Ibid., p. 240.

FIGURE 2–3　The Linking Pin Function

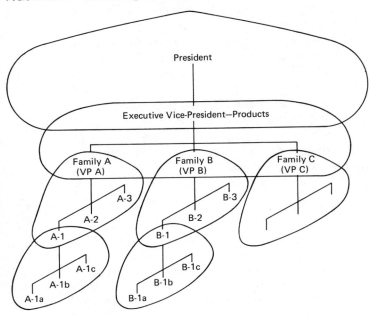

Vertical, Overlapping Group Linkages of Product Departments.

SOURCE: From *The Human Organization* by Rensis Likert (New York: McGraw-Hill Book Company, 1967), p. 166. Used with permission of McGraw-Hill Book Company.

Seventh, in contrast to other types of management systems, e.g., exploitive authoritative, benevolent authoritative, and consultative, the participative group system is most effective. Likert has spelled out in some detail forty-three items whereby these four types of management systems are differentiated.[72] Although the seven major dimensions (motivation, communication, interpretation, decision making, goal setting, control, performance) are more inclusive than the earlier work of Mayo and other Hawthorne researchers, the major emphasis remains on the general quality of the group and organizational "atmosphere" as reflected in day-to-day interactions. Thus, participative organizations provide "a supportive, ego-building atmosphere, one in which people feel valued and respected and in which confidence and trust grow. The atmosphere is permeated by ego-enhancing rather than ego-deflating and threatening points of view toward people."[73]

Management systems can be changed. Measurement on the forty-three items at different points in time suggests that shifts toward the

[72] Ibid., pp. 223–33.
[73] Ibid., p. 238.

participative group style (System 4) results in increased production.[74] Likert further argues that as organizational management systems can be measured, these data, once obtained, could be made available for decision makers to consider. Hence, as a subunit began to drift away from System 4, actions could be taken to assist the subunit to regain its equilibrium. Thus, a continual flow of selected data would be available, which would indicate the "organizational atmosphere." And with this type of continuous feedback system the organization would increase its sense of "self-awareness" greatly beyond what is available through reports limited to financial data.[75]

Illustrative Propositions

1. Organizations that appeal to both economic and social motives will have higher productivity than organizations that rely exclusively on economic motives.
2. Organizations that use group participation and involvement in setting goals will have higher productivity than organizations that do not.
3. Organizations with patterns of frequent upward, downward, and lateral communication will be more productive than organizations with predominately downward communication patterns.
4. Organizations in which members are psychologically very close (in which superiors know and understand problems faced by subordinates) will be more productive than organizations in which members are distant psychologically.
5. Organizations in which decision making is shared widely throughout the structure with well-integrated linking processes provided by overlapping groups will be more productive than organizations in which most decisions are made at upper levels.

Critique

Several criticisms can be made of the human relations perspective. As with classical theorists, human relations researchers are often overly prescriptive rather than analytic. Their accounts seem pushed to describe how organizations *ought* to function rather than how they actually do function. For example, Likert lists performance characteristics such as productivity for each of the four management systems. System 1 (exploitive authoritative) is listed as "mediocre productivity," whereas System 4 (participative group) is listed as "excellent produc-

---

[74] Likert, *The Human Organization*, op. cit., pp. 29–38.
[75] Ibid., pp. 146–55.

tivity." [76] Surely this should be considered problematic until more reasearch is done.

As is implicit above, variables designated are often vaguely defined, frequently highly value laden, and lack comprehensiveness. The very labels used to define the four management systems reflect this value-laden tone. Review of the "table of organizational variables," [77] indicates much concern with "warmth" of interpersonal relations and degree of group participation in decision making. However, the concept of power does not appear in the list or even in the index of either of Likert's major books. Certainly, power can be conceptualized in many other ways.

The "social humanitarian spirit" that is implicit throughout the viewpoint, necessarily presents conflicts as an evil. Conflict, like status differences and competition, may be highly functional at times. Yet the perspective presents us with variables that prevent us from seeing this. Indeed, through this set of lenses, conflict would appear nonexistent except in terms of "personality clashes".

As Etzioni and others have indicated,[78] the view fails to recognize that individuals need not always be adjusted to existing systems. Through the heavy emphasis on warmth in personal relationships, the perspective seems almost to suggest that individuals who might disagree with company policies can be "helped" through group meetings to understand why such policies are necessary. We need not deny the power of group pressure—but might not some policies be wrong, at least from the value perspectives of some persons? Hence, the charge of manipulation: you adjust the worker to understand why it is that he can be paid only so much per hour! It is assumed that there is a basic rightness to organizational policies and structures, if only individuals can be assisted to understand. Of course, presumably individuals agree with policies that they had a part in making, but the model overlooks vast differences in status, life styles, and so on. It fails to recognize that consensus on many matters simply may not be possible nor desirable.

Finally, little mention is made of the environments in which organizations function. Emphasis is on internal functioning rather than on organization-environment transactions. External threats to survival remain unmentioned. Despite these criticisms, however, the human relations model contains many excellent insights.

[76] Ibid., p. 24.
[77] Ibid., pp. 212–29.
[78] Etzioni, *Modern Organizations*, op. cit., pp. 41–45.
See also Curt Tausky, *Work Organizations: Major Theoretical Perspectives* (Itasca, Ill.: F. E. Peacock Publishers, 1970).

Chapter 2. Perspectives in Organizational Theory

A Natural System Perspective

In contrast to the highly rationalistic and mechanistic image implicit in the rational and classical views, other theorists have viewed organizations much like biological organisms—continually changing in efforts to cope with environmental modifications. Most changes are not based on planning. And even planned changes are recognized to precipitate many significant unanticipated consequences. Thus, organizations are viewed as adaptive structures within a changing environment that must be coped with if equilibrium is to be maintained. This perspective, which is used by many, especially sociologists, is best illustrated in the work of Michels,[79] Parsons,[80] and Selznick.[81]

The "Iron Law of Oligarchy," suggested by Michels in *Political Parties,* suggests that liberal and revolutionary organizations become consistently more conservative over time as the leaders are less and less willing to risk any threat to their positions of power. And his analysis of socialist parties and labor unions in Europe before World War I clearly supported this thesis. Over time, the original goals were displaced, and these organizations became concerned with one primary goal, survival.[82]

The use of an organic analogy in studying social organization is certainly not a new idea. It can be traced back at least to Plato's *Republic.* But the analogy has been especially well developed by Talcott Parsons and his colleagues. Thus, Parsons suggests that organizations, like other social systems, have certain needs or functional requirements that must be met if they are to survive. Hence, organizations must attain goals because that is why they were constructed. But they must also have adaptive structures that will permit them to cope with environmental changes. And further, integrative, tension-management, and pattern-maintenance mechanisms must also be present.[83]

[79] Robert Michels, *Political Parties*, trans. Eden Paul and Cedar Paul (New York: The Free Press, 1949), first published 1915.

[80] See especially Talcott Parsons, *The Social System* (New York: The Free Press, 1951); "An Outline of the Social System" in *Theories of Society*, Talcott Parsons et al., eds. (New York: The Free Press, 1961), pp. 30–76; Talcott Parsons, "Suggestions for a Sociological Approach to Theory of Organizations," *Administrative Science Quarterly*, 1: 63–85 (June 1956); and Max Black, ed., *Social Theories of Talcott Parsons* (Englewood Cliffs, N.J.: Prentice-Hall, Inc., 1961).

[81] Philip Selznick, *TVA and the Grass Roots* (Berkeley and Los Angeles: University of California Press, 1949); *Leadership in Administration* (Evanston, Ill.: Row, Peterson and Company, 1957).

[82] Michels' general thesis has received empirical support—e.g., Sheldon L. Messinger, "Organizational Transformation," *American Sociological Review*, 20: 3–10 (February 1955).

[83] Parsons, "An Outline of the Social System," op. cit., pp. 57–66.

Structures to perform these functions must be evolved if the organization is to survive.

In a somewhat different vein, Philip Selznick suggests a distinction between organizational and institutional analysis. *Organization* "suggests a certain bareness, a lean, no-nonsense system of consciously coordinated activities. It refers to an expendable tool, a rational instrument engineered to a job." [84]

In contrast, an *institution* "is more nearly a natural product of social needs and pressures—a responsive, adaptive organism." [85] Selznick is not referring to different empirical objects, but to a mode of analysis. And his perspective, like that of Michels and Parsons, emphasizes the "natural whole" as a living, responsive organism. This is not to say that change is never planned, but only that "living associations" "are complex mixtures of both designed and responsive behavior." [86] The focus is on "dynamic adaptation" as a mode of analysis—i.e., by confronting day-to-day external situations, internal changes are generated that result in new needs and new problems and thereby precipitate changes in the organization's personality or character.

The General Image

These natural-system[87] or functionalist theorists vary greatly in the analytical terminology used, but eight central ideas seem to be emphasized. First, the focus of their analyses is on the organization as a "natural whole." As a structure, it has a history. Historically, events, and the organization's response to these events, have created a "character" or "personality." And an understanding of this "personality" is essential if organizational behavior is to be predicted.

Second, although organizations do have goals, it should be recognized that "every structure has a set of basic needs and develops systematic means of self-defense." [88] Most of the behaviors observed within organizations are not specifically goal-directed, but rather are

[84] Selznick, *Leadership in Administration*, op. cit., p. 5.

[85] Ibid.

[86] Ibid., p. 6.

[87] This term is from Gouldner, op. cit., p. 405. Although the present summary is more detailed, his analysis was most helpful.

[88] Selznick, *TVA and the Grass Roots*, op. cit., p. 252.

Selznick emphasized that his reference was to organizational, not individual needs. "Organizational needs" he defined as ". . . stable systems of variables which, with respect to many changes in organizational structure and behavior, are independent." Ibid., p. 252. Such needs include: ". . . the security of the organization as a whole in relation to social forces in its environment; the stability of the lines of authority and communication; the stability of informal relations within the organization; the continuity of policy and of the sources of its determination; a homogeneity of outlook with respect to the meaning and role of the organization." Ibid., p. 252.

attempts to meet these needs so that equilibrium can be maintained or restored.

Third, organizations exist in environments. And the problem of organizational equilibrium is most directly affected by environmental change. Thus, organizations are confronted with environments in which there are competing organizations, various types of threats to their prestige or economic base, inducements to lure away both existing and potential members, and the like. Yet, to survive, organizations must somehow adapt to their environments.

Fourth, although there are many types of adaptive processes, Selznick placed great emphasis on "cooptation"—that is, "the process of absorbing new elements into the leadership or policy-determining structure of an organization as one means of averting threats to its stability or existence." [89] This process was highly important in Selznick's interpretation of the behavior of TVA officials. Cooptation can be formal (self-governing committees in housing projects, for example), or informal (the appointment, for instance, of a recognized leader of a politically conservative group to a university fund raising effort).[90] In either instance, such behavior represents an organization's effort to adapt better to its environment. But such adaptive responses are often dynamic, i.e., the response precipitates internal change in the structure of the organization.

Thus, fifth, as organizations seek to adapt to their environments, these actions in turn modify their basic structures, and "personality." Hence, day-to-day policy decisions cannot be viewed as short-term goal-directed expedients, as it is the cumulative effect of these actions that defines the very "character" of the organization. Leaders must then be aware that "the setting of institutional *goals* cannot be divorced from the enunciation of governing principles. Goal-setting, if it is institutionally meaningful, is framed in the language of character or identity, that is, it tells us what we should 'do' in order to become what we want to 'be'." [91] Thus, from Selznick's view, institutional leaders are primarily to promote and protect basic values, through the recognition that their organization has a certain character that is the result of historical adaptive responses. Policy decisions, like one to market new "prestige items," will have significant consequences in changing that character. Hence, if organizations are to survive they

[89] Selznick, *TVA and the Grass Roots*, op. cit., p. 13.
[90] James L. Price, "Continuity in Social Research: TVA and the Grass Roots," *Pacific Sociological Review*, 1: 63–68 (Fall, 1958). Price has proposed a helpful refinement of the cooptation concept.
[91] Selznick, *Leadership in Administration*, op. cit., p. 144.
Clark has written three exceptional case studies of Reed, Antioch, and Swarthmore Colleges, in which he describes this process in detail. Burton Clark, *The Distinctive College: Antioch, Reed and Swarthmore* (Chicago: Aldine Publishing Company, 1970).

cannot drift and adapt haphazardly to their environments without running a strong risk of developing segments with contradictory values and objectives.

Sixth, members are viewed as being more or less committed to the general values of the institution. Moreover, changes in the quality of members may precipitate institutional value changes despite efforts of organizational leaders. Thus, in contrast to the Weberian or classical perspective, goal setting and member behavior are viewed as often unplanned, growing out of constraint patterns that have emerged unconsciously through daily routine decisions.

Seventh through the equilibrium concept, interdependence of parts is stressed. Policy changes made by one unit in the organization will, more than likely, have consequences for several other segments. And many of the consequences will be unplanned, undesired, and often unrecognized.

Thus, eighth and finally, the total organization is viewed as a collection of subsystems. And just as the entire organization is fighting for survival and growth, so also is each sub-unit. Hence, in contrast to an efficient machine designed to attain a single, clearly defined goal, these natural system theorists suggest an image of competing systems within systems, each trying to maintain its own equilibrium, each fighting for survival.

Illustrative Propositions

1. Organizations that can most easily adapt to changes in their environment are more likely to survive than those that cannot.
2. Organizations that have a high degree of autonomy in relationship to their environment are more likely to survive than those that do not.
3. All subsystems within organizations are constantly trying to change their structures so as to increase their autonomy.
4. Changes in internal organizational structures are a direct function of changes in external or environmental elements.
5. If threatened by powerful environmental forces, organizations that attempt to coopt key personalities from those forces are more likely to survive than those that do not.

Critique

Among the numerous criticisms that can be raised of this natural system perspective, five are most significant. First, there is a sharp de-emphasis on the formal organizational structure. Rational planning and decision making appear almost not to exist. Whereas the formal structure receives nearly total focus in the rational and classical viewpoints, it tends to be almost deleted here—and it is clear that, although not deserving the emphasis given in the rational model, the formal structure is an important facet of organizational life.

Second, despite the emphasis on informal structures and individual responses to values, and so on, little if any attention is given to the interpersonal relationships among members. As persons interact in organizations, clearly sets of interpersonal relationships emerge that may be very powerful in guiding their behavior as human relations theorists suggest.

Third, the central variables remain highly abstract and vaguely defined. Although there is much discussion of environment, for example, the concept remains unanalyzed, and the result is a series of concepts like equilibrium, dynamic adaptation, integration, tension management, and the like, which seem to fit together but remain extremely vague. Selznick's detailed analysis of "cooptation" as an adaptive process is perhaps the most developed concept, but even it remains more at the "sensitizing" level.

Thus, fourth, operational specification of the concepts remains to be done. As they remain highly vague, efforts to construct even crude operational measurements are probably premature until much conceptual elaboration has occurred. For example, measurement of equilibrium would be most desirable, but a moment of thought reveals the complexities involved in such a task.

Fifth, and finally, largely because of the above difficulties it is hard to know whether or not this set of concepts is at all predictive. Selznick's case study of TVA sounds plausible. Certainly the conceptual tools he constructs are of much help in interpreting the complex phenomena selected for analysis. But the perspective does not provide us with a clear set of mechanisms or even constructs that we might apply to another organization to make predictions. Parsons's work is even less helpful in this regard. Using the "system problems" approach is helpful as a broad and abstract perspective. And of course, Parsons does offer numerous other constructs. But, as Homans concluded, we still have "a language without sentences." [92] And the "words" in that language remain very vague—perhaps impossible to make operational.

A Conflict Perspective

In contrast to natural system theorists with their emphasis on stability and equilibrium, others have focused on conflict. The idea that conflict and its resolution are central facts of society can be traced back into

[92] George C. Homans, *Social Behavior: Its Elementary Forms* (New York: Harcourt, Brace, Jovanovich, Inc., 1961), p. 10.

antiquity, to writers, for example, in ancient China, Greece, and Rome.[93] Although numerous social theorists have viewed conflict as a critical aspect in societal analysis, the work of Karl Marx undoubtedly has proved most significant. But for a variety of reasons, Marx's impact on American sociology was delayed. Some early American sociologists like Albion Small, writing in the early 1900s, emphasized that conflict was "the basic and universal social process. Social life will be structured locally by whatever particular conflicts the individual faces." [94] And since Small, George Vold has made a major effort to explicate and apply a conflict model in the study of criminology.[95] However, despite the efforts of these men and many others, the natural system model prevailed in American sociology through the 1940s and early 1950s.

In 1956, Lewis A. Coser published *The Functions of Social Conflict*[96] and the conflict perspective was reborn in American sociology. Coser argued that researchers who reflected the natural system orientation had too long neglected the study of conflict. For Parsons, Coser states, conflict is to be equated "with deviant behavior, which is seen as a disease in need of treatment." [97] Moreover, other organizational theorists, such as Mayo with his human relations model, had formulated the problem solely in terms of conflict avoidance as viewed exclusively from a management viewpoint. "To Mayo, management embodied the central purposes of society, and with this initial orientation he never considered the possibility that an industrial system might contain conflicting interests, as distinct from different attitudes or 'logics.'" [98] In an effort to correct the imbalance that had existed in American sociology since its beginnings, Coser brilliantly analyzed, integrated, and extended an essay by Georg Simmel that had only recently become available to most American scholars through a translation by Kurt Wolff.[99]

In 1957, *The Journal of Conflict Resolution* made its first appearance. Among the articles published, a statement by Mack and Snyder, which appeared in the first issue, remains useful as a major codification of propositions regarding conflict resolution, the likelihood of conflict,

[93] Don Martindale, *The Nature and Types of Sociological Theory* (Cambridge, Mass.: Riverside Press, 1960), pp. 129–30. See also pp. 127–207.

[94] Ibid., p. 194. See also Albion W. Small, *General Sociology: An Exposition of the Main Development in Sociological Theory From Spencer to Ratzenhofer* (Chicago: University of Chicago Press, 1905, 1925).

[95] George B. Vold, *Theoretical Criminology* (New York: Oxford University Press, 1958).

[96] Lewis A. Coser, *The Functions of Social Conflict* (New York: The Free Press, 1956).

[97] Ibid., pp. 22–23.

[98] Ibid., p. 24.

[99] Georg Simmel, *Conflict*, trans. Kurt H. Wolff (New York: The Free Press, 1955).

intensity of conflicts, and so on.[100] They presented more than fifty such propositions, e.g., "conflict with outgroups increases internal cohesion."[101]

Of course, many have since contributed to the analysis of social conflict, but the works of Coser[102] and Ralf Dahrendorf[103] remain the most helpful. Coser has clearly stated that he feels that an integrated model, emphasizing both consensus and conflict, is needed, and his efforts aided in bringing the insights of Marx and Simmel to American sociologists.[104] Among recent organizational studies that demonstrate the utility of this perspective are Corwin's analysis of staff conflicts in twenty-eight midwestern high schools[105] and Baldridge's descriptive case study of discord and confrontation at New York University.[106]

The General Image

Eight major ideas form the core of the perspective presented by conflict theorists. First, conflict is natural; it should not be defined as

[100] Raymond W. Mack and Richard C. Snyder, "The Analysis of Social Conflict—Toward an Overview and Synthesis," *Journal of Conflict Resolution*, 1: 212–48 (June 1957).

[101] Ibid., p. 215.

[102] Lewis A. Coser, *Continuities in the Study of Social Conflict* (New York: The Free Press, 1967); Ralf Dahrendorf, *Class and Class Conflict in Industrial Society* (Stanford, Calif.: Stanford University Press, 1959).

[103] Ralf Dahrendorf, *Essays in the Theory of Society* (Stanford, Calif.: Stanford University Press, 1968).

[104] Despite his attacks on Parsons and other "integration" theorists, Coser has stated, "I fully agree with Robin Williams, who recently wrote in a spirited rebuttal of such views, that, 'Actual societies are held together by consensus, by interdependence, by sociability, and by coercion . . . . The real job is to show how actual social structure and processes operating in these ways can be predicted and explained.'" Robin Williams, Jr., "Some Further Comments on Chronic Controverseries," *American Journal of Sociology*, 71: 717–21 (May 1966). Coser, *Continuities in the Study of Social Conflict*, op. cit., p. 9.

Dahrendorf's position is less clear, but he appears to maintain the position presented in his highly popular "Out of Utopia: Toward a Reorientation of Sociological Analysis," *American Journal of Sociology*, 64: 115–27 (September 1958). For example, "That societies are held together by some kind of value consensus seems to me either a definition of societies or a statement clearly contradicted by empirical evidence . . ." (p. 120). Thus, he appears to support the separation of the conflict model from an "integration" model with its "utopian bias," and fixed answers. "There are sociological problems for the explanation of which the integration theory of society provides adequate assumptions; there are other problems which can be explained only in terms of the coercion theory of society; there are, finally, problems for which both theories appear adequate." Dahrendorf, *Class and Class Conflict in Industrial Society*, op. cit., p. 159.

[105] Ronald G. Corwin, *Militant Professionalism* (New York: Appleton-Century-Crofts, 1970).

[106] J. Victor Baldridge, *Power and Conflict in the University* (New York: John Wiley and Sons, Inc., 1971).

disease. There is a limit to resources and freedom. Persons value both, and what one person has necessarily limits someone else. Hence, there is an inevitable struggle among groups, as definitions vary among them as to what comprises appropriate allocations of resources and freedom. "Every society displays at every point dissensus and conflict; social conflict is ubiquitous." [107]

Second, groups vary in power. Each group seeks to increase its power over others. "Every society is based on the coercion of some of its members by others." [108] Hence, especially groups of persons subject to greatest coercion by more powerful groups will make efforts to increase their power. Groups form a sense of consciousness, purpose, and cohesion. Individual members come to see their common plight and are willing to make short-term sacrifices if they believe that it might result in better future conditions. Thus, groups constrain member behavior so as to increase group power through conflict. Presumably, increased group power will enhance the gratifications of the individual members, especially economically.

Third, system change can best be understood through analysis of this principal aspect of social life—the conflict resulting from struggles of persons and groups to alter existing power distributions. "Every society is at every point subject to processes of change; social change is ubiquitous." [109] Thus, the nature and quality of system change is primarily determined by the manner and style in which conflicts are resolved.

Coser accepts Parsons' distinction between changes *within* a system and change *of* a system. He indicates that the distinction between the two is somewhat relative because there is always some sort of continuity with the past: "one may claim that all that can be observed is a change of the organization of social relations; but from one perspective such change may be considered re-establishment of equilibrium whereas from another it may be seen as the formation of a new system." [110] But he emphasizes that too often system change has been analyzed in terms of re-establishment of equilibrium, rather than change *of* a system, i.e., "when all major structural relations, its basic institutions, and its prevailing value system have been drastically altered." [111]

Fourth, conflict has many positive functions. For example, data from Corwin's study of conflict in public schools supported his hypothesis that "organizational tension and conflict are positively associated with job satisfaction and satisfaction with the teaching career." [112] By per-

[107] Dahrendorf, *Class and Class Conflict in Industrial Society*, op. cit., p. 162.
[108] Ibid.
[109] Ibid.
[110] Coser, *Continuities in the Study of Social Conflict*, op. cit., p. 27.
[111] Ibid., p. 28.
[112] Corwin, *Militant Professionalism*, op. cit., pp. 277–78.

mitting conflict to occur in regularized and institutionalized manners, flexible systems can allow new solutions to emerge. Of course, for highly rigid systems this is not the case. "The intensity of a conflict which threatens to 'tear apart,' which attacks the consensual basis of a social system, is related to the rigidity of the structure. What threatens the equilibrium of such a structure is not conflict as such, but the rigidity itself which permits hostilities to accumulate and to be channeled along one major line of cleavage once they break out in conflict." [113] Thus, by ventilitating hostilities and locating areas of strain and dissensus, groups are able to maintain a stronger system, which is less likely to disintegrate suddenly because of an accumulation of pent-up anger and disagreements.

Fifth, following from the above point, the absence of conflict is not necessarily a sign of system strength or stability. Quite the opposite, the presence of conflict may be indicative of a highly stable system. For example, "Closeness gives rise to frequent occasions for conflict, but if the participants feel that their relationships are tenuous, they will avoid conflict, fearing that it might endanger the continuance of the relation." [114] Thus, in close relationships, frequency of conflict, except where it concerns basic consensus, can actually be used as an index of stability rather than instability. Empirical support of this theme is found in Corwin's study. He reports that the presence of such "facilitating channels" as high informal interaction rates, e.g., proportion of faculty who lunch together, is correlated positively with frequency of conflict.[115] Similarly, conflict in more secondary relationships may indicate the presence of a "balancing mechanism," which also is indicative of increased stability. "Loosely structured groups and open societies, by allowing conflicts, institute safeguards against the type of conflict which would endanger basic consensus and thereby minimize the dangers of divergences touching core values. The interdependence of antagonistic groups and the crisscrossing within such societies of conflicts, which serve to 'sew the social system together' by cancelling each other out, thus prevent disintegration along one primary line of cleavage." [116]

Sixth, social conflict is a critical process in the maintenance of system vitality. Bureaucratic structures, especially, are likely to become ritualistic and stagnant. "By attacking and overcoming the resistance to innovation and change that seems to be an 'occupational psychosis' always threatening the bureaucratic office holder, it [conflict] can help to insure that the system does not stifle in the deadening routine of

---

[113] Coser, *The Functions of Social Conflict*, op. cit., p. 157.
[114] Ibid., p. 85.
[115] Corwin, *Militant Professionalism*, op. cit., p. 269–72.
[116] Coser, *The Functions of Social Conflict*, op. cit., p. 80.

habituation and that in the planning activity itself creativity and invention can be applied." [117]

Seventh, there are many mechanisms by which conflict may be tolerated and controlled, thus offering an alternative to total group consensus. Eugene Litwak has provided some helpful insight in this regard through conceptualizing four "Mechanisms of Segregation" whereby "potentially contradictory social relations are co-ordinated in some common organizational goal." [118] (1) *Role separation.* For example, hiring and firing are done by a group that has no responsibilities for production, such as the civil service. "In this way, the potential contradiction between positive affect and objectivity can be minimized, while the virtues are maximized." [119] (2) *Physical distance.* Units with different operating philosophies are physically separated, e.g., basic researchers and production staff are often kept physically separate. (3) *Transferral occupations.* An example is engineers who "must move between the world of science, with its colleague relationships, to the world of production, with its formal hierarchical relations, without permitting the attitudes to mix." [120] (4) *Evaluation procedures.* For example, "If the organization contains contradictory social relations and, at the same time, is subject to constant changes, then there must be some procedure for determining points at which one kind of social relations should be replaced by another." [121] Thus, through such mechanisms as these and others, dissensus and contradictory forms of organization can coexist without conflict or an eventual "single-minded consensus."

Eighth, and finally, from the perspective of these theorists, violence need not be viewed as irrational, aimless outbursts. Violence is not an indicator of the intensity of conflict; rather, the two are distinct aspects of any conflict situation: "intensity refers to the expenditure and degree of involvement of conflicting parties." [122] In contrast, "the violence of conflict relates rather to its manifestations than to its causes; it is a matter of the weapons that are chosen by conflict groups to express their hostilities." [123] And "organized conflict groups tend to use less violent means of combat than those that lack organization." [124]

Given these distinctions, violent behavior, such as riots by blacks during the middle 1960s, need not be interpreted as irrational or sense-

[117] Coser, *Continuities in the Study of Social Conflict,* op. cit., p. 24.
[118] Eugene Litwak, "Models of Bureaucracy Which Permit Conflict," *American Journal of Sociology,* 67: 182 (September 1961).
[119] Ibid., p. 182.
[120] Ibid., p. 184.
[121] Ibid.
[122] Dahrendorf, *Class and Class Conflict in Industrial Society,* op. cit., p. 211.
[123] Ibid., p. 212.
[124] Coser, *Continuities in the Study of Social Conflict,* op. cit., p. 3.

less. Rather, they may be viewed as cries "for help in a situation where other means to draw attention to the community's distress seemed socially unavoidable." [125] Analogous to machine-breaking incidents by industrial workers before there were union channels for bargaining, these riots may be viewed as rational conflict strategies whereby vague attitudes were crystallized, discrimination and its consequences exposed, and the change process accelerated. From the view of conflict theorists, American sociology clearly evidenced its weakness by its failure to anticipate or explain the major conflict confrontations of the 1960s by blacks, college students, and others.

Illustrative Propositions

1. "Conflict with another group leads to the mobilization of the energies of group members and hence to increased cohesion of the group." [126]
2. "Conflict serves to establish and maintain the identity and boundary lines of societies and groups." [127]
3. "Groups engaged in continued struggle with the outside tend to be intolerant within." [128]
4. "Rigid systems which suppress the incidence of conflict exert pressure towards the emergence of radical cleavages and violent forms of conflict." [129]
5. "Organizational tension and conflict are positively associated with the rate of informal interaction among a faculty and between a faculty and its administration, and with their participation in employee associations." [130]

Critique

Five major points of criticism have been raised against the conflict perspective. First, there is more to social life than just conflict. Hence, the analysis and the object of study become overly narrow and distorted. Coser seems to recognize this, however, as he has suggested that efforts at combining this view with the natural system perspective must take place (see footnote 104). However, as a conceptual framework, integration of social groups is ignored. What holds groups together aside from fights with outgroups remains unasked. Therefore, the questions raised and the directions of the analysis remain exceed-

[125] Ibid., p. 101.
[126] Coser, *The Functions of Social Conflict*, op. cit., p. 95.
[127] Ibid., p. 37.
[128] Ibid., p. 103.
[129] Coser, *Continuities in the Study of Social Conflict*, op. cit., p. 29.
[130] Corwin, *Militant Professionalism*, op. cit., p. 270.

ingly narrow. One is forced to see conflict everywhere—to the exclusion of anything else.

Implicit in the above criticism, significant processes like cooperation and coordination are ignored. Group cohesion is viewed exclusively as a product of reactions to external threat and hostilities. Mutual respect, shared values, and the like, indeed, any of the variables comprising the bases of consensus proposed by human relations or natural system theorists are absent. Thus, as a consequence of the exclusive focus on conflict, several types of behaviors and explanatory variables are ignored.

The perspective proposes that social change is an outgrowth of conflict resolution. Often, no doubt, it is. However, planned change and changes through consensus are slighted. Analysis of planned change through this perspective would result in excessive concentration on conflict, to the exclusion of changes reached through consensual process. Although the researcher is sensitized to look for conflict, few other conceptual tools are provided whereby efforts at planned change might be analyzed.

A multitude of concepts, like equilibrium and homeostatis, are criticized for their narrowness, vagueness, and political bias. However, when one attempts to conceptualize empirical work of an analytical nature using the central concepts of this perspective, many of the same arguments seem to apply. For example, how is the "rigidity" of a system measured? Indeed, the intensity of conflict, visibility of objects of contention, group tolerance, and rigidity of group boundaries, remain highly abstract and difficult variables to make operational. Thus, while the central variables proposed by natural system theorists can be criticized, the conflict perspective appears lacking as well.

Finally, there is minimal analysis of group or organizational environment. Of course, there is discussion of in-group–out-group conflict, but the processes whereby sectors of an organization's environment constrain and modify member behavior are not analyzed except in a very general fashion. However, the empirical research cited earlier by Corwin, and especially that of Baldridge, emphasize changes in and conflicts with environmental sectors. Thus, there is nothing inherent in the perspective to preclude such analysis.

Despite these criticisms, the insights are important. And the idea that conflict will most likely emerge in rigid systems that resist efforts toward change by subunits is especially useful if viewed in generic terms, i.e., system-environment interaction.

An Exchange Perspective

In contrast to the abstract and theoretical perspectives on which we have focused thus far, several analysts have begun at the observational level. They have proceeded on the assumption that organizations, like other social systems, can best be studied by analysis of the interactions among members. Chapple, for example, suggests that "in factories, it is easily seen that the process of manufacture consists of a series of events connected with the flow of material through the factory in which individuals are in interaction in a fixed and repetitive way." [131] Those subscribing to this "objective" approach have been critical of others who do not observe behavior, but instead seek to ascertain the "functions" of various systems. "Subtle minds and good observers," Chapple argues, ". . . can discuss and dissect the institutions that they are dealing with until they find as many functions as the schoolmen in the Middle Ages found angels on the head of a pin." [132]

This perspective, with its focus on objective description and analysis of patterns of interaction, reflects the earlier work of Simmel.[133] The viewpoint, however, gained increased popularity through the efforts of Eliot Chapple and Conrad Arensberg[134] during the late 1930s. Their work dovetailed in many respects with the emergence of sociometric techniques first introduced by Moreno that greatly stimulated the establishment of the journal *Sociometry* in 1937.[135] Although much broader in scope, this interactional perspective clearly is apparent in C. I. Barnard's work.[136] Despite his focus on cooperation among individuals as a prime requisite for groups and organizations, Barnard emphasized that "it is the *system of interactions* which appears to be the basis for the concept of a 'group.' " [137] Finally, in 1943, William Foote Whyte presented *Street Corner Society*,[138] which clearly reflected the influence of Chapple and Arensberg. In that now classic piece, Whyte applied their perspective in a brilliant fashion and clearly

[131] Eliot D. Chapple, "Measuring Human Relations: An Introduction to the Study of the Interaction of Individuals," *Genetic Psychology Monographs*, **22**: 60 (1940).

[132] Ibid., p. 52.

[133] For example, Kurt Wolff, *The Sociology of Georg Simmel* (New York: The Free Press, 1950).

Both Homans and Blau emphasize the linkage to Simmel's work—e.g., George C. Homans, "Social Behavior as Exchange," *American Journal of Sociology*, **62**: 597 (May 1958); and Peter M. Blau, *Exchange and Power in Social Life* (New York: John Wiley and Sons, Inc., 1964), pp. 12–14.

[134] For example, Alexander B. Horsfall and Conrad M. Arensberg, "Teamwork and Productivity in a Shoe Factory," *Human Organization*, **8**: 13–25 (Winter 1949).

[135] For a detailed discussion of the emergence and reactions to the "Sociometry Movement," see Jacob L. Moreno, *Who Shall Survive?* (New York: Beacon House, Inc., 1953), pp. xiii–cviii.

[136] Chester I. Barnard, *The Functions of the Executive* (Cambridge, Mass.: Harvard University Press, 1938).

[137] Ibid., p. 70.

[138] William F. Whyte, *Street Corner Society* (Chicago: University of Chicago Press, 1943), p. 287.

illustrated the potential power of this viewpoint, which he has continued to modify and refine in his analyses of restaurants, manufacturing plants, and other types of organizations.[139]

In contrast to Whyte's case studies of social structures, George Homans abstracted from the work of Whyte and others, the rudimentary elements of a theoretical model.[140] Reflecting a position voiced by other interactional theorists, Homans was critical of excessive theoretical abstraction. "In sociology we are devoted to 'big' words: status, culture, function, heuristic, particularistic, methodology, integration, solidarity, authority. Too often we work with these words and not with observations. Or rather, we do not wed the two." [141] Using the elemental concepts of sentiment, interaction, activity, and norms, Homans carefully presented a set of hypotheses through which the behavior of human groups might be understood.

In 1958, Homans presented his analysis of "exchange." [142] Declaring himself an "ultimate psychological reductionist," he linked concepts from behavioral psychology (especially that of B. F. Skinner) to his earlier work. During operant conditioning experiments, Skinner's pigeons were engaged in a type of exchange relationship—sequences of pecks for kernels of corn. Men, too, often engage in such exchange relationships. "Each is emitting behavior reinforced to some degree by the behavior of the other." Each finds "the other's behavior reinforcing, and I shall call the reinforcers—the equivalent of the pigeon's corn—*values*, for this, I think, is what we mean by this term. As he emits behavior, each man may incur costs, and each man has more than one course of behavior open to him." [143] With this focus on interaction as exchange, Homans concluded, in the style of *The Human Group*, by illustrating how interaction patterns that were described in a case study by Peter Blau reflected more general and abstract propositions. (Of Blau's case study Homans wrote that it was "almost the only study

---

[139] For example, William F. Whyte, *Human Relations in the Restaurant Industry* (New York: McGraw-Hill Book Co., 1948); "The Social Structure of the Restaurant," *American Journal of Sociology*, **54**: 302–10 (January 1949); *Men at Work* (Homewood, Ill.: Richard D. Irwin, Inc. and The Dorsey Press, 1961).

Although the basic ideas of this perspective remain central in Whyte's work, he has somewhat transcended it. For example, in one of his more recent works he has tried to integrate some of the more abstract conceptualizations of technology, e.g., *Organizational Behavior: Theory and Practice* (Homewood, Ill.: Richard D. Irwin, Inc. and The Dorsey Press, 1969). However, the perspective, not the men, is our focus here.

[140] George C. Homans, *The Human Group* (New York: Harcourt, Brace, Jovanovich, Inc., 1950).

[141] Ibid., p. 10.

[142] Homans, "Social Behavior as Exchange," op. cit., pp. 597–606.

[143] Ibid., p. 589.

I am aware of that begins to show in detail how a stable and differentiated social structure in a real-life group might arise out of a process of exchange between members." [144]) These ideas were expanded, and basic principles from "elementary economics" were added in Homans' effort to explain social behavior "as an exchange of activity, tangible or intangible, and more or less rewarding or costly, between at least two persons." [145]

Alvin Gouldner, also critical of the highly abstract formulations of natural system theorists (e.g., Merton and Parsons), proposed that "some concept of reciprocity apparently has been smuggled into the basic but unstated postulates of functional analysis." [146] Returning to the fundamental question of Malinowski—"Why is it that rules of conduct in a primative society are obeyed, even though they are hard and irksome?"—Gouldner suggested that the answer lay in a more adequate understanding of reciprocity as "the pattern of exchange through which the mutual dependence of people, brought about by the division of labor, is realized. Reciprocity, therefore, is a mutually gratifying pattern of exchanging goods and services." [147] Additionally, there appears to be a "norm of reciprocity" that may be found in all cultures. In simplest terms the norm is this: "people should help those who have helped them and, therefore, those whom you have helped have an obligation to help you." [148]

> such obligations of repayment are contingent upon the imputed *value* of the benefit received. The value of the benefit and hence the debt is in proportion to and varies with—among other things—the intensity of the recipient's need at the time the benefit was bestowed ("a friend in need . . ."), the resources of the donor ("he gave although he could ill afford it"), the motives imputed to the donor ("without thought of gain"), and the nature of the constraints which are perceived to exist or to be absent ("he gave of his own free will . . .").[149]

Presumably, this general norm is applied to numerous transactions and serves as a "kind of plastic filler, capable of being poured into the shifting crevices of social structures, and serving as a kind of all-purpose moral cement." [150]

Acknowledging their debt to Homans but rejecting his position of

---

[144] Ibid., p. 604.

[145] Homans, *Social Behavior: Its Elementary Forms,* op. cit., p. 13.

[146] Alvin W. Gouldner, "The Norm of Reciprocity: A Preliminary Statement," *American Sociological Review,* 25: 163 (April 1960).

[147] Ibid., pp. 169–70.

[148] Ibid., p. 170.

[149] Ibid., p. 171.

[150] Ibid., p. 175.

psychological reductionism, both Whyte[151] and Blau[152] have sought to expand and refine the perspective by moving from description to higher levels of abstraction. Thus, although there are important differences among these theorists, there are many common themes—the most critical being a focus on observing regularities in human interaction that emerge as persons exchange benefits.

The General Image

Nine central ideas comprise the core of this viewpoint. First, analytical focus should be on persons and their interactions. Thus, one first seeks to describe the structure or pattern of observed interaction. By starting in this fashion, one avoids the Don Quixote windmill tilting activity of some colleagues, who begin with a myth and then delight in empirical work that disproves the myth. Although this makes for nice social criticism, it does little to enhance an understanding of actual human behavior. For example, many have chosen to criticize system decision-making patterns, claiming that a conspiratorial elite actually decides everything. And so they seek to discover *the* decision makers.

In contrast, Whyte proposes that we have few empirical analyses of decision making as an interactional process. Through analysis of interaction sequences that culminated in the selection of a university dean, and the Bay of Pigs "decision" by President Kennedy, Whyte discovered "a process in which it is impossible to determine who makes the decision." [153] "Unless we understand what people are included in the process to provide information, what people give advice, what people are involved in discussion of a given decision, and the sequence of the interactions and activities leading up to the decision, our literature in the field of decision making will continue to be a mixture of fact and folklore." [154] Thus, the focus of analysis ought to be member interactions.

Second, interaction patterns can be observed and measured in a rigorous and objective fashion. Through careful counting of the fre-

---

[151] "My own study of *Street Corner Society* makes a great deal of this exchange of favors in the street corner gang. I have a chapter on the exchange of favors in my *Human Relations in the Restaurant Industry*. However, it was only as I read George Homans' *Social Behavior: Its Elementary Forms* . . . that I began to see how these ideas fitted in with the social system of my scheme." Whyte, *Men at Work*, op. cit., p. 45.

[152] "Of the many influences on my thinking, one should be singled out for special recognition since it is so pervasive in the first half of this book despite some fundamental differences in approach: namely, that of George C. Homans' *Social Behavior: Its Elementary Forms*." Blau, op cit., p. vii.

[153] Whyte, *Organizational Behavior: Theory and Application*, op. cit., p. 702.

[154] Ibid.

quency and duration of member interactions, an "interaction structure" can be ascertained. Bales,[155] his colleagues,[156] and many others have provided careful and rigorous analysis of such interaction structures both among laboratory groups and "real" groups meeting in their "natural habitats." Detailed analyses of pair-interaction patterns, sequences of interaction patterns, initiator and receiver rates for each member, and the like can be accurately recorded and rigorously scrutinized in a highly objective fashion.

Third, member interactions, once observed, can be analyzed at several different analytical levels. Whyte proposes that individual personalities can be best understood through analysis of interactional data, using such dimensions as "quickness," i.e., the speed with which a person takes the initiative; "dominance," i.e., the frequency with which a person takes over or maintains control in spite of the attempts of other people to assume control; and "hesitancy" or "inhibitedness." [157] However, "the quantitative description of the roles of interaction of individuals under certain conditions defines a system." [158] Thus, in addition to individuals, interaction systems (i.e., groups or organizations) may serve as the units of analysis. Interaction frequency may be used as an empirical method to determine group boundaries. "It is possible just by counting interactions to map out a group quantitatively distinct from others." [159] Thus, groups and organizations can be distinguished from their environments and can be used as units of analysis by themselves.

In addition, the interrelationships between personality and group structure may be analyzed using interactional data. Whyte, especially, has demonstrated this point in much of his work. For example, he suggests that organizational analysis should begin with observation of the work flow; "the sequence of activities carried out in patterned form whereby the product moves from its earliest stage through to final completion or whereby a series of people perform interdependent tasks in the provision of a service to the customer." [160] Using this perspective, he attempted to discover "why waitresses cry." He concluded that the answer lay in the structural demands of the work situation which was not compatible with certain personality types; "it was those girls who had learned in the course of growing up to take the initiative in managing their relations with other people who were able to structure

---

[155] Robert F. Bales, *Interaction Process Analysis* (Reading, Mass.: Addison-Wesley Publishing Co., 1950).

[156] For example, Theodore M. Mills, *Group Transformation* (Englewood Cliffs, N.J.: Prentice-Hall, Inc., 1964).

[157] Whyte, *Organizational Behavior: Theory and Application*, op. cit., p. 56.

[158] Ibid., p. 72.

[159] Homans, *The Human Group*, op. cit., p. 87.

[160] Whyte, *Organizational Behavior: Theory and Application*, op. cit., p. 56.

the interpersonal relations of the work situation in such a way that they did not break down. The girls who grew up as followers tended to find that they had great difficulty handling the tensions of the work situation." [161] In short, interactional data may be analyzed at the individual, group, or organizational levels and may serve as well as a basis for analysis of the "interfaces" among these levels.

Fourth, just as member interaction may be analyzed at differing levels of system complexity, so also it may be analyzed at a transactional level. At this level, collections of observed interaction are clustered into event sequences of different types. Thus, transactions, i.e., "events involving the giving-receiving of rewards or penalties," [162] may be of seven different forms: (1) positive exchange; (2) trading; (3) joint payoff; (4) competitive; (5) negative exchange; (6) open conflict; and (7) bargaining. The labels are fairly self-explanatory except, perhaps, for positive and negative exchange. This concept has key significance and reflects the work of Gouldner, Blau, and Homans referred to earlier. Essentially, it refers to the notion of normative reciprocity. In short, positive exchange is said to have occurred "if A gives a gift to B, or performs some valuable service for him, and this action creates in B the sentiment of being obliged to A and the need to cancel this obligation in the future by means of a gift or service of like value." [163]

It is to be noted that not all interaction is exchange,[164] nor is there an assumption of "rationalism." Rather, "the only assumption made is that human beings choose between alternative potential associates or courses of action by evaluating the experiences or expected experiences with each in terms of a preference ranking and then selecting the best alternative." [165] Of course, persons rarely, if ever, have complete information but make decisions on the basis of what is available. "Indeed, the need to anticipate in advance the social rewards with which others will reciprocate for favors in exchange relations inevitably introduces uncertainty and recurrent errors of judgment that make perfectly rational calculations impossible." [166]

Thus, fifth, many patterns of interaction may be explained through analysis of exchange transactions. Blau presents a detailed statement

[161] Ibid., pp. 106–107.
[162] Ibid., p. 148.
[163] Ibid., p. 149.
[164] Blau proposes a fourfold typology based on two dimensions: (1) basis of attraction (intrinsic reward, e.g., love, versus extrinsic); and (2) balance or symmetry of transaction (reciprocal versus unilateral).
The four types are (1) *mutual attraction* (intrinsic-reciprocal); (2) *one-sided attachment* (intrinsic-unilateral); (3) *power* (extrinsic-unilateral); and (4) *exchange* (extrinsic-reciprocal). Blau, op. cit., p. 313.
[165] Ibid., p. 18.
[166] Ibid., p. 19.

in which he explicates this complex network of processes. An oversimplified but brief summary of Blau's analysis is as follows. Exchange transactions often produce differentiation in power because of the imbalances of obligations incurred. Also, power may be gained by providing services desired by others who become dependent on the supplier. Collective approval of such power legitimates it, and the relationship may become stabilized as long as the exchange rate is viewed as "fair." Thus, such differentiated power, once legitimated, is the basis for organization. Homans' "principle of distributive justice" suggests that the exchange rate need not be equivalent, for, if the costs are higher to one group, then the rewards should be higher too.[167] Those who assume greater responsibilities and risks (a type of cost) in an exchange relationship should receive higher rewards. But definitions of fair rates are dynamic. Thus, accompanying the differentiation of power are processes of opposition formation that stimulate questioning of the legitimacy of the power imbalance. Thus, Blau concludes that structural change assumes a "dialectical pattern" because it takes time for opposition forces to emerge and develop an ideology to which persons can adhere. "Opposition ideals create a surplus of resources, since devotion to them frees social energies by making men willing to sacrifice material welfare for their sake, and the opposition movement they inspire constitutes a new social investment that brings about social change and reorganization." [168]

Sixth, exchange processes that characterize relationships among persons in small groups have counterparts in more complex systems, but there are important differences as many of the transactions are indirect rather than face-to-face. "Long chains of social transactions occur in complex organizations, in which the work of some members contributes to the performances of others, and which typically do not involve reciprocal exchanges. What these chains of transactions do involve is conformity to official obligations on the part of members of the organization in exchange for rewards received from it." [169] Blau proposes that, just as money permits an enormous expansion of indirect exchange transactions, social values serve as "media" that permit the social processes to extend far beyond face-to-face social contacts and over long periods of time. Finally, a further shift in abstration levels permits conceptualization of transactions among collectivities. Thus, although there are essential differences, exchange processes can be analyzed among persons in small groups; within larger units comprised of such groups; or even among large collectivities.

Seventh, as interaction patterns persist over time, interpersonal rela-

[167] Homans, "Social Behavior As Exchange," op. cit., p. 604.
[168] Blau, op. cit., p. 335.
[169] Blau, op. cit., p. 260.

tionships emerge. People form these abstracted patterns, and they have feelings, likes, and dislikes. Interpersonal conflicts often become converted into interdepartmental conflicts. The formal structure is frequently circumvented, avoided, and by-passed so that the organizational work can get done. Thus, when one actually observes member interaction within organizations, he becomes aware of numerous behavioral processes, like informal information pipelines, that are absolutely critical to the functioning of the unit. Similarly, when other areas, like decision making and coordination, are looked at *behaviorally,* many assumptions of rational or classical theorists become absurdities. For example, decision-making behavior simply cannot be understood through only an awareness of formal rule structures. And interpersonal sentiments, viewed collectively in terms of friendship patterns, hostility patterns, and the like, become highly important in explaining organizational functioning.

Therefore, an understanding of the composition of the interpersonal relations among all of the group members must be ascertained. However, it is the composite of these sentiments that must be understood rather than individual views studied in isolation. Various efforts have been made to measure these sentiments. The sociogram, first introduced by Moreno, is one device whereby this can be accomplished. All group members respond to such instructions as "write down the names of the three group members that you would most like to sit next to." Of course, numerous situations have been used, e.g., "eat lunch with," "work with," and so on. Figures 2–4 and 2–5 present typical examples. However, sociograms are hard to use. More recently, analysts have turned to matrix algebra for assistance in analysis of sociometric data. In this way, friendship patterns, cliques, and so on can be ascertained quickly.[170]

Eighth, groups and organizations maintain stability through a system of norms and sanctions. System stability refers to the degree to which the interaction is repetitive or patterned. As already indicated, Bales and others have demonstrated empirically that as persons interact over time, their interaction becomes more patterned.[171] This emergent patterning of interaction, or system stability, is presumably, caused by the emergence of expectations or norms, held for different group members. Similarly, persons enter groups with expectations they have learned elsewhere regarding how persons in various social positions ought to behave. Thus, a series of interlocking roles, or collections

---

[170] An excellent discussion with applications for organizational analysis is contained in Rocco Carzo., Jr., and John N. Yanouzas, op. cit., pp. 159–77.

[171] Robert F. Bales and Fred L. Strodtbeck, "Phases in Group Problem Solving" in *Group Dynamics: Research and Theory,* Dorwin Cartwright and Alvin Zander, eds. (Evanston, Illinois: Row, Peterson, and Company, 1960), pp. 624–40.

FIGURE 2–4 Sociogram of Steam Laundry Before Reconstruction

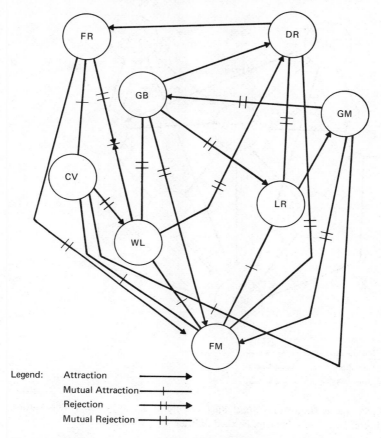

Legend: Attraction ⟶
         Mutual Attraction ⟶|⟶
         Rejection ⟶||⟶
         Mutual Rejection ⟶||⟶

SOURCE: Adapted from *Who Shall Survive?* by J. L. Moreno, M.D., Author, Beacon House, Inc., 1953, Beacon, N.Y., Publisher. By permission.

of expectations, emerge that structure future interaction, thereby making it increasingly patterned. Thus, just as Whyte found that the bowling scores among the boys in Doc's gang were constrained through group expectations, so also is individual behavior in organizations explained through insight into the normative structure and the sanctioning processes used.

Ninth, and finally, all of these writers alert us to an issue heretofore ignored: to what degree does the perspective have utility for analysis of social behavior in places other than the United States? All of these theorists express the hope that they are generating a perspective that will prove useful in crosscultural analysis. Think back to the prescriptive principles advocated by human relations theorists; it would seem that their applicability to other cultural settings is highly problematic.

FIGURE 2–5   Sociogram of Steam Laundry After Reconstruction

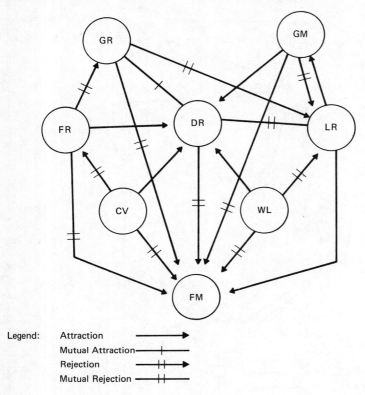

Legend: Attraction   ———————▶
           Mutual Attraction———————|———————
           Rejection   ———————++▶
           Mutual Rejection   ———————++———————

SOURCE: Adapted from *Who Shall Survive?* by J. L. Moreno, M.D., Author,
Beacon House, Inc., 1953, Beacon, N.Y., Publisher. By permission.

These exchange theorists do not propose that there are no cultural
differences. Rather, by starting at this behavioral level and working up
in abstraction levels, propositions such as those proposed by Homans
and Blau can be tested in a variety of cultural settings. Gouldner's
norm of reciprocity may or may not be a universal across cultures, but
at least we are alerted to the issue.

Illustrative Propositions

1. "If the persons are engaged in joint payoff or positive exchange
   transactions, their sentiments toward each other will be positive."
   Or conversely, "If the persons are engaged in competitive, negative
   exchange, or open conflict transactions, their sentiments toward
   each other will be negative." [172]

[172] Whyte, *Organizational Behavior: Theory and Application*, op. cit., p. 225.

2. "The more often within a given period of time a man's activity rewards the activity of another, the more often the other will emit the activity." [173]

3. "The more valuable to a man a unit of the activity another gives him, the more often he will emit activity rewarded by the activity of the other." [174]

4. "The more often a man has in the recent past received a rewarding activity from another, the less valuable any further unit of that activity becomes to him." [175]

5. "The more to a man's disadvantage the rule of distributive justice fails of realization, the more likely he is to display the emotional behavior we call anger." [176]

Critique

Six major types of criticism can be raised with this perspective. First, there are problems with the distinctions used between normative and interpersonal expectations. Although they are analytically distinct, too often the distinction is blurred. Usually, the normative expectations being discussed become expectations associated with particular persons rather than with social positions. And sometimes, especially in Whyte's work, these expectations drift into personality components when measurement is attempted.

Second, despite statements regarding distinctive levels of analysis, efforts to "humanize" the research often result in reductionist strategies. Interaction patterns are noted and defined, but the source of explanation all too often ends up being the personality of the actor. Of course, Homans has taken the position that one must necessarily look to the psychological level to explain group phenomena.[177] Whyte has made a conscientious effort to integrate findings and analyses at different levels. However, he usually places an emphasis on personality factors as the final explanation, as was illustrated under the third point above in the quotation explaining why waitresses cry. Others, like Blau, would prefer to assume that social phenomena are best explained by variables conceptualized at that level.

Third, except in Blau's work conflict is too often viewed as neces-

---

[173] Homans, *Social Behavior: Its Elementary Forms*, op. cit., p. 54.

[174] Ibid., p. 55.

[175] Ibid. Blau explored this proposition by relating it to the concept of marginal utility and applying tools used by economists; see Blau, op. cit., pp. 168–98.

[176] Homans, *Social Behavior: Its Elementary Forms*, op. cit., p. 75.

[177] Homans defended this reductionistic position most vigorously in his 1964 presidential address to the American Sociological Association, "Bringing Men Back In," *American Sociological Review*, 29: 809–18 (December 1964).

sarily undesirable behavior that is to be resolved through better human relations. Although personal likes and dislikes certainly occur, this perspective contains little about ideological differences, their consequences, and their resolution. Thus, the criticisms raised by conflict theorists regarding system stability, absence of conflict, and the focus on conformity are germane here.

Fourth, masses of data are collected, but movement toward generalization occurs too seldom. Descriptive data, be it in the form of "the number of interactions initiated by *A* toward *B*" or the more literary storytelling so well done by Whyte, is too frequently all that remains when we reach the conclusion. Hence, we find ourselves asking "so what?" as Whyte gives us case after case to illustrate a point. We end up knowing much about how Doc, Sally, or Rita feels, but we have few insights as to networks of *analytical* propositions that explain or predict organizational behavior. Of course, this criticism does not hold for Homans or Blau, who have done more than most to push sociology toward explanatory models. But even their work, rigorous as it is, fails to link together into an analytic model with firm closure.

Fifth, those working within this perspective have too often ignored the formal structure of organizations as a set of variables that might be used to account for observed behavior patterns. Whyte underscores this shortcoming in one of his recent works,[178] but says little about remedies. Certainly, any future work completed within this model should place greater emphasis upon the formal structure as a set of constraints that may be highly significant in accounting for member behavior in many types of organizations.

Sixth, and finally, little effort has been made to analyze or conceptualize environmental influences or organizational-environment interaction. Homans did make an internal-external differentiation in *The Human Group*, but dropped it in his later work.[179] But his analysis of environmental conditions is very brief and is presented solely in descriptive, rather than analytical terms.

Like the formal structure, the consequences of technology, are also ignored in the exchange perspective. However, recently several analysts have attempted to conceptualize rigorously and investigate empirically technology as a central variable with which to account for variations in organizational structure and behavior. In contrast to the more literary and humanistic styles of Whyte and Homans, these theorists tend to be extremely analytical and abstract. But it is certainly time that technology be subjected to sociological scrutiny rather than just being mentioned in passing.

[178] Whyte, *Organizational Behavior: Theory and Application*, op. cit., pp. 709–11.
[179] Homans, *Social Behavior: Its Elementary Forms*, op. cit., pp. 230–31.

Chapter 2. Perspectives in Organizational Theory

A Technological Perspective

In 1904, Thorstein Veblen charged: "In a sense more intimate than the inventors of the phrase seem to have appreciated, the machine has become the master of the man who works with it and an arbiter in the cultural fortunes of the community into whose life it has entered." [180] Thus, in a tone of intense social criticism, Veblen warned that machinery necessarily precipitated changes in worker behaviors—and, indeed, in their mode of thought. "There results a standardization of the workman's intellectual life in terms of mechanical process." [181] And this machine discipline, Veblen argued, would result in the death of honest intellectual work. "What can be done to save civilized mankind from the vulgarization and disintegration wrought by the machine industry?" [182] Although Veblen was unable to see much that could be done, we need not necessarily share his pessimism to recognize his use of technology as an independent variable. Technology, as a variable, has been curiously absent from the theoretical perspectives thus far explored.

Since Veblen, several investigators in various sectors of the social sciences have proposed that technology has a critical impact on social organization. For example, Blauner's analysis suggests that technology and the resulting forms of social organization determine the intensity of alienation that workers experience.[183] Similarly, Fullan's data on 1,491 Canadian manual workers indicated a clear link between the type of technology (craft, mass production, or continuous process) and degree of worker integration.[184] Greatest worker integration occurred in organizations with a "continuous process" technology (e.g., an oil refinery); it was lowest in those with a "mass production" technology (e.g., an automobile manufacturer). However, relatively few sociologists have attempted rigorously to conceptualize technology as either an independent or dependent variable in their general theoretical framework for system analysis.

The writings of Gerhard Lenski are a notable exception.[185] Working at the macroscopic level, Lenski has integrated volumes of data from

[180] Thorstein Veblen, *The Theory of Business Enterprise* (New York: Charles Scribner's Sons, 1904), p. 323.

[181] Ibid., p. 308.

[182] Ibid., p. 377.

[183] Robert Blauner, *Alienation and Freedom* (Chicago: University of Chicago Press, 1964).

[184] Michael Fullan, "Industrial Technology and Worker Integration in the Organization," *American Sociological Review*, 35: 1028–1039 (December 1970).

[185] Gerhard Lenski, *Human Societies* (New York: McGraw-Hill Book Co., 1970). For an earlier but more narrowly focused statement, see Gerhard Lenski, *Power and Privilege* (New York: McGraw-Hill Book Co., 1966).

a multiplicity of sources using total societies as his units of analysis. He suggests that a multilineal evolutionary framework, analogous to that used in modern biology, can be a helpful tool. And the key variable that differentiates societies, reflecting a type of sociocultural "progress," is technological advancement. Although technological advancement is used as the central variable for a typology of societies, Lenski does not fall into the pitfall of suggesting a simplistic direct causal relationship. Rather, *a society's solutions to its technological problems tend to function as a set of prior conditions that limit the range of possible solutions to its organizational and ideological problems.* [186] And perhaps the same statement can be made about organizations.

How does the process of evolution operate? Let us look at an example from Robert Murphy and Julian Steward's anthropological work, which closely parallels Lenski's. Tracing the changing patterns of social organization among the fur-trapping Canadian Algonkians and the rubber-tapping Brazilian Mundurucu, Murphy and Steward present a convincing argument of multilineal evolution.[187] They assert that the patterns of social organization that characterized these two societies were different initially, but that, in adapting to new technologies that had common analytical characteristics, similar forms of social organization emerged. Thus, changes in social organization can best be explained by analysis of culture-environment interaction, with special emphasis on available technology.[188] Similarly, Steward has argued that the social structure of the Shosone Indians could best be explained by analysis of their hostile environment and available technology.[189] For example, absence of preservation and storing techniques for meats, and the relative scarcity of rabbits, antelope, and fish demanded a social structure of isolated migratory groups in contrast to large concentrated collectivities that might better meet the demands of a different environment as mediated by different technologies.

In contrast to Lenski and Steward, who use a societal level of analysis, many have built on the insights initially presented by Bavelas regarding communication networks in small groups.[190] By varying the

---

[186] Lenski, *Human Societies*, op. cit., p. 103.

[187] Robert F. Murphy and Julian H. Steward, "Tappers and Trappers: Parallel Process in Acculturation," *Economic Development and Cultural Change*, 4: 335–55 (July 1956).

[188] Murphy and Steward conclude the piece with this idea stated as a specific hypothesis: "When the people of an unstratified native society barter wild products found in extensive distribution and obtained through individual effort, the structure of the native culture will be destroyed, the final culmination will be a culture type characterized by individual families having delimited rights to marketable resources and linked to the larger nation through trading centers." Ibid., p. 353.

[189] Julian H. Steward, *Theory of Culture Change* (Urbana, Ill.: University of Illinois Press, 1955).

[190] Alex Bavelas, "Communication Patterns in Task-oriented Groups," *Journal of the Acoustical Society of America*, 22: 725–30 (1950).

possible communication contact with differing telephone arrangements, he was able to stimulate much research on the consequences of
differing communication structures for group problem solving.[191] Of
course, such structures could intentionally or unintentionally be manipulated through various technological means. However, these observations are very narrow in scope, and as yet they have not been
integrated into a general framework of organizational theory regarding
technology.

Shifting back to a macroscopic level, Stinchcombe has observed that
organizations of different types frequently have been founded in large
numbers at particular points in time. "Thus, there was a rash of savings
bank formations in the 1830's. . . . Railroads, and consequently new
communities and counties, and, of course, great steel companies, had
their great period of organization in the 1850's and again in the
1870's." [192] And once formed, these organizations exhibit structures
that are remarkably stable, almost as if the organization was a captive
of the initial technology used.

Drawing from Rice and Trist's analysis of the Glacier Metal Company and the work of Richardson and Walker at an IBM plant, Price
formulated the proposition that "organizations which have continuous
systems of assembling output are more likely to have a high degree of
effectiveness than organizations which have batch systems of assembling output." [193]

Although rather oversimplified, this generalization points our attention toward types of product-assembling processes. And it was this
dimension on which Joan Woodward and her colleagues focused in an
ambitious ten-year study.[194] To date, it remains the most comprehensive empirical study directed at the relationship of technology and
organizational structure. On the basis of her analysis of 203 firms she
concluded: "Many of the variations found in the organizational structure of the firms did, however, appear to be closely linked with differences in manufacturing techniques. Different technologies imposed
different kinds of demands on individuals and organizations, and these
demands had to be met through an appropriate structure. Com-

[191] For an excellent summary of this literature, see Harold Guetzkow, "Communications in Organizations" in *Handbook of Organizations*, James D. March, ed.,
(Chicago: Rand McNally and Co., 1965), pp. 534–73.

[192] Arthur L. Stinchcombe, "Social Structure and Organization" in March, op. cit.,
p. 154.

[193] Price, *Organizational Effectiveness*, op. cit., p. 39.

[194] Joan Woodward, *Industrial Organization: Theory and Practice* (London:
Oxford University Press, 1965).
Zwerman's partial replication, based on 55 firms in the Minneapolis–St. Paul
metropolitan area, generally supports Woodward's conclusions. William L.
Zwerman, *New Perspectives on Organization Theory* (Westport, Conn.: Greenwood
Publishing Corporation, 1970). See also *Industrial Organization: Behavior and
Control*, Joan Woodward (ed.) (London: Oxford University Press, 1970).

mercially successful firms seemed to be those in which function and form were complementary." [195]

In a rigorous theoretical manner, Charles Perrow has creatively explored strategies whereby organizational technology might be conceptualized. He has underscored the importance of this variable in several articles.[196] For example, Perrow argues rather convincingly that goal changes he observed in a hospital could be directly linked to changing technologies. "Following the shift in power from trustees, representing community goals (e.g., charity cases), to doctors, representing the interests of their business-profession (e.g., a focus upon paying patients and the interests of the organized profession, including research interests), there appears to be a shift of power to the administrative staff, perhaps in uneasy alliance with a revitalized trustee group. . . . It would appear to be a logical transformation for many hospitals, since the growing complexity of medical technologies require increasing interdependence of units, coordination of resources and personnel and rationalization of the supportive structure." [197] And this explanation concerning hospitals seems to fit other types of organizations. For example, what about universities? However, now let us develop these arguments in a more systematic fashion.

The General Image

Six critical ideas summarize much of what Woodward, Perrow, and others have thus far pieced together in an effort to use technology as a variable. First, organizations are viewed "in terms of the work performed on the basic material which is to be altered, rather than focusing upon the interaction of organizational members or the function for society." [198] Organizations are defined, then, "as systems which utilize energy (given up by humans and non-human devices) in a patterned, directed effort to alter the condition of basic materials in a predetermined manner." [199] And technology is defined as "the actions that an individual performs upon an object, with or without the aid of tools or mechanical devices, in order to make some change in that object. The object, or 'raw material,' may be a living being, human or otherwise, a symbol or an inanimate object." [200] Given these focal definitions, the

---

[195] Ibid., p. vi.

[196] Charles Perrow, "Hospitals: Technology, Structure, and Goals," in March, op. cit., pp. 910–71; and Charles Perrow, "A Framework for the Comparative Analysis of Organizations," *American Sociological Review*, 32: 194–208 (April 1967).

[197] Perrow, "Hospitals: Technology, Structure, and Goals," op. cit., p. 959.

[198] Ibid., p. 913.

[199] Ibid.

[200] Perrow, "A Framework for the Comparative Analysis of Organizations," op. cit., p. 195.

hypothesis emerges that technology determines structure. That is, as persons go about changing the "raw material," they interact with one another. The pattern of this interaction is the structure of the organization. This structure is largely constrained by the technology used.

Second, technology can be best conceptualized by abstracting properties of the transformation process through which the "raw materials" are manipulated. At a rather low level of abstraction, Woodward devised a continuum on which eleven types of production systems were identified. Her classification scheme is presented in Figure 2–6. In a much more abstract fashion, Perrow proposes that a useful but not necessarily exclusive alternative is to focus on two aspects of technology: (1) "the number of exceptional cases encountered in the work, that is, the degree to which stimuli are perceived as familiar or unfamiliar"; [201] and (2) "the nature of the search process that is undertaken by the individual when exceptions occur." [202] Putting these two dimensions into a two-by-two table we derive the relationships presented in Figure 2–7.

Third, "the state of the art of analyzing the characteristics of the raw materials is likely to determine what kind of technology will be used." [203] Thus, types of raw material can be differentiated analytically by assessing characteristics of the perceptions held about it. Perrow proposes two dimensions: (1) the degree to which the raw material is perceived to be understood; and (2) the degree to which raw material is perceived to be stable so that it can be treated in a standardized fashion. These are, of course, interrelated, but they provide some refreshing insight as examples of how raw material might be conceptualized in a more abstract fashion. Moreover, "If the technology of an organization is going to move from cell 2 to any of the other cells, it can only do so either by reducing the variability of the material and thus the number of exceptional cases that occur or by increasing the knowledge of the material and thus allowing more analytic techniques to be used, or both." [204] Reviewing a diagram similar to that presented in Figure 2–8, Perrow concluded: "If technical knowledge increases, increasing the reliability of search procedures, one may move from Cell 2 to Cell 3. If both things happen—and this is the aim of most organizations—one may move from Cell 2 to Cell 4." [205]

Fourth, comparative analysis of organizations can best proceed using technology rather than other variables, e.g., goals, prime beneficiary, compliance structures, and the like. Most commonly, attempts

[201] Ibid., pp. 195–96.
[202] Ibid., p. 196.
[203] Ibid., pp. 196–97.
[204] Ibid., p. 197.
[205] Ibid.

FIGURE 2–6   Woodward's Typology of Production Systems

(A) Integral Products	Number of Firms	Production System	Number of Firms	Production Engineering Classifications
Unit & Small Batch Production	5	I Production of Units to Customers' Requirements	17	Jobbing
	10	II Production of Prototypes		
	2	III Fabrication of Large Equipments in Stages		
	7	IV Production of Small Batches to Customers' Orders	32	Batch
Large Batch & Mass Production	14	V Production of Large Batches		
	11	VI Production of Large Batches on Assembly Lines		
	6	VII Mass Production	6	Mass
(B) Dimensional Products				
Process Production	13	VIII Intermittent Production of Chemicals in Multipurpose Plant	13	Batch
	12	IX Continuous Flow Production of Liquids, Gases, & Crystalline Substances	12	Mass
(C) Combined Systems (Total Firms = 92)	3	X Production of Standardized Components in Large Batches Subsequently Assembled Diversely		
	9	XI Process Production of Crystalline Substances, Subsequently Prepared for Sale by Standardized Production Methods		

SOURCE: From Joan Woodward, *Industrial Organization: Theory and Practice* (The Clarendon Press, Oxford, 1965), p. 39. By permission.

FIGURE 2–7   Perrow's Technology Variable

Nature of the Search Process	Number of Exceptions Encountered in Work	
	Few Exceptions	Many Exceptions
Unanalyzable Problems	Craft Industries (Specialty Glass) 1	Nonroutine (Aerospace) 2
Analyzable Problems	4 Routine (Tonnage Steel) Mills, Screws and Bolts)	3 Engineering (Heavy Machinery)

SOURCE: Adapted from Charles Perrow, "A Framework for the Comparative Analysis of Organizations," *American Sociological Review,* **32** (April 1967), 196.

FIGURE 2-8   Perrow's Raw Material Variables (People-Changing Examples)

Perceived Nature of Raw Material	Perceived Variability of Material	
	Uniform and Stable	Nonuniform and Unstable
Not Well-understood	Socializing Institutions (e.g., some schools) 1	2 Elite Psychiatric Agency
Well-understood	3 Custodial Institutions, Vocational Training	4 Programmed Learning School

SOURCE: Adapted by permission from Charles Perrow, "A Framework for the Analysis of Organizations," *American Sociological Review*, 32 (April, 1967), 198.

at comparative analyses have used organizational goal as the criterion establishing a research base, e.g., a comparative study of several prisons. Perrow does *not* propose that his conceptual scheme be used as a simple typology to establish four basic organizational types. Rather, he asserts that the variables be viewed as continua, and that technology be included as one of the variables to form a more complex basis for comparative study. He is, however, emphatic that organizational goal as a single criterion for differentiation is not adequate. To "assume that you are holding constant the major variable by comparing several schools or several steel mills is unwarranted until one looks at the technologies employed by various schools or steel mills. In fact, the variations within one type of organization may be such that some schools are like prisons, some prisons like churches, some churches like factories, some factories like universities, and so on." [206]

Fifth, many variations in organizational structure can be directly related to and explained by variations in technology. Woodward's detailed longitudinal studies of four firms suggested that a variety of changes in organizational functioning occurred with change in technology, e.g., patterns of interactions, status relationships, and the control system.[207] For example, managers and supervisors found themselves much busier and more conscious of pressure after various changes were made. Woodward explained this by proposing that the shifts from unit to batch production necessitated a more complicated network of communications both within and among each of the subunits. Hence, managerial personnel experienced this through sharp

[206] Ibid., pp. 203–204.
[207] Woodward, *Industrial Organization: Theory and Practice*, op. cit., pp. 210–26.

changes in their interaction patterns. Similarly, Perrow's analysis concludes with numerous hypotheses whereby technology is related to aspects of task structure and social structure using such variables as degree of discretion, power, coordination within groups, interdependence among groups, and the like. Finally, Harvey's empirical data on 43 industrial organizations suggest that greater technical specificity, as measured by the number of product changes during a ten-year period, is directly related to various structural patterns.[208] Harvey conceptualized organizational technology as a continuum with polar extremes labeled "technical diffuseness" (i.e., many product changes) and "technical specificity" (i.e., few product changes). And this dimension was consistently related to such structural variables as the number of levels of authority and the number of specialized subunits.

Sixth, and finally, different theoretical models may define different organizational "types" where technology is used as the basis for defining "types." This point is similar to the observation regarding comparative analysis, except that it goes a bit further. As Harvey put it after briefly reviewing alternative decision-making models: "In short, we would suggest that the models of decision making referred to here are not antithetical orientations but, rather, refer to decision making under different conditions. The question is not one of rational decision making versus non-rational decision making, but rather a question of identifying the kinds of technical and organizational conditions which serve to enhance rationality in some circumstances and impede its operation in others." [209] Thus, synthesis of alternative theoretical perspectives may occur through increased emphasis on this dimension in that different models may be more or less relevant to organizations with comparable technological structures.

Illustrative Propositions

1. As technical specificity increases (i.e., when there are fewer product changes), there will be increases in the number of specialized subunits, the number of levels of authority, the ratio of managers and supervisors to total personnel, and the amount of program specification.[210]
2. "[F]irms characterized by the sociotechnical mode of 'technical diffuseness—low internal structure' tend to exhibit flexibilities of organization and general readiness for change which facilitated innovation when the need for it arose." [211]

[208] Edward Harvey, "Technology and the Structure of Organizations," *American Sociological Review*, 33: 247–59 (April 1968).
[209] Ibid., p. 258.
[210] Adapted from Harvey; Ibid., p. 250.
[211] Ibid., p. 258.

3. As organizations "advance" technologically (i.e., shift from Type 1 to Type 11 on Woodward's typology of production systems), there will be increases in the length of the line of command and the span of control of the chief executive.[212]

4. In organizations processing raw materials that are perceived to be non uniform and not well understood (Perrow's Cell 2), "the discretion of both those who supervise the transformation of the basic raw material, and those who provide technical help for this process, must be high." [213]

5. In organizations processing raw materials that are perceived to be uniform and well understood (Perrow's Cell 4), the discretion of both technical and supervisory groups will be low, but "the power of the technical group over the supervisory group is high." [214]

Critique

Five types of criticisms may be raised. It should be emphasized at the outset, however, that the analysts we have used. (e.g., Perrow, Woodward, and Harvey), also have made explicit many of these criticisms. First, the perspective is extremely narrow. Clearly, technology does not explain everything about organizational behavior. None of the above writers claims that it does; all express reservations. However, viewing technology as one type of constraint, one factor, is not enough. The variable must be conceptualized so that it can be integrated with others. Only a complex cluster of variables will form a usable model to guide future research. This is not to say that any existing perspective must be used as the integrative base, but only that we are left at present with some highly refreshing insights regarding a single dimension that remains rather isolated.

Moreover, this narrow focus may lead researchers to exaggerate the importance of their findings because they are not viewed in a larger context. Slight shifts in structural dimensions may be correlated with changes in technological process, but are overemphasized as few other variables are included in the analysis. For example, data from fifty-two diverse work organizations led Hickson, Pugh, and Pheysey to conclusions that appeared to contradict Woodward's findings. Careful comparison and criticism of Woodward's study led them to conclude: "Comparison with the apparently contradictory findings by Woodward, linking technology with a wide variety of structural characteristics, leads to a final hypothesis which, concisely stated, is that *variables of*

---

[212] Woodward, *Industrial Organization: Theory and Practice*, op. cit., p. 51.

[213] Perrow, "A Framework for the Comparative Analysis of Organizations," op. cit., p. 199.

[214] Ibid., p. 200.

operations technology will be related only to those structural variables that are centered on the workflow. The smaller the organization, the wider the structural effects are confined to particular variables, and size and dependence and similar factors make the greater overall impact." [215]

Second, future empirical research can be completed only after techniques have been developed for operationally specifying the variables. Woodward and Harvey have used extremely simplistic operational measures. It is not clear that future work using such crude procedures necessarily will prove productive. And alternative strategies are not self-evident. In contrast, Perrow's approach appears more attractive conceptually, but most difficult operationally.[216] Perrow justifiably criticizes Woodward and suggests that he was unable to incorporate her analysis into his.[217] And Harvey's use of the number of product changes, although creative, is hardly much of an indicator of technical specificity. He also proposed—but did not use as an operational measure since it correlated highly with product change—"The average number of different kinds of products offered during the last ten years." [218] This sounds a bit better, but takes us little further.

Third, Perrow underscores a difficulty raised by Udy as to whose perceptions are to be used in assessing technology or raw material— the respondent or the analyst? As Perrow notes, "Few organizations will characterize themselves as routine, and most employees emphasize the variability of their jobs and the discretion required." [219] Whereas obvious operational difficulties are raised by this point, it would appear that Perrow's conceptual work needs to be extended so as to incorporate both actor expectations and some "objective" criteria for assessing the degree to which search processes, for example, are routinized.

Fourth, organizational environment, except as an input for new technology, is ignored. Perrow recognizes this, and emphasizes that

[215] David J. Hickson, D. S. Pugh, and Diana C. Pheysey, "Operations Technology and Organization Structure: An Empirical Reappraisal," *Administrative Science Quarterly*, 14: 395 (September 1969).

[216] Hage and Aiken have reported an empirical study in which they discuss their operational procedures for measuring technology as conceptualized by Perrow. Although not a "final answer," their work provides some helpful leads for measurement and empirical support for some of the hypotheses implicit in this perspective —e.g., "Organizations with routine work are more likely to be characterized by centralization of organizational power" (p. 370); "Organizations with routine work are more likely to have greater formalization of organizational roles" (p. 371). Jerald Hage and Michael Aiken, "Routine Technology, Social Structure, and Organizational Goals," *Administrative Science Quarterly*, 14: 366–76 (September 1969).

[217] Perrow, "A Framework for the Comparative Analysis of Organizations," op. cit., p. 207.

[218] Harvey, op. cit., p. 252.

[219] Perrow, "A Framework for the Comparative Analysis of Organizations," op. cit., p. 208.

environmental factors also should be treated as independent variables, especially "the product environment—customers, competitors, suppliers, unions, and regulatory agencies." [220] Yet, again, how this might be conceptualized and integrated with organizational technology awaits another day.

Fifth, the informal structure, emphasized so much by exchange and human relations theorists, and ideological conflict, pushed so hard by Coser, remain ignored.

In brief, we obtain some critical insights and some highly creative efforts at conceptualizing an important organizational variable that has been conspicuously absent as either an independent or dependent variable in any of the other theoretical perspectives. To be unduly critical of the authors cited here for ignoring other organizational variables would be most unfair in that they have noted this in their respective works. It is clear that future research must explore the inter-relationships of technology with other clusters of more commonly used variables. But it is equally clear that much conceptual work remains to be completed before such efforts will meet with much success.

In contrast to an intensive focus on a single variable, others have followed a strategy of working in broad terms in an effort to develop an integrative framework for organizational theory, sociology, and all of the sciences—including the physical, biological, and social. Let us turn now to this open system perspective and examine some attempts to apply it to organizational analysis.

An Open-System Perspective

Ludwig von Bertalanffy writes that in the early 1920s he "became puzzled about obvious lacunae in the research and theory in biology." [221] He advocated then that biological research could best be conceptualized within a framework which "emphasizes consideration of the organism as a whole or system, and sees the main objective of biological sciences in the discovery of the principles of organization at its various levels." [222] Bertalanffy has used and elaborated this position and now envisions "general system theory" as a means to integrate all of the sciences, not just biology.

But Bertalanffy's views received little attention until shortly after World War II. In the early 1950s, numerous groups throughout the United States began exploring "system theory," and many reached the

---

[220] Ibid., pp. 202–203.

[221] Ludwig von Bertalanffy, *General System Theory* (New York: George Braziller, 1968), p. 12.

[222] Ibid.

conclusion expressed by Kenneth Boulding in a letter to Bertalanffy dated 1953. "I seem to have come to much the same conclusion as you have reached, though approaching it from the direction of economics and the social sciences rather than from biology—that there is a body of what I have been calling 'general empirical theory' or 'general system theory' in your excellent terminology, which is of wide applicability in many different disciplines." [223] Although this was applicable in different disciplines, Boulding noted that crossing disciplinary boundaries was most difficult. The following year these two men, along with Anatol Rapoport and Ralph Gerard, established a "Society for General System Theory," which later became an affiliate of the American Association for the Advancement of Science (AAAS) under a less pretentious name—"Society for General Systems Research."

About 1949, another group at the University of Chicago began similar work with a focus on construction of a general theoretical framework for the behavioral sciences—including both the biological and social areas. Some members relocated at the University of Michigan, others dropped out, and new ones were added throughout the early 1950s. James G. Miller presented a progress report on the group activity in 1955, in which he emphasized: "Of the various possible integrations of the relevant data, we have found most profit in what we call *"general behavior systems theory."* [224] The efforts continued for another ten years, when Miller presented a lengthy and systematized outline of the various components of this theoretical framework.[225] Of course, numerous researchers in a wide variety of disciplines were now conceptualizing their work within somewhat similar frameworks.[226]

Sociological applications of aspects of this framework were best summarized by Walter Buckley in a formal statement (1967)[227] and a widely diverse collection of readings (1968).[228] In contrast to natural system theorists, such as Parsons, Buckley emphasized that open systems theory did not assume the "postulate of consensus" regarding social roles and expectations; that is, actors were to be viewed as interacting within normative systems that varied greatly in specificity, ambiguity, and perceived legitimacy. These structures were subject to

[223] Ibid., p. 14.

[224] James G. Miller, "Toward a General Theory for the Behavioral Sciences," *American Psychologist*, 10: 514 (September 1955).

[225] James G. Miller, "Living Systems: Basic Concepts," *Behavioral Science*, 10: 193–237 (July 1965).

[226] An excellent and helpful summary statement of the systems viewpoint is F. Kenneth Berrien, *General and Social Systems* (New Brunswick, N.J.: Rutgers University Press, 1968).

[227] Walter Buckley, *Sociology and Modern Systems Theory* (Englewood Cliffs, N.J.: Prentice-Hall, Inc., 1967).

[228] Walter Buckley, *Modern Systems Research for the Behavioral Scientist* (Chicago: Aldine Publishing Company, 1968).

continual negotiations and frequently contained critical contradictions. Hence, in contrast to the more static and highly reified perspective of Parsons, Buckley emphasized process.[229] And the most critical consequence of this was to begin to view systems as *interacting* with environmental sectors rather than as *mere reactors*.

Several impressive applications of the insights of this perspective to complex social organizations appeared almost simultaneously with Buckley's work. We will draw heavily from the integrative efforts of James D. Thompson,[230] and also those of Daniel Katz and Robert L. Kahn,[231] who forged ahead to apply aspects of general systems theory to human organizations. Equally helpful is the impressive empirical study by Paul R. Lawrence and Jay W. Lorsch, who applied this perspective to ten organizations that functioned in different types of environments.[232] Finally, Crozier has been most effective in integrating descriptive and survey data with the process and negotiation themes that characterize this perspective.[233]

The General Image

Although it is somewhat similar to the natural systems perspective, open systems theorists emphasize several points of divergence. The following eight points will give us a broad picture that can be contrasted with those thus far presented.

First, organizations are to be viewed as systems within systems. The image is something akin to the layers one sees upon peeling an onion. Systems are "complexes of elements standing in interaction."[234] The focus is on the *relations* among these interacting elements. And because the elements are interacting, they comprise a whole that cannot be understood by investigation of the various parts in isolation.

Second, these systems are open systems; they cannot survive in isolation. In contrast, closed systems—i.e., those isolated from their environment—comply with the second principle of thermodynamics, which states that "a certain quantity, called entropy, must increase to

---

[229] Ibid., pp. 499–508.

[230] James D. Thompson, *Organizations in Action* (New York: McGraw-Hill Book Co., 1967).

[231] Daniel Katz and Robert L. Kahn, *The Social Psychology of Organizations* (New York: John Wiley and Sons, Inc., 1966).

[232] Paul R. Lawrence and Jay W. Lorsch, *Organization and Environment* (Homewood, Ill.: Richard D. Irwin, Inc., 1969).

[233] Michel Crozier, *The Bureaucratic Phenomenon* (Chicago: University of Chicago Press, 1964), French publication, 1963; and Michel Crozier. *The World of the Office Worker*, trans. David Landau (Chicago: University of Chicago Press, 1971), French publication, 1965.

[234] Bertalanffy, op. cit., p. 33.

a maximum." [235] Thus, the conclusion is that "the general trend of events in physical nature is toward states of maximum disorder." [236] But an open system "maintains itself in a continuous inflow and out-flow, a building up and a breaking down of components, never being, so long as it is alive, in a state of chemical and thermodynamic equilib-rium but maintained in a so-called steady state." [237] Open systems can thereby "avoid the increase of entropy, and may even develop towards states of increased order and organization" [238] (negative entropy). Through environmental interaction, open systems, "restore their own energy and repair breakdowns in their own organization." [239]

Third, open systems follow the principle of equifinality. That is, "the same final state can be reached from different initial conditions and in different ways." [240] And no single final state or structure is assumed to be best for all organizations, as the qualities of their environments are different. Thus, similar to the multilineal evolutionary argument of Lenski and Steward, this view emphasizes that differences in organiza-tion-environment interaction will be reflected in organizational struc-ture.

This idea was verified empirically in the study by Lawrence and Lorsch. They found that effective plastics organizations (in contrast to less effective ones) that function in dynamic and diverse environments were highly differentiated structurally. In contrast was the lesser differentiation of an equally effective container industry, which func-tioned in a more stable environment. However, structures character-ized by high differentiation still must be successfully integrated. Thus the plastics organization "had developed an elaborate set of formal devices (both an integrating unit and cross-functional teams) to facili-tate the resolution of conflict and the achievement of integration. Be-cause market and scientific factors were uncertain and complex, the lower and middle echelons of management had to be involved in reaching joint departmental decisions; these managers were centrally involved in the resolution of conflict." [241]

Thus, variation in environment requires variation in organizational structure. Looking at the data from another vantage point, Lawrence and Lorsch summarize their findings as follows:

[235] Ibid., p. 39.
[236] Ibid., p. 40.
[237] Ibid., p. 39.
[238] Ibid., p. 41.
[239] Miller, "Living Systems: Basic Concepts," op. cit., p. 203.
[240] Bertalanffy, op. cit., p. 79. Buckley takes us one step further with his concept of "multifinality," i.e., ". . . similar initial conditions may lead to dissimilar end-states." Buckley, Sociology and Modern Systems Theory, op. cit., p. 60.
[241] Lawrence and Lorsch, op. cit., pp. 151–52.

In contrast to the plastics organization, the container organization was in a relatively stable and homogeneous environment. Thus its functional units were not highly differentiated, which meant that the only formal integrating device required was the managerial hierarchy. But in using this device this organization also met the determinants of effective conflict resolution. The sales and production units, which were centrally involved in the crucial decisions related to scheduling and delivery, both felt that they had much influence over decisions. Around these issues influence was concentrated at the top of the organization, where top managers could centrally collect the relevant information to reach decisions. Middle managers, particulary those dealing with technical matters, did have some influence. The great influence of the top managers stemmed not only from their position, but also from their competence and knowledge. Finally, conflicts between departments were resolved and decisions reached through problem-solving behavior.[242]

Fourth, open systems have complex feedback and regulatory mechanisms that permit adaptive responses to many types of environmental change. And, in turn, these provide the system with a basis for judging whether or not its efforts at environmental manipulation have accomplished the desired purposes. Of course, to imply that cells, fish, or men have "purposes" is a risky, perhaps even foolish, strategy. The issue is a complex one and deserves careful thought. However, the view that emerges from these theorists is that it is useful to view systems as varying in degrees of self-direction. Hence, Miller suggests: "But if 'purpose' is defined not in terms of the observer but in terms of specific values of internal variables which systems take corrective actions in order to maintain in steady states, then the concept is scientifically useful." [243]

It is in this context that Thompson's and Crozier's emphasis on uncertainty takes on added importance. Because humans are presumably characterized by complex symbol manipulating skills, through which enhanced self-awareness is possible, human organizations can be viewed as efforts to *cope with* uncertainty. Uncertainty from within, but especially from the environment, is assumed as a given. "The most advanced organizations, because they now feel capable of integrating areas of uncertainty in their economic calculus, are beginning to understand that the illusion of perfect rationality has too long persisted, weakening the possibilities of action by insisting on rigorous logic and immediate coherence." [244] And reflecting the assumption of equifinality, there is a critical implication; persons do not seek the one best way. "Man has never been able to search for the 'optimum' solution. He has always had to be content with solutions merely 'satis-

[242] Ibid., p. 152.
[243] Miller, "Living Systems: Basic Concepts," op. cit., p. 232.
[244] Crozier, *The Bureaucratic Phenomenon*, op. cit., p. 159.

factory' in regard to a few particularistic criteria of which he was aware."[245]

Thus, through feedback processes, degrees of self-regulation become possible, and in turn, degrees of self-direction. But these states are dynamic, continually subject to threat, and consistently participants seek to expand them whenever possible. The simple feedback model presented in the upper portion of Figure 2–9 illustrates the type of analysis implied. And through increased understanding of such complex feedback circuits, as illustrated by the lower diagram in Figure 2–9, we can begin to grasp an understanding of organizational behavior.

Fifth, organizations, within this open system perspective, are to be viewed as patterned sets of events. The focus is not upon individual actors, but rather upon patterns of activity. One "begins by identifying and mapping the repeated cycles of input, transformation, output, and renewed input which comprise the organizational pattern."[246] Thus, implicit in the discussion of feedback are definitions of organizations as cycles of events, patterns of events, and the like. It should be noted that these events referred to are observable behaviors. This is a sharp contrast to the "abstracted system" view of Parsons, which defines organizations as systems of roles. Roles are viewed as patterned behaviors, which leads one to talk of roles interacting with one another. But by the behavioral focus of these theorists, the question of the degree of convergence between role behavior and role expectation remains problematic. Thus, Miller argues that we should focus on "concrete systems" that are based on behavioral observations rather than abstracted systems.[247]

Sixth, organizations do have boundaries that differentiate them from various environments. However, as was implicit in the discussion of this topic in Chapter 1, organizational boundaries are somewhat difficult to conceptualize. Defining the organization as a patterned set of events suggests little regarding boundaries. But if any system is to be studied as a whole, then some types of decision regarding boundaries is required. "Strictly speaking," Bertalanffy suggests, "spatial boundaries exist only in naive observation, and all boundaries are ultimately dynamic."[248] Given this, however, Hall and Fagen take us a step further by emphasizing that decisions regarding which objects or relationships that are to be included within the boundaries of a system depend on the problem at hand. "The decision as to which relationships are important and which trivial is up to the person dealing with

[245] Ibid.
[246] Katz and Kahn, op. cit., p. 28.
[247] Miller, "Living Systems: Basic Concepts," op. cit., 204–206.
[248] Bertalanffy, op. cit., p. 215.

FIGURE 2–9   Bertalanffy Illustration of Feedback Scheme

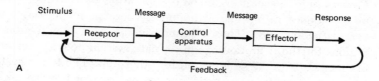

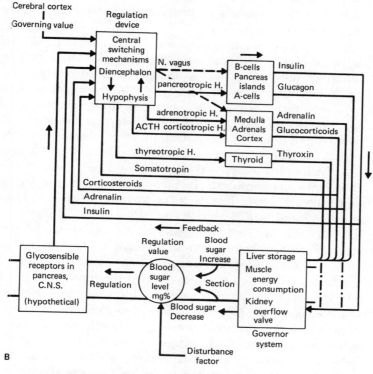

A – Simple Feedback Scheme.   B – Homeostatic Regulation of the Blood Sugar Level.

SOURCE: George Braziller, Inc. From *General Systems Theory* by Ludwig von Bertalanffy; with permission of the publisher. Copyright © 1968 by Ludwig von Bertalanffy. Material in diagram B follows H. Mittelstaedt, "Regelung in der Biologie," *Regelungstechnik*, **2** (1954), 177–81.

the problem; i.e., the question of triviality turns out to be relative to one's interest." [249]

One further note regarding boundaries provided by Katz and Kahn is especially important; boundaries vary in the degree to which they

---

[249] A. D. Hall and R. E. Fagen, "Definition of System," pp. 81–92, in Buckley, *Modern Systems Research for the Behavioral Scientist*, op. cit., p. 82.

are permeable and the degree to which this permeability is specified. For example, a secret organization operating in a hostile environment may evidence rather closed boundaries except to persons who know various code words. Thus, "Boundaries are the demarcation lines or regions for the definition of appropriate system activity, for admission of members into the system, and for other imports into the system. The boundary constitutes a barrier for many types of interaction between people on the inside and people on the outside, but it includes some facilitating device for the particular types of transactions necessary for organizational functioning." [250]

Seventh, system interaction, without and within, reflects differing layers of control and autonomy. For example, Miller proposes that a variety of subsystems may comprise any given system, but nineteen processes must be carried out by system components or be performed by some other system: "reproducer, boundary, ingestor, distributor, decomposer, producer, matter-energy storage, extruder, motor, supporter, input transducer, internal transducer, channel and net, decoder, associator, memory, decider, encoder, and output transducer." [251]

Activities of these various critical subsystems must be coordinated. How is this accomplished? To follow Miller's chain of logic, "Characteristically, in hierarchies of living systems, each level has a certain autonomy and to a degree is controlled by levels above and below it." [252] Power and control are exerted through intra and inter system messages that evoke compliance. Messages contain five critical characteristics: (1) an address; (2) a signature (sender identification); (3) legitimacy indicator, i.e., "evidence that the transmitter is a *legitimate* or appropriate source of command information to influence decisions of the receiver" [253]; (4) expectations of compliance, i.e., thus messages are often in the form of commands or in imperative mood; and (5) action specifications. Such messages elicit compliance "at lower levels because the electrical or chemical form of what is transmitted sets off a specific reaction. At higher levels because the receiving system is part of a suprasystem that can transmit rewarding and punishing inputs to it. The receiver has learned that, because the signature indicates that the message is from a legitimate source capable of influencing some part of the suprasystem to make such inputs, there is a certain significant probability of receiving such rewards or punishments, depending on how it responds." [254]

In short, some systems have varying degrees of power over others.

[250] Katz and Kahn, op. cit., pp. 60–61.
[251] Miller, "Living Systems: Basic Concepts," op. cit., p. 222.
[252] Ibid., p. 229.
[253] Ibid., p. 230.
[254] Ibid.

Miller proposes that power might be measured by looking jointly at: (1) the percentage of acts of a system that are controlled, i.e., changed from one alternative to another; (2) how critical the acts controlled are to the system; (3) the number of systems controlled; and (4) the level of systems controlled, as control of one system at a high level may influence many systems at lower levels. [255]

However, these degrees of power are dynamic and are continually subject to renegotiation. Crozier puts it most clearly with his image of the organization as a network of groups that comprise a complex bargaining system.[256] A series of bargaining strategies are used by these groups. And our understanding of organizational phenomena can be enhanced through analysis of these negotiation processes.[257]

Eighth, and finally, open systems analysis need not be reductionistic. Despite Bertalanffy's interest in developing a framework that might be applicable to most scientific disciplines, he is emphatic regarding reductionism. "A unitary conception of the world may be based, not upon the possibly futile and certainly farfetched hope finally to reduce all levels of reality to the level of physics, but rather on the isomorphy of laws in different fields." [258] Thompson's work clearly reflects this viewpoint; however, he does deal very briefly with the interactions between individual and organizational levels. Katz and Kahn also reflect this position, but as social psychologists they are especially interested in questions that focus on the interactions between the social and psychological levels. Hence, they include such topics as "personality factors as determinates of role expectations and response," "personality as affected by role behavior," and the like. At times, however, the distinctions become blurred, and they proceed to explain organizational phenomena using only individual characteristics. This has led some critics to cry "reductionism." [259] In general, however, most working within the perspective appear to agree in principle with Bertalanffy's position.

> We come, then, to a conception which in contrast to reductionism, we may call perspectivism. We cannot reduce the biological, behavioral, and social levels to the lowest level, that of the constructs and laws of physics. We can, however, find constructs and possibly laws within the individual levels. The world is, as Aldous Huxley once put it, like a Neapolitan ice cream cake

---

[255] Ibid.

[256] Crozier, *The Bureaucratic Phenomenon*, op. cit., pp. 145–74.

[257] This view is also reflected in Moore's imagery of social systems as "tension-management units." Wilbert E. Moore, *The Conduct of the Corporation* (New York: Random House, 1962), pp. 93–136; and Wilbert E. Moore, *Social Change* (Englewood Cliffs, N.J.: Prentice-Hall, Inc., 1963), pp. 10–21.

[258] Bertalanffy, op. cit., p. 48.

[259] Joseph W. Lella, "Review of *The Social Psychology of Organizations*," *American Journal of Sociology*, **72**: 677 (May 1967).

where the levels—the physical, the biological, the social and the moral universe—represent the chocolate, strawberry, and vanilla layers. We cannot reduce strawberry to chocolate—the most we can say is that possibly in the last resort, all is vanilla, all mind or spirit. The unifying principle is that we find organization at all levels.[260]

Illustrative Propositions

1. "Organizations will tend to elaborate and subdivide units that cope with the more problematic or uncertain sectors of their environments." [261]
2. "The locus of influence to resolve conflict is at a level where the required knowledge about the environment is available. The more unpredictable and uncertain the parts of the environment, the lower in the organizational hierarchy this tends to be." [262]
3. "Organizations with capacity in excess of what the task environment supports will seek to enlarge their domains." [263]
4. "When the range of variation presented by the task-environment segment is known, the organization component will treat this as a constraint and adapt by standardizing sets of rules." [264]
5. "When the range of task-environment variations is large or unpredictable, the responsible organization component must achieve the necessary adaptation by monitoring that environment and planning responses, and this calls for localized units." [265]

Critique

Several criticisms can be raised with this open system perspective. First, although it does provide a useful broad overview, actual attempts to use it as a basis for empirical research instantly produce complex operational problems. Few propositions are given that tie the various components of the complex vocabularies together. And propositions offered contain terms that may be impractical to make operational. For example, looking at the perceptive propositions offered above from Thompson's book, how might we make operational "organizational capacity"? Terms like *boundary, adaptation, feedback,* and the like are useful as organizing concepts, but difficult to use operationally. Predictive statements are hard to make.

Ideology and belief systems too frequently are conspicuously absent.

---

[260] Bertalanffy, op. cit., p. 49.
[261] Lawrence and Lorsch, op. cit., p. 100.
[262] Ibid., pp. 157–58.
[263] Thompson, op. cit., p. 46.
[264] Ibid., p. 71.
[265] Ibid., p. 72.

Although most writers do include some notion of stress or strain, this does not become central to the analysis. Hence, the insights from Coser, Dahrendorf, and other conflict theorists await notice.

Although interpersonal expectations are used by Katz and Kahn, few others have followed their lead. Even if patterned activity or event systems are identified, how are they to be explained? Most analysts have not included the interpersonal structure, or when they have it has been reduced to the psychological level, i.e., personality characteristics.

Technology has not been successfully integrated into any of the frameworks within this model. Thompson has made some minimal effort in this direction, but it remains greatly lacking. Others have ignored it in any analytical sense. They write about inputs, through-puts, and outputs, but take us no further.

Despite the focus on patterned event systems, little effort has been made to categorize analytically types of event systems wherein different processes might operate, except in the crudest of terms, e.g., people-changing versus thing-changing organizations.

Finally, as with all of the other perspectives presented, empirical studies that would sharpen the concepts and test some of the hypothesized relationships are almost totally absent. What kinds of studies need to be done? Buckley gives us some important leads. For example, ". . . a) specifying much more adequately the distribution of essential features of the component subsystems' internal mappings, including both self-mappings and their mappings of their effective environment, b) specifying more extensively the structure of the transactions among these units at a given time, the degree and stability of the given structuring seen as varying with the degree and depth of common meaning that are generated in the transaction process, and c) assessing, with the help of techniques now developing, the ongoing process of transitions from a given state of the system to the next in terms of the deviation-reducing and deviation-generating feedback loops relating the tensionful, goal-seeking, decision-making subunits via the communication nets partly specified by b)." [266]

In short, we find numerous important insights provided by this perspective. And many of the concepts, despite their vagueness, seem to relate to one another and tie together many loose ends. However, this cluster of ideas, as they are developed thus far, is more of a becoming than a being. But this is always true, in a sense, of all scientific endeavors. This should be kept in mind as we move into the next chapter where we will present our own effort to expand on this open systems perspective and pick up on some of the insights provided by other theorists discussed in this chapter.

[266] Buckley, *Modern Systems Research for the Behavioral Scientist*, op. cit., p. 511.

Chapter 3

ORGANIZATIONAL ANALYSIS: OVERVIEW OF A STRESS-STRAIN PERSPECTIVE

As indicated in Chapter 2 several theoretical perspectives have been constructed to guide organizational analysis. Although there are difficulties with all of these, many important insights are provided. But how might they be synthesized? Obviously, future investigators will propose many different answers. But now let us explore a conceptual framework that we have developed over the past several years. It should not be seen as any kind of final answer, but rather as an additional, general perspective that may provide a helpful starting point in thinking about organizations.

In Chapter 1, we emphasized the utility of viewing organizations as interaction systems. Let us now sketch in the basic elements of a theoretical framework that emerges when this view is taken. Although brief and fast-moving, this chapter will serve as a road map for the next several chapters in which all of the concepts will be elaborated and discussed in much greater detail. As you are reading later chapters, it may be useful to return here so as more easily to place discussions of specific concepts into the context of the entire framework.

Performance Structures

Following the suggestion of exchange theorists, let us start by observing. Assume that we are watching several police officers who comprise a communication unit. As citizens telephone the police organizations, their calls are directed to officers in this department. Depending upon the nature of the request, officers will act differently. However, if we watched them over a period of time, we would find consistency in their behavior. Patterns would become apparent as many behavior sequences reoccur.

These patterns can be described systematically. Often, a flow chart, such as that presented in Figure 3–1, can be most helpful in summarizing behavior patterns. Thus, complaints, inquiries, and requests for police action are filtered by the communication officer (complaint clerk) who may act on them in a variety of ways depending upon the content of the request. If the request requires cruiser action, necessary data are obtained; a form is filled out; and the data are communicated to the dispatcher, who then relays this information to a cruiser officer. System feedback loops emerge as the cruiser officer contacts the citizen initiating the request or otherwise handles the complaint. He then informs the dispatcher by radio of how the complaint was handled; or he may request from the dispatcher additional assistance, e.g., a tow truck to remove a wrecked automobile from a busy intersection. Finally, the disposition of the complaint is referred back to the complaint clerk, who records this data and forwards it to the records department for storage and general analysis.

Note that in this illustration interaction took place by several means. Information was exchanged through telephone calls, paper forms, radio messages, and face-to-face conversation. As emphasized earlier, organizational interaction is most complex. Often, if not typically, it assumes some form other than face-to-face. And frequently the interaction is indirect or nonperson-oriented. For example, an individual who has just experienced an automobile accident usually telephones the police department rather than a specific person or individual within the department. Events that take place within a specified geographical area are assigned to cruiser operators located in that region, rather than to officers as individuals.

After watching officers deal with the public for a time, we might move into another segment of the police organization where persons are busy with payroll checks. And as we observe, we note that there is a specific routine by which checks are handled. With little more than a few questions, we would discover that from the time a new candidate enrolls in the police training school, members of this department know of it. They have continual and up-to-date knowledge of the financial remuneration to which he is entitled. Note that we are referring here to behavior—not to reasons for it. And we can detect patterns of behavior; that is, there are sequences that exist. These *patterns in interaction sequences* are referred to as the organizational *performance structure*.

When we observe even a very small organization, however, it becomes apparent rather quickly that the performance structure is highly

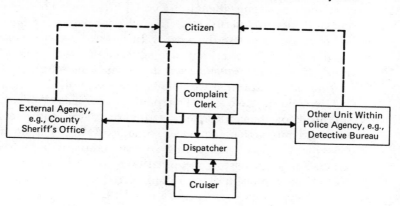

FIGURE 3–1   Flow Chart of a Typical Police Communication System

complex and that all aspects of it are interrelated. Yet, this reality of patterned events is exactly the reality that we have isolated for study. But to talk of "the" organizational performance structure is accurate only to a point; the complexity must be faced.

One way of dealing with this complexity is to subdivide the performance structure into smaller and smaller observable units. For example, we might subdivide on the basis of departmental boundaries. By using an organizational chart as our map, we could write brief descriptions of the patterned sequences of behavior that were observed in each department. This can be done, but the results tend to be of limited value because the portrait of the organization that emerges is often that of a collection of relatively isolated subunits. The interrelationships among the units may remain unclear. Also, some units intuitively seem to be worth more analysis than others, but if we are to analyze each individually we have little theoretical basis for making such selections. What we must develop from our observations are sets of categories that help us observe behavior and note its sequential nature in detail.

If not description by department, then what? Whyte gives us a helpful idea. "No one can make sense out of organizational behavior in a large restaurant, for example, unless he examines the flow of work from customer to waitress, from waitress back to customer." [1] Thus, similar to our description of the police interaction, we can focus on the work flow or *task process*. By using this process approach we might follow a product in a manufacturing firm, in and out of several departments. But we thereby gain a clear picture of organizational

[1] William F. Whyte, "Parsons' Theory Applied to Organizations," in *The Social Theories of Talcott Parsons*, Max Black, ed. (Englewood Cliffs, N.J.: Prentice-Hall, Inc., 1961), p. 264.

activity that is based on actual behavior rather than *prescriptive devices* such as organizational charts. Clearly, such charts are but one type of device to describe what the behavior pattern *ought* to be: they do not necessarily describe what *is*. In this way we can *make problematic the degree of correspondence between observed behavior patterns and participant ideas about what the behavior patterns ought to be.*

From this perspective we maintain our view of the organization as an interaction system—a set of patterned events.[2] And although we can speak of the performance structure as the entire collection of patterned interaction sequences, complexity forces us to use smaller units for analysis. After trying several alternatives such as departmental boundaries as a conceptual unit, it has become clear that the most effective procedure is to think of the performance structure as a series of interrelated processes. By *process*, we mean only to imply a sequence of interactions with common content that recur over time.[3]

Thus, we can think of task processes as those sequences of behaviors related directly to the central tasks of the organization. Note that this does not refer to ideas about organizational goals, i.e., desired future states. Instead, sets of behaviors are identified that *we as analysts* have grouped together as being most related to central tasks. In this way, we can go from the descriptive level directly to more abstract statements about rates and patterns of task performance, and thereby include both quantitative and qualitative dimensions of the task process. Also, we have linked not only activities of several persons but perhaps also of several departments into a central set of variables that have much operational potential because they are directly related to observable behavior.

From this perspective, the organizational analyst begins with observations of behavior. As incumbents are observed over time, certain patterns in their behavior are noted. Because of the complexity of all of the behavior patterns that constitute any organization, we subdivide our analysis into a series of processes. And behavior patterns are then grouped, to be analyzed in terms of these processes.

[2] These patterned interaction sequences are similar to, but less inclusive than the concept of "patterned event structures" proposed by Daniel Katz and Robert L. Kahn in *The Social Psychology of Organizations* (New York: John Wiley and Sons, Inc., 1966).

Given our broad interpretation of interaction, we will use the two terms interchangeably, but our emphasis will be on human interaction.

[3] The concept of process has a long history in sociological thought and at different times has had varied meanings. Brief but illuminating discussions can be found in Russell L. Langworthy, "Process," in *A Dictionary of the Social Sciences*, Julius Gould and William Kolb, eds. (New York: The Free Press, 1964), pp. 538–540; and Max Lerner, "Social Process," in *Encyclopedia of the Social Sciences*, Edwin Seligman and Alvin Johnson, eds. (New York: The Macmillan Company, 1934), Vol. 14, pp. 148–51.

This is rather similar to the viewpoint that emerged when Hammond and his colleagues completed a series of discussions focused on the administrative process:

> A focus on administrative processes seems to offer the best assurance against the temptation to be content with association, and reduces our reliance on the particular genius of the investigator. In the definitional context already advanced, those *patterned sequences of behavior* which bring about, maintain, or curtail organizational structure would constitute an administrative process. Likewise, those *sets of behavior* related to establishing, maintaining, or dropping organizational purposes constitute an administrative process. The *patterned sequences of behavior* which provide or deny modes of interaction with the relevant environment would also constitute an administrative process. In each case, the crucial question is *how* one pattern of behavior leads to another pattern of behavior, and so on through a chain until a functional requirement is satisfied.[4]

Three points of clarification are necessary before we proceed. First, data on organizational performance structures need not be limited to direct observation of persons. Although we have defined performance structure as patterned sequences of interaction, such sequences may be ascertained using a variety of research methods. Direct observation is only one alternative. Questionnaires, interviews, primary source materials such as interoffice memos, records of telephone conversations, or budgets may all be used singly or in combination. In fact, as we will argue in detail in Chapter 9, the best strategy is to use a variety of data collection techniques so as systematically to crossvalidate all sources. Thus, although direct observation of incumbent behavior may be used exclusively, the perspective does not require this. What is required, however, is that behavior patterns be ascertained in some manner, and that the degree of correspondence and divergence between these patterns and participant ideas about how these patterns *ought* to be, be viewed as problematic.

Second, in order to cluster behaviors into analytical processes, we must invent a series of categories. As such, they are imposed on what we have observed so as to organize it in a manner that permits us more easily to record, keep track of, and group the complexity of the numerous interrelations. Just as we use language as an organizing tool that creates our very definition of reality, so we invent these categories. Some behaviors may be classified into more than one analytical category. Although the categories are analytically distinct, behaviors may be treated differently at different points in analysis. For example, when

---

[4] Peter B. Hammond, et al., "On the Study of Administration," in *Comparative Studies in Administration*, James D. Thompson et al., eds. (Pittsburgh, Pa.: University of Pittsburgh Press, 1959), p. 11.

analyzing communication processes, many of the same behaviors will be regrouped to constitute decision-making processes. Once decisions are made, they must be communicated, and the very act of making decisions usually requires a series of communications. This should be recognized at the outset to avoid confusion.

Finally, how many processes are to be used, and which ones are they? At the present stage in theory development, we suggest that different analysts with varying interests may want to handle this question in alternative ways. We do not think that the present state of theory permits us to propose a list of four, six, or ten fundamental organizational processes. And how each of the more general processes is subdivided is subject to even more variation. Unfortunately, specific propositions relating variables in a systematic fashion are not found in excessive numbers within the literature. Thus, as yet we do not have a sufficient theoretical base with which to make any definite statements as to how these processes can be conceptualized most effectively. Hence, the following guidelines are offered with clear recognition that other analysts may want to use, refine, and reformulate any one or all of them.

Organizational Processes

It appears that the performance structure can be subdivided into at least eight processes: task, maintenance, communication, decision making, coordination, control, adaptation, and conflict. Let us briefly explore each of these.

1. *Task processes* include all activities specifically related to central organizational tasks. As the entire organization is our focus, we would not refer to tasks of specific departments because they would be included elsewhere in the analysis. And it is clear that attempts to identify central tasks for many organizations will be difficult because they may be highly diffuse. Thus, rate of task performance, pattern of task performance, degree of task specificity, and other such categories might be used as operational variables when we wished to shift levels of abstraction beyond the descriptive. Note that we are not referring to the criteria that members might use in establishing levels of task performance, but only to behavior identified by the analyst as being relevant to organizational tasks.

In keeping with our emphasis on the organization as an open system, analysis of task processes cannot be viewed as being confined solely within an organizational boundary. Dill's work is especially illuminating in this regard. He proposed that the "task environment" might be conceptualized into four components: (1) customers or clients; (2)

suppliers of materials, labor, capital, equipment, and so on; (3) competitors for both markets and resources; and (4) regulatory groups, e.g., unions, associations, governmental agencies.[5] Thus, by viewing the environment as being composed of a multiplicity of structures, those most related to task are included here. This perspective provides us with a more open model of organization and forces us to recognize the significance of behavior patterns that transcend what traditionally have been treated as excessively tight boundaries.

Finally, more abstract conceptualizations of technology, such as Perrow's (see pp. 72–78), often will prove useful in thinking about task processes especially as they are interrelated to other aspects of the performance structure. Thus, the degree to which task processes are perceived by participants as being highly certain and involving few exceptions will have consequences for other processes, such as maintenance and control. We shall pursue this point in a while, but let us now turn to the other processes used to analyze organizational performance structures.

2. *Maintenance processes* are comprised of such subprocesses as recruitment and socialization. Specific behavior patterns usually can be detected in all organizations that might be categorized into these areas. Thus, new members must be obtained (recruitment), and once obtained they must be taught the ways of organizational life (socialization). Note that we are using these terms only as possible categories for grouping behavior analytically. Although the categories to some degree will affect our perception of that behavior, as do all categorical systems, we must start with something. However, we see these as categories to be used in grouping existing, observable behavior, and not as prescriptive ideas as to what *ought* to exist in an organization if it is to be efficient or well managed. Thus, some behavior sequences that an analyst might include in his description of socialization processes might not be so defined by organizational members.

3. *Communication processes* have long been researched by organizational specialists. We have become aware of the complexity of the multitude of channels that exist within organizations, including both official and unofficial channels. Also, laboratory research has provided some interesting insights into effectiveness of various types of communications nets.[6] For example, if members are forced to communicate in a certain pattern, we now have some evidence as to what to

---

[5] William R. Dill, "Environment as an Influence on Managerial Autonomy," *Administrative Science Quarterly*, **2**: 409– 443 (March 1958).

[6] Alex Bavelas, "Communication Patterns in Task-Oriented Groups," *Journal of Acoustical Society of America*, **22**: 725–30 (1950), is generally recognized as the seminal piece.

anticipate in terms of speed in problem solving and the like.[7] Also, the significance of the organizational grapevine as a communication channel has been researched. However, although we have many ideas concerning communication patterns, rates of flow, and type of information communicated, we lack sets of interrelated and precisely stated hypotheses.

When such findings are stated in hypothesis form and are empirically tested, we may be in for many surprises as to what actually goes on in organizations. For example, it is commonly assumed that most communication within organizations is vertical, i.e., between subordinates and their superiors. However, Simpson's study in the spinning department of a synthetic textile mill strongly suggested that this was not true.[8] His evidence indicated support for his thesis "that writers on formal organization have overemphasized vertical communication, in which instructions are given and reports are made, while underemphasizing horizontal communication, in which problems are ironed out and work flow processes are coordinated." [9] Future research must be directed at conceptual formulation that will permit precise empirical testing of hypotheses so that myth can be separated from fact.

4. *Decision-making processes* have likewise received much study, but other than statements somewhat similar to Dewey's initial formulation[10] as to how decisions ought to be made, these research studies have left us with limited insights as to how decision-making processes might be conceptualized for future empirical work. Elaborating on Dewey's formulation of this process, Katz and Kahn have posed several questions that should guide future research.[11] For example, how do organizational members first come to decide that here is a problem? How are priorities assigned? To what degree are incumbents aware of the constraints within which they must work? Similarly, March and Simon propose that "the existing pattern of communication will determine the relative frequency with which particular members of the organization will encounter particular stimuli, or kinds of stimuli, in

[7] Outstanding summaries of research since Bavelas are Murray Glanzer and Robert Glaser, "Techniques for the Study of Group Structure and Behavior: II Empirical Studies of the Effects of Structure in Small Groups," *Psychological Bulletin*, 58: 1–27 (January 1961); and Harold Guetzkow, "Communications in Organizations," in *Handbook of Organizations*, James G. March, ed. (Chicago: Rand McNally and Company, 1964), pp. 534–73.

[8] Richard L. Simpson, "Vertical and Horizontal Communication in Formal Organizations," *Administrative Science Quarterly*, 4: 188–96 (September 1959).

[9] Ibid., p. 194.

[10] John Dewey, *How We Think* (Lexington, Mass.: D. C. Heath, 1933). He suggested that decision making proceeded through five stages: (1) felt need; (2) analysis of problem; (3) search for alternative solutions; (4) consideration of consequences of solutions; and finally (5) selection of a particular solution.

[11] Katz and Kahn, op. cit., pp. 274–82.

Chapter 3. Organizational Analysis: Overview

their research processes."[12] Most of this analysis, however, is at the psychological level and is concerned with the specific psychological processes that characterize individuals involved in decision-making activity. Analysis of the process at the social level awaits clear conceptualization and sets of hypotheses relating specific variables in a clear and concise manner.

5. *Coordination processes* refer to those sets of behaviors through which the complex network of interrelated events are maintained. And findings from studies such as Simpson's strongly indicate that much coordination is accomplished in a horizontal fashion rather than vertical.[13] Department heads and other administrative personnel often may resemble the supervisors in Simpson's study who "seldom had to communicate with each other, since the work relations between their sections were coordinated mainly through horizontal contacts between their subordinates."[14] Through our focus on specific patterns of observed behavior, we may learn much that will alter the image too often found in management and administration texts, which emphasizes the major responsibility of the administrator as *the* organizational coordinator.

Certainly, there are a multitude of coordination or integration processes in operation. And as Lawrence and Lorsch point out, whereas high levels of interaction are required for all organizations, the behavioral processes may vary considerably. Thus, in plastics and foods organizations, where innovation was a key concern, integration had to occur at lower levels. The research units had to be linked closely with both production and sales quite far down in the organization structure. In contrast, container organizations, characterized by task processes of high certainty and relative stability, demonstrated major integrative processes at the upper levels.[15]

6. *Control processes* are related closely to those of coordination. But here we are identifying interaction sequences primarily characterized by: (1) a participant or groups (A) announcing an intention; (2) that leads to attempts to influence other participants or groups (B); (3) that results in behaviors of the others (B); (4) that fulfill the original intention of (A).

This view of the control process reflects Floyd Allport's "event-structure" theory wherein control is viewed as a cycle of events.[16]

---

[12] James G. March and Herbert A. Simon, *Organizations* (New York: John Wiley and Sons, Inc., 1958), p. 168.

[13] Simpson, op. cit.

[14] Ibid.

[15] Paul R. Lawrence and Jay W. Lorsch, *Organization and Environment* (Homewood, Ill.: Richard D. Irwin, Inc., 1969), pp. 151–58.

[16] Floyd H. Allport, *Theories of Perception and the Concept of Structure* (New York: John Wiley and Sons, Inc., 1955).

Moreover, it has been elaborated and used for a large number of empirical research studies that have been summarized by Likert[17] and Tannenbaum.[18] Although descriptive analysis could be completed of the control process within the performance structure, this research provides us with some important conceptual insights. For example, Likert suggests that management systems can be conceptualized as four general types: exploitive-authoritative, benevolent-authoritative, consultative, and participative group.[19] He further argues that forty-three "operating characteristics" of an organization can be measured so as to ascertain which management system is in operation. His findings clearly suggest two things. First, there are linkages among the variables; that is, particular communication patterns and decision-making processes are intercorrelated with the management system typology. Second, participative group management systems (System 4) "are more productive and have lower costs and more favorable attitudes than do . . ."[20] the other management systems. Similarly, firms using participative group management "show high productivity, low scrap costs, low costs, favorable attitudes, and excellent labor relations."[21] And shifts over time toward participative group management resulted in structural changes that were correlated with changes in these same variables. Clearly, the type of control process is related to many other structural variables.

In contrast to Likert's work, which appears to be directed to highlight findings that prove the "positive" consequences of System 4, Tannenbaum's summary is much more analytic. He presents several leads regarding measurement of control processes.[22] Comparative research across organizations again suggests that the distribution of control does vary both within and among organizations.[23] And, as suggested by Likert, this distribution is related to numerous other variables.

Another lead that aids in analysis of control processes is gleaned from Gerald Bell's creative work on the concept of discretion.[24] An in-

[17] Rensis Likert, *New Patterns of Management* (New York: McGraw-Hill Book Co., 1967).

[18] Arnold S. Tannenbaum, *Control in Organizations* (New York: McGraw-Hill Book Co., 1968).

[19] Rensis Likert, *The Human Organization* (New York: McGraw-Hill Book Co., 1967), pp. 13–46.

[20] Ibid., p. 46.

[21] Ibid.

[22] Tannenbaum, op. cit., pp. 23–25.

[23] Ibid., pp. 73–112.

[24] Gerald D. Bell, "Formality Versus Flexibility in Complex Organizations," in *Organizations and Human Behavior*, Gerald D. Bell, ed. (Englewood Cliffs, N.J.: Prentice-Hall, Inc., 1967), pp. 97–106.

cumbent may be permitted discretion in one or more of the following areas: "1) *which task* he performs during a given period of time, 2) *how or by which methods,* and 3) *in which sequence he performs* his tasks." [25] Bell concluded his analysis with a series of perceptive hypotheses. Thus, "in organizations in which employees exert a high degree of discretion there will be: 1) less rigid lines of authority, 2) high vertical communications, 3) low coordination, 4) high normative control by supervisors, 5) high normative commitment by employees, 6) high affectivity in interpersonal relationships, and finally 7) relatively high productivity";[26] and further, "that discretion is determined by predictability, management control, and extent of professionalization of jobs." [27] Thus, Likert, Tannenbaum, and Bell provide us with several conceptual and methodological clues with which we might explore control processes. And they suggest several linkages among these processes and others.

7. *Adaptation processes* again highlight environmental factors. As we observe organizational incumbents over time, certain activities would be directed at ascertaining changes in the environment. Those patterned activities most related to task would be viewed as part of the task process, but the focus here is on patterned behaviors directed at modifying organizational elements given certain environmental changes. Also included are behaviors by organizational incumbents that *act on* elements of the environment and thereby modify it in some way.

Using Dill's basic concept of task environment, Thompson has formulated a series of propositions that are illustrative of the type of work that can be done in this area.

1. "Under norms of rationality, organizations facing heterogenous task environments seek to identify homogeneous segments and to establish structural units to deal with each."
2. "Under norms of rationality, boundary-spanning components facing homogeneous segments of the task environment are further subdivided to match surveillance capacity with environmental action."
3. "When the range of variation presented by the task-environment segment is known, the organization component will treat this as a constraint and adapt by standardizing sets of rules."
4. "When the range of task-environment variations is large or unpredictable, the responsible organization component must achieve the necessary adaptation by monitoring that environment and planning responses, and this calls for localized units."
5. "Under norms of rationality, organizations facing dynamic task en-

[25] Ibid., p. 98.
[26] Ibid., p. 105.
[27] Ibid.

vironments seek to score favorably in relation to comparable organizations."

6. "When organizations find it difficult to score on intrinsic criteria, they seek extrinsic measures of fitness for the future."
7. "When task-environment elements lack technical ability to assess performance, organizations seek extrinsic measures of fitness for future actions."
8. "When cause/effect knowledge is believed to be incomplete, organizations seek extrinsic measures of fitness for future action." [28]

Let us return to the behavior patterns in the police department that we discussed earlier. Some of these descriptive observations can be recast using hypothesis statements such as these by Thompson. For example, separate communication units are found in most large police departments (number 1, above). Environmental changes are monitored by such units. Different types of events are referred to various specialized divisions, such as juvenile, detective, internal security, or narcotics. Thus, although there is variety in the situations that police confront, the communication unit narrows the range of variation by filtering and sorting incoming messages to the appropriate substructure. Similarly, sets of rules have been established that specify organizational actions that are to be taken in a wide variety of circumstances. For example, rules specify standardized operating procedures for handling automobile accidents, burglary reports, and the like (number 3, above). Keeping crime-rate statistics and putting emphasis on extrinsic measures, such as awards won, are handled perceptively in the above hypotheses (numbers 6 and 7). Additional work of this type is exactly what is needed if a theory of organization is ever to emerge.

8. *Conflict processes* refer to those patterned sets of behavior that designate internal and external conflict disagreements and efforts at resolution. Employee grievance behavior that remains internal, and that which might involve union officials, are typical examples. Our view of organizations as interaction systems permits focus on such conflict patterns. Although empirical research in this area is minimal, we can build on studies like Scott's, in which he analyzed employee appeal systems in several business and nonbusiness organizations.[29] At a more abstract level, Boulding has suggested that analysis of conflict processes probably requires four sets of concepts, related to the parties involved, the field of conflict, dynamics of conflict situations, and con-

---

[28] The propositions were extracted from James D. Thompson, *Organizations in Action* (New York: McGraw-Hill Book Co., 1967), pp. 70–92.

[29] William G. Scott, *The Management of Conflict: Appeal Systems in Organizations* (Homewood, Ill.: Richard D. Irwin, Inc., 1965).

flict management.[30] But it is clear that much additional conceptual work will be required before extensive sets of hypotheses will be generated.

It should be emphasized that we do not imply that all or even most of the conflict within organizations, or among organizations, can be resolved. Rather, behavior patterns that we might choose to deal with in this aspect of the performance structure are always present at varying levels and degrees of frequency and intensity. Further, certain activities that we as analysts might select to include here might not be regarded by the participants as having anything to do with conflict. Often, conflict is a latent consequence of behavior initially motivated by very different aims. However, it is important to recognize that some conflict behavior may be generated purposely by organizational incumbents for a variety of motives.

Organizational performance structure—i.e., patterned sets of interaction sequences—can be subdivided into the above eight processes. There is no intention of implying that these eight are the only eight, or that there is any reason to suspect that there are eight basic organizational processes. They are presented as sensitizing concepts, which, given the present state of organizational theory, seem to be helpful. Over time, it may be discovered that none of these eight categories is especially useful in organizing observation of the performance structure. At present, however, they appear to be the most promising routes through which the complex reality of patterned interaction sequences can be analyzed. Each general process must be divided into a series of subprocesses and then finally into a collection of specific hypothesis statements, before we begin to approach a comprehensive theory of organizations.

As we have emphasized throughout, each of these processes is interrelated. For example, task processes appear to be directly related to control. As the degree of uncertainty and the number of exceptions encountered increase, to use Perrow's notion, the type of control processes that will be found will vary.[31] Certainly, the leads from Likert, Bell, and Tannenbaum suggest this. Communication patterns, conflict resolution strategies, and coordination processes also appear to be related to certain characteristics of the task processes. Recall some of the insights provided by Lawrence and Lorsch's research. And similarly, as highlighted by Thompson, adaptation processes whereby organizations seek to cope with and act on their environments are interrelated with other aspects of the performance structure.

[30] Kenneth E. Boulding, "A Pure Theory of Conflict Applied to Organizations," in Robert L. Kahn and Elise Boulding, eds., *Power and Conflict in Organizations* (New York: Basic Books, Inc., 1964), pp. 136–45.

[31] Charles Perrow, "A Framework for the Comparative Analysis of Organizations," *American Sociological Review*, 32: 194–208 (April 1967).

But the closeness of interrelationship among the various processes will vary greatly in functioning organizations. And some organizations may be hindered consistently because the participants fail to appreciate these types of linkages. For example, we might categorize task processes into people changing versus object changing. Prisons are regarded by some optimists as people changing institutions. However, as Etzioni's analysis reveals, there are sharp limitations on task performances in prisons because of the control processes employed.[32] Thus, prisons that emphasize alienative involvement and coercive power relations are thwarted structurally in rehabilitative efforts. Moreover, as Duncombe has emphasized in applying this view to nursing home organizations, changes in one processual dimension of the performance structure (e.g., decision making) will establish intense strain unless corresponding changes are made in the other dimensions as well.[33] Such strained structures are inherently unstable and reflect pressures to reach consistency among the total set of processes in one way or another. For example, if changes are made in the mode of decision making and nowhere else, pressure will emerge to force changes in other sectors of the performance structure so as to make them consistent with the altered decision making process. Efforts to introduce widespread participation in decision making probably will fail if control processes remain highly authoritarian and excessively tight. Thus, we suspect that many efforts at organizational change are thwarted because the piecemeal alterations are not accompanied by change elsewhere in the structure. Rather, the unchanged processual sectors of the performance structure exert sufficient pressure so that either the changed process returns to its original state or the organization experiences high turnover as incumbents find that the strained, inconsistent structure will not work.

Although such general statements can be made and somewhat defended, what we lack is a clear set of conceptual categories for each process area and networks of propositions that relate each of them systematically. Such propositions, in a collective form, would serve to describe the patterned interaction sequences found in organizations of different types. This idea of multiple forms of linkages among these eight processes is illustrated in Figure 3–2.

In spite of the present lack of such a network of propositions, we can at least now see the directions in which we must go. But why do the patterns of behavior persist as they do? At one level of explanation, they persist because they are interrelated. However, we can shift to

[32] Amitai Etzioni, "Dual Leadership in Complex Organizations," *American Sociological Review*, 30: 688–98 (October 1965).

[33] Margaret Duncombe, "A Theoretical Model of the Interaction Between Total Institutions and Their Inmates," paper at the Annual Meetings of the Rocky Mountain Social Science Association, in Fort Collins, Colorado, May 7, 1971.

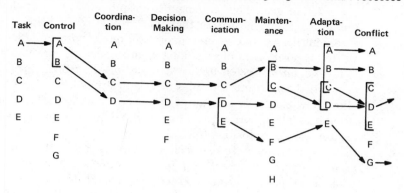

FIGURE 3–2   Illustrative Interrelationships Among Organizational Processes

another level of abstraction in seeking an explanation of the perform-ance structure—of both its persistence and change.

Explanatory Structures

In our analysis of an organization, assume that we have mapped out the performance structure. That is, after observing and perhaps interview-ing organizational members we have developed a relatively clear pic-ture of the central behavior patterns in which we are interested. This analysis may be rather limited in scope, e.g., only decision-making processes, or it may be comprehensive and include all aspects of the performance structure. At any rate, specific interaction sequences and the interrelationships among them have been noted. We now want to develop some idea of why these patterns recur over time. Why do they persist? And when they do change, why does this happen when it does and in the way it does?

We propose that through refinement and elaboration, three inter-related analytical structures may account for the performance structure. It appears to us that these structures operate simultaneously to produce the patterned interaction sequences that we have defined as the reality for study. That is, the performance structure is an observable behav-ioral phenomenon that we seek to *explain* through characteristics of and fluctuations in the normative, interpersonal, and resource struc-tures. Clearly, our goal of explanation is far from being accomplished. *Hopefully the following sets of "orienting statements"* [34] *and the few low-level propositions that comprise this stress–strain perspective will*

---

[34] Homans' discussion of the process of explanation is most helpful. Orienting statements, comprised of relationships among "whole clusters of undefined vari-ables" are not "real propositions." They may serve the purpose, however, of ". . . telling us what we ought to look into further or how we ought to look at it"

prove useful in assisting some to conduct research that might carry us closer to our goal. This statement is not intended as an apology; rather, our intent is to emphasize that what follows is a brief sketch of an emergent *perspective—not a theoretical model* with explanatory power. With this position emphasized, let us proceed with our overview.

1. The *normative structure* consists of the entire array of social norms that constitute the rules of organizational life. *Norms* are *ideas* about how classes or categories of persons ought to behave in specified situations. Thus, norms are *categorical,* i.e., they apply to categories of persons—e.g., professors, husbands, or wives. They are situational, i.e., they are relevant only to specific situations rather than to all. Norms *vary in degree of specificity* in that some are narrow and specific whereas others are vague and loosely defined. Norms are ideas about how persons ought to behave rather than being the actual behavior. Thus, they are *ideational.* Some norms specify behavioral actions that are to be enacted if behavior deviates from other norms. Norms that specify how rule violation is to be responded to are called *negative sanctions.*[35] Similarly, when certain norms are followed, *positive sanctions* are in order.

Because the normative structure is such a crucial aspect of our perspective, an example may help to clarify this mode of analysis.[36] Assume that we have been invited to attend our first hockey game.[37]

(p. 17). Thus, we use the term *explanatory structures* to emphasize our belief that further analysis in this general direction may prove productive in developing explanatory systems. George C. Homans, *The Nature of Social Science* (New York: Harcourt, Brace, Jovanovich, Inc., 1967).

See also Eugene J. Meehan, *Explanation in Social Science: A System Paradigm* (Homewood, Ill.: The Dorsey Press, 1968).

[35] A classic illustration of this concept is the "binging" device discovered in the Hawthorne studies. Workers identified as rate busters were in jest hit on the arm or "binged" by other workers. While done in a joking context, the act served to inform the rate buster of his failure to comply to the group norm, and if he continued rule violation, the work rate was slowed by a sore arm. Fritz J. Roethlisberger and William J. Dickson, *Management and the Worker* (Cambridge, Mass.: Harvard University Press, 1939). Detailed discussion of norms, and a proposed typology is found in Richard T. Morris, "A Typology of Norms," *American Sociological Review,* **21:** 610–13 (October 1956).

[36] Among more detailed and extensive empirical analyses using this concept of normative structure in an organizational setting are the following.

Neal Gross et al., *Explorations in Role Analysis: Studies of the School Superintendency Role* (New York: John Wiley and Sons, Inc., 1958).

Robert L. Kahn et al., *Organizational Stress: Studies in Role Conflict and Ambiguity* (New York: John Wiley and Sons, Inc., 1964).

Jack J. Preiss and Howard Ehrlich, *An Examination of Role Theory: The Case of the State Police* (Lincoln, Neb.: University of Nebraska Press, 1966).

[37] Goffman's insights into game analysis and its relevance to sociology have been most helpful, especially Erving Goffman, *Encounters* (Indianapolis, Ind.: Bobbs-Merrill, 1961); and Erving Goffman, *Presentation of Self in Everyday Life* (Garden City, N.Y.: Doubleday Anchor, 1959).

As the play develops, we notice that there are certain behavior patterns that recur time after time. As a new player enters the ice, another leaves. Some leave and sit alone in a small box. Two types of uniforms are represented, but there are two individuals with striped shirts who blow whistles from time to time. To account for this behavior we might invent many explanatory devices. However, we would suggest that in contrast to attitude tests, psychological scales, or motivational inventories, the most powerful explanatory device would be to derive some understanding of the normative structure. That is, what are the rules of the game? As we understand these rules, which exist apart from any of the individual players, we can begin to predict and understand their behavior. And it is important to note that all players are subject to these rules even though they may be unaware of any one of them. The rules exist as a reality apart from the conceptions of them by any individual player. They represent a constraint structure that will be highly influential in shaping these behavior patterns.

As we listed these rules, many of which might be inferred from actual behavior, it would be convenient to group them in certain ways. Following what is gradually becoming a somewhat standard usage in sociology, we might construct *a role*. A role is *a cluster of norms that applies to any single unit of social interaction.*[38] Thus, those norms that specify the nature of the relationship between a player and the referee would constitute a role or role relationship. Again, these are rules or ideas about how each is to behave toward the other; their actual behavior we refer to as role behavior. Roles are always reciprocal in nature. Thus, reference might be made to the player–referee role, the player–player role, player–coach role, coach–referee role, and so on.

As we began explicating the norms that compose the player–referee role, for example, five general categories would emerge. First, some norms specify appropriate *tasks*—what they are, how or when they are to be carried out, and so forth. Second, other norms designate the *authority* dimension of the relationship. Players ought to follow orders from the referee, not the other way around. Third, the relative *status* of each is reflected in many ways. Unique uniforms for the referee and players are required so that they can easily be distinguished. But more importantly, these uniforms reflect differential status. In other settings, the type of office furniture, the presence of an expensive carpet, the use of titles ("sir" or "Doctor," for example) reflect status differences. The ways of expressing deference are many and complex. Fourth, the

---

[38] J. Eugene Haas, "Role, Position, and Social Organization: A Conceptual Formulation," *Midwest Sociologist*, **19**: 33–37 (December 1956); Gross, op. cit., pp. 3–69; Robert K. Merton, *Social Theory and Social Srutcture*, rev. ed. (New York: The Free Press, 1957), pp. 368–84; Robert K. Merton, "The Role-Set: Problems in Sociological Theory," *British Journal of Sociology*, **8**: 106–20 (June 1957); and Bruce J. Biddle and Edwin J. Thomas, eds., *Role Theory: Concepts and Research* (New York: John Wiley and Sons, Inc., 1966), pp. 3–62.

affective nature of the relationship is specified. Hockey referees ought to remain emotionally uninvolved with players. A wife ought to love her husband, be he player or referee. Fifth, and finally, some norms specify appropriate *sanctions* when rule violation occurs.

Each of these general categories can be further subdivided for greater precision. For example, Richard Scott and his colleagues [39] have suggested that four types of "authority rights" can be differentiated: (1) allocating rights, i.e., "the right to assign an organizational goal to a participant"; (2) criteria-setting rights, i.e., "the right to specify those performance properties to be considered, their weights or relative importance, and the standards to be used in determining a performance evaluation"; (3) sampling rights, i.e., "the right to select aspects of performances or outcomes that will be observed to provide information for an evaluation"; and (4) appraising rights, i.e., "the right to decide how the level of performance is to be inferred from the sample and to apply the criteria to arrive at a performance evaluation." [40] These writers and others have emphasized that incumbents may grant that their superiors may exercise certain controls over them, and yet believe that their particular superior should not be accorded such rights. Thus, subordinates may comply with demands from their superiors even though they may feel that the superior is not technically competent or should not have this right. The hockey player must obey the referee's decision even though he may disagree with it. His only recourse would be to leave the game.

A role is a cluster of norms that applies to any single unit of social interaction. And there are several roles into which the norms of a hockey game are clustered. The entire collection of roles that are commonly thought to go together define a *position*. The player position is composed of several role relationships: player–referee, player–player (same side), and player–player (opposite side). Persons enact positions in the sense that they behave in certain expected ways while in interaction with a series of other position incumbents. Any position incumbent is thus expected to behave in accordance with an entire set of norms that specify the role relationships between his position and a series of other positions.

Note Figure 3–3 which presents the three role relationships that compose the position of hockey player. Of course, we could shift to a lower level of abstraction and follow this same form of analysis, but in greater detail. Thus, depending upon the specific task the player was to complete (e.g., goal tender, forward, or the like), the specification

[39] W. Richard Scott, et al., "Organizational Evaluation and Authority," in W. Richard Scott, *Social Processes and Social Structures* (New York: Holt, Rinehart and Winston, Inc., 1970), pp. 392–98.

[40] Ibid., pp. 394–95.

FIGURE 3–3   Position of Hockey Player

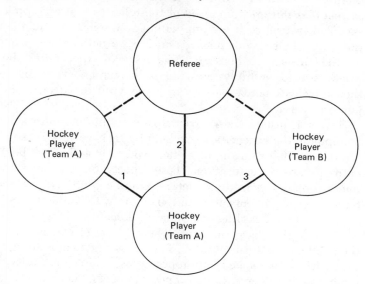

of the position, component roles, and norms would be much more specific.

Organizational charts and tables of organization are examples of written versions of official normative structures. Such devices are intended to provide guidelines for position incumbents. In this way, authority relationships, task assignments, and the like are specified. Such official norms are both written and unwritten. They are official in the sense that they are enforced by a position incumbent who has been designated as a legitimate authority. But other norms, equally important in guiding incumbent behavior, may be unofficial. For example, as human relations theorists are quick to point out, industrial workers may establish work standards among themselves. These workers are not an official authority in the hierarchy of authority, but nonetheless their norms may be powerful determinants of behavior. Failure to comply with the going rate results in being labeled a rate buster or chiseler, and appropriate sanctions will be employed in an effort to bring about conformity. Although official norms are more likely to be written than those originating from unofficial sources, we have found it desirable to keep the two dimensions separate. Thus, norms may be of three types: (1) written, official; (2) unwritten, official; and (3) unwritten, unofficial (although a logical possiblity, unofficial norms that are written would appear to be rare at best).

Shifting to a higher level of abstraction, we see norms clustered into expectation sets for entire networks of positions. Although they are often more abstract than those at the dyadic (role relationship) level, *system domains* are comprised of those norms that are applicable to a specified system, be it a group within an organization or the organization as a whole. If our house is on fire we notify the fire department, not the barber shop, because we have sets of expectations about appropriate tasks for entire systems. Similarly, incumbents seeing an error on their paycheck notify persons in the payroll department and not the janitorial services.

However, just as we see participants within organizations trying to manipulate the expectation sets held by their coworkers, so also do we see them trying to manipulate the expectations that are held for their entire group or organization. These expectation sets, like those at more microscopic levels in the structure, are in a continual process of negotiation as incumbents test and bargain with subunits and environmental sectors regarding definitions of domain.

What do they bargain about? The same set of five categories used at the dyadic level are applicable. Thus, system domains are comprised of expectations that specify appropriate task, status, authority, and sanctioning activity for *entire systems*. Moreover, incumbents may, as at the dyadic level, seek to increase the autonomy, security, and prestige of their organization by altering these expectation sets.

In summary, then, the normative structure is composed of norms that are ideas about how classes or categories of persons ought to behave in specified types of situations. They are clustered into roles, positions, and system domains. They vary in content so as to specify task, authority, status, affect, and sanctioning dimensions of role relationships, positions, and system domains. They may originate and be enforced through either official or unofficial sources. Much of the patterned behavior sequences for which we wish to account can be explained by the normative structure. But, in contrast to those sociologists who stop here, we propose that two additional explanatory structures are necessary.

2. The *interpersonal structure* is composed of sets of relatively stable person-to-person understandings and orientations. It is clear that as persons interact over time, they do not relate to one another merely as position incumbents. These orientations and understandings emerge, and they are noncategorical and are not related to positions enacted. Instead, they are a function of the relationships that exist between *persons as persons*. It should be emphasized that we are not referring to what is popularly labeled personality with this concept. It does not denote characteristics of individuals, but rather types of relationships that exist between persons, independent of the positions they enact.

Thus, as persons interact, orientations emerge of a variety of types. Reflecting the leads from Moreno and the abundance of sociometric research done to date,[41] even knowledge of the interpersonal structure based on a "like–dislike" continuum can be valuable in predicting certain behavior patterns. This is especially true when the pattern is a deviation from what one would expect given the normative structure. Why is it that certain assistant professors within a university may know of decisions made at a board of trustees meeting before their department chairman or dean? Often, the answer lies in understanding the organizational grapevine, which reflects the interpersonal rather than the normative structure.

How can we categorize interpersonal relationships? We will treat this question in detail in the next chapter, when five continua will be discussed: (1) like–dislike; (2) dominance–submission; (3) trust–distrust; (4) extensive–limited; and (5) respect–disrespect. The designation of polar points on the continua are self-explanatory except possibly number 4—which is extensive–limited. Here we refer to the degree to which the relationship is segmental—that is, do I know you only in terms of our job (limited), or do I know you more intensely regarding your family life, leisure time pursuits, and the like (extensive)?

Although there may be consistency among these five dimensions in a relationship between two persons, there need not be. Relationships characterized by the first term in each of the continua—e.g., like or trust, or equalitarian in number 2—are predicted to have greatest stability. Interaction among persons in this type of interpersonal structure will be mutually-satisfying and will be desired in the future. Various degrees of avoidance patterns will be found where interpersonal relations are characterized by other points on the continua.

One last point requires emphasis. Persons confront both the normative and the interpersonal structures simultaneously. Thus, inconsistencies or strains, both within and among these structures, result in instability in behavior patterns. If there is high normative consensus between two position incumbents, then there is a much greater likelihood that positive interpersonal relationships will emerge and persist. Similarly, absence of normative consensus may precipitate interpersonal hostility, friction, and conflict. And likewise, if interpersonal relations are intensely positive, a much wider degree of normative dissensus may be tolerated: "Yes, we intensely disagree on what de-

---

[41] Following Moreno's classic work—Jacob L. Moreno, *Who Shall Survive?* (New York: Beacon House, 1953)—sociometric data have given insights but are difficult to analyze. Excellent discussion of mathematical strategies for such data, which are written for nonmathematicians, are found in John G. Kemeny et al., *Introduction to Finite Mathematics* (Englewood Cliffs, N.J.: Prentice-Hall, Inc., 1956), pp. 307–15; and Rocco Carzo, Jr. and John N. Yanouzas, *Formal Organization: A Systems Approach* (Homewood, Ill.: Richard D. Irwin, Inc. and The Dorsey Press, 1967), pp. 157–77.

fines a good teacher, but we *like* each other." Analysis of interactions among these structures is critical and requires much additional research.

3. The *resource structure* is composed of physical resources currently being used or known to be available for use by organizational personnel. Presence of the objects themselves, however, is only one aspect. Ideas about proper and improper usage are also important. Thus, two levels are implied here, i.e., physical and ideational.[42] For example, a hospital manual in which procedures for establishing emergency electrical power are outlined is more than just a physical object. It represents a codification of the belief system that specifies appropriate (normative) usage. If the normative or ideational system does not specify a particular usage, there is a probability that the object will not be used.

It has often been found in community disaster, for example, that actual physical resources were available, but were not used in certain ways that would have greatly increased organizational effectiveness. Following a large explosion in Indianapolis in 1963, the efficiency of the community emergency social system was drastically reduced because there was no communication link among the hospitals to which nearly 400 injured persons were being taken.[43] No one knew how many patients were sent to any hospital, and patient dispersal efforts from the scene were largely ineffectual. As might be anticipated, some hospitals received large numbers of patients and others received few. Police cruisers could have been stationed at each hospital and thereby have created an interhospital communication network, but this was not done. Technology existed, but the idea did not occur to those in positions of authority during the initial emergency period.[44]

One further point requires elaboration. Small group and other research areas have demonstrated that interaction is affected by how persons are socially arranged even around a small table.[45] Analysis of how architectual style, office location, and the like affects interaction has not yet received sufficient attention from social scientists except to indicate that "it is a factor." Future work on conceptualization of the resource structure must include this dimension.

[42] Bakke makes a similar distinction between levels. See E. Wright Bakke, "Concept of the Social Organization," in Mason Haire, ed., *Modern Organization Theory* (New York: John Wiley and Sons, Inc., 1959), pp. 40–43.

[43] Thomas E. Drabek, *Disaster in Aisle 13* (Columbus, Ohio: College of Administrative Science, Ohio State University, 1968).

[44] In this instance, written disaster plans had been distributed to all involved agencies by the local civil defense office in which this very tactic was specified. Thus, written aspects of the normative structure often may not be as relevant as is commonly thought. Ibid., pp. 156–59; 171–73.

[45] For example. Fred L. Strodtbeck and L. Harmon Hook, "The Social Dimensions of a Twelve-Man Jury Table," *Sociometry*, 24: 397–415 (December 1961).

In brief, the resource structure includes all physical objects being used or known to be available for use, their spatial arrangement and the ideational or normative expectations defining appropriate use. At a low level of abstraction, three different kinds of objects can be differentiated: (1) persons; (2) buildings and equipment; and (3) information. Depending upon the problem at hand, one can count the number of persons and measure relevant abilities of each. These measures can be aggregated so as to characterize the entire collectivity. Similarly, at a descriptive level, floor plans, maps, and the like can be used to analyze features of buildings and the placement of persons and equipment. At a very abstract level, a variable like technology, which can be conceptualized as varying in degrees of certainty or variability,[46] points us in the direction we must head in shifting to more analytic characteristics of the resource structure.

The Basic Framework

These three explanatory structures, i.e., normative, interpersonal, and resource, are viewed as interacting with one another. Thus, a particular normative and interpersonal structure will not result in the same behavior pattern if the physical setting is severely altered, e.g., participants moved from a single room into individual offices. If viewed jointly, however, the three structures may provide a basis for understanding and predicting the patterns of interaction that we define as the organization, i.e., the performance structure. As outlined earlier, the performance structure is comprised of eight general processes. Figure 3–4 summarizes the relationships.

Organizations do not exist in vacuums, however. Organizational participants interact with participants in other groups and organizations. And these interaction patterns must be analyzed because they often greatly affect the internal functioning of the focal organization. Thus, we must elaborate our framework so that these environmental interactions are included. Moreover, corresponding environmental interactions are also to be understood and predicted through analysis of the appropriate normative, interpersonal, and resource structures. When elaborated in this way, the framework may be summarized as presented in Figure 3–5.

Note the inclusion of the boundary spanning processes. As indicated in Chapter 1, there are interaction patterns wherein one part of the interaction unit lies within one system and the other in another.

---

[46] Perrow, "A Framework for the Comparative Analysis of Organizations," op. cit., and Charles Perrow, "Hospitals: Technology, Structure, and Goals," in March, op. cit., pp. 913–16.

FIGURE 3–4 Interrelationship Among Structures

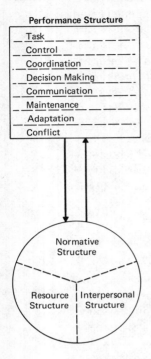

Performance Structure

Task
Control
Coordination
Decision Making
Communication
Maintenance
Adaptation
Conflict

Normative
Structure

Resource | Interpersonal
Structure | Structure

FIGURE 3–5 The Basic Framework

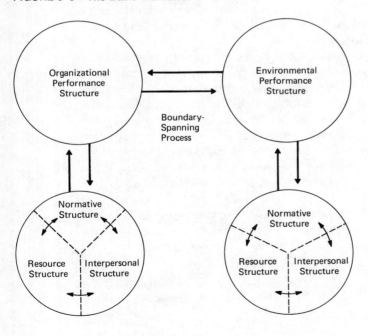

Organizational
Performance
Structure

Environmental
Performance
Structure

Boundary-
Spanning
Process

Normative
Structure

Resource | Interpersonal
Structure | Structure

Normative
Structure

Resource | Interpersonal
Structure | Structure

With these concepts we seek to understand the persistence of the performance structure. The concepts guide us in work at a descriptive level. Thus, we can look at the specific content of the normative structure in a particular organization and "overlay" the interpersonal and resource structures so as to begin to understand task or conflict behavior patterns. Increasingly, however, we must seek to shift levels of abstraction in our theorizing so as to develop multivariant hypotheses that relate analytic qualities of these structures to behavior patterns. For example, the degree of consensus about the norms is one characteristic. As the degree of normative consensus decreases, we hypothesize that the behavior pattern will become less stable. Conversely, as the degree of consensus increases, behavior patterns will exhibit greater stability regardless of the content of the norms involved. Thus, we make problematic the degree of correspondence between the various explanatory structures and the behavior patterns. And the behavior patterns, like the explanatory structures, are viewed as being in a constant state of flux; their stability is always a matter of *degree*.

The basic theme of the framework is that persistence and change in performance structures covaries with patterns of stress and strain among and within the explanatory structures. The linkages among degree of stability in performance structures and strain patterns are complex, and much empirical research awaits completion before we will have even a vague understanding. However, we have pieced together a series of ideas that it is hoped will guide future research in this direction. These ideas are detailed in Chapters 7 and 8. But before we leave this overview to turn to detailed treatment of each of the components of the framework, let us explore the stress–strain theme very briefly.

The Stress–Strain Analogy

Picture yourself driving an automobile out of a parking lot. As you drive down the street, you are thinking about the pattern of cracks in your windshield, which was hit by a large rock while the car was parked. You now turn onto the entrance of the freeway system and begin to accelerate. As you gain speed, the windshield gains your attention. Will it be able to withstand the increased wind pressure? You reach the upper level of the speed limit and breath a sigh of relief —the windshield is holding fine. After driving for about five miles, without warning, you hit an area under construction. You try to slow down, but the loose gravel prevents a quick change of speed. The road is rough, and you bounce across several holes. Suddenly, the windshield breaks. The demands were more than the strained, fractured windshield could tolerate.

In simplest terms, we propose that organizations can be viewed as analogues to that windshield. Of course there are many important differences, which we will elaborate in later chapters. But let us briefly explore the analogy. Organizational normative, interpersonal, and resource structures are never totally consistent. Strains of varying intensity are always present. By *organizational strain* we mean inconsistencies among and within the three explanatory structures. For example, a type of strain we might find pervasive in many high schools would be reflected in the normative dissensus between professional and bureaucratically oriented teachers about the degree to which faculty ought to participate in decision making. Thus, like the cracked windshield, there are many patterns and types of strain within organizational structures. The windshield confronted wind pressure, that is, in interacting with its environment, certain *demands* were made on it. And it could cope with those demands up to a given level; it had a certain *capacity* to meet those demands. As the demand level increased when the car accelerated, the discrepancy between demands and capacity was altered. We define the degree of discrepancy between demands and capacity as *stress*. Thus, as the level of stress increased, because of increased demands and constant capacity, the structures eventually disintegrated. And the points or initial lines of disintegration coincided with the pattern of cracks.

We propose that an understanding of organizational behavior, both persistence and change, requires an understanding of stress and strain. Environmental changes do occur and exert pressure for change on the organization, but there is not a one-to-one correspondence. Changed norms may stimulate a new behavior pattern in one sector of an organization's environment. Organizational incumbents confront this new behavior pattern and must devise some means of coping. Their range of options is great, but is constrained by the pattern of strain within the organization. Thus, the coping strategy selected will reflect the present pattern of strain. And these coping behaviors, directed at this individual situation, in turn, alter the future performance structure and the strain pattern. Thus, the process is dynamic.

From our perspective then, organizations are viewed as patterned interaction structures that vary in stability, both in degree and over time. Likewise, the normative, interpersonal, and resource structures that permit us to understand and predict the behavior patterns also are dynamic and interdependent. Strains within and among these structures give us clues as to how the structure will fare as demands from the environment are altered.

We believe that organizational participants often find themselves trapped in structures that fail them. As participants try to maximize the autonomy, security, and prestige of their own subsystem, larger objectives become blurred and misplaced. They proceed to make changes in local operations, but fail to realize the consequences of these efforts on the pattern of strain for the larger structure. And so the organization drifts, like a ship with a faulty rudder, responding moment by moment to the most pressing demands. Greater knowledge of strain patterns would provide clues to where change efforts should be directed given specified objectives and missions—clues to where change is most critical. Consequently, we believe that future research guided by this perspective can increase our ability to renew organizational structures that no longer permit us to cope effectively with highly dynamic environments. If organizational participants can gain an understanding of strain patterns, this may provide the self-knowledge that will permit self-renewal.[47] For organizational freedom, like that of individuals, requires such self-awareness and continual energy devoted to renewal.

Sensitized by this broad overview, now let us explore each aspect of the perspective in detail.

---

[47] John W. Gardner, *Self-Renewal: The Individual and the Innovative Society* (New York: Harper and Row, 1963).

Chapter 4

GROUPS
WITHIN
ORGANIZATIONS

In the previous chapters we have presented an overview of organizational theory and selected research findings. Drawing ideas from most of these theoretical perspectives, we have attempted to recast and integrate them into an emergent synthesis. This synthesis was discussed briefly in Chapter 3.

In this chapter we will examine the internal dynamics of groups within organizational settings. In the next chapter the focus will be on the dynamics internal to organizations as social systems, followed, in Chapter 6 by an analysis of the organization in a broad environmental setting.

In an effort to make the conceptual framework most meaningful, we will begin by indicating how one might go about looking at the performance structure of an organizational group. We will then point out how the explanatory concepts, normative structure, interpersonal structure, and resource structure and their interrelations may be used to explain change and stability in the performance structure.

A Perspective on Group Interaction

Imagine that we are observing human behavior in an office setting. There are five persons seated at desks in two adjacent rooms. A man named Brown calls a lady named Harper indicating that he wishes to dictate a letter.[1] He talks, pauses, and talks some more while she continues to write on a pad. Soon she returns to her desk, types the letter from her notes, and places the letter on his desk for signature without making any further comment. Brown says "thank you" and signs the letter. Harper, returning to her desk, prepares the letter for mailing. This pattern is repeated six times throughout the day.

One of the other participants, Green, has two lengthy discussions with Brown, and by midafternoon has written a ten-page document that he gives to Harper for typing. He then hands a copy of the typed document to Brown, a brief discussion follows, and Brown initials the document before it is sent to another person in the organization. A fourth person, White, interacts with Brown and Harper in much the same manner.

The fifth person, Clark, is busy much of the day operating a desk calculator. While she converses occasionally with Harper, her principal discussions are with Green and White. At various times one of them hands a sheaf of papers to her and discusses the contents with her, whereupon she returns to her desk and runs a series of computations apparently utilizing the information on the papers. Following the computations, she hands him a single sheet of paper containing the results.

Let us use this hypothetical setting to illustrate a way of analyzing a group in an organizational context. First, it should be noted that the description as presented emphasizes *patterned interaction sequences*. Brown and Harper repeat the letter production interaction sequence six times. Different kinds of interaction sequences are repeated several times daily, whereas others may be repeated once or twice a week or perhaps only once a month.

Now, if we were to observe the interaction in this office setting over a period of weeks, we would notice that Brown and Green, for example, are involved in other kinds of interaction sequences. On a number of occasions Green, at the suggestion of Brown, reads various written reports that have come to the office, prepares summaries, and gives oral reports to Brown. On other occasions, after lengthy discussions, Green represents Brown at committee meetings outside the group but within the organization and reports to Brown after each meeting. Thus, we note that over time there are a number of different patterned interaction sequences that take place between Brown and Green. The interaction sequences of Brown and White are essentially the same. Although the sequences vary in frequency of occurrence and content, they all have the common feature of having taken place between Brown and either Green or White. The problem we now face is that, although we are satisfied that the interaction between Brown and Green is basically the same in content as that between Brown and White, we are inadvertently using different labels (Brown–Green and Brown–White)

---

[1] We observe that on each desk is a small plaque with a name inscribed on it. We will use these labels to indicate who the participants are.

for the same interaction phenomena. Our labels are person oriented rather than interaction-content oriented.

In an attempt to simplify the labeling process, we recall that on several occasions we have heard Brown referred to as the "boss" whereas both Green and White have been referred to as "assistant." We decide, therefore, that we will use the common label "boss–assistant" to refer to the kind of interaction that occurs for both pairs of participants. Furthermore, using the common label reminds us that similar or identical interaction sequences may exist among several different pairs of persons, and therefore the behaviors exhibited are not necessarily strictly person-oriented. We can summarize these various sequences and any other similar interaction by using the phrase "boss–assistant *unit of social interaction.*" In a similar manner, we can summarize the other observed sequences as boss–secretary unit of social interaction, assistant–secretary unit of social interaction, clerk–assistant unit of social interaction, and so forth.

In this particular illustration we see that the office group is an interaction system composed of seven identifiable units of social interaction. We call this a *system* not because of the physical proximity of the persons in the adjoining offices, but because these are continuing units of social interaction that are to a greater or lesser degree *interdependent.* What transpires in one unit of social interaction is clearly and directly related to what occurs in the other units. For example, after an assistant discusses with the boss the need for a particular kind of report, he assigns work to the clerk and utilizes her output to prepare the report, which is then typed by the secretary before it is discussed in detail by the assistant and the boss. Where units of interaction are interrelated (interdependent) in some demonstrable fashion, we have a social system—a system of interaction. If there is a change in one unit of interaction that is followed by a subsequent change in another, we take this as evidence of interdependence. If the clerk fails to give the needed information to the assistant and as a result the assistant cannot complete the report for the boss, this fact suggests that the boss–assistant unit of interaction is dependent in part on the assistant–clerk unit of interaction. However, as stressed in Chapters 1 and 3, the degree of interdependence varies among systems, among various subunits within systems, and over time for any given system.

Moreover, if a work group such as we have been discussing is part of a larger social system called an *organization,* we would anticipate that there would be some ongoing connection between the group and other organizational units. There would be *intergroup* units of interaction also, and therefore, as seen in Chapter 1, we have to come to grips with the concept of group boundary. If we start with the units that we are confident make up the core of the group and if we continue to look for other units that are linked to those in some demonstrable way, we will eventually be dealing with units of interaction that are clearly outside of the core group. Somewhere between are those units that may be

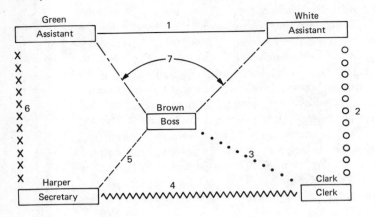

meaningfully labeled as boundary units of interaction. We have argued that boundary units should be designated by the researcher and that different points in the network of interaction units may be treated as *the* boundary depending on the substantive theoretical interests of the researcher (see Figure 1–4 for a diagram of this idea).

Once we have a well-developed notion of the specific units that make up the group to be analyzed, we can take a closer look at the content of the various units. We need not, however, just describe the content in fairly concrete terms. We can prepare the way for the testing of propositions by applying some slightly more abstract concepts that would be applicable across many groups and organizations. These concepts center on the notion of *process*. As noted in the previous chapter, there is as yet no finite list of processes that are always used by group and organizational analysts. But there are some that have been used repeatedly with at least moderately fruitful results. In addition to the obvious task process, we should be aware of the *decision-making, conflict*, and *coordination* processes as well as others, which will be treated later in this text. What is going on in any group can and should be viewed in process terms if the study of organizations is to advance beyond the compiling of case studies.

When we speak of an interaction system, we will be thinking primarily of the patterning and relevant processes observable in the behaviors. But we may also want to inquire *why* the patterning exists as it does and *why* it persists or changes over time. In order to keep clear the distinction between the patterned interaction and that which produces it, we use several different terms. The patterned interaction taken as a totality we shall call the *performance structure*. Where we attempt to *explain* persistence or change in the performance structure, we shall be describing and analyzing the *normative structure, interpersonal structure,* and *resource structure.*

Now, if we look again at our hypothetical office group at a later point in time—say, six months after our earlier observation period—we might note that a different person is now an assistant and that there is a new secretary as well. However, after careful comparison with our record of the previous period we conclude that there has been relatively little change in the interaction patterns. The frequency and content of the interaction sequences has not changed significantly, even though two of the participants are new. With such a change in personnel, why should the persistence of the patterning be so marked?

Although it is possible that the personal habits or personalities of the two new participants just happen to be nearly identical to those of their predecessors, sociologists would suggest that a more useful concept to explain the persistence in patterning is *social norm.* Thus, we would want to determine if a set of social norms held in common by both sets of participants concerning required and appropriate behaviors for interaction in this office setting was an important factor in producing the patterned interaction that we observed during both of our observation periods. If our research showed that in fact the participants at both time periods did have such norms in mind and that their office behavior was significantly influenced by such normative ideas, we would conclude that the *normative structure* was an important determinant of the persistence in the *performance structure* that we had observed.

Social norms are ideas held by two or more persons about how categories of persons should behave in specified types of situations. There are two general ways by which the analyst can find out what the norms are for any group. He can ask questions about the norms directly of the participants in interviews or questionnaires, and he can, by careful observation over extended periods of time, discover what the norms are by noting the use of rewards and punishments (positive and negative sanctions) in response to certain behaviors. Both approaches have certain inherent weaknesses, however, so a combination of the two approaches should be used when possible. The extent to which behavior actually complies with the norms of a group is discussed later in this chapter.

We would not want to leave the impression that the sole effect of the normative structure is the stability of the performance structure. If the normative structure had changed somewhat during the two time periods, then we might anticipate resulting changes in the performance structure also. For example, in early discussions between the new assistant and the boss, it was agreed that face-to-face interaction between them should take place only at the beginning of each day, urgent matters being the only exception to this new norm. The observed change in a part of the performance structure, the boss-assistant unit of social interaction, would thus be explained by noting the change in the normative structure. We conclude, then, that stability in the normative structure produces persistence in the performance structure, but that when the normative structure is altered there will be consequent change in the performance structure.

Actually, the normative structure of a group is seldom completely static over long periods of time. As will be seen later, there are a variety of ways by which norms may be changed or replaced. It is probably safe to assume that although many norms persist without significant modification over extended time periods, negotiation of some norm or other can probably be seen in interaction almost weekly. Rule books may change very slowly, but what might be called the day-to-day operational norms nearly always show a more dynamic quality.

The interpersonal structure also helps explain both persistence and change in the performance structure. To be sure, the normative structure provides a context in which the interpersonal structure develops. Even in an organization where the prevailing theme is "do everything by the book," where there is a serious effort made to have a rule (norm) for almost every situation that may arise, it is clear that there is still a considerable degree to which a person can stay within the rules and yet follow his own inclinations in interaction. Where there are relatively fewer and less restrictive norms, the latitude is even greater. The point is that interaction is based on more than the guidelines and constraints inherent in the normative structure.

Interaction comes to be patterned in part because of the reciprocal perceptions that persons have of one another as *individuals*. As time passes, two persons may come to some common understandings about how to get along, which is to say that they have worked out a *modus vivendi*. In many cases they will even develop a way of thinking about their relationship in fairly abstract terms; e.g., "it is a competitive relationship" or "underlying much of our interaction is mutual mistrust". Note that these understandings and conceptions refer to the *relationship between particular persons*; they are interpersonal rather than interpositional phenomena. If one of the persons is replaced by a successor, new and different understandings and expectations will develop, and the resulting patterned interaction will be changed somewhat. When two persons continue to interact over a period of time, the developing sets of understandings and orientations are called an *interpersonal relation*. If we wish to refer to the total configuration of interpersonal relations underlying the performance structure, we speak of the *interpersonal structure* of the group.

When there is no turnover of personnel in the group, we would expect that the interpersonal structure would be relatively stable. However, we do not assume that the interpersonal structure is ever completely static, just as we would not expect the normative structure to remain static over an extended period of time. To the extent that the interpersonal structure remains relatively stable, that part of the performance structure which is a reflection of the interpersonal structure will not change either.

It is a common observation that an individual changes over time as the result of physical maturation and the experience he has. We would anticipate also that with individual change there would be some type of concomitant change in the interpersonal relations in which the person is involved. Thus, in our illustration, we would not be surprised to find that over time the interpersonal relation between the secretary and the clerk has changed somewhat as a result of the changes in the two individuals. But even if there were no changes in the two women as individuals, it is likely that some change, however slight, would take place in the interpersonal relation simply because the longer they interact the more they learn about each other. And in the process, their perceptions of each other will be modified and their understanding and expectations will be adjusted accordingly. We have all seen instances where two persons were good friends at one point in time but had a much more distant relationship later. It is our impression that for most groups within an organization the interpersonal structure is more dynamic and shifting than the normative structure. We must anticipate both continuity and change for both, however.

The third general explanatory concept is the *resource structure*. As we shall see, both the social and nonsocial aspects of the resource structure help determine the characteristics of a group's performance structure. The reports that come into our hypothetical office setting are a resource that provides the basis for much of the observed interaction. And quite apart from the norms that may have developed regarding who should interact with whom about what subjects, the fact of physical separation of the boss in a separate office and the physical proximity of the other persons in a single room will provide opportunities and incentives for interaction as well as constraints on potential interaction. These constraints are different from what would be the case if each person had a separate office or if all five of them were located within the same room.

Hare and Bales, for example, conclude from their own research findings and that of others that interaction patterns in small discussion groups can be predicted successfully from an analysis of the seating positions of participants.[2] Even jury decisions, according to Strodtbeck and Hook, are influenced by who sits where around the rectangular table. Persons who sit in the least central positions, near the corners of the table, contribute significantly less to the discussion and hence to the outcome.[3]

[2] A. Paul Hare and Robert F. Bales, "Seating Position and Small Group Interaction," *Sociometry*, 26: 480–86 (December 1963).

[3] Fred L. Strodtbeck and L. Harmon Hook, "The Social Dimensions of a Twelve-Man Jury Table," *Sociometry*, 24: 397–415 (December 1961).

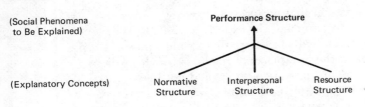

FIGURE 4–2   Diagram of Relation of Explanatory Concepts to the Performance
Structure

(Social Phenomena   **Performance Structure**
to Be Explained)

(Explanatory Concepts)   Normative   Interpersonal   Resource
                           Structure   Structure   Structure

Figure 4–2 provides a simple representation of the relation between
the ongoing interaction system and the explanatory concepts discussed
so far.

The basic concepts for analyzing the dynamics of organizational
groups have been introduced briefly. It is clear that each concept is
complex and thus requires further elaboration. Moreover, the nature of
the relatedness among the explanatory concepts needs to be examined.
We shall proceed, therefore, to look at these ideas in greater detail.

Normative Structure:
Norms, Roles, Positions, and Domain

In outlining a perspective on group interaction we have tried to make
a distinction between the observable, interrelated units of social interaction and those forces that shape the interaction, the normative, interpersonal, and resource structures. In this section we shall examine the
various elements of the normative structure and show how they shape
the patterning of the interaction system.

Participants in any group know what is usually done. They also have
fairly specific ideas about what should be done, may be done, and
should not be done by the various members under a variety of circumstances. These ideas we call the social norms of the group. Examination
of the norms of any group will almost certainly show that some norms
are more specific than others. For example, in a military group the norm
usually specifies that you should use as a specific form of address: "sir"
or the name of the appropriate rank, such as "Colonel." The norm does
not permit much latitude in behavior. However, another norm may
simply indicate that the officer in charge should direct the activity of
those in the squad. There are a number of ways in which that direction
may be given, each of which falls within the limits permitted by the
norm. Thus, there is a range of norms, from those that are very specific
to those that are quite general.

The various norms that specify the kinds of *reciprocal behaviors* that
should take place for a given unit of social interaction are called a *role*.
Those normative ideas held by a particular person we call his conception of the role or simply *role conception*. When we wish to speak of the

degree of congruence between the role conception held by one person and the conceptions held by others for the same role, we speak of the *level of role consensus*. If our main interest is in the congruence of views held by two persons regarding a particular role, the term *dyadic role consensus* is appropriate. If we wish to contrast and compare the role conceptions of all the participants of a particular social system, we would use the terms *group role consensus* or *organizational role consensus*.

Once we have delimited the boundaries of a group we will want to make a distinction between *intragroup roles* and *intergroup roles*. The same distinction is useful when the object of study is an organization. Thompson[4] and others[5] have attempted to articulate the unique problems faced by "boundary personnel" who must perform in both intra-organization and interorganization roles. For the moment, however, we shall limit our discussion to intragroup and intergroup roles. It is clear that persons in most groups are required to perform more than one role. Typically, they are involved in several different units of social interaction within the group, and they may be involved in one or more such units outside the group. A different role guides their behavior in each case. As a continuing participant in a particular social system (group), each person is required to perform several roles.

A *position* is a cluster of roles that are usually defined as belonging together. They are thought to go together in the sense that, if a person carries out the requirements of one of the roles, it is generally held that he should enact his part of the other roles as well. Thus, in a college, the professor–student, professor–department chairman, professor–dean, and professor–registrar roles are defined as belonging together in the sense that if a person acts as a professor in the professor–student role he should also act as a professor in the other roles as well. Now, if a class is the focus of our interest, then the professor–student role is an intra-group role, whereas the professor–dean role is intergroup. Figure 4–3 illustrates these ideas.

It should be clear that it takes at least two persons to enact any role. Since every position is composed of more than one role, any position holder or activator must, according to the norms, participate in the performance of each of the other relevant roles. Any professor who participates in the professor–undergraduate student role and ignores the requirements of the professor–registrar role will soon be in trouble!

There are also norms about *who* may activiate any position. Elected public officials must meet certain age and residency requirements *before* taking office (activating the position). In order to function as a physician, a person must first meet certain educational and certification

[4] James D. Thompson, *Organizations in Action* (New York: McGraw-Hill Book Co., 1967).

[5] Robert L. Kahn et al., *Organizational Stress: Studies in Role Conflict and Ambiguity* (New York: John Wiley and Sons, Inc., 1964).

FIGURE 4–3   Diagram of Roles and Positions in a Classroom Group

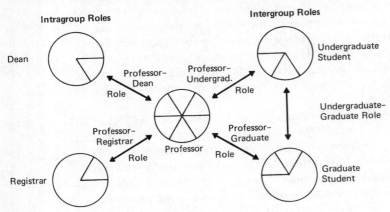

requirements. The imposter is the person who pretends to meet the requirements for position incumbency when in fact those demands have not been satisfied. Even though his role performance may have been adequate, he has still violated those norms that designate criteria that must be met by those enacting the position.

Dimensions of Role

Any well-developed role is composed of a large number of norms, some of which are quite broad and general in nature, others being quite detailed and specific. If we were to make a list of all of the norms in a single role, there could well be dozens of them. A careful examination of the content of the norms of any role would reveal that some of them deal principally with *tasks* or activities—the kinds of things that the participants should be doing. (We use the label *task* rather than *work* because it is more general and seems to apply to all roles.) As we can recall from our experiences in groups, there are times when it is not clear who should do what, when the norms are not specific in assigning tasks and activities. There is, then, another category of norms that comes into play—those dealing with *authority*.[6] Such norms indicate how problematic situations should be resolved. In the supervisor–worker role, for example, the norms may stipulate that at the beginning

---

[6] Hopkins suggests that, although much attention has been given to the authority dimension, there has been a tendency to overlook the other significant aspects of role. "Social systems are composed of roles of which authority is only one of the properties or basic dimensions. . . . The 'commanding' and 'complying' aspects of the actions of each role hardly exhaust the significant content of the roles." Terrence K. Hopkins, "Bureaucratic Authority: The Convergence of Weber and Barnard," in Amitai Etzioni, *Complex Organizations: A Sociological Reader* (New York: Holt, Rinehart & Winston, Inc., 1961), pp. 95–96.

of each work shift the supervisor should assign the tasks to be accomplished and the worker should carry them out. Later, the worker should report to the supervisor the extent of completion. In other roles, such as husband–wife in the equalitarian family, the norms may call for discussion among the participants of the problematic situation until a mutually acceptable agreement is arrived at regarding who should carry out the various activities. In any event, it seems that there are always some sort of authority norms present in every role.

Norms describing the extent and nature of *deferential behavior* among role performers are also a part of each role. Some roles call for extensive and detailed displays of deference (monarch–citizen), whereas others stipulate that each participant should show courtesy but avoid other forms of deference, as in the friend–friend role. Traditionally, the roles in military and governmental organizations have included a greater emphasis on the deference dimension than roles in production and sales organizations.

Interestingly, there are even norms about how role participants should feel about each other. Husbands and wives, children and parents should love each other, whereas doctors and nurses interacting in a hospital should have neutral or professional feelings toward each other. Actually, the norms go further than specifying the feelings that should exist. They indicate the extent and manner in which these affective ties should be evidenced in behavior. Certain words of endearment and special tones of voice are acceptable or even required in certain roles but clearly forbidden in others. This *affect* dimension is present in every role, although it may be a dominant part of some and a minor element in others.

Finally, there is the *sanctioning* dimension of role. Colleagues and subordinates in one's work group should be complimented and perhaps rewarded in other ways for excellence of role performance. Those who break the norms should be handed negative sanctions of some kind. We will explore in more detail such norm violations and the application of sanctioning norms later in this chapter.

Group Domain

The norms of all the appropriate roles for a group, when viewed as a whole, provide an overview of what the group should be doing. The sales department should be engaged in selling products, not producing them. The chemistry department should be teaching chemistry, not English literature. These normative notions of what a group should do, may do, and should not do, make up what we will call *group domain*. The definitions of *domain* that group members hold come into play on a number of occasions. Such definitions are particularly relevant when the possibility of adding new positions and roles to the group is under consideration. Some members might argue: "This new position makes sense and is needed in the organization but it should not be a part of our group; it should be the responsibility of some other group." Domain provides the general normative framework for making decisions regarding appropriate positions and roles.

In the next chapter we shall discuss in detail the relevance of group domain for intergroup relations.

Peripheral and Intrusive Roles

Think of the appropriate roles for a classroom group, the roles that you think should be the primary determiners of interaction in the classroom. Should the roles be limited to professor–student and student–student? Or, if there are both graduates and undergraduates in the class, should it include professor–graduate student, professor–undergraduate student, and graduate student–undergraduate student roles? What about male–female, father–son, and friend–friend roles?

In almost any group there are what we might call *peripheral roles*. Such roles are not considered to be central to the main focus of the interaction but are recognized as being necessary appendages. They are considered to be peripheral in importance. In most classroom groups, for example, the male–female role would be considered peripheral but should not be ignored entirely. When someone says, "You shouldn't tell dirty stories to a mixed class," he is saying that you should not ignore the male–female role entirely. The professor should take it into account in telling stories, but he should not consider it in teaching basic subject matter. Other roles that are often considered peripheral for a class group are age-related, such as older person–younger person, and ethnic related, such as white–black.

There are also *intrusive roles*. These are roles that are considered not to be relevant at all for the particular group or organization but that in fact occasionally come into operation anyway. The concept of teacher's pet is a reflection of the intrusive friend–friend role into a class group. The father–son role is often thought to be an intrusive role when rapid promotions are given to the employee who is also the son of the president of the company. "It is not what you know but who you know" is a recognition that the friend–friend role is frequently an intrusive one.

The patterns in any interaction system are largely shaped by the central or dominant roles, but the influence of peripheral and intrusive roles is seldom negligible.

Sources of Group Norms

Norms do not suddenly appear out of the blue. We shall point to three major ways in which norms come to be group norms. Some are brought to the group by entering participants, some are initiated by identifiable outside sources, and others emerge from interaction within the group itself.

The "Carry In" Phenomenon

Although we speak of *group* norms, it should be remembered that we actually wish to refer to those norms that make up the various roles utilized by participants in a discernible interaction system that we call a group. They are, if you like, the operational norms of the system. In most groups not everyone follows all of the same norms, as there is usually more than just one role involved. The secretary–clerk role differs somewhat from the secretary–boss role. Some of the norms appear in all of the roles in a group, some in several roles, and some in only a single role.

But where do these norms come from? Surely, they are not all invented *de novo* everytime a new group comes into existence. Clearly, many of the norms are "carried into" the group as generalized role conceptions that the members had learned before participation in that group. These role conceptions are in part a reflection of the general culture of the larger society or societies in which the members have lived since birth. A beginning college student has learned a great deal about the professor–student role requirements long before he first encounters a professor in a classroom setting. It is a part of the general culture that he carries with him and is prepared to use when the appropriate situation arises.

In addition to the general culture of a society, we know that there are numerous subcultures in existence. Ethnic, religious, regional (e.g., the Deep South), and even age (e.g., adolescent) subcultures have been documented in our society. The role conceptions held by group members may be shaped also by these subcultures.

Even the different institutional settings seem to have an impact on the role conceptions brought to a group. A career military officer who upon retirement takes a position in a university may gradually discover that some of his conceptions are resented by colleagues. Nevertheless, some of these norms have become so much a part of his map for behavior that he has great difficulty in altering his role conceptions.

Although to a more limited extent, this carry-in phenomenon occurs when a person changes work groups within the same organization or between two similar organizations. Perhaps it is most obvious when a completely new work group is formed where the various participants are drawn from a broad spectrum of previous groups. Initially, each member of the new group tends to utilize the norms he knows best and deems appropriate. Many of these, of course, are norms that he has internalized as the result of his interaction in previous work groups. Each person comes to the new group "wearing a suit of norms" acquired for and used at length in previous interaction systems. "The way we used to do it" (translation: "the norms that I'm comfortable with") is a commonly heard phrase in such new groups.

Norms Promulgated by Outside Sources

Some group norms are initiated from sources outside the group. To the extent that such norms do in fact become part of the operational norms of a group, they help determine some of the interaction patterns within the group.

It is easy to cite examples of outside organizations and agencies that promulgate such norms. Local, state, and national legislative bodies enact laws, which may become part of the normative structure of many groups. Frequently, courts interpret these laws, making their meaning more specific. A host of regulatory agencies also promulgate norms for other groups to follow (FCC, PUC, ICC, FAA, and so on). Many administrative units of government do likewise. Health, fire, and building departments in cities are further examples. A state department of education lays down regulations that must be followed if the local school wishes to receive state financial aid. Research fund granting agencies in the United States have drastically increased the rules that must be followed in research groups. College athletic programs are often hemmed in by rules of an athletic conference to which the college belongs. Pick any work group at random, and upon investigation you will probably discover a dozen or more such norm-making organizations that contribute to its normative structure.

As in the phrase *wheels within wheels*, there are organizations within organizations. Many church congregations are part of a district organization, which is part of a state organization, which is part of a national organization. Corporations often have wholly owned subsidiaries. Rarely do these parent organizations refrain from handing down rules or at least guidelines.

Finally many, many norms come from the immediate organization in which the group operates. More specifically, the norms come from various other subsystems within the organization. The business and accounting department is a major source of this type in almost every organization. The personnel office is not far behind. The formulation of policies and rules is a major activity of the various line offices. Thus, the boundaries of groups are penetrated from all sides. Of course, groups vary considerably in the degree to which their boundaries can be so penetrated. We will pursue this important point in a later chapter.

We can see, therefore, that many norms that shape group interaction are in fact initiated from sources outside the group itself. Many writers, especially those who take a rational model–closed system perspective on the study of organizations, seem to believe that practically all norms emanate from the top management level of an organization. We have argued that that is only one of many outside sources. It is true that managers frequently accept and condone the norms coming from outside the organization, but that acceptance should not be confused with the point of origin of the norms.

The Group As a Source of Norms

We have argued that a group is an on-going interaction system. Participants in such a social system do not simply receive norms from various outside sources and carry them out in a rote fashion. Persons in interaction are not the equivalent of the mechanical parts of an engine. For one thing, we have already seen that members bring to the group normative structure definitions for various relevant roles. In most instances, a member brings in role conceptions for the roles he will personally help enact. But he also has ideas about roles that he believes others in the group should use as guidelines for their interaction and activity. Over time, the differing conceptions of the various members are welded into a set of interlocking roles and positions about which there may be a fairly high level of consensus among the participants. This compromise version represents one process whereby norms emerge. There are also other ways in which norms develop within the group.

It is generally understood that each group within an organization will have a head, a position composed of roles specifying that the incumbent has the right and obligation to promulgate new norms and to alter established norms on occasion. One might conclude that such norms are simply introduced by a single position incumbent, and, if accepted by the other participants, become group norms. Indeed, that may happen on occasion, but a different series of events occurs with much greater frequency. The head or even another member of the group will initiate discussion about the need for a change in norms. The discussion may involve only the head and a few of his more trusted subordinates, or it may include almost all members of the group. In any event, whether or not a new norm is introduced depends upon, and is an outgrowth of, these discussions. Furthermore, the content of the norm as introduced will be determined in part by this type of interaction. Once the norm has been introduced, there is always the further question of its exact meaning for the behavior of group members. It will be interpreted by the various group members. This interpretation usually involves a time span of at least a few days, perhaps several weeks. In time, there will usually be general agreement as to the significance and content of the norm. It is in this sense that a norm may be said to be a genuine product of the group. It grew out of interaction; it is an emergent group norm.

This discussion of norm formation is a modification of the more classical "top down" perspective so frequently used by some authors. It suggests that superordinates do not and perhaps cannot simply impose norms on a group. Rather, they *initiate the process* whereby new norms come into existence. It is also clear that other group members, not just the head, may initiate a norm formation process. One or several participants may initiate the process by discussing some problematic situation with the head of the group, suggesting that certain policies or procedures need to be altered. Frequently, the problematic situation is discussed at length within the group before any of the issues are raised with the head. Where it is generally thought that the head would be unsympathetic to their ideas, he may not be contacted at all. But failure to consult with the head does not necessarily mean that a norm change will not take place. Over time, the concerned members may simply take matters into their own hands, agree that certain procedures or rules should be revised, and gradually shift their behavior until it is congruent with the new norm or norms. This ignoring of the head in the norm formation process is most likely to occur when the behaviors in question are not readily observable by the head. It is also more likely to occur when the interpersonal structure among the members, excluding the head, is characterized by a high level of mutual respect and trust. One or two highly influential members frequently serve as a catalyst in this process.

Finally, we should note that not all new norms follow from shared concerns and planning. What might be called minor procedural norms often seem to develop from slow accretion. One member changes his way of doing something; the change, if noticed, is tolerated; gradually, other members make similar changes until all or nearly all have done so. Over time, what has slowly become an accepted practice becomes a preferred or even required practice. To the extent that it is preferred or required, it is, by definition, *normatively* based. Who among us has not seen the official norm specifying that the coffee break should not exceed fifteen minutes gradually changed until the normatively supported limit is thirty minutes? And "You should be at work no later than 8:30" often changes to "you should be in the building sometime between 8:30 and 8:45"!

Two Components of the Normative Structure

The notion that the normative structure of an organization is composed of only the policies and rules laid down by management has been rather thoroughly discredited. As indicated in Chapter 2, Mayo and his colleagues were among the first to show that many norms emerge within work groups. These nonmanagement norms, it was discovered, often are not even known to second-line supervisors and higher management personnel. Some of these operational norms even contradict norms enunciated by supervisory and managerial officials. Norms that specify the upper and lower limits of production are among better known examples. Dalton[7] and Dubin,[8] among others, have suggested that these norms are in fact inevitable as no set of management-developed rules is ever so complete that it provides a blueprint for any and all situations that may arise.

Research findings suggest, then, that there are two major facets of the normative structure of a group within an organization.[9] There are the obvious, often written *official* norms and the less obvious (at least to the casual observer) *unofficial* norms. In every organization there are a certain number of positions whose incumbents are understood to have both the right and obligation to promulgate norms. The specifications of their various roles require them to be norm makers, within limited spheres of activity, of course. We suggested earlier that organizational groups often have an official head who may be actively involved in the development of new norms. He does so because his roles require it of him.

Official norms are those that are *supported* by group and organizational *officials*. We have seen that norms may come from many different sources. But those that come from "appropriate officials" within the group or organization usually have a unique status: there is often a persistent belief that such norms should be enforced. The interaction and activity of members should be congruent with these norms. Thus, certain officials by virtue of their role definitions do attempt to enforce these norms.

However, there are also some norms that have had a different life history. They have come from other than official sources, but over time they have been given the stamp of approval by officials, or at least by the officials immediately involved in their implementation. They have become part of the official normative structure in the sense that officials now attempt to enforce them just as they do norms that emanated from official sources. So, although the source of a norm may help explain why officials attempt to enforce it and why members are more or less

[7] Melville Dalton, *Men Who Manage* (New York: John Wiley and Sons, Inc., 1959).

[8] Robert Dubin, *The World of Work* (Englewood Cliffs, N.J.: Prentice-Hall, Inc., 1958).

[9] Daniel Katz and Robert L. Kahn, *The Social Psychology of Organizations* (New York: John Wiley and Sons, Inc., 1966), pp. 80–81; Peter M. Blau and W. Richard Scott, *Formal Organizations* (San Francisco, Calif.: Chandler Publishing Company, 1962), pp. 89–100.

FIGURE 4–4   Components of Group Normative Structure

Enforcement Attempts by	Analytical Designation:
Relevant officials only	Official norms
Relevant officials and other members	Official norms
Other members only	Unofficial norms

prone to comply with it, the critical distinction between an official and an unofficial norm is based on *who tries to enforce it*. If officials work for enforcement, the norm is, by definition, an official norm—part of the official normative structure. Other group members may or may not assist in enforcement efforts.

Every group in an organization also has some unofficial norms in its normative structure. These are norms whose enforcement attempts come from group members who have no official, management-designated responsibility for enforcing them. Such norms may supplement and/or contradict official norms. These unofficial norms exist as part of the total normative structure of the group *only* because a significant number, usually a majority, of group members other than the head of the group do in fact make fairly consistent efforts to enforce them. If these norms are known to the head of the group, he may try to ignore them or fight them, but so long as he does not openly approve of them they remain unofficial norms. Figure 4–4 outlines the components of the normative structure.

Perhaps the sharpest distinction between official and unofficial norms may be seen in the prison cell block. The guard is required to enforce official norms, many of which he had no hand in formulating. But the inmate participants in that social system almost universally reject those official norms while believing that their own set of unofficial norms is fully justified. Cell block guards quickly learn that if they want a semblance of peace—e.g., absence of extreme noise, which is necessary to make good impressions on superiors—they must adjust to some unofficial norms. One common technique is to avoid being in a position to discover infractions of certain official rules. Further, they may permit powerful inmate leaders to enforce the unofficial norms so long as they do so unobtrusively and without significant violence. Clearly, the operational norms in the cell block are a weird mixture of the official and the unofficial.[10]

Lack of consistent enforcement efforts sometimes brings confusion concerning whether certain official norms are still to be taken seriously. Perhaps as a product of wishful thinking, some college students have assumed that because dormitory supervisors were ignoring the presence of various drugs, the official rule prohibiting their use had been abandoned. Apparently, many students believed that their unofficial

[10] Gresham M. Sykes, "The Corruption of Authority and Rehabilitation," *Social Forces*, 34: 257–62 (March 1956).

norm, which said that drugs in the dormitory were to be tolerated so long as they were used discretely, had become the official norm. When college officials later cooperated with and assisted police in raiding the dormitory and violators were arrested, many of the students were outraged. Gouldner has documented the emergence of this type of indulgency by officials in a gypsum plant and the consequences of the definitions of injustice that occurred when new supervisors began enforcement efforts of the official norms.[11]

Where members of an organizational group are hostile toward and suspicious of higher level officials, there is almost certain to be a sizable unofficial norm component in the total normative structure of the group. And many of those norms will require or at least approve of behaviors that are forbidden by official norms. But even where hostility and suspicion are largely absent there will still be some unofficial norms, simply because the total of all official norms can seldom be all-encompassing. No set of planners and norm makers outside of a group, or even the head of a group, can ever anticipate all possible situations that may arise within the group; thus their catalog of official rules, no matter how large, will never be complete. Unofficial norms develop to fill the gap for normative guidelines. And it is the emergence of these and other norms that provide an important aspect of the dynamic quality of organizational functioning.

Factors in Level of Compliance

It is clear even to the casual observer that there is variation in the degree to which norms are followed in day-to-day interaction. There appears to be frequent and general norm violation in some groups, whereas, in others, violations are few and far between. Within a particular group some norms are adhered to religiously and others are not. How can we explain such variation?

We lack a tight theoretical model for such explanation, but several factors appear highly significant. Before exploring these, however, let us explicate some of the assumptions that we are making.

We are speaking of groups within an organization. It is assumed that: (1) for most participants, the attractiveness of the group and organization is high; i.e., there is high cohesion; (2) there is an absence of competing and/or conflicting cliques within the group; and (3) the norms in question are relatively unambiguous—there is relatively high member consensus regarding the meaning of their norms. Clearly, all of these assumptions may not hold for the majority of organizational groups, but by applying the assumptions in our discussion we can more readily illustrate the propositions we wish to consider.

Given these assumptions, we would expect the level of compliance to be highest under the following conditions.

[11] Alvin W. Gouldner, *Wildcat Strike* (New York: Harper & Row, 1965).

1. The norm has been internalized by the participants. As a result of past experience, the members have come to believe that the norm is important, crucial, right, and best for a range of stipulated circumstances. The worth of the norm is pretty much taken for granted. Compliance is almost automatic. Reconsideration of its value seldom occurs. Norms dealing with courtesy, the provision of nonsensitive information upon request, and worker level of effort are examples of norms that are often internalized.

2. Compliance will be higher when the norm is seen as being reasonable. Norms that are defined by participants as being irrelevant, bothersome, demeaning, silly, or unnecessarily time consuming will be labeled as unreasonable. New norms that require additional paper work are often seen in this light.

The criteria used to determine the reasonableness of a norm will, of course, vary from group to group and may even vary somewhat within a given group. Often, the criteria may not be verbalized among members, the norm simply being labeled as "silly" by one or more members who proceed to ignore it whenever possible. But the tendency to label norms as reasonable or not seems to be a frequent factor determining the degree of compliance.

3. One of Max Weber's significant contributions to the subject was his emphasis on the legitimacy of the source of a norm. He pointed out that in the "rational-legal" basis of authority, subordinates would carry out commands that came from officeholders who were understood to have the right to direct the behavior of others within limited spheres of activity. The right of command is attached to the office (position), not to the person, he argued.

A norm will be considered legitimate when it comes from a duly constituted source, one that is defined as having the right to make that kind of norm. If the head of the sales department tells a production group that they should change the procedures used to assemble a product, the suggested norms are almost certain to be rejected because they came from a nonlegitimate source. If those very same proposed norms had come from the head of the production division, the likelihood of compliance would be much greater as this source probably would be considered legitimate. In short, the degree of compliance to a norm is based to a large extent on the perceived legitimacy of the source of the norm.

The concept "source" should not be conceived of in a narrow sense. It should be understood to include the notion of standing committees or specially designated ad hoc committees that cut across departmental lines. In certain organizations, especially those that approximate Likert's System Four model,[12] it would include the idea that the norm maker must have consulted at length with all interested parties before

[12] Rensis Likert, *New Patterns of Management* (New York: McGraw-Hill Book Co., 1961).

promulgating the norm. In the case of a highly autonomous group with a tradition of intragroup democratic decision making, most norms can come from only one source that will be considered legitimate—the group itself. Suggestions may be considered from extragroup sources, but it is clearly understood by members that they are only suggestions. Professional groups within hospitals and universities exemplify this approach to the concept of legitimacy.

4. Compliance will be greater when the enforcement agent is viewed as legitimate. A janitor attempting to enforce a no smoking rule in a classroom usually has less success than the professor. The latter but not the former, say the group members, has the right to enforce such a norm. The team captain or the manager may replace a faltering baseball pitcher; but should the first baseman try to do it, he may be told to mind his own business even if all team members agree that a new pitcher is needed. In some groups, enforcement efforts are seen as the responsibility of all members rather than just the duty of one or two position holders; each person is seen as a legitimate agent. In other groups, only members with high seniority are viewed as legitimate norm enforcers.

As used here, legitimacy is included within the concepts of position and role. However, position may involve more than the usual connotations of office or job (such as supervisor and assistant supervisor). Age, sex, and years of experience may be considered relevant characteristics of a position, and as such they may influence the definition of what is legitimate or nonlegitimate behavior.

5. When a norm is supported by the head and by other group members, compliance will be greater. When both fellow workers and the boss indicate by word and deed that a norm ought to be followed, noncompliance will be infrequent. In certain respects, the boss may be a majority of one, especially in an authoritarian group. But in most groups it is the proportion of all members supporting the norm that is crucial. Even prison guards using physical coercion soon learn the significance of member support for rules. An official norm without significant member support may be followed on occasion, but consistent compliance will be absent.

6. Compliance will be greater when norms are supported by relevant reference groups.[13] Some norms are followed by other, similar work groups within the same organization or are given verbal and other support by labor unions and various occupational and professional associations. These norms seem to have a special kind of merit among group members. Although compliance is certainly not automatic, such norms

[13] Extended summaries of reference group theory and empirical research are contained in Robert K. Merton, *Social Theory and Social Structure*, rev. ed. (New York: The Free Press, 1957), pp. 225–386; and Muzafer Sherif and Carolyn W. Sherif, *Reference Groups: Exploration into Conformity and Deviation of Adolescents* (New York: Harper & Row, 1964).

are often followed with little or no questioning about their significance or worth.

7. The greater the observability of norm-relevant behavior, the higher will be the level of compliance—i.e., while a worker has a private office, he may goof off on occasion without anyone else knowing about it. Where colleagues can see easily what a worker is doing, the frequency of such behavior will decline unless it is normatively approved.[14] Even where the fear of severe negative sanctions is not involved, being observed by other knowledgeable persons still seems to have a sobering effect. Walls may reduce the general noise level in a plant and may reduce visual distractions, but they also are associated with lower levels of conformity.

Observability includes more than the visual. A silent typewriter in the office typing pool conveys as clear a message as does the sight of a sleeping night watchman. There are many jobs where the actual behavior of a group member is not easily observed by others but where the consequences of that behavior are immediately obvious. When a television show is being produced, the actions of the cameraman may not be seen at all by his colleagues; however, the results of his behavior are immediately obvious on the television monitor. The results of his work are even more visible than those of a chief surgeon in a hospital. Where behavior is linked to outcome in such an unequivocal manner, observing the product has the same effect as direct observation of the behavior itself.[15]

8. Conformity to norms will be greatest when the norms are supported by powerful sanctions, both positive and negative. Everyone is familiar with the carrot and stick concept. When significant positive sanctions (rewards) are in fact applied on appropriate occasions by both peers and superordinates, compliance tends to be high. When significant negative sanctions (punishment, withholding of favors, and so on) are also applied consistently by significant others, the level will be even higher. As Etzioni[16] and many others have pointed out[17] sanctioning behavior may range from physical coercion and threats of coercion

[14] Rose L. Coser, "Insulation from Observability and Types of Social Conformity," *American Sociological Review*, 26: 28–39 (February 1961).

[15] Support for this hypothesis and more detailed analysis of the process involved are reported by Donald I. Warren, "Power, Visibility, and Conformity in Formal Organizations," *American Sociological Review*, 33: 951–70 (December 1968).

See also the critique by Harry Perlstadt, "Comments on 'Power, Visibility and Conformity in Formal Organizations,'" *American Sociological Review*, 34: 937–41 (December 1969); and Warren's reply, "Reply to Perlstadt," *American Sociological Review*, 34: 941–43 (December 1969).

[16] Amitai Etzioni, *A Comparative Analysis of Complex Organizations* (New York: The Free Press, 1961).

[17] Exchange theorists such as Blau and Homans have analyzed this process most carefully. See Chap. 2 (pp. 60–72).

on the one extreme to subtle verbal and nonverbal expressions of approval and disapproval on the other.

What do we mean by "powerful" sanctions? To be sure, there is individual variation regarding what is considered to be a really worthwhile reward and a really severe negative sanction. It is clear, however, that within particular cultures or subcultures there is often a fair level of consensus regarding what are defined as significant rewards or severe punishments. Favorable mention in a story in a publication of the organization is almost certain to be viewed in a favorable light, especially if the complimentary statements reported are made by knowledgeable and respected persons. If such a story is also carried in the general news media of the community, the sanction is even more powerful. Expulsion from the group is almost always considered to be a severe negative sanction. The same may be said for what is known as the "silent treatment" administered by peers.

9. Compliance will be greater for norms that reinforce the desirable characteristics of the group. Every group has a configuration of salient characteristics as understood by all or by a significant proportion of the participants; examples: "We are . . . a professional group," ". . . a creative group," ". . . a group where everybody pitches in when the pressure is on," ". . . a group that can outproduce all others." Not all of the recognized characteristics are viewed as desirable, of course, but norms that support and reinforce the desirable group characteristics will be complied with more consistently than will other norms.

10. When group members participate in norm formation, the level of conformity will be greater. Research evidence suggests that the extent of member involvement in the making of group norms is positively associated with the extent of member compliance to those norms.[18] This seems to be the case for persons reared in western cultures and may, or may not, be true universally. There is always the possibility, of course, that the norms agreed upon by the members may not be desired by a supervisor or manager. Similarly, the behavioral approximations of such norms may not be the most efficient way of working, but they will be norms that are violated less frequently than others.

Variation in Role Consensus and Its Consequences

A characteristic of role enactment in a group and organizational setting is that it takes more than one person to do so. Life in an organization would be so much simpler and less fraught with frustration if each of us could learn the norms of each of our roles and carry them out at the

[18]Likert and other human relations theorists emphasize this point. See Chap. 2 (pp. 42–48).

times and places thought to be appropriate by us without any interference from other group members. But just as it "takes two to tango," it also takes at least two persons to perform a role.

Any role performance involves patterned *interaction*, reciprocal behaviors carried out in an interdependent fashion by two or more persons. When one is learning the norms of a role, he will learn what he is supposed to do in a variety of settings when enacting his part of the role, and he will also learn what the other(s) involved in the role should be doing. He will learn what his *obligations* are to them; what each of the others should be doing by way of response to his actions; and what they should be initiating so that he can respond. He will learn that he has a *right* to expect certain behaviors from them, just as they have a right to expect certain behaviors from him. In short, his rights are their obligations, and vice versa.

To be sure, role performance often involves more than just interaction. There are activities that a person carries out alone. A janitor, machine operator, secretary, supervisor, middle-level manager, and even the president of an organization will perform duties that are called for by the norms of one or more roles but that are carried out for the most part by a single person working alone for a period of time. Such activities are also part of the role requirements. But it should be noted that such activities flow from and are systematically related to the interaction element of the roles. A first-line supervisor may spend several hours alone compiling a weekly or monthly report (activity), but much of the information he uses in the report was secured in talking with his employees (interaction). And when he completes the report he hands it to his boss and discusses its contents with him (interaction). If he fails to complete the report on time, the supervisor may be contacted by his boss and as a result may speed up his report-preparing activity. The boss may tell him that the next monthly report should omit information normally included and that he should add several new items of information. Thus, the activity of preparing a report may be altered by the interaction that resulted from the norm, "prepare reports as directed by the boss."

Now, we have said that each group member has a mental image or role conception of each role, which includes his understanding of the reciprocal rights and obligations of anyone engaged in the role enactment. He has a conception of what is required, what is appropriate, and what is permitted behavior for each of the roles that are the normative base for the performance structure of the group. When a person is new on the job and learning a great deal about the various nuances of the different roles that he is supposed to help perform, his role conceptions may be somewhat fluid, with redefinitions and new definitions occurring from day to day. As his understanding of the details of the role requirements becomes more complete over time, his role conceptions will become more stable and less subject to fluctuation. Renegotiation and redefinition continue, of course; the degree of stability is relative and variable.

Each member, then, has in mind a series of role conceptions that for him act as a blueprint for the activities and interaction in which he believes he should be participating. This same blueprint also specifies the nature and extent of activity and interaction that his colleagues should be pursuing. To the extent that his blueprint of the roles relevant to him is complete and unambiguous, he knows in detail what he ought to be doing and what reciprocal behaviors others ought to be carrying out. To the extent that he is capable of conforming to his role conceptions, his performance in interaction and in the conduct of related activity should develop smoothly and with a minimum of frustration, providing that his colleagues are using the same role conception blueprint that he is attempting to utilize. This is the critical point to remember in attempting to understand and explain the interaction and activity that actually occurs during any given time period. Other persons in his group may in fact be operating from slightly different or even markedly different role conceptions.

To the extent that there is not complete consensus among group members in role conception regarding the relevant roles, there will be, at the very least, a decided lack of meshing in the resulting interaction and activity being attempted. And as complete consensus probably never occurs, there always is some degree of mismatch. The lower the level of consensus, the more incongruous become the various attempts at interaction and activity. Lower consensus levels tend to lead to interaction attempts that may be defined as "confusion" or perhaps "conflict." If I am attempting to interact with you and I find many of your responses to be irrelevant, ridiculous, or clearly at odds with the role norms that I hold, I may make some minor adjustments in my behavior in order to try to bridge the gap. But if these fail, our mutual attempts at interaction will have a sporadic unpredictability about them.

Role Consensus and Friction

In most work groups each member can observe readily many if not most of the activities of the other members. He can certainly observe the behavior of others with whom he interacts directly. Thus, violations of his role norms will be quite obvious in many cases. Some of these violations he may consider to be relatively unimportant, as the norms involved may not be viewed as particularly critical. Other violations will meet with unequivocal disapproval, and we should expect some type of negative sanctions to be evident. So where there is a low level of role consensus among group members, there should be observable behavioral evidence of that fact in the day-to-day interaction.

Specifically, what kinds of behavioral consequences do we expect to flow from low role consensus? Whether we use such terms as *friction, disharmony, conflict,* or the more narrow concept of *negative sanction,* we must be aware of the cultural context in which these behaviors occur. Behavior that is defined as clearly aggressive and inappropriate in one culture may be commonly defined in another culture as permissible or even appropriate. Similarly, certain roles may permit or even require a great deal of verbal aggressiveness (e.g., the prosecutor–witness role in the court room), whereas other roles may have much narrower limits (e.g., the patient–physician role). The behavioral consequences of low role consensus would include culturally approved negative sanctions and also behavior that, in the context of the situation, is generally defined as discordant, nonharmonious, or conflictive. If an observer is sufficiently familiar with the subculture of the group(s) being observed, he should be able to report such friction events, his knowledge of the group's norms being more complete than that of even an astute and experienced observer. Stated succinctly, the proposition would be: *For groups which persist over time, level of role consensus among members is inversely related to the incidence of friction.*

Jacobson, Charters, Lieberman, reporting on a study of industrial work groups, conclude that low consensus was associated with "strain and a lack of ease in interpersonal relations." [19] Haas conducted a study of nine work groups in two hospitals. The level of role consensus was computed for each group, and the number of friction events occurring during a five-day period was recorded for each group. The findings indicate that for such groups, which persist over time, the lower the level of group role consensus the higher the incidence of friction. [20]

Consensus and Evaluation of Role Performance

We know, of course, that in any group some persons have more patience and practice more discretion than others. Not every person is equally prone to display openly his disapproval of another member's role performance. Some subordinates in a work group seldom express such disapproval of the boss to others, let alone criticize him to his face (thereby being party to a friction event). But although discretion or fear may dampen the tendency of a person to express *overt* disapproval when another member has violated a significant role norm, the recognition of such violations will still have discernible, though indirect, consequences.

[19] Eugene Jacobson, W. W. Charters, Jr., and S. Lieberman, "The Use of the Role Concept in the Study of Complex Organizations," *Journal of Social Issues,* 7: 18–27 (1951).

[20] J. Eugene Haas, *Role Conception and Group Consensus* (Columbus, Ohio: Bureau of Business Research, Ohio State University, 1964).

To the extent that a role partner has a different role conception from mine, he is likely to carry out his part of our mutually relevant role(s) in a manner that does not fit my role blueprint. The role norms that I hold specify what he should and should not be doing; and, if he occasionally or frequently violates my norms, I am certain to evaluate that part of his role performance in a negative manner. Thus, the lower the level of role consensus between us, the more frequently we are likely to violate each other's role norms and the lower will be the evaluation each of us has of the other's role norms and the lower will be the evaluation each of us has of the other's role performance. If this hypothesized relation exists, we ought to find support for the proposition that *role pairs or dyads with lower role consensus more frequently have negative mutual role performance evaluations than dyads with higher levels of role consensus.*[21]

Haas attempted to test this hypothesis by comparing level of role consensus and mutual role performance ratings for more than 800 dyads in hospital work groups. Each person was asked to rate the following aspects of the other's role performance: (1) correctness of procedures and techniques; (2) initiative; and (3) general attitude toward work. The findings generally support the hypothesized relation despite the fact that the proportion of dyads with low consensus was exceedingly small as contrasted to the proportions with moderate and high consensus. When position was held constant (e.g., general-duty nurse–general-duty nurse role) the results provide strong support for the hypothesis.[22]

Although this general hypothesis appears to hold, other research suggests a more complex relationship when units other than dyads are used. For example, Gross, Mason, and McEachern investigated the role definitions held by 105 paired units of school superintendents and school board members serving in Massachusetts during the early 1950s. Their data led them to modify the above hypothesis, because the primary variable appeared to be the degree of consensus among board members. Thus, they concluded: "A board whose members agree among themselves on the expectations for their own and the superintendent's positions, will rate the superintendent highly on how well he performs his job, whether or not they agree with the superintendent on the role definitions for his and their positions." [23]

These findings suggest that even in cases where low consensus does not result in overt friction within the work group, it frequently results in measurable negative evaluations of performance among pairs of persons who work together regularly. This seems to be especially true among colleagues where the work to be done is identical or nearly

---

[21] Bond L. Bible and James D. McComas, "Role Consensus and Teacher Effectiveness," *Social Forces*, **42**: 225–32 (December 1963).

[22] Haas, op. cit., pp. 65–72, 88–94.

[23] Neal Gross et al., *Explorations in Role Analysis: Studies of the School Superintendency Role* (New York: John Wiley and Sons, Inc., 1958), p. 220.

identical for each of the role partners under consideration. This suggests that low consensus is most critical in work groups where there is little or no variation in tasks performed by the members (high homogeneity in work tasks). A closely related factor ought to be examined also. The extent to which the member has detailed knowledge about the role partner's work may be significant in the performance rating he gives the partner. If he has such detailed knowledge and concomitant detailed role norms for his partner's work, the possibility of observing violations would seem to be enhanced. The greater the number of violations observed, the more likely he is to give the partner a negative role performance evaluation. In short, for example, the more I know about what you *should* be doing, the more critical I am likely to be of what you *are* doing.

Consensus and Sociometric Preference

If role consensus affects evaluation of role performance, it may have other consequences as well. Could the level of role consensus affect group cohesion? More specifically, is the amount of attractiveness that various group members have for one another influenced by the degree of role consensus they possess? The evidence from a number of studies indicates that such a relationship may exist.

In a review of small group research, Riecken and Homans conclude that the evidence supports the following proposition: "A member 'O' of a group chooses or likes a member 'P' to the degree that 'P's' activities realize 'O's' norms and values." [24] As roles are composed of norms, the proposition would indicate that level of role consensus is related to sociometric preference. Hare, in a more recent review of small group research, concludes that "common interests or values" are an important determiner of "interpersonal choice." Other factors listed by Hare as influencing sociometric choice are proximity, similar social characteristics, and similar personality.[25] Newcomb found consensus on values to be related to the formation of friendship groups among college men.[26]

How is role consensus related to sociometric choice? First of all, it is relatively clear that extreme deviants from what are considered to be important societal norms are thoroughly disliked. Hostility expressed toward the child molester, the murderer, and the arsonist are prime examples. To a lesser degree, but still clearly evident, is the dislike ex-

[24] Henry W. Riecken and George C. Homans, "Psychological Aspects of Social Structure," in Gardner Lindzey, ed., *Handbook of Social Psychology* (Cambridge, Mass.: Addison-Wesley Publishing Co., Inc., 1954), p. 794.

[25] A Paul Hare, *Handbook of Small Group Research* (New York: The Free Press, 1962), pp. 139–40.

[26] Theodore M. Newcomb, *The Acquaintance Process* (New York: Holt, Rinehart, & Winston, Inc., 1961).

pressed toward persons who "don't do things our way"—persons whose life style is clearly different from that which we advocate as the ideal or right way of behaving. Pressures on members to conform to certain group norms are always in evidence, and repeated violation by a member usually brings negative sanctions of one kind or another. One frequent negative sanction is the withdrawal of positive affect.

Because roles are composed of social norms, at least some of which are thought to be important or crucial norms by the person holding the role conception, violation of these role norms by significant others ought to produce a negative response similar to that which occurs when general societal or general group norms are violated. In short, when significant others violate what is believed to be right, there is a tendency to dislike them for it. Two persons who have low role consensus are likely to carry out their roles in different ways, and the behavior of each will to some extent be in violation of the role norms of the other. They can be expected, therefore, to like each other less, on the average, than dyads where consensus is greater. *For dyads in groups that persist over time, low consensus is associated with low sociometric preference.*

Occasionally, a comment such as the following is heard: "Chively is not only a good worker, but he is also a very likable chap." Research evidence suggests that a person can and frequently does distinguish between his evaluation of another group member as a role performer and his evaluation of him as a person in a more general sense.[27] In the Haas study referred to above, each respondent was asked to express both a role performance rating and a sociometric preference for each of the other members of the work group. Three separate sociometric questions were used: "How do you feel about working with this person?", "How do you feel about eating with this person at coffee break or at lunch?", and "How do you feel about associating with this person outside of work and having him or her as a friend?" The responses to each of the three questions were significantly associated with dyadic consensus level. Paired members with low consensus expressed lower sociometric preference for each other than did paired members with a higher consensus level. This relationship was most clearly evident in the "consensus–friendship outside of work" findings. Although some persons may have hesitated to state a frank personal preference when asked about interaction in the work setting, they were less reluctant to give such frank preferences when asked about associating with colleagues outside of the work arena. Only 8 out of 44 low consensus dyads deviated from the expected pattern when asked about their preferences for friendship outside of work.[28] For work group members, level of role consensus apparently does influence the choice of such members as friends.

[27] Hare, op. cit., pp. 115–16.
[28] Haas, op. cit., pp. 72–77, 89–94.

Role Performance Ratings and Sociometric Preferences

The theoretical perspective presented thus far and the evidence from research suggest that role partners with low consensus will tend to express a less favorable evaluation of each other's role performance and will have less positive affect for each other than will high consensus dyads. If both performance ratings and sociometric preferences are determined to a significant extent by level of consensus, then we would anticipate that *performance evaluation and sociometric choice will be statistically associated.* They may or may not be causally connected.

Again, data from Haas' study of hospital work groups support the anticipated association of the two variables. Dyads that express little preference for working together (sociometric preference) also tend to give negative ratings to each other on work attitude, initiative, and correctness of procedures and techniques. And even when the sociometric choice involves expressed preferences for associating with each other at lunch and outside of the work setting, dyads showing mutually low sociometric preference also give each other lower performance ratings than do more friendly dyads.[29]

It is not clear whether a person first develops a dislike for a colleague and as a result becomes more critical of his work performance or first notes his colleague's lack of excellence at work and then begins to like him less. Or perhaps the initial explanation offered at the beginning of this section is the best representation of the causal linkage—low consensus produces low ratings and low sociometric preference with each, being a reflection of a basic process. That is, low role consensus produces both overt friction in interaction and covert orientations that can be tapped by role performance and sociometric rating instruments.

Summary

Patterned interaction within a group is a reflection of the normative structure known to and internalized by the members. That structure is composed of positions and connecting roles. The role conceptions held by each participant specify what each role partner should do, may do, and should not do in all intragroup interaction and related activity. Each role is composed of a unique configuration of norms, which are to be followed by any participant regardless of who he may be. These norms are, therefore, categorical imperatives for behavior in the group setting.

Role partners do not necessarily have identical conceptions of the relevant role(s). Thus, any given dyad may have relatively higher or lower consensus on their role conceptions. Some groups taken as a whole may have a higher level of role consensus than others, even when the tasks of the several groups are comparable. Groups with lower

[29] Ibid., pp. 75–77, 94–95.

levels of consensus evidence more frequent instances of friction or conflict.

Role partners (dyads) with lower levels of role consensus, when contrasted with high consensus dyads, more frequently give each other negative role performance evaluations and express less positive affect toward each other on sociometric preference ratings. Furthermore, those dyads who like each other least also are most critical of each other's work performance.

It would appear that group efficiency may be enhanced by higher levels of role consensus. If nothing else, the time consumed in the expression of intragroup friction and conflict would seem to inhibit efficiency. Also, high role consensus among group members is probably a necessary but not a sufficient condition for effectiveness. Although high consensus may reduce disharmony and contribute to member satisfaction, it does not necessarily insure *effectiveness*. There may be high consensus on either effective or ineffective norms. The members of a business firm may move harmoniously into bankruptcy! High consensus on norms that optimize effectiveness would appear to be the ideal for which the administrator should strive.

However, efficiency and effectiveness may be viewed in both a short-term and longer-term perspective. Short-term inefficiency resulting from verbal quarrels that reflect low role consensus may in fact produce greater efficiency and effectiveness over the long haul. A group member with unusual or deviant role conceptions may and probably will be the instigator of some conflict, but it is also possible that out of that conflict will come ideas for group interaction that would otherwise not have come to the fore. To the extent that such unprogrammed ideas are valuable to the group when measured against some set of criteria such as efficiency or effectiveness, conflict must be considered at least potentially worthwhile.

Certainly, an analysis of the normative structure of any group can take us a long way in understanding member behavior. But often we need to go beyond this area of analysis. We turn next to the second of the three general explanatory concepts, the interpersonal structure.

Person to Person: The Interpersonal Structure

We have argued that the patterned interaction is, to a very significant degree, the product of normative structure. Norms specify preferred and required interaction for *categories of persons* in kinds or *types of situations*. When a member knows the appropriate person–situation set, he has a general blueprint for his own behavior and that of others involved in the interaction. Norms are categorical imperatives. One needs to know very little about other participants as persons to be a norm-abiding member.

But as interaction continues over time, participants do in fact learn a great deal about one another as persons. They do not respond to each other *strictly* as members of various relevant categories. Let us examine what we shall call the interpersonal structure (IPS) of a group.

We start by noting that individual differences do exist. Some persons smile more than others, some speak rapidly, others slowly and some are very quiet. In discussion, some persons arrive at conclusions very quickly whereas others are more cautious. Some members seem to want others to make the first move in getting acquainted, others do not hesitate to take the lead. One could compile a long list of such individual differences.

There is an interesting phenomenon that is important in this regard. Not all of these behaviors are normatively defined. We recognize that there are individual preferences with regard to such behaviors, but we also know that there are no generally recognized norms that stipulate that such behaviors should or should not occur. I may enjoy persons who express their emotions readily, persons who express annoyance and elation frequently; you may prefer the cool type. Being consistently cool is neither more nor less laudable than being expressive. Normatively, it is simply a matter of *personal* taste or preference for most situations. There is, then, a whole range of such behaviors where we note the actions of others and have an evaluation of them, but it is an evaluation based strictly on our own personal preferences rather than on normative standards.

In a group setting, therefore, each participant will notice (perceive) certain attributes of every other person. Those attributes that are not normatively defined will be evaluated on a personal basis. In any given instance, the evaluation may range from very positive, through neutrality, to very negative. The person doing the evaluation may or may not be able to express the reasons for his response. Frequently, it is a "that is just the way he strikes me" expression. But if an attribute is noticed, there will be some type of evaluative response.

Each person noticing and evaluating certain attributes will have an initial orientation toward the other as a person. In most cases, this initial orientation will be composed of positive, neutral, and negative elements. In a dyad (pair), both persons will have such an initial orientation toward each other. Each will get clues from time to time concerning the "person orientation" of the other toward him. These clues, in turn, will influence the orientation of each as time passes.

The person orientation of each will influence the character and frequency of interaction in the dyad. If I find some of your actions disgusting, I will probably try to minimize contact with you. As a result, the orientations will be reinforced in some respects and probably revised in other respects. There is a dynamic element to this process. We have all had experiences where we rather liked another person at first, but later felt differently about him. In other cases, we disliked a person for a time, only to become close friends at a later time. Thus, the initial orientations are often altered, sometimes drastically, as persons become better acquainted.[30]

As interaction continues over time, relative stability develops in these person-to-person orientations. Along with this, each member of the dyad develops some conception of the nature of "our relationship." The conception of this relationship may be quite vague, or it may be quite specific and detailed. It might be described by the participants as "competitive," "friendly," "distant," "strictly businesslike," "intimate," or perhaps "supportive." Persons with a more reflective disposition can probably describe their relationships in more detail and with more color (see Figure 4–5).

Bales and his students have concentrated on developing descriptive concepts and recording techniques for interpersonal behavior. Their ideas are relevant for the suggestion here of the concept of interpersonal relation, but there are distinct differences. The focus of Bales's work is on behavior enacted in the presence of others.[31] But the prime interest of the observer-analyst is still on *individual* behavior, not on the interpersonal relation as a separate conceptual unit. For example, in *Interaction Process Analysis,*[32] each behavioral *act* is coded in one of twelve categories, such as "shows tension," "asks for orientation," "disagrees," and so on. In his more recent work, Bales goes beyond the person–act as the basic unit of analysis.[33] But he does not go far beyond it. Although modifying slightly his categories for interaction process analysis, he presents a new typological system, which may be used to characterize the expressed behaviors of each participant in a group. Each *person* is rated on twenty-six different dimensions. The rating on each dimension is accomplished when the rater attempts to answer a specific question about the behaviors of the member being rated—e.g., "Does he seem warm and personal?", "Does he seem to feel that others are generally too conforming to conventional social expectations?" The combined answers to all twenty-six questions provide a descriptive *profile of the person as he generally behaves in that group.* The basic unit of analysis is still the individual, but now the unit covers a longer time span. It is an attempt to characterize an individual's set of behavioral acts across time in a specific group context. For self-analytic groups, Bales suggests that each group member will profit by rating every other member on the twenty-six question "Interpersonal Rating" form.

[30] Newcomb, op. cit.

[31] Robert F. Bales, *Interaction Process Analysis* (Cambridge, Mass.: Addison-Wesley Publishing Co., Inc., 1950).

[32] Ibid.

[33] Robert F. Bales, *Personality and Interpersonal Behavior* (New York: Holt, Rinehart & Winston, Inc., 1970).

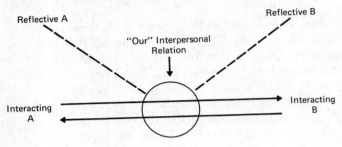

One implication of the Bales approach is that each person has a standardized mode of acting within a specific group. It implies that John
acts essentially in the same manner when he is interacting with Mary
as he does when he is interacting with Sally or Helen or Patricia. Our
observation of interaction in groups leads us to the conclusion that few
persons are so insensitive to the variation in individual differences
among other group participants. Although John may have some standardized ways of behaving, he will almost certainly respond to each
individual in a slightly or even markedly different fashion. John and
Mary may tease each other, whereas John and Sally challenge each
other in intellectual matters. John and Helen tend to ignore each other
whenever possible. In short, each pair interacting over time develops a
set of mutual understandings and orientations that are unique to them.
Each interpersonal relation has at least some unique characteristics. If
such interpersonal relations do in fact develop among dyads within
each group, as they seem to, then the concept of interpersonal relation
ought to be useful in explaining interaction patterns.

It is clear that some persons, such as a child, may have difficulty in
describing the character of an interpersonal relation. But quite apart
from the members' conceptions of their relations and their ability to
verbalize the conceptions they hold, the observer-analyst can utilize
the concept to understand and explain both stability and change in
observed interaction. We define an *interpersonal relation* as a *set of
emergent and relatively stable person-to-person orientations and understandings between two persons, where the reciprocal orientations are
based on perceived personal attributes.* These orientations are independent of positions held and relevant roles typically enacted. They are
person-based idea sets. In a hospital setting, for example, we would
speak of the doctor–head nurse role as defined and enacted by Dr.
Sharp and Nurse Clean, but in considering interpersonal aspects we
would speak of the John Sharp–Sarah Clean interpersonal relation.

An organizational group does not carry on interaction in splendid isolation. Some, if not all, members of such a group also interact with varying frequency with persons who are members of other groups in the organization. Thus, we need to recognize that there will be intergroup as well as intragroup interpersonal relations. It is not difficult to recognize the significance for the group of certain intergroup interpersonal relations. Where there is distrust between the department chairman and the dean of a college, for example, that department is probably going to suffer when money and space are being allocated among competing departments. The significance of intergroup interpersonal relations will be discussed in greater detail in the next chapter.

The *interpersonal structure* of a group is composed of the complete set of interconnected interpersonal relations. In a rudimentary sense, the IPS is simply a summary term for the set of interpersonal relations, but in another sense it is more than that. IPS also refers to the *characteristics of the configuration* and the way in which the interpersonal relations are interconnected. The IPS of Doc's gang in *Street Corner Society* was more than just the sum of the various interpersonal relations.[34] The characteristics of the Doc–Long John interpersonal relation were a reflection of the other interpersonal relations in which both men were involved. If the various interpersonal relations are viewed simply as a list in a catalog, much will be missed. Rather, we should use a three-dimensional, multicolored map as an analogy. An IPS map does permit us to view particular segments, interpersonal relations, in great detail, but it also allows us to look at the characteristics of the whole. This is a different perspective. Just as we make qualitative comparisons among two or more oil paintings we can also compare the IPS of several groups and show, it is hoped, how that structure relates to such variables as level of productivity or stability of membership over time.

It should be remembered that when we speak of an interpersonal relation we are *not* attempting to characterize reciprocal behaviors or interaction per se. We wish rather to point to the mutual understandings and orientations that underlie and produce the observable interaction. We want to use the concepts interpersonal relation and IPS to explain stability and change in group interaction patterns. Although there is some reference in the literature to what we are calling interpersonal relations, there is as yet no adequate vocabulary for discussing the various types of interpersonal relations. There are some words in common use that are used to denote some interpersonal relations, but they are limited in number. We speak of love and hate, of mutual respect and jealousy. And in so doing, we imply an underlying relation that may be expressed in a variety of actions by the persons involved.

[34] William F. Whyte, *Street Corner Society* (Chicago: University of Chicago Press, 1943).

Thus, a wife may say, "If you love me, why don't you express it more often?"

On Sorting Out Interpersonal Relations

We may comment that one person consistently dominates another. In so doing, we imply two related but different levels of abstraction. The first and more obvious meaning associated with that comment is that the one person has undue influence and control over the thinking and overt behavior of the other. It is an attempt to characterize the nature of the *interaction* and its consequences. But quite apart from attempting to describe interaction, we can also use the term *dominance* to characterize one aspect of an interpersonal relation. We can say that, as we understand it, persons *A* and *B* have a strong dominance–submission dimension to their interpersonal relation. It is a significant part of their mutual understandings and orientations. Extending this idea a bit, we might take words from our everyday vocabulary that are frequently used to summarize aspects of interaction. Where they are appropriate we can use them to denote attributes of interpersonal relations.

In order to emphasize that we are referring to a *relation* between two persons, rather than just the orientation of a single person, we shall use hyphenated labels. Thus, we will use *dominance–submission* rather than just the word *dominance*.

Let us look at a brief outline of a hypothetical interpersonal relation using five illustrative dimensions.

Characteristics of a Hypothetical Interpersonal Relation	Other Related Possible Characteristics
Dominance–Submission	Dominance–Dominance Submission–Submission
Like–Like	Like–Dislike Dislike–Dislike
Trust–Trust	Trust–Distrust Distrust–Distrust
Extensive–Extensive	Extensive–Limited Limited–Limited
Respect–Respect	Respect–Disrespect Disrespect–Disrespect

In our hypothetical case we have mentioned only five of many possible significant characteristics of the interpersonal relation. The relationship is one of mutual liking, respect, and trust. There is a tacit understanding that in most matters influence will be somewhat unequal (dominance–submission). In addition, each recognizes that it will be quite acceptable to the other to discuss almost any possible topic of conversation. There are very few subjects that need to be avoided. The relationship is seen by both of them as extensive in character rather than limited.

Balanced and Unbalanced Characteristics of an Interpersonal Relation

If we were actually to observe and make notations concerning such a relationship in a real life setting, we would probably predict that this particular interpersonal relation stands a good chance of remaining stable over an extended period of time. There is a kind of balance or symmetry about it that leads us to such a forecast. We might say that, as far as we can tell, the persons involved are now and will continue to be good friends.

But suppose that we had studied the interpersonal relation, looking at the same dimensions, and had found that the following were the significant features:

Dominance–dominance
Like–dislike
Trust–distrust
Extensive–limited
Respect–disrespect

What forecast would we make about the stability of such an interpersonal relation and the continuation of interaction over time? We would probably estimate that the relation would not continue indefinitely. Either the attributes of the interpersonal relation would change to a more balanced configuration, or the level of interaction would decline markedly and perhaps cease altogether in time.

The point to be considered in using the concept of balance in assessment of the characteristics of an interpersonal relation is this: How can knowledge of the attributes of an interpersonal relation assist us in *explaining* the nature and frequency of dyadic interaction as it is occurring at any point in time; and to what extent can such knowledge be used successfully to *predict* the type and frequency of interaction in the near future? In short, as social scientists we want to develop a theoretical framework that is useful in explaining and predicting both stability and change in group interaction. The concept of balance would seem to offer some hope in this regard. If we examine the same set of five characteristics mentioned above and now apply the balance concept, we get the following distribution:

CONTINUUM OF BALANCED–UNBALANCED ATTRIBUTES OF INTERPERSONAL RELATIONS

Balanced		Unbalanced
Equalitarian–Equalitarian	Dominance–Submission	Dominance–Dominance
		Submission–Submission
Like–Like	Dislike–Dislike	Like–Dislike
Trust–Trust	Distrust–Distrust	Trust–Distrust
Extensive–Extensive	Limited–Limited	Extensive–Limited
Respect–Respect	Disrespect–Disrespect	Respect–Disrespect

The attributes listed on the *balanced* end of the continuum, once developed between two persons, would tend to produce a continuation of the established patterns of interaction within the dyad and perhaps within limits yet to be specified, to increased frequency of interaction. The attributes listed on the *unbalanced* end would seem to produce the opposite outcome. An interpersonal relation with unbalanced characteristics as the predominant ones is inherently unstable; the relationship is not likely to continue unchanged for very long. And if the relationship changes, then so will the characteristics of the observable interaction. During any given time period, we would expect more day-to-day fluctuations in interaction patterns. Over a longer period of time, the unbalanced attributes will either change to some that are more nearly balanced, or, failing that, the interaction will decrease to some absolute minimum. In an organizational setting, both persons may be forced to continue minimal interaction in order to carry out basic job requirements. They may seek transfer to other positions in the organization or even resign from the organization in order to escape from the setting. Change in some form would seem to be a near certainty.

Attributes appearing near the midrange of the continuum tend to be reflected in a relatively low level of interaction. Where the attributes of an interpersonal relation are predominately of this type, the relation would be more stable than for the unbalanced type, but less stable than the balanced. Day-to-day interaction will probably be distant, cool, and segmental in nature. Such a mixed configuration is not uncommon. But when there is mutual dislike, disrespect, and distrust, especially if these orientations are *intense*, the ingredients for some instability seem to be present. Where these orientations are *mild*, the relation could continue with little change for an extended period of time. Here, the intrusion of some catalytic event may be crucial. A colleague of both persons could exacerbate the relation by revealing negative comments made to him in confidence. On the other hand, a colleague sensing the nature of the relationship could pursue a course of action that would gradually result in change to a more balanced relationship.

A word of caution is in order. This notion of *balance in interpersonal relations* has not been utilized so far in research on actual groups in an organizational setting. There have been a few related laboratory studies, but for our purposes they would appear to have a significant defect.[35] They do not deal with interpersonal relations that continued over any extended period of time. Two persons, subjects in a laboratory experiment, may recognize the beginnings of an unbalanced interpersonal relation. Their interaction in such a setting is usually controlled to a significant extent by the experimenter. Even more crucial is the fact that they know that the interaction series is relatively temporary. For a setting that they define as "strictly an experiment," which will last for a few hours or days at most, their overt behavior can be held in line with what they understand to be the relevant "laboratory norms." They are most unlikely to walk out in the middle of an experiment. A subject seldom goes to the experimenter with a request that he be placed in a different experimental group because he cannot stand to work with another subject.

Interaction in a work group that is part of an organization has a different set of constraints and opportunities. Such a group is more than and different from an encounter, to use a distinction made by Goffman.[36] What is needed, then, is a series of longitudinal studies of interpersonal relations and the related interaction that takes place in on-going organizational groups.

The Interpersonal Structure: Understanding a Network

The analysis of interpersonal relations is, of course, only the first step in understanding the IPS of a group, at least for groups with more than two participants. We want to be able to characterize the entire IPS of a group. How can this be accomplished? As a start, we can analyze the IPS with regard to its balance characteristics. To what extent is it composed of balanced versus unbalanced and mixed interpersonal relations? What are some of the possible consequences flowing from high versus low balance characteristics of an IPS?

There is some evidence to suggest that the following propositions may be both valid and significant for the understanding of groups in an organizational setting.

1. The higher the degree of balance[37] in the IPS of a group, *the more stable are the interaction patterns* over time.

[35] Timothy J. Curry and Richard M. Emerson, "Balance Theory: A Theory of Interpersonal Attraction," *Sociometry*, 33: 216–38 (June 1970).

[36] Erving Goffman, *Encounters* (Indianapolis, Ind.: Bobbs-Merrill, 1961), p. 8.

[37] Degree of balance refers to the general extent of balance in the overall configuration of interpersonal relations. As we do not yet know what weights ought to be given to the various dimensions, we will simply hold that for this discussion the more closely all five characteristics come to the balanced end of the scale, the higher the degree of balance.

Where the interpersonal relations are balanced for the most part, group members have no particular incentive or reason for trying to alter the existing relations. But where even a few dyads within the group have relatively unbalanced relations, we would expect some kind of efforts to be made to increase the level of balance. Those efforts may take a variety of forms, most of which would produce *variation* in the patterned interaction of the group. For example, when John comes to realize that there is not the degree of mutual respect that he had hoped for in one of his interpersonal relations, he may alter his behavior in a variety of ways. He may try harder to gain the respect of the other person (Jim). He may try to initiate more and perhaps somewhat different interaction with Jim, or he may consciously reduce the level of interaction with Mary and seek increased interaction with both Sally and Helen. We need not posit particular individual needs to anticipate that unbalanced interpersonal relations will tend to produce variation and less predictable patterns of interaction than will balanced interpersonal relations.

2. The higher the degree of balance in the IPS of a group, the *more consistent is the level of group productivity*.

To the extent that productivity in a group is in part a consequence of the level and modes of interaction, then the balance features of the IPS ought also to be related to *consistency* of productivity. The *level* of productivity may be high, medium, or low for any particular group during some designated time period. But whatever the level of productivity might be, it will have a tendency to remain constant in groups with higher balance than those with lower balance in their IPS. The connection being suggested can be represented thus:

High degree of balance in interpersonal structure → stable interaction patterns over time → consistency of productivity over time.

Summary

In responding to each other as individuals rather than merely as position incumbents, sets of emergent and relatively stable person-to-person orientations and understandings develop. Each set between any two members is called an interpersonal relation. The network of interpersonal relations among group members is the interpersonal structure of the group. Any given interpersonal relation as well as the total interpersonal structure may be balanced to a greater or lesser degree, and that level of balance is apparently related to the stability of the performance structure over time.

The interpersonal structure of a group is a second "explanatory" concept. It remains an "orientating statement," as does the "normative structure." But it helps direct our attention toward an area where future conceptual refinement may be most profitable. The notion of balance, and the five dimensions cited (dominance–submission; like–dislike; trust–distrust; extensive–limited; and respect–disrespect) appear helpful. But much future empirical work and conceptual elaboration are necessary before we will have sets of propositions whereby the complex of variables subsumed within this very general concept can be integrated.

Let us move now to a discussion of the resource structure of the group. It is our third explanatory concept and the one most frequently ignored in sociological research. Although the authors are convinced of its importance, it remains the most underdeveloped as a concept. Clearly, there are numerous variables that will have to be sorted out and conceptualized before we will have much of a handle on this dimension, which appears so crucial.

The Resource Structure

Immediately after the 1964 Good Friday earthquake in Anchorage, the Alaska Disaster Office was without electric power and only sporadic, and partial telephone service was available.[38] Their standby, diesel-powered electric generator, purchased with just such a contingency in mind, would not function. The head of the small organization and one of his deputies were in fog-bound Juneau, and he could not be reached even by radio for several hours. Although a draft version of a state "disaster plan" had been completed several months previously, it did not include statements regarding the procedures that should be followed within the Alaska Disaster Office itself if a natural disaster were to occur. Within a few hours, the small office building was jammed with volunteers whose skills and efforts were needed but for whom space, desks, and supplies were totally inadequate. Sanitary facilities were inoperative because of breaks in the city water system. Even drinking water was in short supply for a time.

It was clear to any observer in this setting that the resources at the Alaska Disaster Office were a critical element in determining the interaction and activity that followed the earthquake. On the one hand, the resources severely limited the character and extent of interaction. And on the other hand, the resources, especially the volunteers, provided

---

[38] For more extended discussion of this event see the following.

Daniel Yutzy and J. Eugene Haas, "Chronology of Events in Anchorage Following the Earthquake," in National Academy of Sciences, Committee on the Alaska Earthquake, *The Great Alaska Earthquake of 1964: Human Ecology*, Vol. 7 (Washington, D.C.: National Academy of Sciences and National Research Council, 1970) pp. 403-24.

Daniel Yutzy, *Community Priorities in the Anchorage, Alaska, Earthquake 1964* (Columbus: Disaster Research Center, The Ohio State University, 1969).

opportunities for activity and interaction that would not have been possible otherwise. Clearly, the resources of a group do influence in significant measure the performance structure of the group.

What do we mean by "resource structure"? It is easy to recognize equipment and other physical objects as resources. But the concept also includes the available physical space and the way that such space is broken up by walls, corridors, steps, and so on. Information and records, whether in written form or not, also serve as a resource. The number of participants and their relevant skills clearly make a difference in performance. *The resource structure of a group, then, consists of the physical materials, space, and information under the jurisdiction of or available for use by members as well as the number and relevant skills of members.*

There is an additional point that needs to be clarified if the concept "resource" is to be useful. Although there may be a few instances in which the researcher may need to catalog all of the resources of a group, usually he will want to take note only of those resources that are relevant to the problem or problems under study. Where group productivity (one characteristic of the performance structure) is a central concern of the researcher, he will want to examine those resources that may function to limit or enhance the quantity and quality of product or service output. On the other hand, if his principal interest is on sanctioning procedures used within the group, he may want to examine a different and perhaps much more limited set of resources. There is probably no single check list of possible group resources that can serve equally well for research on any and all researchable issues.

Limitations on Interaction and Activity

In order to portray the significance of the resource structure, we shall attempt to illustrate how it may limit and shape three of the most basic organizational processes: task, coordination, and communication.

Let us first consider *task processes*. Although machines and automated equipment of various kinds have served to reduce the number of workers required to accomplish many tasks, there are still numerous tasks that require a minimal number of persons working together or separately for their accomplishment. In some cases, the task could conceivably be accomplished with fewer than the "minimum" number of workers, but the length of time required to do so would be thought to be unacceptable. If allowed sufficient time, one man could even assemble an automobile by himself, but it seldom happens that way. Other tasks, such as constructing a large building, performing heart surgery, or running a ship, simply cannot be completed by a single individual regardless of the amount of time allowed. At least, such tasks cannot be performed with our current level of technology. So, quite apart from skill specialization among the persons in a group, the tasks that can be performed are limited by the number of members available at any point in time.

The significance of relevant skills is so obvious that it hardly needs mentioning. When only the secretary can type clean copy, few letters will be sent out when she is ill. When the man who can repair malfunctioning equipment is absent and there is no back-up man available, the chances are good that the interaction patterns involved in task performance will be altered drastically if his absence is extended.

Both the speed and quality of task performance appear to be related to observability. When my fellow workers can observe readily my work efforts and I am aware of that fact, my behavior is very likely to stay within the limits of what is normatively acceptable. As discussed earlier, my behavior is, in part, normatively based. But we must recognize the significance of visual and auditory barriers. Most tasks that require extended periods of intense concentration will not be done well, if at all, when noise and visual distractions abound. The breaking up of space in work areas with walls or other barriers may be an expression of what is considered appropriate or proper within a given culture, but the manner in which it is done sets very real limits on how and how well various tasks can be carried out.

Some tasks require essentially only relevant motor skills, tools, and materials to be worked on. Others may require mostly intellectual or creative skills. Many tasks require the performer to have access to information of various kinds. The recent boom in data storage and retrieval equipment and techniques suggests that an increasing proportion of tasks require the performer to have frequent and easy access to many kinds of information. For many work groups, the loss of even modest amounts of information stored in filing cabinets or on magnetic tapes would be more than an annoying inconvenience; it means that some tasks simply would become impossible. In an extreme case it would be comparable to the task facing the Coroner's Office after the Vaiont Dam disaster in Italy in 1963. More than two thousand persons had been killed, and the recovered bodies had to be identified before burial. But as all legal, medical, dental, and even family records had been washed away in the deluge, most bodies simply could not be identified. Efforts at identification went on for many months, but that was after the mass burials had taken place.

When written records have not been kept or have been lost or destroyed, the memory skills of individual members become recognized as a very significant resource. Member knowledge about where certain kinds of information are stored and how to get access to such information is often a limiting factor—limiting what can be done and how rapidly it can be accomplished.

Next, we will consider how resources may limit *coordination processes*. The concept of coordination implies that interaction and activity ought to take place in some specifiable time sequence and spatial relationship. Thompson holds that there are three general approaches to coordination.[39] Coordination may be achieved by *standardization*, establishing routines or rules that apply to relatively stable, repetitive situations. Where the task situation is more dynamic, coordination may be by *plan*, which involves the setting of schedules by which various activities may then be governed. Where the situation is highly variable and unpredictable there is likely to be coordination by *mutual adjustment*. In this setting, the sequence of activities cannot be scheduled in advance, so there must be repeated transmission of information among those involved in the various activities if the final desired outcome is to be achieved. For example, if the object is to apprehend a criminal suspect who is roaming the city in a stolen vehicle, police cruisers equipped with two-way radios make coordination by mutual adjustment possible.

Whatever the mode of coordination being attempted, the extent and nature of the resources of the group will limit the success of coordination efforts. Even where there is coordination by standardization, an absence or shortage of necessary materials needed by a single member or a subgroup will reduce the level of coordination. Where oral communication is a prerequisite for coordination, the use of space and the ease of direct access to persons and to phone, radio, and intercom equipment will place restrictions on the coordination that is possible. In a group in which each member has the skills necessary to perform any one of the required tasks, the absence of one or a few members on a given day may not produce serious coordination problems because persons can be shifted to the various tasks as necessary. But with increasing skill specialization among members, absence will make coordination much more problematic. Where coordination by mutual adjustment is being attempted, the skill factor becomes even more crucial. The effectiveness of a football team on the field is a good example. Each player may know what his basic assignment is, and each may be able to carry out that part of his task superbly. But the success of the team is also dependent on how well each player can send and receive mutual adjustment cues. A substitute player, even one with superb skill in the fundamentals of football, may not have equal skill in the subtleties of cue handling, and such cues are essential for coordination. If the substitute player has not worked with the other members of the team regularly, he cannot be as highly skilled as a regular player in handling cues because many of the cues are idiosyncratic to particular players and to the team as a whole. Although it may be a less obvious phenomenon than some others, coordination cue skills are a significant resource for many groups.

Quite apart from coordination processes per se, *communication processes* are influenced by group resources. For many groups the receipt,

[39] Thompson, op. cit., pp. 51–65.

encoding, summing, compiling, storing, interpreting, and sending of information is the central task of the group. Clearly, the amount and kinds of information that can be processed is dependent on the nature and extent of group resources. Experimental groups using Y-shaped communication nets perform better than groups using circle nets.[40]

However, most organizational groups do not have information processing as their central task. In such groups communication is a facilitating process, and that process is shaped by the resources. If we consider physical space and barriers, evidence suggests that the frequency of communication declines as distance and the number of barriers increases.[41] But even in groups in which physical conditions for inter-communication are optimized, spatial location still plays some part. For example, members tend to address more communication to persons seated opposite to them at a table than to those next to them, presumably because of easier eye contact. It may also be true that even when telephone and intercom devices are within easy reach, a person is less likely to initiate communication with another group member than he is if the other member works in the same room or in one immediately adjacent. Even such a simple device as a printed form for writing messages apparently affects the communication rate.

It seems clear also that intragroup communication is also shaped by the ready accessibility of written records of various types. The secretary who controls such records will be contacted much more frequently than will other group members.

We have attempted to illustrate the significance of the resource structure by discussing its relevance for task, coordination, and communication processes. Other processes are undoubtedly also influenced by the resources of the group. We shall now treat the concept of the resource structure in more detail.

Resources and Domain

No organizational group is totally self-sufficient. In every complex interaction system there is a division of labor as well as a concomitant division of resources. Ideally, each group has assigned to it those resources that are required for the day-to-day accomplishment of its tasks. Each group has direct jurisdiction over its central, critical resources—at least, there is a strong tendency for this to exist in most organizations.

Now, many of the things we view as group resources come from outside the group. Decisions regarding such concerns as size of budget,

---

[40] Joseph E. McGrath and Irwin Altman, *Small Group Research: A Synthesis and Critique of the Field* (New York: Holt, Rinehart & Winston, Inc., 1966), p. 140.

[41] Hare, op. cit., p. 273.

number and kind of positions or slots, raises for personnel, space allocation, or equipment and supplies are usually made by persons who are not full-time participants in the group. The group head may make recommendations and may engage in complicated negotiation strategies, but at best he has only partial control over these resource decisions. Normally, when such decisions are made, these resources take on the status of semiproperty of the group to which they were allocated. In some cases, these resources "belong to" and are under the jurisdiction of the group for a specifiable period of time. The monies allocated to the group usually have a life span of one year. (Technically, money per se is not a resource. Rather, as with "good will" and "past favors rendered," it is a means for securing resources.) The space assigned to the group may be for some designated period, or it may be for an indefinite period of time. Typically, equipment belongs to the group until it is worn out or replaced by newer models. Supplies are seldom returned or taken away from the group. In publically financed organizations, the number of personnel positions usually comes up for consideration once a year, whereas in other organizations the period of time is less definite.

The significant feature of this resource allocation and control process is that at any given point in time, there is usually a high degree of consensus concerning which resources belong to which group. In any group it is understood that "we" have certain resources over which "we" have control and outsiders do not (should not) have access to them unless "we" give explicit permission for such use.

There are some interesting partial exceptions to this principle. One exception involves certain centralized service facilities such as computer installations. Instead of allowing each group, department, or division to have its own computer facilities, a single computing center is established and computer specialists are assigned to the facility to assist all legitimate users. On the face of it, an observer might conclude that these computer resources belong to no single group but rather to the organization as a whole. In actual practice, what usually evolves are claims by several groups to partial ownership, each group claiming that it has (should have) at least partial jurisdiction. An additional complication lies in the fact that the computer specialists who work with the facility regularly come to think of themselves as a group and tend to view these resources as belonging to "their" group. Unless such persons have a strong service orientation, they will not view their group as the caretaker of the resource but as legitimate owner in the usual sense of group ownership. Thus, any given user group will not only have to compete with other user groups for partial jurisdiction, but also with the caretaker group, which claims total ownership. These competing claims over jurisdiction often are the basis for continuing intergroup expressions of hostility. An upper-level manager will occasionally be confronted with the comment, "We can't get our work done on schedule because those characters at the computer facility act like they own the equipment and they think that they are doing us a big favor in letting us use the facility." University libraries share this dilemma.

The following propositions seem to be valid and ought to be subjected to a rigorous empirical test. Space occupied and used regularly by a group will be claimed by the group as theirs. Equipment located within such space, even when used occasionally by other groups, will be viewed as the property of the occupying group. The ownership rights of the occupying group will be consistently defended by that group even against the claims of an officially designated user group. Where there is significant multiple-group use of space and/or equipment, low consensus regarding ownership rights will be a major source of hostility among the competing groups.

The discussion of group ownership of resources suggests the relevance of the concept of group domain. Group domain, as we suggested earlier in this chapter, consists of normative ideas about what the group has the right and responsibility to do. But notions of task and function inevitably get linked to the space, equipment, and personnel thought necessary to get the job done. Thus, the normative structure of a production group will include ideas about *what* should be produced, the range of *techniques* or *procedures* that should be employed, the types and amount of *equipment* and *space* that should be allocated to the group, the number and types of *personnel* that should be provided, and even the amount and type of compensation that the group members should receive. (For example, members of a professional group should receive salaries rather than wages, and the total compensation should be greater than that given to semiskilled workers.)

The resource structure of a group then should be viewed through the notion of domain. Where a group has effective control over who may use the resources we shall speak of resources within the domain or simply *domain resources*. Resources not under the effective control of the group but to which the group usually has access we shall call *domain-shared resources*. Access to these resources may be based on a variety of considerations. There may be consensus on official or unofficial norms that specify accessibility. There may be specific bargains between groups, regarding the mutual sharing of resources. (Bargains are based on norms of reciprocity.) In rare cases, access may be permitted because the request has a high level of urgency involved, as when there is a dramatic emergency and a special set of norms apply to the situation. Those relevant resources clearly beyond the domain of the group, but still within the organization, we call *domain-relevant resources*.

We would anticipate that some groups would have a wealth of

domain resources whereas others may be relatively poor. The same variation is likely to be present with respect to domain-shared and domain-relevant resources. Where the members of a group believe that their resources are marginal or inadequate for the tasks that they believe they are to perform, we would expect to see a variety of efforts made to increase the adequacy of the group resources. Where domain-shared resources are considered more than adequate and domain resources less than adequate, efforts to secure additional domain resources will be less intense than when the shared resources also are considered marginal. In sum, it is the perception of total group resources, that will be the best indication of the total effort that will be expended to increase the resource level. Where the total resource level is considered adequate, little, if any, effort will be expended in a search for additional resources even if one segment (e.g., domain-shared resources) taken alone is less than adequate. Where the total is considered inadequate, the segment that is least adequate will get the greatest amount of attention.

These ideas about group resource structures just "scratch the surface" of this complex and highly abstract conceptual area. Clearly, much future theoretical work must be directed here if we are to extend our understanding of organizations or even smaller units within.

Up to this point we have discussed separately the nature and significance of the normative structure, the interpersonal structure, and the resource structure for stability and change in the performance structure of organizational groups. However, we emphasized at the outset that we viewed these three general explanatory concepts as interrelated. Each is "overlaid" on the other, thereby constraining the emergent patterns of interaction. Clear understanding of the interdependencies among these three concepts must await more conceptual elaboration within each. But the idea of interdependence is crucial. Let us explore a few brief examples at a descriptive level of abstraction.

Interdependence of Structures

We have tried to demonstrate that the stability and change of a group's performance structure might be explained by utilizing the notions of the normative structure, interpersonal structure (IPS), and resource structure. But if the resource structure is altered, what will be the consequence for the normative structure? Can a change in the normative structure be expected to produce a revised IPS? What can be said about the interdependence existing among the three underlying structures?

Some of the links among structures are not too difficult to illustrate. Others are more difficult, because most of us are not accustomed to thinking about the manner in which these structures are interrelated and hence we are seldom alerted to note events that illustrate the linkages. The research and conceptual base needed to formulate valid and reasonably specific propositions dealing with interstructure interdependence simply are not yet available. However, it is possible to provide illustrations that suggest the various ways in which these structures are linked.

Resource Structure → Normative Structure

In a production group there are norms that specify both the quantity and the quality of the group output. The supervisor hears frequent complaints from other user groups within the organization about the quality of the output of his group. He has tried to make occasional spot checks on the product quality but has found that he simply does not have sufficient time to check consistently on quality without neglecting other equally important responsibilities. His production workers, knowing that the quality is only sporadically checked, do not take the relevant norms too seriously even though they view the norms as reasonable. The supervisor finally convinces management that the personnel resources of his group need to be strengthened, and a new employee is assigned the responsibility of systematically observing and reporting on product quality of the group. The availability of the additional personnel resource produces at least two kinds of changes in the group normative structure: (1) The norms dealing with product quality are now seen by the production workers as norms that should be closely and consistently adhered to; and (2) the new position of product quality inspector brings into the group normative structure a whole new set of official and unofficial norms that spell out the rights and obligations of the new inspector vis-à-vis other position incumbents within the group. New roles have been added, and the configuration of the normative structure has been significantly altered.

Normative Structure → Resource Structure

One of the traditional norms of a hospital station group specifies that not more than 50 per cent of the members may be gone from the station for lunch at any one time. The norm has now been changed to "at least two staff members must be on duty at all times." In practice, it now develops that the two or three persons remaining on the station during coffee break and lunch periods are almost always just aides or orderlies rather than some professional nurses. The obvious result is that during such periods the station resources are sharply reduced in both the number of personnel available for patient care and the range of skills available. If an emergency arises and the demand level increases, there will be fewer persons to cope with the demand, only a limited range of skills will be available, and much of the technical equipment on the station will not be available for use because those members present have not been trained to use it. (The moral is, if you are a patient on the station, don't have a cardiac arrest during normal coffee or lunch break periods!)

Resource Structure → Interpersonal Structure

Groups having a high proportion of resources that must be shared by various members have more extensively developed interpersonal structures. In some groups, the tasks involve frequent use of records, reference sources, space, and equipment where most members of the group must share these resources in carrying out their work. If the resource structure included multiple sets of records and duplicate sets of equipment, less sharing among members would be necessary. Where a high level of sharing is necessary, more intragroup interaction will take place and, as a consequence, a more extensively developed interpersonal structure will evolve.

Interpersonal Structure → Resource Structure

Some group members tend to hoard group-relevant information. Others are very possessive about equipment with which they normally work. In an office work group, the nature of the interpersonal structure will determine, in part, which members have easy and quick access to such resources. The close friends of the hoarders and possessors will usually have easy access to relevant information and equipment, whereas other group members will not. To the extent that certain members do not have ready access to what are nominally group resources, those resources have in fact been reduced. That which is not available cannot serve as a resource.

Normative Structure → Interpersonal Structure

For a group, any set of norms that significantly controls the frequency, content, and mode of interaction among members will shape the nature of the IPS. Norms that encourage or specify open and completely free interaction among all members will produce an IPS quite different from one resulting from role requirements that call for channeled and segmented communication. Official norms for many military groups are formulated specifically to limit interaction between officers and enlisted men, so that close friendships will not develop.[42]

---

[42] For more detailed analyses of relationships within military groups and how they vary under conditions of combat and Cold War, see Morris Janowitz, *Sociology and the Military Establishment* (New York: Russell Sage Foundation, 1959), pp. 64–72; and Rodger W. Little, "Buddy Relations and Combat Performance," in *The New Military*, Morris Janowitz, ed. (New York: Russell Sage Foundation, 1964), pp. 195–219.

Interpersonal Structure → Normative Structure

Earlier, we discussed the concept of balance in interpersonal relations. It was suggested there that the network of interpersonal relations —i.e., the IPS—of any group, could be viewed as a point on a continuum representing the extent to which the structure was balanced.

Consider the case of a teaching department in a university. Here, by common agreement, group norms are developed or discarded through a process of discussion in faculty meetings. Upon examination, we conclude that the IPS of this group can best be represented by a point near the highly balanced end of the continuum. At a later point in time we note a significant change in the IPS. There is now clearly less mutual trust, liking, and respect. The IPS is less balanced than before. We also notice a distinct change in the norm-making propensities of the group. The group now is bent on developing more and more norms. Issues concerning member behavior, which were seldom discussed before, now are the focus of lengthy discussion and norm making. It is tentatively concluded that a change in the balance level of the IPS produces a change in the *pervasiveness* of the normative structure.

Summary

Organizational groups exist within a larger social system or systems that provide both opportunities and constraints for group activity and interaction. These constraints and opportunities will vary, of course, from one organizational setting to the next. In this chapter we have tried to treat group internal dynamics per se.

A group may be viewed as a small social system where the interdependent units of social interaction are seen as the basic elements of the system. The observable, repetitive patterns of interaction make up the performance structure of the group. When we want to understand the stability and change that occur in the performance structure of a group, we utilize three interrelated concepts: normative structure, interpersonal structure, and resource structure. Each explanatory structure provides a partial explanation. We noted also how the explanatory structures are interrelated in that a change in one of them will produce change in the others as well.

The chapter, then, offers a general conceptual framework for understanding organizational groups, a view that stresses dynamic rather than static considerations of group life. In the next chapter we will discuss the organizational context in which these groups operate.

Chapter 5

INTERNAL DYNAMICS
OF ORGANIZATIONS

Let us suppose for a moment that we know practically nothing about what an organization is and its specific internal operations. Further, let us suppose that for the moment we have no interest in any exchange or interaction that might be taking place between the organization and any outside social units. When we look within an organization, *what do we see, what is actually going on?* We suggest this perspective because all of us have notions about what should be going on in any organization. Thus, often what we think we see is colored too much by our prescriptive view of organizational life. For the moment, let us try to put our prescriptive view aside and try just to look at a hypothetical organization.

The Continual Struggle for ASP

Making only a minimal number of inferences, we would probably say that we see:

1. Identifiable subsystems or groups. The activities of each distinguish it from all of the other groups. Each group is doing its own thing!
2. Interaction among the groups.
   a. movement of physical objects.
   b. movement of messages, which include requests, reports, and instructions.
3. Variations among the groups as to size, types of physical surroundings, and equipment.

4. A few groups specialize in the preparation of directives for the day-to-day activities of other groups.
5. At varying intervals, almost all groups prepare reports on their activities and submit these reports to other groups.
6. A very few groups make financial, personnel, space, and equipment decisions for all of the other groups.
7. Over extended periods of time some groups are dissolved, some new ones formed, some grow in size and sphere of activities, whereas others decline.

What shall we make of these observations? What is the real core or nub of what is going on?

From a structural perspective, we would say that there is a division of labor among the groups and a ranking or hierarchical arrangement. From a process perspective, we would note that communication, coordination, and decision making and various other processes are in operation. But what is the driving force that is in operation, what is it all about? We suggest that underlying the structural arrangements and processes of organizational life is a *continuing struggle by each group for autonomy, security, and prestige.*

Within any organization we find functional interdependence among the groups. The activities of each group are *directly* dependent on the activities of some of the other groups and *indirectly* dependent on most, if not all, of the remaining groups. The *autonomy* of a group, therefore, is limited by the fact of dependence. Furthermore, recognition of this interdependence throughout the organization usually means that some mechanism has been established to try to assure optimal coordination among the interdependent activities. Those responsible for insuring proper coordination may or may not be overzealous in their efforts, but such efforts will almost certainly place limitations on the potential for autonomy of any group whose efforts are being coordinated.

The *security* or survival potential of a group is threatened by scarce resources and by notions of the functional significance of its activities. If the resources allocated to a group within an organization are cut repeatedly over time, it is often a sign that the group is being phased out of existence. Where the opposite resource trend is in evidence, the group's security is enhanced. Notions about the importance of a group's activity to the success of the organization as a whole often are critical for resource allocation. When an organization is contracting rather than expanding, those groups involved in the least essential activities are the first to be dismantled. And knowing this, we can expect participants to make efforts to manipulate the normative expectations that others hold about the importance of their activity for the security of the organization as a whole.

The *prestige* rank of any specific group is directly dependent on the ranks of the other groups within the organization. No group aspires to a lower rank, all aspire to higher ranks. Higher, rather than lower, group prestige rank is a situation desired by most members of a group. Higher rank means that in day-to-day interaction, group members will be treated with more deference and respect. They will receive fewer demeaning and derogatory comments. Furthermore, high rank is normally documented by desirable perquisites of office: pleasanter working conditions; more convenient equipment and facilities (e.g., a carpet on the floor in private offices); and more flexible work schedules. The concern for group prestige enhancement may be called a silly game, but there is good reason to recognize it as a major driving force shaping intergroup interaction.

In this chapter we want to provide an inside look at the dynamics of organizational life. We will attempt to do this by focusing on the continuing struggle by each group for autonomy, security, and prestige. While describing the struggle we will try to highlight some of the basic social processes that are in operation in all organizations. We hope thereby to explicate the nature of organizational life as it really exists on a day-to-day basis rather than simply describing how an organization would function if it were an ideally rational system.

Strain, stress, conflict, and normative expectations that are continually in a process of renegotiation are central to the basic imagery of this view. In part, then, organizations are the patterned interaction networks that emerge from the bargaining struggles among groups within. But clearly these struggles among groups cannot be comprehended through simplistic analyses of individual political orientations or attitudes. These processes are not a product of liberal, change-oriented participants, battling against conservatives. Rather, vacillating with the issues, participants in each group emerge as liberal or conservative, depending upon the implications of the issue for the autonomy, security, and prestige of their group.

Drawing upon his descriptive analyses of a large Parisian administrative organization and a French government production organization, Crozier proposed a theoretical perspective with similar imagery.

> Directors and assistant directors, socially conservative, fight with great passion for technical change and modernization. At the same time, technical engineers, who would like to transform the present social order, are very conservative about technical matters; they do whatever they can to keep their skill a rule-of-thumb one and to prevent efforts to rationalize it. This is the reason that they like to act as trouble-shooters, even if it means always running to patch things up, and that they oppose any kind of progress which could free them from certain of their difficulties. Their only solution has always been to ask for an assistant, and they are quite ready to remain overworked if this demand cannot be met.

What is the common thread among these diverse strategies? *Each group fights to preserve and enlarge the area upon which it has some discretion, attempts to limit its dependence upon other groups and to accept such dependence only insofar as it is a safeguard against another and more feared one, but finally prefers retreatism if there is no other choice but submission. The groups' freedom of action and the power structure appear clearly to be at the core of all these strategies.*[1] (Emphasis added.)

Dimensions of Group Domain

James Thompson presents a cogent argument for the usefulness of the notion of organizational domain.[2] In noting the exchange that occurs between an organization and elements of its environment, he points out that exchange agreements rest upon prior consensus regarding domain. The domain of an organization consists of a set of specifications and understandings both for members of the organization and for others with whom they interact, about what the organization will and will not do. "It provides, although imperfectly, an image of an organization's role in a larger system, which in turn serves as a guide for the ordering of action in certain directions and not in others." [3]

The concept of domain would seem to apply equally well to any group within an organization. It is composed of the generally recognized normative specifications regarding the range and types of activities and interaction that should be performed by an established group. Thus for any group within an organization, the domain-relevant question is: Given the character of the parent organization, what is it appropriate for the group to *do*—what *must* be done, what *may* be done, what should *not* be done?

Often the major features of the domain of a group are so taken for granted that discussion is relatively unnecessary. But if a procurement group attempts to arrange for the sale of the organization's product or a sales group tries to dictate the production schedule, these deviations from the relevant domain specifications will be met with negative sanctions. Each group, it is insisted, should stick to its own business!

Thus, it is easy to recognize that group domain deals with normative ideas about appropriate tasks for each group. Are there other dimensions of group domain that are also specified? Let us consider the possibility that the dimensions of group domain are, in fact, analogous

[1] Michel Crozier, *The Bureaucratic Phenomenon* (Chicago: University of Chicago Press, 1964), p. 156.

[2] James D. Thompson, *Organizations in Action* (New York: McGraw-Hill Book Co., 1967).

[3] Ibid., p. 29.

FIGURE 5–1   Dimensions of Role and Domain

Dimensions of Role	*Dimensions of Group Domain*

Task:
   Example: The foreman should assign work tasks to workers at the beginning of each day.
	Task:
	   Example: The production group should give the order for materials to the procurement group the third week of each month.

Authority:
   Example: When the physician prescribes medications for a hospitalized patient, the nurse should see to it that the medications are given to the patient on schedule.
	Authority:
	   Example: When there is a vacancy at a nonexecutive level, the personnel department should evaluate the qualifications of candidates and arrange for the three best candidates to be interviewed by the employing group. One of the three candidates *must* be accepted by the employing group.

Prestige (Deference):
   Example: In most situations, the lower-level worker should use an appropriate title in initiating a conversation with the head of the oganization.
	Prestige (Deference):
	   Example: When the janitorial staff of a university wants professors to enforce more systematically the no smoking rule in classrooms, that desire should be expressed as a request not a demand.

Affect:
   Example: An elementary school teacher who doesn't really care about the personal problems of her students is in the wrong occupation.
	Affect:
	   Example: In written reports when one group is commenting on the cooperativeness of another group, guarded expressions of annoyance are acceptable but blunt expressions of hostility are not acceptable.

Sanctioning:
   Example: A supervisor who persistently fails to enforce important rules should be warned once and then demoted, transferred, or fired.
	Sanctioning:
	   Example: If a group has adequate resources and still doesn't get the job done, the activity in question should be transferred to a group that will perform appropriately.

to the dimensions of role as discussed in Chapter 4. Figure 5–1 outlines the parallels to be considered.

When the dimensions of role are applied to the concept of group domain, the labels do seem to make sense. This should not be too surprising. Just as there are norms for individual activity and interaction, so too are there norms that specify how groups should act. Under normal conditions a family group should not behave as if it were a military squad.

In one sense, of course, a group does not act; only persons act. From a social system perspective, however, persons do act *for* and *in* the name of a group and, therefore, the conception of group action need not entail reification. Furthermore, the patterned interaction that can be observed does vary from one group to another. To describe these differences requires labels, and our ordinary language usage reflects this requirement. We do, in fact, have rather well-developed ideas about what different groups should do, about what action should be performed by various groups.

The task dimension of group domain is readily understood. And a glance at the table of organization for most organizations suggests that some groups have the responsibility and authority to direct the activities of other, lower groups. Likewise, groups within an organization do vary in subjective prestige rank, and that perceived ranking is usually reflected in the interaction among them. In an egalitarian society the expressions of deference may be subtle, but they are not absent. The affect dimension may seem problematic. However, as Marwell and Hage point out, "In the midst of business; man constructs intimate, *gemeinshaft*-types of relationships with his co-workers." [4] Affective orientation within an organizational setting may tend toward affective neutrality, but there is variation, and some of that variation may be caused by normative notions about how well certain groups *should* be liked. Participants in production groups often express hostility toward the time and motion study group. It would be surprising if these production people did not really believe that the hostility was deserved and, therefore, appropriate. Some groups ought to be disliked, it is thought.

The right of one group to sanction others is not equally distributed throughout an organization. Groups on the same level seldom have a normatively based right or obligation to sanction each other. The finance office should, and frequently does, sanction negatively groups that fail to stay within the budget. Groups that show outstanding performance should be sanctioned positively by the news and information staff through favorable mention in appropriate publications. Such sanctioning is part of the domain of the news staff.

A wide variety of normative ideas then, associated with groups or subsystems within organizations, comprise the domain of each. These normative ideas, or group domains, serve to constrain, channel, and shape the direction and flow of struggles among groups. Although increased autonomy and security are desired, notions included within the domain of each group specify the limits wherein actions are at the group's discretion. Of course, some groups gain wider ranges of action

[4] Gerald Marwell and Jerald Hage, "The Organization of Role-Relationships: A Systematic Description," *American Sociological Review*, 35: 898 (October 1970).

than others. And this may enable the organizational collectivity to make a somewhat more coordinated assault on the environment. As Crozier puts it: "No organization can function, indeed, without imposing some check on the bargaining power of its own members. Thus certain individuals must be given enough freedom of action to be able to adjust conflicting claims and to impose decisions about general development—in other words, to improve the game they are playing against their environment." [5]

Thus, we have suggested that group domain is an important factor in the dynamics of organizational life. These normatively based ideas are spread across a range of dimensions, which parallel those used to conceptualize role relationships. Clearly, the established domain of a group has implications for the autonomy, security, and prestige of that group. It is to a group's advantage, therefore, to have a domain that at least permits the development of desired levels of autonomy, security, and prestige.

In Chapter 4, we noted that within any group there are a number of recognized roles that are generally accepted as relevant for intragroup interaction and activity. But we also saw that member consensus on the general features of those roles does not necessarily mean that there is complete consensus on the details of the role specifications. Where role consensus is perceived to be lacking, members directly involved as role participants, and perhaps other group members as well, will often be involved in attempts at manipulation of the divergent role definitions of others. Thus, if you are the head of a department in a university and you believe that a department head should have the final say in decisions to promote faculty members within a department, and if you suspect that some of the faculty in your department do not share that view of the professor–department head role, you will probably devise a variety of approaches, arguments, and explanations to get them to adopt your perspective on the role definition.

The same tendency toward manipulation seems to apply where there is low consensus among several groups regarding the characteristics of the domain of a focal group. When members of a group feel that the group is not being granted as much prestige as is appropriate, there will be attempts to change the views held by key persons in other groups. Efforts will be made to show that "our group is just as productive as the best of them" and that "what we do requires much skill and concentrated effort." Thus, group domains, like sets of norms that comprise roles and positions, are rarely characterized by total consensus and are frequently subjected to renegotiation.

Another important parallel to role relationships is the characteristic of specificity. The norms that comprise group domains vary

[5] Crozier, op. cit., p. 163.

greatly in level of specificity. Ranges of tolerable action that are permitted for group members are quite narrow and specifically defined in some instances and very broad in others. For example, payroll forms ought to reach the payroll office before a specified date. Other groups must act in accordance with that norm or live with the sanctions. In contrast to such norms with high specificity, participants in many organizations may dress pretty much as they please. Of course, in some organizations even the manner of dress or other aspects of personal attire may be subject to high specificity for members of certain groups.

Similarly, norms comprising group domains may be written or unwritten. Clearly, organizations vary greatly in the degree to which norms are written or formalized. We need empirical research directed at the *processes* whereby norms that comprise group domains become formalized. But it would appear that formalization often reflects past areas of conflict and dissensus. Where the issue involves group activities that were highly interdependent with other groups, such conflicts might stimulate negotiation efforts. And the results of the negotiation are written down—i.e., formalized, so as to clear the air and to avoid such situations in the future.

However, interdependence need not always be present. Clearly, some norms reflecting the prestige dimension of domain can appear as rather bizarre departures from classical notions of rationality. For example, think of military dress codes. These, like those in some public schools, may be formalized to demarcate various social positions. And teacher–student conflict regarding the limits of acceptable dress may precipitate increased formalization of norms so that the ranges of tolerable behavior become specified for all parties, including parents. Of course, as in the instance of hair length for male students or employees, organizational officials may find that the products of their internal negotiation efforts are overruled by a higher authority located in the environment, e.g., a school board or court. Thus, in negotiations dealing with many aspects of group domains, environmental sectors weigh heavily, both directly and indirectly. "We'd like to change our payroll procedures to meet the programming of your graduate students, but the IRS [or some other outside monitoring agency] wouldn't approve it." Real, imagined, or fabricated? Certainly, limited access to information and outside groups can be a most powerful resource in such bargaining negotiations.

It should be clear that group domain is a central concept with which we can begin to gain some understanding of many aspects of organizational life. If the domain of each internal group was fixed, or perceived to be beyond the possibility of alteration, organizational life would be rather quiescent, but that is seldom the case. And the environment of the organization, as we shall see later, is a major stimulus of internal organizational change. The normal processes of personnel turnover tend to contribute to internal fluidity also. Often, executives who have been promoted within the organization, and especially executives new to the organization, want to demonstrate their competence, and a frequent tactic is to try to change things. Such attempted changes threaten some groups while appearing to be advantageous to other groups. For these and other reasons the domain of any group is seldom clearly established and generally understood over long periods of time. Group domains in organizations are almost always being buffeted in some manner. Group autonomy, security, and prestige, therefore, are seldom taken for granted for long.

On Being Born and Becoming

Many writers in the field of complex organizations define an organization as a social system that is *established* to achieve certain specific goals or objectives.[6] It is designed as a rational tool to accomplish what the originators have in mind. Just as a space vehicle may be designed and built to carry men to the moon and back, so also every organization that is born is designed to accomplish objectives at least some of which have been specified in advance of its birth.

We believe that this perspective is somewhat simplistic and certainly incomplete. It is incomplete at least in the sense that the objectives for the organization that the founders have in mind are often anything but highly specific. They are seldom as specific as "taking men to the moon and back." Furthermore, as with the founding of a university or a city government, there are often *multiple* objectives in view. Although we cannot cite data that would document what is the typical case when an organization is formed, our hunch is that in many, if not most, cases the founders have multiple, relatively nonspecific objectives for the organization. If that is an accurate assessment of what transpires before an organization's birth date, the design of the organization flows from the application of several criteria, only some of which are a direct function of conceived objectives for the organization.

[6] For example: "Organizations are social units (or human groupings) deliberately constructed and reconstructed to seek specific goals." Amitai Etzioni, *Modern Organizations* (Englewood Cliffs, N.J.: Prentice-Hall, Inc., 1964), p. 3.

Hall backs away somewhat, but retains goal as a central concept. "An organization is a collectivity with relatively indentifiable boundary, a normative order, authority ranks, communications systems, and membership coordinating systems; this collectively exists on a relatively continuous basis in an environment and engages in activities that are usually related to a goal or a set of goals." Richard H. Hall, *Organizations: Structure and Process* (Englewood Cliffs, N.J.: Prentice-Hall, Inc., 1972), p. 9.

In contrast to those who emphasize goal consensus as the critical aspect of organizational birth, Weick poses a provocative counterposition in which the processes of organizing are viewed as much more complex than is usually acknowledged. The whole process is much looser and more erratic than would be suspected, given the imagery or theoretical perspectives where the concept of goal is emphasized.

The common assertion that people organize in order to accomplish some agreed-upon end is not essential to an explanation of the orderliness found in concerted action, nor is goal-governed behavior that evident in organizations. Goals are sufficiently diverse, the future is sufficiently uncertain, and the actions on which goal statements could center are sufficiently unclear, that goal statements exert little control over action. Visible features such as profit, wages, productivity, and share of the market can be treated as the reasons for an organization's existence, but this begs such questions as why these particular goals were formulated, how widely they are diffused, and with what intensity they are held. The view common to most organization theories attributes to goals more stability than they seemingly have. It is probable that goals are tied more closely to actual activities than has been realized, and that they are better understood as summaries of *previous* actions. Much of the organization's work does not seem to be directed toward goal attainment. Instead, it can be understood more readily as actions with a primitive orderliness, this orderliness being enhanced retrospectively when members review what has come to pass as a result of the actions.[7]

Less skeptical than Weick, Blau and Meyer also express sharp reservations with a highly rationalistic, goal-oriented view of organizational development.

While it is true that all formal organizations have objectives, many such goals are stated only in general and imprecise ways, and their relevance for day-to-day activities is not always clear. Public bureaucracies in particular are characterized by uncertain and sometimes conflicting goals. . . .

When organizational objectives are uncertain, there is a tendency to determine goals and activities according to the resources available. As a high government official has remarked, goals were once determined by *"starting with a budget and sending it off in search of a program."* [5] Funds were allocated for personnel costs, materials, overhead supplies, and the like; no attempt was made to link expenditures with objectives.[8] (Emphasis added.)

[7] Karl E. Weick, *The Social Psychology of Organizing* (Reading, Mass.: Addison-Wesley Publishing Co., Inc., 1969), p. 37.

[8] Peter M. Blau and Marshall W. Meyer, *Bureaucracy in Modern Society*, 2nd ed. (New York: Random House, 1971), p. 123.

Footnote 5 in the quotation is David Novick, "The Department of Defense," in *Program Budgeting*, D. Novick, ed. (Cambridge, Mass.: Harvard University Press, 1965), p. 97.

What, then, are some of the criteria used in the initial planning of an organization? During this conception and gestation period, the focus is on the design of the official normative structure and the resource structure. With respect to each of these structures the planners lay out what they think is required to produce and distribute the organizational product or service (output) and what they think is required to secure on a regular basis the necessary inputs to the organization. Here efficiency and effectiveness are presumably taken into account. But it is well to remember that there are numerous variations in the blueprints that *could* be designed to satisfy these two general requirements. There are any number of ways to skin the cat! It is here that at least two other factors come into play. Frequently, design decisions are based on what is considered to be "appropriate for this kind of organization." Appropriateness in this context means that which is traditional or that which is currently the fashion for the *type* of organization being designed. Where it is not at all clear which is the best of many roads that lead to Rome, there is a strong tendency to use the most heavily traveled route! Top executives should have private offices and personal secretaries, while middle and lower-level executives may share an office and utilize a secretarial pool. Why? Because it is appropriate to have that type of arrangement!

A second much used criterion is "perceived convenience." There are physical and social considerations that make some proposed structural arrangements seem more convenient than others. The designers do not know in any definitive sense which of several alternatives being considered will in fact be the most convenient, but they are almost certain to have views on the matter of relative convenience and will utilize those views on numerous occasions.

Whereas necessity may be the mother of invention, it is clear that the designers' objective for the organization is not its sole father. And now we come to what every founder of an organization knows but may hate to admit: designing an organization does not necessarily insure that it will become what the designers had in mind at the time. *Once the social system is set in operation, an increasing proportion of the evolving official normative structure and resource structure develops in response to the jockeying among the organizational groups for autonomy, security, and prestige.* When this "rational tool" begins to function, the unofficial normative structure and the IPS slowly emerge at all levels and within all groups. These emergent structures shape the performance structure in ways not envisioned by the organization's founders. One year after organizational birth, the baby has developed features that were not included in the conception blueprint. In the ensuing struggle for autonomy, security, and prestige, norms are altered and resources redistributed to reflect more nearly the emerging power relations among the organizational groups.

View from the Top

Seldom, if ever, does the head of an organization operate in isolation away from the claims, suggestions, and pressures emanating from the various groups and coalitions throughout the organization. As with some United States Presidents who have taken the position that the buck stops here, some organizational heads may have a sense that they thoroughly direct the affairs of the organization and that what is accomplished is a direct reflection of the carefully considered decisions of the head. Without suggesting that the head of an organization is "just another participant" in the system, it should be remembered that such a person is, after all, a member of several top management groups. He is subject, therefore, to most of the normative, interpersonal, and resource constraints that participation in any group brings. In many organizations the head can, if he is willing to live with the consequences, alter the size of "his" group, vary the frequency of group meetings, and control to a very substantial degree the mode and content of interaction within the group. But even here his viable options are usually quite limited if he wants loyalty and productive responses from his immediate subordinates. Thus, over a period of time it is typical for the head to see the organization as a whole through the perspective of "his group." Group members report on the activities, plans, recommendations, and requests of other organizational groups.

The characteristics of the communication process of the organization as a whole influence the view that top level personnel have of the organization. Participants in this top management group also soon learn how much detail to omit (filtering and screening of information) in making reports to the group, which of the other organizational groups are fair game for critical comment, and how to make the strongest possible case for requests for resources that come from competing groups.

The first thing to remember, then, about the view from the top is that the view, whatever its specific character, is shaped by the same basic intra- and inter-group processes that shape such views in other parts of the organization. It is, after all, an ongoing component of a larger system. And if the search for maximum autonomy, security, and prestige is the major driving force for other groups in the system, it is certainly not going to be absent in a top management group.

It is tempting for the organizational analyst as well as organizational members to conclude that because the amount of discretion permitted a member usually increases as level in the organization increases, therefore persons and groups near the top of the hierarchy must have almost complete autonomy so long as what they do is in "best interests" of the organization. It may well be that if we could develop and apply meaningful, rigorous measures of group autonomy we might find that such autonomy is greater near the top. But even if that were the case, we would still have to consider the difference between the autonomy that each group has and the amount of autonomy that its members believe that it ought to have. There is always the matter of relative deprivation.

To overstate the point slightly, one of the most persistent concerns of a top management group deals with setting precedents. Time and again, a particular solution to a problem under consideration is rejected, even though it is agreed that from almost every point of view it is the *best* currently available solution. Why then is it rejected? Because adopting this solution *now* will set a precedent that will come back to haunt them many times in the future! But why the concern with precedent? Simply because setting a precedent involves explicit or implicit commitments regarding future decisions. It thereby reduces the options for action that would otherwise be available in the future. In short, it reduces the group's autonomy. Autonomy for a group means the freedom to do what it wants now and at all foreseeable points in the future; it means operating without constraints. Obviously, group autonomy, as that of an individual, is never total; but there is marked variation in a relative sense—from high to low. Although top level groups may have to live with fewer constraints that are imposed *directly* on them by other organizational groups, they are destined by the very nature of their function to have to operate within a set of constraints that are indirect and often self-imposed.

If all of top managements' decisions could be kept secret, the problem of autonomy maintenance would be greatly reduced. Members of the group might ask, "In what we are deciding here today, are we being consistent with our past decisions?" but that self-imposed constraint would be minor. The real threat to autonomy for the top level group comes from the fact that much of what is decided must be made known if the decisions are to be implemented at all. Add to that the pattern whereby groups contributing reports and recommendations, which are used in the management decision process, have a claim to knowing what was decided. And finally, throughout the organization part of the search for group security takes the form of trying in various ingenious ways to look over the shoulders of top management. Each group in the organization has one or more links that, it is hoped, will provide information on what top management has decided or is about to decide. Top level groups learn, therefore, that it is almost impossible to keep knowledge of decisions from spreading throughout the organization. This means that in a very literal sense many, if not most, decisions are made in full view of a sizable organizational audience. Such an audience is not likely to forget decisions that have implications for group security and prestige. Top management will not, therefore, be allowed to conveniently ignore past decisions.

It seems, then, that the more decisions that the top group makes and the more explicit the reasoning for each decision, the greater the threat to its autonomy. Thus, there is a strong tendency to protect the future autonomy of the group by avoiding or postponing decisions when possible, by playing down the significance of certain decisions ("This is really nothing very new"), by attempting to minimize the publicity given to certain decisions, and by substituting plausible reasons for the real ones behind some decisions when they are being explained.

Obviously, not all decisions once made are equally significant for group autonomy. Some decisions may even serve positively to buttress future autonomy; e.g., adopting a policy that bases promotion to top positions in the organization "strictly on individual merit" rather than on some combination of seniority and merit. As we have shown, making decisions has within it the potential for reduction of group autonomy, and all groups, certainly a top management group, will maneuver in a variety of ways to minimize that threat.

Perhaps one of the most troublesome aspects of group domain for top management is contained in the *control process*. For most organizations the threat or the use of physical coercion as a basis for control is out of the question. There is general consensus that it may not be used. Even in most prisons the threat of solitary confinement must be used sparingly, if for no other reason than that the physical facilities for the implementation of the coercive threat are always limited.[9] Thus, even in those few organizations where the societal norms permit the use of physical coercion, the application is limited in type and scope. It is rare that coercion and coercive threat are used on a day-to-day basis except on lower participants in the organization.[10]

Authority, by far the most common basis of top management control, rests on consensus, just as do other aspects of group domain.[11] Generally speaking, commands and requests for action will be followed, so long as they are deemed to be within the range of that which is considered to be legitimate. Borderline cases may or may not bring compliance, depending on a variety of other considerations. It is probably a safe guess that most top management groups would prefer to have the authority dimension of domain enlarged. Any experienced administrator has learned that the views held by subordinate group members on the authority relation is a hard rock of reality with which

[9] Gresham M. Sykes, "The Corruption of Authority and Rehabilitation," *Social Forces*, 34: 257–62 (March 1956).

[10] Amitai Etzioni, *A Comparative Analysis of Complex Organizations* (New York: The Free Press, 1961).

[11] In general, a superordinate who is granted a generalized right to enforce certain necessary but "annoying" rules may obtain more control over subordinate groups by occasionally *not* enforcing such rules. This strategy of "strategic leniency" is discussed in Blau and Meyer, op. cit., pp. 62–65.

he must live. It is not only the heads of many religious congregations and college deans who have to live with the lack of domain consensus on authority matters; even military executives have to consider whether an order will be considered legitimate, as when they are considering the use of force to overthrow the government in power of a nation.

There are two approaches frequently used by the head of a superordinate group to handle domain-based limitations in the control process. In cases where he believes that an order or a new program that he wishes to initiate may be resisted by subordinate groups because they view it as borderline or nonlegitimate, he may attempt to persuade them that this case is in fact a legitimate application of the authority specifications of the intergroup relation. This attempt at persuasion may be expressed by explaining the *need* for the proposed action ("this is necessary in order for our company to remain competitive"), the *reasonableness* of the request ("this is a standard approach under these circumstances"), the *benefits* that will accrue to the subordinate groups by complying, or by pointing to other justifications. This may be called the ad hoc approach to persuasion in regard to a specific issue.

A second approach may be called "persuasion for long-term domain enlargement." Here a variety of tactics may be used. One common technique is repeatedly to weave into various written materials statements that stress the breadth of responsibility delegated to the focal group ("this office has been charged with the responsibility to lead and supervise all plans and programs to meet objectives X, Y, and Z"). Again, the necessity of always working together may be stressed ("only as we work together as an integrated team can we master the challenges that face us all"). There is also the appeal to pride in accomplishment ("the subordinate group" has always carried out its responsibilities with excellence, and we know that they will do so in the future regardless of the task given them"). And there is the reiteration of the "times are changing and we must all be flexible" approach.

So persuasion is a necessary component in the control process even when dealing with subordinate groups. The more divergent the views on the authority dimension of group domain, the more frequent will be the attempts at persuasion.

View from the Line

Usually, every group down the line is required to submit reports upward. Such reports are required periodically, usually on a set time schedule, although there may be special reports also. These reports represent both a threat and an opportunity for the group. Any report may include a description of what the group has been doing, and it may also indicate what the group plans to do. Such information is normally reviewed by officials at the levels immediately above the reporting group, often summarized and integrated with information coming from other groups and sent up the line. The summarizing and integrating may be repeated several times before the resulting document reaches the top.

Even if the initial report, upon being submitted to the first higher level group, is complete and objective in the description of past activities and plans for the future, there is no assurance that those characteristics of the report will be maintained as it moves up to the top. Thus, both the autonomy and security of the group may be threatened as a result of this upward communication process. The process does not permit the group to present its own case to top management. Instead its case may be distorted by omission or emphasis, and the result may be additional infringement by management on the rights of the group to continue to do what the group's members consider most desirable. As a consequence of this perceived threat to the group's autonomy and security, reports are often more of a public relations document than a factual account.

But the reporting process also provides an opportunity for the enhancement of autonomy, security, and prestige. If the message that goes up the line and arrives at the top says in effect, "we are doing good work now, but we could contribute even more to the organization if the constraints placed on our operations were relaxed," there is the possibility that the constraints may in fact be reduced and the autonomy of the group thereby enhanced. If a message that gets through to the top includes convincing arguments that "only members of *our* group are really qualified to perform this function," top management may in fact decide in the group's favor, and the security of the group is buttressed as a consequence.

The relative prestige rank of any organizational group is based on and associated with several different dimensions. Some of these dimensions are relatively independent of group autonomy and security. The general prestige rank of the group members accorded by society, the economic and related rewards received by individual members, and the esoteric nature of their work, all contribute to group prestige rank.[12] But group autonomy and security also have an effect on group prestige. There appears to be an interactive effect among autonomy, security, and prestige. The greater the level of autonomy and security of a group, the more relative prestige it is accorded by its competitors; and the higher the prestige rank, the easier it is to maintain or gain security and autonomy.

[12] Kingsley Davis and Wilbert Moore, "Some Principles of Stratification," *American Sociological Review*, **10**: 242–49 (April 1945).

The reporting process, therefore, provides both a direct and indirect approach to prestige enhancement. If the reports that get through (i.e., messages received *and* believed) indicate clearly that the group has been unusually productive while giving excellent cooperation to other groups in the organization, the prestige of the group will be maintained or enhanced as a direct function of the communication process. Of course, if that message does not get through, the direct effect may be prestige degradation. The indirect effect comes through the consequences via the reporting process for group autonomy and security. To the extent that such reporting succeeds in maintaining and/or enhancing autonomy and security, it does the same, indirectly, for prestige.

A prime example of the relation between autonomy and security on the one hand, and prestige on the other, is the United States Supreme Court in comparison to the United States Senate. The Court as a body has almost complete autonomy and security, and along with that it has the ultimate in group prestige rank. The Senate in some respects is more powerful than the Court, but it has less autonomy in that it must on frequent occasion bargain with the House of Representatives if legislation is to be enacted. One apparent consequence of that need to bargain is the lower prestige rank of the Senate.

An important arena in the continuing struggle for group autonomy, security, and prestige is the reporting process. The view from the line is a perspective that centers on the reporting "game." That game has as much salience for the organizational group on the line as does the dating game for the marriage-oriented male or female!

Perhaps one of the most basic ideas that comes to mind when thinking of organizations is the concept of coordination. If there is to be a division of labor among a series of groups or departments, it is generally argued, there must be coordination among the various activities. Because coordination must be so central, there need to be several focal units in the organization where the responsibility for coordinating rests. Whether we are concerned with coordination by standardization, by plan, or by mutual adjustment,[13] some group or groups other than those whose activities are being coordinated will be expected to initiate and to conduct surveillance on coordination procedures and their consequnces.

For any group, coordination means working within constraints—time constraints, quantitative constraints with respect to input and output, and type of activity constraints. To the extent that these constraints are self-initiated—i.e., intragroup—or are a reflection of the group's preferences for intergroup interaction, they will not be a threat to the autonomy of the group. Indeed, in such a case these normative requirements for coordination may serve as a handy buffer against

---

[13] Thompson, op. cit., pp. 55–65.

demands from other groups to use alternative procedures for handling interdependence problems. They are a guaranteed rationale for rejecting the special requests that inevitably come from other organizational groups.

However, as with other kinds of rules or normatively based plans, coordination norms may serve as a shield on some occasions and as a straitjacket on other occasions. It is a fair guess that for most groups, most of the time the straitjacket analogy is the more accurate one.

Thompson's discussion of the relation between type of interdependence and kind of coordination is a most useful one.[14] Although he does not treat directly the issues of autonomy and coordination, our consideration of the impact of coordination efforts on group autonomy suggests that for groups where the prime orientation is coordination by standardization, the coordinators will be viewed as more of a threat than in the case of attempts at coordination by plan or by mutual adjustment. Standardization involves more rules and more detailed specifications for action and, therefore, permits less room for the group to maneuver in behalf of its autonomy. From a management point of view, coordination by standardization may seem to be the most desirable approach. But when used, it is certain to foment some hostility that will be directed toward the group or groups responsible for coordination enforcement. Enforcing numerous specific rules is a direct challenge to the drive for group autonomy, and the challenge will be met in a variety of subtle and on occasion even open ways. When viewed from the top, the group's action will be seen as recalcitrance. The view from the line, however, is quite different. The response is justified as being necessary to "get the job done" and to "keep peace with the guys that we have to work with every day." Members of line groups will readily agree that some coordination arrangements are necessary and even desirable, but, as in the television commercial, their attitude is, "Please, Mother, I'd rather do it myself!"

Coordination by mutual adjustment is less threatening to a group. There is less interference by a third party (the group responsible for insuring coordination). Those constraints that seem unsatisfactory to one or more of the line groups involved can be negotiated directly as part of the on-going exchange relationship.

Coalitions, Constituencies, and Natural Enemies

"Some form of social organization emerges implicitly in collectivities as a result of the processes of exchange and competition, in which the

[14] Ibid.

patterns of conduct of individuals and groups and the relations between them become adjusted." [15]

All groups within an organization are interdependent, but they are not equally dependent on each other. The symbiotic relation is much stronger among certain pairs or sets than among others. This variation in interdependence is reflected in the conflict process in the organization. Typically, in a manufacturing firm, the production department is quite dependent on procurement, and sales is often dependent on production. In such cases where there is a strong one-way dependency relation between two groups, the prevalence of bickering and conflict may be seen. Failure of the sales department to produce the budgeted level of income will be blamed in part on the alleged failure of production to provide the products or services on time or with the stipulated quality. The very nature of the dependency relation seems to make the two groups natural enemies.

Where the dependency relation is weak, neither group being dependent on the other, and balanced rather than one-sided, the groups are more likely to work together as a coalition in the larger competitive struggle within the organization.[16] Such groups tend to define each other as neutrals with respect to day-to-day concerns of mutual interest. Thus, when the big issues come up they are more likely to combine forces than are groups that are natural enemies.

The whole notion of big issues and coalitions may seem strange to a reader who thinks of an organization as a well-planned, highly rationalized system. The "dispute over issues" concept may seem to smack of participative management at its worst. Let us examine briefly how broad policy decisions are actually reached in a complex organizational setting.

Top executives, who are responsible for broad policy matters, could in a hypothetical situation order the relevant data summaries and reports that are needed to consider carefully the various alternatives and the probable consequences flowing from each alternative. But the persons who must prepare such reports are not usually isolated individual specialists. They are participants in one or more established groups within the organization, and each group has its own vested interests to be protected and promoted. Thus, any nonroutine request for information will be viewed as a clear signal that "something is about to happen and we had better find out what it is." The subsequent intense activity in the grapevine may include a lot of noise and relatively little information, but the reports that are prepared are not likely to be neutral

[15] Peter M. Blau, *Exchange and Power in Social Life* (New York: John Wiley and Sons, Inc., 1964), p. 199.
[16] Richard M. Emerson, "Power-Dependence Relations," *American Sociological Review*, 27: 31–40 (February 1962).

documents. They will include implied if not explicit recommendations as well as data summaries. Groups not requested to prepare a special report soon are aware of the fact and are likely to try to influence the content of the reports so that their interests will be protected. Other efforts to influence the major policy decision by means of direct contact with top executives may also take place.

Thus, on major policy issues, some form of participative decision making does occur even when it is not so intended. The only questions are in regard to the *extent* to which it occurs and whether or not such participation is supported by the official normative structure. Although it is rare that a proposed policy is openly submitted to a referendum among all interested groups within an organization, a set of events obliquely akin to that process seems to occur with great frequency. Therefore, the context for possible coalition formation is repeated at intervals. Particular coalitions may form and disappear from time to time, but the process continues to have relevance for every organizational group. This need for allies "the next time around" has a moderating effect on the open expression of hostility toward a group that refuses to join the coalition in the current power play. Thus, an adequate model of organizational decision making must include recognition of the arena of conflicting groups, coalition formation, and even semi-permanent schism between certain groups.

The normative structure of any organization requires each group to perform a minimum number of services for other groups. Such services must be supplied within the context of time schedule and quality requirements. Where the performance of such services goes beyond those minimum requirements, social obligations are created.

Staff units, such as a personnel department, in an organization typically do not have a direct, line authority relation to groups below them in the hierarchy. Nevertheless, they are charged with supplying a service to many such groups. As with an elected public official, such groups have a constituency to look after. When information is wanted from constituent groups, requests rather than commands are the mode of communication. The staff group can increase the responsiveness to such requests by operating in a manner to create social obligations just as the politician uses "past favors rendered" to elicit appropriate voting behavior at election time. One way of creating such social obligations is *occasionally* to provide certain services ahead of schedule. When these favors are duly noted by constituent groups, there is an implied obligation to be cooperative in the future and perhaps to come to the defense of the staff group if its budget or programs come under attack.

Task processes provide the context in which constituent groups may be served, and by providing special services at crucial times a group can create social obligations that in turn provide an added measure of group security.

Everyone Wants to Help: Imperialism Is Not Dead

In most organizations the desirability of growth is seldom questioned. "Grow or die" is a common cliché. That expression may not be an established scientific principle of organizational life, but it certainly is an indication of what is generally considered desirable.

Just as growth for the organization as a whole is considered good, so too is it a persistent theme of group life. There is one difference, however. When executives of an organization express a preference for and openly plan for organizational growth, their colleagues in the enterprise seldom have any concern for what that growth will do to competing organizations. Within a single organization, however, the growth of one group is often accomplished at the expense of other groups. At least, that is the typical perspective taken.[17] To proclaim openly that "our group intends to achieve above average growth in the next few years" is to invite negative responses from other groups in the organization, responses that will reduce the likelihood of that growth taking place. The point of the game, then, is to achieve growth and thereby increased security and prestige but to do so without fanfare, without arousing the suspicion and hostility of competing groups. Of course, growth may bring with it new definitions of group domain and new security and autonomy problems. Generally, however, the larger the group the more clout it has.

Within the organization, growth of a group is best justified verbally by the explanation that it is simply a by-product of the increased contribution that the group is making or will soon make to the organization as a whole. It is akin to the *nouveau riche* explaining that all that wealth came from hard work, frugality, and concerted attention to the more subtle aspects of the business world.

A common approach to group growth is through enlargement of the task element of domain. Finding ways of taking on new tasks or increased responsibility for current task areas is a major avenue to growth. But a group can enlarge its task domain only if other relevant groups accept the revision of domain specifications or if those relevant groups are relatively powerless to do anything about the enlargement effort. Thus, if rumor has it that top management is considering diversification of organizational efforts or quantitative enlargement of some current functions, the most likely response of various intraorganizational groups is an effort to get word to top management that says, in effect, "our group is ready, willing, and able to take on the additional tasks that may be required; indeed, our record of productivity is such that it is only natural to assign the additional responsibility to us."

[17] Harrison White, "Management Conflict and Sociometric Structure," *American Journal of Sociology*, 67: 185–99 (September 1961). See especially p. 187.

This tendency to expand is also evident in another way. Where there are no new tasks up for grabs, the eyes of a growth-oriented group will be on those tasks being performed elsewhere in the organization. Where a task is not being performed well in another group, capture of the right to take over the performance of that task becomes a target. The effort may be slow and not too obvious. But the potential opportunity to expand the task domain is seldom ignored if the task is one that is not too foreign to the capability of the expansionist-oriented group.

To succeed in capturing the right to perform the tasks of other groups requires that, at a minimum, the relevant decision-making bodies be convinced that the expansionist group has the necessary skills and other characteristics relevant to the performance of the desired task(s). The expansionist group, therefore, will find it advantageous to project an image of an enlarged group capability. Thus, when replacements are hired for the group, an effort may be made to hire persons who not only have the skills for the position to be filled but who also have other skills that may be needed in the expansionist process. By planning for the development of additional kinds of competence within the group, it is possible to move to a point later when the group will in fact have the specialists necessary to take on new tasks. The trick then is to anticipate correctly what the new task opportunities will be and to build the appropriate group strengths at the right times. With the special strengths in hand, the job then is to get relevant reference groups to recognize that the special strengths are indeed already in existence.

This is the process of working actively to alter the group domain so that other units will accept the fact that the group is competent to handle tasks that it is not now performing. To the extent that this type of effort succeeds, the likelihood of success in capturing the right to new tasks is increased.

Not every group actively seeks new tasks in such a calculated fashion. But few groups resist the taking on of additional tasks if the necessary resources are promised. We can see that, whereas the approach to new tasks may vary from group to group, there is always the intermingling of *task processes and decision-making processes.*

Task Performance and Visibility

Consider the following propositions. (1) The more visible the performance of a task is to organizational personnel outside the performing group, the greater will be the effort made by the group to insure high-level performance of the task. (2) The higher the level of performance of a task, the greater will be the attempt to make that activity visible to organizational personnel outside the group. (3) For tasks not being performed well, a consistent group effort will be made to reduce the visibility of the task performance.

Because performance of many tasks is not readily observed by non group members, visibility can be selectively controlled.[18] Records may be kept on only those performance indicators that are likely to show the group in the most favorable light. Written reports and oral presentations are likely to include mostly favorable data. Norms on what should be reported do place some limitations on the strategies used in manipulating the data, however. Where the available quantitative data do not reflect favorably on group performance, qualitative summaries are more likely to be used. Where all else fails to support the group performance halo, selected anecdotes will be presented to illustrate what is alleged to be the typical excellent performance.[19] Groups as well as organizations attempt to project a favorable image. Thus, we should expect that each group will try to attain or preserve the right to determine the criteria by which its performance will be evaluated. The presentation of self is not just an individual phenomenon.[20]

We have argued that domain is a central concern in the continuing struggle to enhance group autonomy, survival, and prestige. The activities of a group and the visibility of those tasks contribute substantially to the development and maintenance of a desirable domain. "If we look good, people will believe that we are good," is a common group perspective. We would anticipate, therefore, a tendency among groups to try to make the group strengths more visible and the weak-

---

[18] Warren's research highlights the importance of task visibility. For example, both attitudinal and behavioral conformity appear to be related to various types of power bases in different ways depending upon the degree of task visibility. "Expert power failed to obtain a significant correlation with any type of conformity under high-visibility conditions, just as Coercive and Reward power failed to achieve significant correlations with any type of conformity under *low* visibility. . . . Coercive power is the only power base significantly correlated with behavioral conformity under high-visibility conditions." Donald I. Warren, "Power, Visibility, and Conformity in Formal Organizations," *American Sociological Review*, 33: 968 (December 1968). See also Thompson, op. cit., pp. 90–91.

[19] Thompson proposes several related propositions:

"When organizations find it difficult to score on intrinsic criteria, they seek extrinsic measures of fitness for the future."

"When task-environment elements lack technical ability to assess performance, organizations seek extrinsic measures of fitness for future action."

"When cause/effect knowledge is believed incomplete, organizations seek extrinsic measures of fitness for future action." Thompson, op. cit., pp. 91–92.

[20] Erving Goffman, *The Presentation of Self in Everyday Life* (Garden City, N.Y.: Doubleday Anchor, 1959).

nesses less visible, and thereby to increase the acceptance by other groups of the desired domain definition.

Overload and Growth

An overload now means growth later. At least, that is frequently the perspective. The notion is that if a group takes on more than its fair share of work now, then those allocating organizational resources will have an implied obligation to increase the personnel and other resources allocated to that group in the near future. Additional resources are equated with growth. This is a common working assumption of groups in organizations.

We would anticipate that groups having slack, where demand level is significantly less than capacity, would seek to hide that fact under most conditions. But we would also expect them frequently to seek additional work. Securing a moderate amount of additional work makes it possible for such a group to handle the additional load without being overwhelmed. Also, it puts the group in a position in which to bargain for and justify additional resources. Groups operating at or near capacity may seek or accept additional work less frequently, especially if doing so in the past has not been followed by the hoped-for added resources. But somehow the opportunity to grow by taking on additional assignments seems more often sought than shunned even by groups already performing near capacity.

The overload–growth process can be illustrated by summarizing a report prepared by a research group within a large research agency. The group had taken on an additional, somewhat novel task, which had not been budgeted for in advance. It was an overload, as their normal research activities continued during the same period. At the conclusion of the special task, the report sent to the top administrative group in the organization contained the following points: (1) The staff and funding of this laboratory are inadequate to conduct a program like the one just finished without major sacrifices of our important research goals. (2) The modest success of this special effort has created and will create demands for similar efforts in other parts of the country. (3) Exportation to other parts of the country of the special techniques we have just developed cannot be adequately accomplished without the extensive involvement of our research staff. (4) If the resources and staff of our laboratory were approximately doubled, then we would manage our basic research commitments, a modest training program for interested scientists, and sound exportation tests in other areas, both United States and foreign.[21] *The group received a significant increase in resources and staff.*

[21] Paraphrased from an internal report made available to one of the authors while conducting research on the social implications of planned weather modification.

Coordination and Authority

A plum frequently sought is the right and responsibility to co-ordinate certain selected activities of other groups. Although such coordination efforts pose the risk of generating hostility from the other groups, the potential for increasing group survival and prestige looks more like a plum than a lemon.

The basic premise is that the *obligation to coordinate requires commensurate authority*. If higher-level executives ask why the activities among the relevant groups are not better coordinated, the answer can often be that the group responsible for the coordination has yet to be given the necessary (commensurate) authority. Additional authority vis-à-vis other groups means added control, however limited in scope, in the management of intergroup relations. Added control, if used wisely, directly increases survival potential. Additional authority is usually associated with an increase in group prestige, and so there is both a survival and prestige pay-off potential. The group that is granted the authority to coordinate is alive and well and probably climbing the prestige ladder.

Please Pass the Dollars

A working organization consists of conflicting claims on available resources. . . . This is as true of the federal bureaucracy as it is of any private firm.[22]

Corporate resources for internal allocation are never inexhaustible, and whenever scarcity exists relative to claims, some vying for position is virtually certain.[23]

Very few organizational analysts have given much serious attention to the budgeting process and its social consequences. Zald's case study of the YMCA is a notable exception.[24] But although he included a wealth of budgetary information and tried to link various types of organization changes to altered patterns of income sources, his work is only a beginning. "Although several sociologists have emphasized the relation of technology and task differentiation to polity, few have examined the relation of accounting rules and procedures to resource

---

[22] Victor A. Thompson, "How Scientific Management Thwarts Innovation," in *American Bureaucracy*, Warren G. Bennis, ed. (New York: Aldine Publishing Company, 1970), p. 132.

[23] Wilbert E. Moore, *The Conduct of the Corporation* (New York: Random House, 1962), p. 119.

[24] Mayer N. Zald, *Organizational Change: The Political Economy of the YMCA* (Chicago: University of Chicago Press, 1970).

allocation and organizational power.[25] This is an exceptionally fertile field for sociological analysis, one whose surface has barely been scratched by this study." [25] Others who have focused on organizational budgets have concentrated largely on the social psychological or individual aspects.[26]

Budgeting, or at least some process of resource allocation, is a universal activity in organizations. Perhaps one reason that so little research on the budgeting process has been done is that in private firms budget figures are supposed to be a well-kept secret lest competitors gain an advantage. Whereas some company officials may be willing to permit social research on the budgetary *process*, it would be exceedingly difficult to conduct such research without the researcher becoming privy to these company secrets. Although the final budget figures for most public organizations are considered public information, elaborate attempts are normally made to keep the figures secret until the budget has reached the final stages. By that time, the initial internal negotiations have been completed and the figures released are for broad categories only. Thus, systematic analysis of the interaction involved in the internal budgeting process would be forbidden to the outsider in almost all cases and dangerous for the insider except under very unusual circumstances.

Zald provides some insights into how budgeting policies can have multiple consequences. Based on his in-depth analysis of the Chicago YMCA organization, he concluded that the particular type of budget policy used "promoted maintenance and growth, regardless of the relationship of maintenance and growth either to need or to the YMCA's abstract goals." [27]

How did the process operate? Zald interpreted it as follows:

The basic justification for the annual budget system, with its strict emphasis on balanced budgets, was that it constituted good business practice. By

[25] Ibid., p. 238. Footnote 25 in the quote reads: "But see Reginald S. Gynther, 'Accounting Concepts and Behavioral Hypothesis,' *The Accounting Review,* 42: 274–90 (April 1967). For an empirical study see Harvey M. Sapolsky, 'Decentralization and Control: Problems in the Organization of Department Stores' (Ph.D. diss., Harvard University, 1966)."

[26] G. H. Hofstede, *The Game of Budget Control* (Assen, The Netherlands: Van Gorcum & Company, 1967); Chris Argyris, *The Impact of Budgets on People* (Ithaca: School of Business and Public Administration, Cornell University, 1952); Selwyn W. Becker and David Green, Jr., "Budgeting and Employee Behavior," *Journal of Business,* 4: 392–402 (1962); Gordon Shillinglaw, "Divisional Performance Review: An Extension of Budgetary Control," in *Management Controls,* C. P. Bonini et al., eds. (New York: McGraw-Hill Book Co., 1964), pp. 149–63; Andrew C. Stedry, *Budgetary Control: A Behavioral Approach* Publication No. 43 of the School of Industrial Management (Cambridge, Mass.: Massachusetts Institute of Technology, 1964).

[27] Zald, op. cit., pp. 120–21.

conceiving each department as an autonomous unit with equal relevance to Association goals, the budget process gave to the board of managers and the general secretary a consistent standard with which to determine when a branch was not performing adequately. If a deficit was foreseen, a department had to cut costs. *The basic criterion for expansion or contraction of service thus became the local department's ability to finance itself.* Community Fund monies, of course, were distributed partly with regard to conceptions of community needs nevertheless, Metropolitan office decisions were influenced by a department's ability to balance its budget. At the end of each year deficit loans could be used to balance the budget, but the interest charges would contribute to future deficits.[28] (Emphasis added.)

Clearly, budgeting is a very serious game known to almost all organizational participants above first-line supervisors. For the head of a group, the budget change from year to year is perceived to be almost as significant an indicator of his worth to the organization as his own salary. Budgets have symbolic as well as real significance. "Even if an increased budget carries no direct financial benefit to the manager or to any of his present personnel, being entirely intended for new faces and new furniture, the increase is a sign of success, reward for well-doing, a mark of approval."[29] Although other members of the group may not have as much ego involvement and career potential riding on the budget as does the head, they are unlikely to consider it irrelevant.

Budgets are one of the few evaluation indicators that are always in writing and therefore less subject to distorted perception than many others. Every division, if not every work group, has as a minimum an overall budget figure. The change in that figure from year to year is taken as an indication of what the top executives think of the group. An increase in the budget is likely to be taken as proof of top management support and satisfaction with the work of the group *provided* that the percent increase is at least as great as that allocated to the appropriate reference groups in the organization. Relative deprivation is the key. A 5 percent budget increase may be considered a reprimand to the group if the reference groups have been granted a 12 per cent increase or more. A 10 percent decrease may be defined as a commendation if relevant others get an 18 percent decrease. Comparison is inevitable and the outcome of the comparisons is important for group prestige rankings.

When budget request time comes around, the aim is to look poor but promising—or, even better, lean and promising. Asking budgets typically start among production units and among various staff units and divisions. These initial budget requests go up the line as recommendations. Now, it is common knowledge that when the asking budgets are

[28] Ibid., p. 120.
[29] Moore, op. cit., p. 119.

totaled, the sum is almost certain to exceed the figure that has any chance of being approved at the top level. Therefore, the expectation is that the initial budget request will not be granted regardless of the merits of the case, and what ensues is the tendency to start by asking for an impossibly high figure in the hope that what is *really* needed will be preserved after the fat and frills have been deleted. Given these communication and decision-making processes, the development of the budget for the organization resembles in many ways a game of poker. The initial inflated set of figures represent a bluff, and most experienced participants understand that, even though it is seldom discussed openly. At some levels, if not at all, the budget figures must be defended or documented. Now the game gets more serious, because adequate justification is seldom as easy to locate as imaginary needs. Preparing documentation for various budget items can be time consuming and costly, and this situation contributes to the temptation to defend budget items by referring to the self-evident nature of the need. The descriptions of such needs then tend to be overstatements, and they too tend to be discounted somewhat as they pass up the line. Justification is the second element of the bluffing game. It is not unusual for these excess budget requests to be handled by a cut across the board in which the biggest bluffers come out of the competition in the best condition.

Where there are few hard measures (e.g., counting widgets or bodies) to certify the extent of need, the opportunity for bluffing is the greatest. Given the processes described, the security and prestige of the group are dependent on bluffing. Playing the game honestly when other groups are not almost certainly means coming in last in the race when dollars are being passed around.

In this chapter we have pointed out what seems to be the major driving forces in the internal dynamics of organizations. We have seen that an organization is composed of groups that both cooperate and compete with each other. Group commitment to the overall organizational objectives may range from weak to intense and should not be ignored as a potential predicator of group action and response. We have chosen, however, to emphasize three principal concerns of any organizational group—the struggle to maintain or enhance group autonomy, security, and prestige. The manipulation of group domain is one arena in which these struggles occur.

In the next chapter we will survey the nature and consequences of interaction between the organization and relevant social units in the external environment.

Chapter 6

ORGANIZATIONAL ENVIRONMENTS

For groups within most organizations, the environmental sectors of most relevance are its colleague groups. It is these surrounding groups that make group life interesting, challenging, and, at times, problematic. In a somewhat similar fashion, what an organization is or becomes depends in large measure on the interaction that occurs between the organization and its significant environmental sectors.

The boundary of any social system, as we have pointed out before, is not necessarily obvious and clear-cut. For an organization, the problem of boundary identification is perhaps even more difficult to handle than it is for a group within an organization. Should the contacts with patients, clients, and inmates be treated as units of interaction within the organization, as part *of* the system, or as a boundary-spanning unit? How about interaction with students and customers? Different researchers have handled these questions in different ways. Clearly, someone must make the boundary identification decision, and we have maintained that the researcher-analyst should do so based on the particular theoretical problem that is guiding his investigation.

How do the environmental considerations of an organization compare with those of a group within an organization? The similarities seem obvious. In both instances there is a continuing struggle to maintain and improve the autonomy, security, and prestige of the group or organization. But there are some significant differences also. On the whole, the continued existence (security) of most organizations is more problematic. With the exception of organizations that have a monopolistic position—e.g., public school systems, electric utility companies, or city police departments—the typical organization faces competitors who specialize in the same product or service. The buyer or client has alternatives from which to choose. The security of the seller organization, therefore, is directly dependent on both the potential buyer and other seller organizations. A group in an organization seldom faces this type of competition. With few exceptions, any organizational group provides a specialized product or service to user groups within its immediate environmental setting. The "sale" function is quite predictable and secure. Not so the organization.

But if the organization's security is more problematic, its autonomy is usually greater, at least in one direct way. Within any organization there are always efforts at coordination—informing, guiding, and controlling efforts to see to it that the activities of various groups dovetail in time and place and complement each other. Many, if not most, organizations do not have to put up with such imposed coordination efforts. The organization may have a four-, five-, or six-day work week, but the length of the week is not usually dictated by some high level, supraorganization coordination body. From the point of view of imposed scheduling, and in many other ways, an organization has more autonomy than a group within an organization.

The prestige game among groups within an organization also differs somewhat from the environmental setting in which the organization exists. The division of labor within an organization means that each group engages in its own specialized activity or set of activities. The adequacy of its performance, therefore, cannot be easily compared with other groups carrying out the same functions. To make such a performance comparison (one of the bases for prestige ratings) requires information about how *the same kind of group* in other organizations performs. For example, how do sociology departments throughout the United States compare in quality of graduate education?[1] Such information is not normally readily available. Thus, comparative performance ratings among groups within an organization are difficult to make except in cases where the performance is obviously very good or extremely poor. Prestige ranks among the groups within an organization, therefore, tend to be based less on performance criteria and more on criteria that can be applied across groups.

[1] The following are among several articles that question the criteria used in such ratings:
Dean D. Knudsen and Ted R. Vaughn, "Quality in Graduate Education: A Reevaluation of the Rankings of Sociology Departments in the Cartter Report," *The American Sociologist*, 4: 12–19 (February 1969); Don H. Shamblin, "Prestige and the Sociology Establishment," *The American Sociologist*, 5: 154–56 (May 1970).

Most organizations have at least one counterpart in the immediate community. A church congregation is ranked in prestige relative to other churches in the area. A retail grocery firm is compared to others of its kind. The Lions Club is contrasted to the Rotary and Kiwanis clubs, and so on. Because organizational prestige rankings can be based more readily on performance criteria, it is important to make good organizational performance as visible as possible. Organizational image building is indeed a significant activity where prestige is concerned.[2]

What Must an Organization Do?

Many analysts implicitly assume, drawing on a natural system or functionalist perspective, that existing organizations are a reflection of the needs or requirements emanating from the environmental context or larger social systems of which they are a part. Any organization arises and continues to exist over time, the argument goes, only when it provides a needed contribution to another system or systems.

This basic notion is usually expressed in several, more specific assumptions:

1. An organization must secure a minimal input of (some combination of) money, material, services, and personnel from the environment.
2. The minimal level of input can be assured only if the organization provides an adequate output of (some combination of) money, material, services, and manpower to one or more sectors of the environment.
3. The recipients of the output may or may not be the same environmental elements that provide the inputs to the organization.
4. The character and level of both the input and output transactions must be approved of or at least tolerated by the general community or societal norms.

A casual reading of these assertions may lead to the view that they are so self-evident that it is pointless even to examine their implications for organization–environment interaction. Perhaps. But first, let us see how well they seem to fit what can be *observed*, even casually, regarding organization–environment interaction.

Consider the first assertion that all organizations must have some minimal input level. Certain voluntary associations have no money income, own no physical facilities or equipment, do not purchase any

---

[2] Charles Perrow, "Organizational Prestige: Some Functions and Dysfunctions," *American Journal of Sociology,* **66**: 335–41 (January 1961).

services, nor consume material products—e.g., an Old Order Amish Congregation. Where is the input to such an organization? It is sometimes argued that contributed actions of the participants constitutes input to the system. But such patterned interaction *is* the organization. Thus, the organization and its input are now synonymous by definition.

What about required output? What is the nature of the output for an organization that produces no tangible product or service? Is it the assumed satisfaction experienced by the participants in the patterned interaction? [3] If so, then is participant satisfaction to be considered an output of all organizations? When input and output are defined in such broad terms they become rather meaningless.

And what of the purported "necessary" approval or tolerance of the general community norms? Can organizations carry on interchanges that are not acceptable under generally held normative standards? Organized criminal syndicates have been operating protection rackets for decades. Local law enforcement personnel may or may not be accepting pay-offs to look the other way. And it is apparently not uncommon for city officials to get kickbacks from business firms that obtain contracts to do work for city government. Competing business firms engage in price fixing agreements, and only rarely are they brought into court. Real estate firms and financial institutions cooperate in racial discrimination in the rental, sale, and financing of housing, which is clearly in violation of both state and federal law. And so it goes. Clearly, observed social reality is much more complex than this assumption set suggests.

Now, in some cases it may be that the laws do not in fact reflect general community norms. That is a matter for empirical investigation. But as we have tried to illustrate in the preceding paragraph, it is not uncommon for organizational members to participate in repeated interchanges that clearly are in violation of community standards.

It seems, therefore, that vague assertions about what an organization must do vis-à-vis its environment is not a very useful way to proceed if our aim is to develop a better understanding of how organizations relate to environmental sectors and the consequences of various modes of relating. Turk, for example, has shown that it is possible to predict the activity levels and complexity of *new* interorganizational networks if you know the prior degree of local and extralocal integration among organizations in an urban area. Whereas natural system theorists might argue that new interorganizational networks develop because there is a system need for them, Turk's data show that, in fact, community-

---

[3] Howard E. Aldrich, "The Sociable Organization: A Case Study of Mensa and Some Propositions," *Sociology and Social Research*, **55**: 429–41 (July 1971).

wide "normative demand" made positive contributions to such prediction only where the prior levels of integration were high.[4]

When we speak of an organization and its environment, we are, of course, speaking of linkages and exchanges between two or more social systems. Dependency is a way of talking about system need, but dependency is only one aspect of what is involved in intersystem linkage. It seems to us that examination of the *total scope of intersystem linkage* is the critical first step. Answering the question of how various systems *do* relate should take precedence over carefully worded treatises on how they must relate.

Characterizing Organization–Environment Relations

If all organizations or even most organizations of a certain type operated within a comparable social setting, our task of developing useful theory to predict the broad features of organization–environment interaction would be considerably less difficult. Unfortunately, even casual examination reveals that organizations vary greatly in their internal characteristics, and their respective environments apparently vary even more. A public school system in New England faces a social milieu rather different from its counterpart organization in the Deep South or rural Alaska. Or so it seems on the surface. And just as the environment shapes an organization in that it provides opportunities for and places limitations on its activities, so too the organization may and often does have an impact on at least some segments of its environment.[5] The interesting question, then, is, How does the two-way influence or impact work? *How can we meaningfully conceptualize organization–environment relations?* Relational concepts always seem vague and difficult to formulate with clarity and specificity. The organizational literature is replete with terms describing the characteristics of organizations, and in the last decade or so there have been

[4] Herman Turk, "Interorganizational Networks in Urban Society: Initial Perspectives and Comparative Research," *American Sociological Review*, 35: 1–19 (February 1970). See also F. E. Emery and E. L. Trist, "Causal Texture of Organizational Environments," *Human Relations*, 18: 21–32 (February 1965).

[5] Perrow in particular is explicit on this latter point. "Society is adaptive to organizations, to the large, powerful organizations controlled by a few, often overlapping, leaders. To see these organizations as adaptive to a 'turbulent', dynamic, ever changing environment is to indulge in fantasy. The environment of most powerful organizations is well controlled by them, quite stable, and made up of other organizations with similar interests, or ones they control." Charles Perrow, *Complex Organizations: A Critical Essay* (Glenview, Ill.: Scott, Foresman and Company, 1972), p. 199.

attempts to characterize organizational environments, but relational concepts are notable for their near absence.[6]

Power

One can, of course, speak of power as a central element in such relations, but the danger of falling prey to tautological explanations is great. We note, for example, that such organizations as General Motors and the Department of Defense[7] seem to dominate most if not all of their environmental units. Why can they be so dominant? Because they are so powerful. How do we know they are so powerful? Because they appear clearly to dominate their significant environmental units!

It soon becomes evident that any meaningful discussion of the power dimension of organization–environment relations must consider the various bases of power. Adequate treatment of that topic would require much more space than can be given to it here. But let us note some of the principal features. *Coercion* or the threat of coercion may be a basis of dominance. Law enforcement agencies, including the Federal Bureau of Investigation, the Selective Service System,[8] the National Guard, labor unions, and even the Internal Revenue Service have been known to make their views prevail on this basis. Closely related is the threat or use of *unfavorable publicity*. Apparently, both General Motors and Ralph Nader's organization have tried to gain leverage through this method, sometimes on each other. The threat of or the actual *withholding of critically needed products or services* can bring desired results under certain conditions. *Bribes* and *kickbacks* give some "competitors" a distinct advantage, at least for a time. Providing *favors* can develop into a basis of power because at some future point in time the favors can be withheld. *Collusive agreements* among a few firms permits them to drive others out of competition. Effective

[6] Where relational concepts have been suggested, they have dealt primarily with interorganizational relations, which is only one subset of the broader organization-environment relations set. Helpful analyses of interorganizational relations include William M. Evan, "The Organization Set: Toward a Theory of Interorganizational Relations," in *Approaches to Organizational Design*, James D. Thompson, ed. (Pittsburgh, Pa.: University of Pittsburgh Press, 1966), pp. 173–88; Harold Guetzkow, "Relations Among Organizations," in *Studies on Behavior in Organizations*, Raymond V. Bowers, ed. (Athens, Ga.: University of Georgia Press, 1966), pp. 13–44; and Roland L. Warren, "The Interorganizational Field As a Focus for Investigation," *Administrative Science Quarterly*, 12: 396–419 (December 1967).

[7] A cartoon illustrates the point nicely. Around a long table are seated U.S. senators, a bemedaled general and his aides. The general has his hand extended. The committee chairman is saying, "Yes, of course, General, you will get your money but you must allow us to hold the hearings first, you know."

[8] James W. David and Kenneth M. Dolbeare, *Little Groups of Neighbors: The Selective Service System* (Chicago: Markham Publishing Co., 1968); Gary L. Wamsley, *Selective Service and a Changing America* (Columbus, Ohio: Charles E. Merrill Publishing Co., 1969).

use of huge resources to *influence* significant others by means of *advertising,* publicity, and *lobbying* activities can provide the basis for domination. The Republican or Democratic National Committee may not buy votes directly at election time, but resources used for mass media campaigning seem to produce almost the same results. *Interpersonal influence* can also be a factor in forming coalitions and power blocks, which then become dominant. And then there is normatively based power called *authority.* Even in the absence of threatened coercion, many governmental agencies can get their way largely because there is general consensus regarding their obligations and rights to make and enforce certain types of decisions.

It is a reasonable assertion that seldom does the power dimension of any specific organization–environment relation rest exclusively on only one of these power bases. The authority of a court system in dealing with citizens is backed up by the threat of coercion so long as the relevant law enforcement agencies respect the authority of the court, i.e., respect the right of the court to have its orders carried out. Labor union power is based in part on the threat of withholding services, in part on legally based rights, and in part on the threat or use of unfavorable publicity. State-supported universities are relatively powerless vis-à-vis the legislature. But some leverage can be generated by favor giving (e.g., giving choice season tickets to football fans who are members of key legislative committees, admitting otherwise unacceptable student applicants at the request of influential legislators, giving honorary degrees for support on critical issues). Leverage can also be achieved through interpersonal influence, by getting interest groups outside the university to contact legislators, and by the threat or use of unfavorable publicity ("Look what the legislature is planning to do to *your* university!"). The normatively based authority of the legislature, especially regarding appropriations, makes almost any struggle between the legislature and the university an uneven contest, however.

In general terms, then, it is possible to assess and describe the *power balance* between two or more social units. But any meaningful statement about the balance has to be in concrete terms and will have to include descriptions of the bases of power. Only by considering the bases of power can the analyst begin to develop tentative explanations as to why the power balance is tipped the way that it is and why the balance may in fact differ significantly from one set of issues to another.

Let us now consider additional alternatives with which we might conceptualize organization–environment relations.

Individuals and group or organization representatives who are external to the focal organization may initiate requests and make demands of an organization. They may be standard demands, such as ordering a product or service or requesting information. But some demands may be nonstandard in some respect. A demand may be nonstandard in that it is a request for an unusual product, service, or compilation of information but still within the general realm of the organization's domain—i.e., the set of expectations for the organizational system that are held by organizational participants. Or a particular demand may call for a response that is generally regarded as outside the domain of the organization receiving the demand. Other things being equal, it is easier to reject the "outside of domain" request than it is the unusual demand. Where the requested action or response is seen as falling outside of the organizational domain, the typical pattern is to refer the demander to some other, more appropriate, social unit.[9]

However, the character of the demand itself is not the only determinant of acceptance, referral, or outright rejection. Demands from very powerful social units such as the governor's office or from the head office of the largest industrial firm in the area will be treated with considerable care, whereas requests from some other units may receive short shrift. Despite such known variation, it may be worthwhile to consider the common or typical mode of responding to demands from the environment, responsiveness, as one of the significant concepts for treating organization–environment relations.

Responsiveness

Some organizations provide products or services in a monopolistic setting; others, such as an auto manufacturing firm, are part of an oligopoly; whereas many organizations operate in a setting where there are numerous other organizations offering essentially the same products or services to the same consuming population. It is often assumed by the student of organizations that an organization that has a monopolistic relation with customers or clients will be less responsive to their demands. It seems logical that this should be the case. But it may be well to remember that there are probably a number of variables that influence organizational responsiveness in addition to the monopolistic dimension. Experience suggests that some monopolies are indeed quite responsive, whereas some organizations surrounded by numerous competitors are considerably less responsive.[10] Some retail firms, for example, seem to treat most of their would-be customers with indifference.

---

[9] Drabek's description of how police processed incoming telephone calls from citizens illustrates this point. Thomas E. Drabek, *Laboratory Simulation of a Police Communications System Under Stress* (Columbus, Ohio: College of Administrative Science, The Ohio State University, 1969).

[10] John G. Craig and Edward Gross, "The Forum Theory of Organizational Democracy: Structural Guarantees as Time-Related Variables," *American Sociological Review*, **35**: 19–33 (February 1970).

It may be that organizational *ideology* plays a significant part in determining responsiveness. The responsiveness of certain religious and political organizations suggests that beliefs about organizational mission and related values do indeed make a difference.[11] Presumably, responsiveness should also be related to the *survival potential* of the organization. If some environmental segments are known to have a considerable measure of power to enhance or threaten the survival of the organization, one would expect organizational actions to reflect attention and concern rather than indifference responses to such segments.[12] This view assumes, of course, that organizational participants recognize the existence and relevance of such power centers.

Activism

Responsiveness as discussed above implies demands from or initiatives taken by units or persons external to the organization. Organizations vary, we have argued, in the ways and to the extent to which they respond to such demands and initiatives. The ongoing relations between an organization and sectors of its environment may be described in part by the typical way of responding on the part of the organization. In that context, the environmental units are viewed as the initiators and the organization as responder.

However, it is also useful to turn the perspective around and to ask about the extent and ways in which various organizations probe, monitor, and attempt to manipulate their relevant environmental units. The variation in such organizational activism is interesting and sometimes puzzling. Until recent years, the Hershey Chocolate Corporation spent no money at all on mass media advertising while competitors were spending small fortunes on that mode of activism. Some corporations and associations have fulltime legislative lobbyists on the payroll, others spend no money at all for such efforts.

On the whole, monopoly organizations are probably less active, but there are numerous striking exceptions to that generalization. A company that has a monopoly on both gas and electric power within a region may spend several hundred thousand dollars annually on mass media advertising. A large federal agency that has had a near monopoly on the provision of weather information for more than a century has yet to develop even a rudimentary procedure to ascertain who its relevant and potentially powerful interest groups are. Other federal agencies, such as the Department of Defense, seem to be as activist as General Motors.

[11] Mayer N. Zald, *Organizational Change: The Political Economy of the YMCA* (Chicago: University of Chicago Press, 1970), pp. 146–54 and 166–77.

[12] For an illustration of an apparent exception to this generalization, see James R. Wood, "Unanticipated Consequences of Organizational Coalitions: Ecumenical Cooperation and Civil Rights Policy," *Social Forces*, 50: 82–95 (June 1972).

Economic considerations would suggest that level of organizational affluence would be associated with activism. The very poor organization can scarcely afford the costs of activism. A downturn in the economy often seems to be followed by reduced efforts actively to monitor and manipulate the environment.

Large organizations may be somewhat more active than their smaller counterparts in the same sector of the economy.

It is tempting to point to ideology as an explanatory factor. Some religious congregations and associations clearly display more activism than others. Are their ideologies really significantly different with respect to beliefs about the importance of activism? For national religious organizations (denominations), there does appear to be a relation between ideology and social activism.[13] At the congregational level the picture is less clear.

Concern with organizational survival and prestige may well influence significantly the level and modes of aggressive effort. Other factors being equal, the very secure organization and the one with very high relative prestige is less likely to be among the most active of its type.

Opportunism

Organizational opportunism is the practice of adapting the organization's actions to immediate and short-term circumstances without regard to basic principles or long-term consequences. "We will deal with anybody if we can make a quick profit" is one expression that reflects the opportunistic approach to interchange with environmental sectors. It is one thing to note that some organizations are more alert to opportunities in the environment and pursue them more consistently and diligently than do other organizations, but that phenomena we would include under the dimension of activism. What we wish to point to in this section is opportunism in its most generic sense. Some organizations seem far more opportunistic than others. They consistently take actions vis-à-vis environmental segments that appear to reflect organizationally an *immediate* self-interest orientation. Some universities, for example, will take on almost any research or consulting activity that will provide significant income. And this is done with little or no consideration being given to longer-term implications for the organization. An opportunistic retail firm, for instance, will take on a new product line without examining its quality or checking its continued availability; a local city council or chamber of commerce may encourage and even offer large financial incentives to potential new

---

[13] James R. Wood, "Authority and Controversial Policy: The Churches and Civil Rights," *American Sociological Review*, **35**: 1057–1069 (December 1970).

firms without looking into the probable environmental and public expenditures consequent upon their establishment.

Other organizations, sometimes called conservative, take such actions only after careful soul searching and peering into the future. They will occasionally, if not frequently, forego apparent short-term gains because it is believed that the character of the organization must be preserved and/or that longer-term risks to the organization are too great.[14]

For some organizations, opportunism may be viewed as the key to survival, whereas in others it is seen as a threat to survival.

Security and Benevolence

Another significant dimension of organization–environment relations is the environmentally based continuity and certainty of support for an organization. Except under very rare circumstances, in the United States certain kinds of organizations will continue to exist into the indefinite future. Examples: public school system, prison, postal service, city government, electric utility company, police department, fire department, telephone company, and the court system. Organizations of this type may be called public monopolies. The view on all sides is that the product or service that they provide is so basic and the demand for it so consistent that somehow or other the organization must be kept going. Within any community or area there is only one of each type of public monopoly. Thus, once established, each organization has what might be termed *maximum security* in that its relations with most of its relevant environmental segments simply will not be terminated. Its survival is not in doubt. The dependency of environmental units on the product or service is almost total, and, therefore, the organization is extremely secure.

To say that an organization's survival is insured does not, however, say anything about its degree of affluence, size, prestige, or autonomy. Some police departments appear to be both anemic and held in generally low esteem. And the department's autonomy may be relatively low, as the mayor, city council, and citizens' review boards repeatedly force personnel and policy changes on the organization. Nevertheless, the organization is not about to expire. It is clear, at least for these organizations, that maximum security is not necessarily associated with maximum autonomy and prestige.

Now, consider the converse of the public monopoly; think of organizations that appear to be the least secure. Organizations such as the Black Panthers, Communist Party, U.S.A., and nudist associations

[14] Philip Selznick, *Leadership in Administration* (Evanston, Ill.: Row, Peterson and Co., 1957), pp. 142–49.

espouse unpopular beliefs that contribute to their insecurity. In recent years, we have witnessed the demise of many elementary and secondary parochial schools. Small retail firms have an even higher death rate.[15]

Some organizations exist and die in a hostile environment. Their product or service may or may not be respectable. They may have many competitors or few. They may be the object of hostility, pity, disinterest, or even some concern. But whatever the specific character of their relations with environmental sectors, the summation of the relations may be expressed as organizations whose *survival is continuously in jeopardy*. Their critical interchanges are on the verge of being severed.

Although maximum security does not necessarily insure high autonomy and prestige, minimum security is almost certainly accompanied by low autonomy and low prestige. Beggars cannot be choosers, and most beggars are held in low esteem. Until the threat of imminent demise is reduced, few organizational resources are going to be devoted to attempts to wrest more autonomy and respect from environmental segments.

Clearly, generalizations that purport to summarize how organizations attempt to manipulate the environment and respond to demands of environmental units need to take the security dimension into account.

Let us summarize some of the propositions implicit in the foregoing discussion.

1. Decreasing security is associated with increasing opportunism.
2. Increasing security is associated with increasing proportion of resources devoted to efforts to increase autonomy and prestige.
3. The level of activism and overall responsiveness tend to increase or decrease concomitantly.
4. Decreasing security is associated with increasing responsiveness.
5. As security increases with a concomitant emphasis on autonomy, responsiveness becomes more selective.

It is evident that more work is needed to develop additional concepts for characterizing organization–environment relations. Not only are additional relational concepts needed, but attention should be given to the manner in which the various dimensions do or do not covary under a variety of organizational and environmental conditions. Let us turn next to consideration of the external performance structure of an organization.

[15] Kurt Mayer and Sidney Goldstein, *The First Two Years: Problems of Firm Growth and Survival* (Washington, D.C.: Small Business Administration, 1961).

The External Performance Structure

The primary focus in this chapter is on organization–environment *interaction*. We could use the term *interorganizational interaction*, but that would exclude the numerous instances of interaction with individual customers, clients, and so on, so we shall stick with the somewhat cumbersome but more exact term *organization–environment interaction*.

Organization–environment interaction includes the full range of interaction that takes place between any particular organization and all social units in the environment. That interaction may involve the transfer of *products*, as in the purchasing of supplies; the provision of *services*, such as a daily supply of laborers or the provision of liability insurance; and the transmission of *symbols*, as when a highway department receives customized weather forecasts for which it pays a price, or when two agencies exchange statistical summaries at the end of every month. Thus we want to consider here what may be called the *external performance structure* of the organization.

If we were to map out the external performance structures of a wide range of organizations, we would note variation among them in the extent to which products, services, or symbols were dominant in the interaction. We might also note variation in the *extensiveness* and *intensiveness* of such interaction. Extensiveness refers to the number of different types of interaction engaged in, whereas intensiveness refers to the frequency with which any given type occurs. A municipal government has more extensive interaction than an electric power company. A wholesaler of Christmas greeting cards has less intensive interaction with customers than does a retail grocery firm. Thus, as Aldrich has pointed out, some populations (types) of organizations have a markedly different environment than do others.[16] The survival potential of an organization with a more extensive external performance structure would seem to be greater than for those with less extensive interaction. Intensiveness as a separate variable may also be related to survival potential, in that frequent interaction provides for possible short-term feedback on the satisfaction and intentions of environmental units such as customers, thereby making adaptive innovation by the organization more feasible.[17]

Organization Domain and External Performance Structure

At any given point in time the domain of any organization may or may not be identical with its external performance structure. Included

---

[16] Howard E. Aldrich, "Organizational Boundaries and Interorganizational Conflict," *Human Relations*, **24**: 279–82 (August 1971).

[17] Betty B. Roe and James R. Wood, "Adaptive Innovation and Organizational Security in Solidary Organizations," n.d., mimeo.

within any organization's domain is a set of normative ideas that outline (and sometimes specify in detail): (1) the activities in which an organization may and should engage; and (2) with whom external interaction may and should take place. For example, the legal charter of a corporation may authorize the organization to conduct more than a dozen different activities with numerous environmental sectors. However, at any point in time the number of activities and environmental sectors in contact may be far fewer than those authorized. On the other hand, an organization may take on new contacts in the environment that have not previously been approved as part of its domain.[18] The leaders of several American church bodies took such actions involving the civil rights movement in the 1960s.[19] Thus, there may be internal and external pressures to bring the external performance structure into line with the organization's domain as it is most commonly defined by interested persons and environmental units. In recent decades, governmental organizations seem to be under more pressure to expand their external performance structure than to contract it. Citizens always want more services, not fewer, say many public officials. Persons and groups opposing such expansion frequently appeal to the domain concept, arguing that government has (should not have) no business getting involved in the proposed new or expanded services. An organization seeking to enlarge its external performance structure beyond that approved by its domain will probably either attempt to persuade relevant environmental sectors to reinterpret the meaning of the current domain, or enlarge the domain definition, or attempt to carry out the new activities and associated interaction in secret.[20] Public information and advertising campaigns may be used in an effort to manipulate domain definition. Also, organizational personnel in boundary-spanning roles may be carefully coached on the new approach to be used in extraorganizational interaction. At least in certain settings, such interaction can influence the views of some classes of persons in the environment. For example, in their role as boundary personnel, policemen were found to transmit their perceptions of the city government to the small businessmen on their beat.[21]

[18] In a recent work, Baldridge does an excellent job of illustrating the usefulness of the domain concept and of documenting how the domain of a university changed over time. See J. Victor Baldridge, *Power and Conflict in the University* (New York: John Wiley and Sons, Inc., 1971), especially pp. 123–35.

[19] Wood, "Authority and Controversial Policy: The Churches and Civil Rights," op. cit.

[20] Sol Levine and Paul E. White, "Exchange as a Conceptual Framework for the Study of Interorganizational Relationships," *Administrative Science Quarterly,* **5**: 583–601 (March 1961).

[21] Howard E. Aldrich and Albert J. Reiss, Jr., "Police Officers as Boundary Personnel: Attitude Congruence Between Policemen and Small Businessmen in Urban Areas," in *Police in Urban Society,* Harlan Hahn, ed. (Beverly Hills, Calif.: Sage Publications, 1971), pp. 193–208.

Domain and External Normative Structure

We speak of normative structure when there is a consensual base for sets of normative ideas and where those ideas are relatively stable over a period of time. We thus exclude from consideration the ephemeral fads and fashions.

The character of the *internal* normative structure of an organization is primarily, though certainly not exclusively, the business of those who participate directly in the system. But the normative structure that applies to organization–environment interaction is quite another matter. Many different persons and social units have something to say about if, when, and how such interaction should and may occur. This *external* normative structure may not be everybody's business, but for most organizations there is a broad range of persons, groups, and organizations including governmental agencies from which such normative ideas emanate. Few, if any, organizations are powerful enough simply to ignore all of the sources of these normative ideas.[22] Even public welfare recipients have shown that their rights must be respected. Like it or not, when organizational members have outside contacts, those being contacted have their own notions about the form and frequency with which such interaction ought to occur. Thus, the norms that matter are the norms held by the organization's significant others, its role partners, so to speak.

Domain is the broad umbrella under which the more specific normative notions operate. It provides the rationale and justification for policy agreements and extraorganizational roles from which flow standardized patterns of interaction. The normative structure as a whole provides the general script for the organization–environment drama.

We suggested in previous chapters that the dimensions of role (task, authority, prestige, affect, and sanctioning) also seem to apply to the concept of group domain. Included in the domain of any group are normative notions about what it should do, whose activities it may legitimately control, and so forth. It appears to us that the same perspective is useful in summarizing the kinds of norms that make up the domain of an organization. Application of the *task* dimension is relatively straightforward. The teaching staff of a school system, when acting as representatives of the school, for example, should not get actively involved in noneducational political issues. The *authority* of a

---

[22] Selznick's analysis in depth of the Tennessee Valley Authority shows that the U.S. Department of Agriculture, the Farm Bureau Federation, local land grant colleges and universities, and the Agricultural Extension Service are among the many environmental units whose views had to be taken into account.

Philip Selznick, *TVA and the Grass Roots* (Berkeley and Los Angeles: University of California Press, 1949).

city council does not include the right to dictate the content of instruction offered at a nearby state university. The norms specify in some detail how the *prestige* of the Federal District Court is to be exemplified in courtroom behavior. Expressions of positive *affect* toward the work of the Society for the Prevention of Cruelty to Animals are appropriate, but not for the work of the local criminal syndicate. And, at least in some communities, it is considered appropriate, if not highly desirable, for churches to *sanction* negatively firms that practice racial discrimination by refusing to buy their products or services. There may, of course, be less than complete consensus among interested parties regarding any of these norms. That is to be expected when an organization faces a heterogeneous environment.

The external normative structure, like all other normative structures, is in a continual process of *negotiation*. The head of an organization may be able to establish certain official internal policies and rules with a relatively free hand, but he has considerably less freedom to be arbitrary in establishing the external normative structure. There are instances, of course, where the outside organization is a wholly owned subsidiary or in some other manner a captive organization, and in such cases they can be dictated to within limits. However, we know that most organizations are dependent on some, and often many, outside organizations and groups. Such environmental units must be depended on for needed raw materials, supplies, personnel, services, and information as inputs. And on the output side, they provide services, such as distribution and advertising, and also purchase the organizational products and services. Or, at a minimum, they facilitate the acceptance and professed utilization of the service, as in the case of governmental agencies. Thus, when there is a high degree of dependency, we would expect that attempts at persuasion and negotiation on the *undetermined* aspects of the external normative structure would be more likely to occur than unilateral insistence on the nature and frequency of interaction.

As Thompson[23] has pointed out, dependency is an important factor for many aspects of organizational life. Its relation to the development and stability of the external normative structure is perhaps one of the most critical areas. Where there is only one local supplier of the one main product or service (high dependency, limited scope) or a limited number of suppliers for a whole range of needed products or services (moderate dependency, broad scope), organizational officials must do more negotiating than where there are multiple suppliers for all needed inputs with potential suppliers bidding against one another on price, quality, and convenience of delivery.

But just what is there to negotiate about? After all, many aspects of

[23] James D. Thompson, *Organizations in Action* (New York: McGraw-Hill Book Co., 1967), pp. 25–38.

the external normative structure are in a very real sense preset. There are established and traditional modes of interaction that have the halo of custom on them and, in some instances, the force of law behind them. For example, practitioners of the medical and legal professions should not use direct advertising in offering their services to potential clients, and they must be certified by the appropriate state boards before providing their services. Potential college students are usually required to pay an application fee. Governmental agencies are supposed to award contracts after the receipt of sealed bids. Thus, for any organization a large part of the external normative structure must be taken as a given.

However, other parts of that normative structure are the subject of occasional or periodic discussion and negotiation. A state-supported college or university will negotiate with the relevant committees of the state legislature regarding the *criteria* to be used in determining the amount of income to be appropriated by the legislature; e.g., $350 per undergraduate and $700 per graduate student enrolled. A business firm or its advertising agency may dicker with radio station or newspaper personnel over the interpretation of truth in advertising policies. City planning commissions and land developers often hassle over the meaning of the policy that requires the latter to present "adequate information" regarding plans for the development of an area proposed for rezoning. A business firm seeking large loans from banks may find it necessary first to reach agreement concerning internal accounting practices or investment policies. A university seeking accreditation of a new Ph.D. program may engage in lengthy discussions with members of the visiting accreditation committee concerning how the criteria are to be interpreted in that specific case. And tax experts can cite numerous instances where it took months of negotiations with the Internal Revenue Service before agreement was reached on acceptable *procedures*[24] for computing corporation profits and losses for tax purposes.

In our earlier discussion of the internal normative structure of organizations, we made a distinction between the official and the unofficial components of that structure. The official norms are those openly supported by those incumbents (officials) whose position definition calls for them to be norm enforcers. The same notion would seem to apply equally well to the external normative structure. Those norms, whether they be contract stipulations, oral agreements between firms or agencies, written memoranda of understanding and so on, receiving open support from the relevant officials, make up the official norm component of the larger set called the external normative structure.

---

[24] It should be noted that environmental units may also shape the *internal* normative structure of an organization. Thus, in the examples cited, the banks and the Internal Revenue Service are able also to shape the internal organizational norms.

Are there also unofficial norms? If there are, they would be agreements and commitments entered into by certain nonofficials in an organization and their counterparts in outside social units. Such norms often, but not always, contradict the officially sanctioned norms. On those rare occasions when corporation executives have been hailed into court on charges of conspiring to fix prices within a segment of an industry, the defense has argued that official company policy forbids engaging in price-fixing agreements. Nevertheless, the prosecution counters, the evidence is clear that such agreements were made and the prices were fixed. Because such agreements are seldom put in writing, it is very difficult to ascertain who acted for the companies in reaching the agreement. It is at least possible that the agreements were in fact arranged by nonofficials acting without the knowledge and approval of top executives. If so, the agreements constituted part of the unofficial, external normative structure for the companies involved. Similarly, organizational personnel from several governmental agencies may agree to exchange certain types of information off the record. The exchange is off the record precisely because official policy in each agency forbids or at least does not authorize such exchanges. Nevertheless, the participants have developed a supporting rationale to justify in their minds the necessity for such unofficial information exchanges. Another example involves the agreement reached between a student recruiter from a high-status university and selected high school student counselors. The recruiter agrees to see to it that the counselors' top candidates get favored consideration in university admissions in exchange for special treatment for the recruiter when he comes to the high school for interviews.[25] The recruiter's boss may be quite unaware of these agreements or, being aware, chooses to look the other way.

We can see, then, that both official and unofficial norms may exist even though the official ones may be more readily identified by the outside observer or researcher. Where such norms do exist, they will shape and direct organization–environment interaction.

Boundary Positions and Roles

Much, but not all, organization–environment interaction involves personnel in officially designated boundary positions. The range includes top executive, purchasing agent, recruiter, public information, telephone answering, sales, shipping, contracting, and receptionist positions, among others. Role specifications for some of these boundary-spanning roles are very detailed—as, for example, instructions on

---

[25] The *interaction* culminating in such an agreement is an illustration of what Thompson calls a "side transaction." James D. Thompson, "Organizations and Output Transactions," *American Journal of Sociology,* **68**: 309–24 (November 1962).

how to answer the most frequently asked questions from customers.[26] In other roles, only general guidelines are provided, or perhaps only a preferred outcome is noted, as when a private welfare agency professional is in contact with a multiple-problem family. Thompson refers to the former as a "programmed" role and the latter a "heuristic" role. The continuum from completely programmed to entirely heuristic role definitions is said to reflect the *specificity* of organizational control over boundary personnel when they are engaged in output transactions.[27] The implication is that these are the characteristics of boundary roles as *officially* defined by the focal organization. As with norms and roles in general, officially boundary-spanning roles may vary considerably in specificity.

But there is another whole arena of organization–environment interaction that has not been treated in the discussion of boundary roles. For many organizations, the number of persons holding officially designated boundary positions is only a small fraction of the total number of members engaged in organization–environment interaction. Yet those persons in nonboundary positions (at least as officially defined) may have frequent and extensive interaction with outsiders, and in those interactions they are representing the organization. For example, *any* employee of a university may be called on by friends, neighbors, and even casual acquaintances to discuss the current status of student unrest in the university, the prospects for the football team, the adequacy of the graduate program in one of the academic departments, or the competency of a newly appointed dean. Perhaps the most frequent topic of conversation centers on whether a particular son or daughter has a good chance of getting admitted to the university. Almost every employee of a large industrial firm is likely to be asked about the overall financial status of the company, whether the firm is doing any hiring, and, if so, what types of skills are being sought. Clearly, it is not only officially designated boundary personnel who in fact interpret the organization to nonmembers. Almost everyone engages in organization–environment interaction, but only a limited number of roles, the officially designated boundary roles, seem to reflect explicitly this fact of organizational life. (Possible partial exceptions to this observation may include organizations engaging in activities considered to be "sensitive" or confidential.)

We have argued earlier in this book that *all* frequently occurring units of social interaction have a normative (role definition) base. How, then, can we account for this employee–outsider patterned interaction? Can it occur in the absence of *any* role definition? Although we

[26] George F. Lombard, *Behavior in a Selling Group* (Boston: Harvard Business School, 1955).

[27] Thompson, "Organizations and Output Transactions," op. cit., p. 310.

know of no systematic research dealing with this issue, it seems likely to us that there exists for such units of interaction a set of unofficial norms that are part of the general normative structure of the community and societal culture. If I repeatedly vilify my university in such conversations, I am likely to be told that if I think it is such a miserable place to work I should look for employment elsewhere! Such a comment is probably intended as a negative sanction to inform me of my role violation.

It is interesting that organizations that make a fetish of written standard operating procedures, job descriptions, rule manuals, and detailed role specifications—i.e., the internal normative structure—are far less comprehensive with respect to the external normative structure. It is almost as if the employee is thought to turn off his "organizational self" when he departs from his place of work!

The External Interpersonal Structure

Select at random 1,000 adults in any community of a population of 50,000. For each person, identify the organization in which the largest single block of his time is consumed as a participant. Then, from among the 1,000 persons, find out who interacts with whom where a part of the interaction deals with organizational matters, where they deal with information, issues, services, or products of mutual interest to their organizations. This exercise will give you a first partial glimpse of an organizationally relevant interaction network in the community. Upon examining that network in detail, you will discover that some of the units in the net represent repeated interaction that could not be predicted from knowledge of the external normative structure. The interaction takes place not because of boundary-spanning role requirements, but because these sets of persons have become acquainted with one another and have developed interpersonal relations that are utilized in an interorganizational context.

The interpersonal relations provide the *preconditions* for such interaction. My company begins to purchase supplies from a particular store because my friend has recently become the firm's manager. In trying to assist my graduate student advisee in finding a job, I write to specific universities because I have acquaintances who are on the faculty there. I do not write to all "good" universities nor to a random sample of universities. My letters may include personal comments, but the principal focus in such correspondence is on interorganizational matters. Typically, I do not write to department chairmen or to the heads of departmental recruiting committees. I write to my friends.

In other instances, the interpersonal relation may have developed out of interaction that was initiated in boundary role enactment. The interaction had only a normative base in the beginning but as the participants came to know one another and developed a distinct interpersonal relation, the frequency and character of the interaction is altered. Thus, the interpersonal relation has a *shaping influence* on the interaction. Where the interpersonal relation that has developed is essentially congruent with the role specifications, its effect is not easily discerned. Where there is marked incongruence, as when two engineers from competing firms develop a high level of mutual trust when the role calls for extreme caution in discussing research and development activities, then the potential shaping influence of the interpersonal relation becomes obvious. Indeed, revolutionary organizations often take this potential incongruence into account and try to inhibit the development of interpersonal relations between members and non-members.[28]

Now, consider the total network of organizationally relevant interactions in a community. Think of it as including the external performance structure of every organization in the community. It would include all organization–organization, organization–group, and organization–individual units of interaction. Perhaps it should be called the Organizationally Relevant Community Performance Structure. Some proportion of the total interaction units are based principally on position and role specifications (normative structure), some principally on an interpersonal relations base (interpersonal structure [IPS]), but the majority of such units are a reflection of a combination of the normative and the interpersonal structures. Figure 6 suggests these distinctions.

It should be recognized that probably no patterned interaction is totally lacking of some normative base. Some conceptions of role, however vague, are probably operating. But in this discussion of interaction flowing from interpersonal relations we are speaking of *organizationally relevant* interaction for which there are few, if any, organizationally based norms (role definitions). *The interaction is organizationally relevant but not to any significant extent organizationally shaped.* It is primarily a reflection of the unique interpersonal relations that have developed among specific sets of persons. Thus, a research chemist in a local laboratory operating from his niche in the community IPS may succeed in generating widespread organizationally based support for a proposed ordinance controlling stream pollution. Similarly, two industrial executives, who were once friends but are now distinctly cool toward each other, might see to it that their respective firms never endorse and support the same community projects: if one does, the other will not.

The external IPS of an organization has potentially great impact on

---

[28] Philip Selznick, *The Organizational Weapon: A Study of Bolshevik Strategy and Tactics* (New York: McGraw-Hill Book Co., 1952), pp. 25–29.

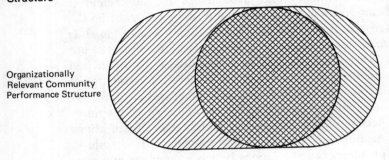

FIGURE 6–1   Bases of an Organizationally Relevant Community Performance Structure

Organizationally
Relevant Community
Performance Structure

Normative Structure Base Only

Interpersonal Structure Base Only

Based on Combination of Normative and Interpersonal Structure

its external performance structure. It is little wonder, therefore, that personnel officers and others dealing with recruitment often place heavy emphasis on hiring persons who can get along well with all kinds of people. The IPS can aid or detract from organizational survival and prestige. These interpersonal links develop and are retained over time in a largely officially unplanned fashion for most organizations. Of the three primary structures determining external organizational performance, the IPS is least amenable to manipulation by an organization's top executives, or by anyone else for that matter.

We turn now to consideration of the significance of the resource structure for organization–environment interaction.

Resource Structure: Keeping the Environment in Line

Organizations vary in the extent and characteristics of their resource structure. Included in the concept of an organization's resource structure are its *physical facilities* and *equipment* (owned, leased, or otherwise under its control), its *aggregate skills* and *competencies* (e.g., 50 engineers representing 6 major specialties, 3 experienced investment analysts and a contract with an advertising firm), and its accumulated *information* and *knowledge* as reflected in the organization's records (e.g., by keeping a detailed record of sales, weather conditions, and advertising effort for certain geographical areas, a major soft drink producer was able to determine under which weather conditions advertising costs could be reduced because purchase of the product would peak anyway due to the thirst producing weather).[29]

As we noted in earlier chapters, it is not difficult to see how the resource structure of an organization may limit or in other ways shape the internal performance structure. The question now is, how can this concept, resource structure, aid in understanding the external performance structure?

Let us note some of the more direct ways in which this concept is useful.

First, the range of member skills and competencies limits the extent and ways in which the organization can *monitor* relevant sectors of its environment. Indeed, some organizations seem not even to know which are the most relevant sectors of their environment. The range of member skills does not include persons who know how to think critically and systematically about a problem of that kind. Where there is adequate understanding of which of all the sectors are the really significant ones, there is frequently no one to plan and direct the monitoring of those sectors. This is most obvious in the arena of market research. But the range of environmental monitoring that could be important for an organization goes beyond that. It includes the possible desirability of monitoring what the competitors are doing and the monitoring of proposed legislation that, if enacted, would have a significant impact on the organization. For example, at a meeting of the heads of a number of small, highly specialized business firms, it became apparent that they were unaware of a proposed regulatory measure that had already passed the United States House of Representatives and was being considered by the Senate. The legislation was specifically aimed at regulating their type of organization and could, depending on the interpretation of the measure, require expensive data gathering, record keeping, and reporting efforts. Indeed, these added costs could very well force a number of these firms out of business. These organizations were unaware of the legislative development primarily because of the absence of relevant skills among their personnel.[30]

Second, the range of skills affects the extent and manner in which an organization can actively *manipulate* its environment. Many an organization takes a beating in the political arena because it has no skilled lobbyists on its staff or its would-be lobbyists are clumsy or

---

[29] From an interview taken during research on "User Needs and Dissemination Requirements for Atmospheric Information," with financial support from the National Science Foundation, Grant No. GA–31298, J. Eugene Haas, principal investigator.

[30] Personal observation by J. Eugene Haas at a meeting of the Weather Modification Association, Oklahoma City, Oklahoma, October 21, 1971.

ineffectual. Experienced, skilled public relations personnel can manipulate mass media coverage of their organization with considerable finesse. Many electronics firms have learned that to be successful their sales representative must have at least three basic skills. He must have an engineer's knowledge of the extremely complex products being offered, skill in presenting the merits of the product to potential customers, and an adeptness in coming to understand quickly the complex character of the customer's problems.

As with a boxer, being strong is not enough. The extent to which an organization can keep its environment in line depends in large measure on the specific kinds of skills that it has in its resource bag. It cannot use what isn't there.

Third, the size and character of the physical facilities affects the overall *rate of external interaction,* and especially with certain sectors. For example, a new bank opens for business after appropriate advertising. Its offices are located on the second floor of a large office building. After several years, the offices are moved to the first floor of the same building, whereupon its business transactions increase markedly. Many an entering college student, selecting among the several colleges that have accepted his application, finally decides on the one that has the nicest campus or most comfortable dormitories. The more affluent customers, it is said, will only patronize restaurants, clothing stores, and auto dealers offering real atmosphere.

Fourth, *information* regarding the effectiveness of *previous organizational efforts* can limit or enhance future attempts to control the environment. The utility of such information appears to be greatest when considering large-scale but nonroutine organizational efforts. A church congregation that remembers that the last building-fund drive surpassed the goal set for it, but that has "forgotten" how the drive was conducted, is of necessity starting with a handicap in planning a new effort. In such cases, retained information about the procedures used and especially about who the large contributors were is an exceedingly valuable resource. The same principle would apply to school boards seeking to have a bond issue passed. In an approaching flood, city officials can plan and mobilize more effectively if they have available detailed information on which areas were flooded first and most extensively on the last previous occasion and information on how long it took to complete evacuation.[31] It is records of just such nonroutine actions that are least likely to be kept. Organizations that do store such information and have it in readily retrievable form, however, have a

---

[31] Daniel Yutzy, *Authority, Jurisdiction and Technical Competence: Interorganizational Relationships at Great Falls, Montana, During the Flood of June 8–10, 1964* (Columbus, Ohio: Disaster Research Center, Ohio State University, 1964).

distinct advantage in efforts to cope with relatively unusual problems in the environment.

Despite the statements from some company executives about their constant worry of having company secrets stolen and their skilled specialists pirated by competitors, most organizations do not seem to exist in an entirely hostile environment. In many communities, organization leaders have developed limited forms of cooperation such that the combined resources of their organizations are utilized to control the outcome of many major community-wide issues that concern them. The findings reported by Perrucci and Pilisuk provide an excellent illustration.[32] They looked at power in terms of interorganizational ties. They theorized that "the power to shape significant community decisions resides in a number of organizations, each containing *some* of the resources required to initiate influence or constrain decisions; when the resources of these organizations are combined, they can be instrumental and most likely decisive in shaping decisions."[33] In the midwestern city where they conducted the research, they found that those persons who were known to have been influential in past community issues of major proportion and who were similarly identified as having a general reputation for power were organizational leaders, each of whom held executive positions in two or more organizations. These executives held common views regarding community issues and had close social ties. Not surprisingly, this community power elite was composed primarily of top officials from banks and industrial firms. They held overlapping high executive positions in other organizations such as an advisory commission to city government, a hospital board, an educational board, a welfare organization, and voluntary associations.[34] Unfortunately for our purposes, the report does not describe the extent to which these executives succeeded in using the outside organizations as tools to control the outcome on issues, but the fact that they held policy-making positions in them suggests that they were probably not ineffectual in their efforts. Also, it is not clear which of the organizational resources other than executive skills were mobilized from time to time to keep the environment in line with their wishes. Nevertheless, the general pattern is clear. Organizational resources can be used cooperatively to keep unwanted trends in the environment from developing ,and to change aspects of the environment in desired directions.

---

[32] Robert Perrucci and Marc Pilisuk, "Leaders and Ruling Elites: The Interorganizational Bases of Community Power," *American Sociological Review*, 35: 1040–1057 (December 1970).

[33] Ibid., p. 1053.

[34] Ibid., p. 1054.

The application or use of an organization's resources vis-à-vis the environment may show a variety of emphases. A few industrial firms are still flailing away at labor unions as if the organization's very life depended on crushing the unions. Some others, notably electric utilities, keep hacking away at "big government." In some cases, the particular emphasis taken is primarily a reflection of the intense ideological beliefs of the top policy makers. In other cases, the emphasis probably reflects the broad normative standards of the industry or class of organization. University administrators and faculty are supposed to view with alarm any purported attempts by legislatures or governmental agencies to interfere with policy or the operations of any university. Perhaps the best way to sum up is to point out that an organization's resource structure provides the horsepower that *can* be used on the environment. The way it is used is shaped by the organization's internal normative and interpersonal structures as well as the external normative and interpersonal structures. But saying that these structures *shape* the utilization of the resources should not be taken to mean that they have complete control. Sometimes, resources are applied in violation of the normative order. Sometimes, interpersonal understandings are violated. Sometimes, there is a lack of consensus on norms. The intriguing question is, Under what conditions do the actions of the organization surprise the analyst who knows the normative and interpersonal structures? Here is another interesting research arena.

Control Configurations in Multiorganizational Systems

It is not unusual for two organizations to make a binding, long-term commitment for the supply or exchange of products, services, or information. In addition, they may make similar commitments to take coordinated action toward some aspect of the environment. Each organization is still a relatively independent entity, but such a binding commitment does limit its options for action and may indicate significant dependency. Thus the partner organization becomes a very special part of the environment. Making such commitments is one way of trying to reduce uncertainty in the task environment. Such commitments are clearly normative in nature. Contained in the documents or understandings are specifications regarding what each party is obligated to do. Often there also is specification of the rights of one party if the other fails in some way to live up to the terms of the commitment.

From the perspective of the analyst, the presence of such a commitment suggests the beginning of a simple, small-scale multiorganizational system. In some cases, the carrying out of the terms of the agreement is largely self-enforcing. The factory will not continue to receive the needed, scarce, raw material unless it pays its bills. But in other cases the enforcement of the commitment is much more problematic. Let us briefly review some of the more common ways used to handle the control problem in multiorganizational systems.

First, we should recognize that few multiorganizational systems have the comprehensive, detailed, "tight," authority-based control mechanisms that are fairly common within a single organization. Almost by definition, subunits within an organization have, on the average, less autonomy than the organizations within a multiorganizational system. Departments within an organization, being highly specialized, simply could not survive if they withdrew from the organization, whereas survival is not quite so tenuous for the organizations within a multiorganizational system. How, then, are the relevant actions of these "voluntary" organizational participants coordinated? How are the agreements and commitments enforced?

The range of such super systems includes trade associations, councils of governmental agencies, United Fund, AFL–CIO and innumerable religious, educational, professional, industrial, and fraternal systems within a country and almost as many international associations covering the same spectra of organizational types. Sometimes the member organizations are in direct competition with each other, as with members of the New York Stock Exchange and petroleum companies participating in a consortium, but for others, such as a state association of school boards, there is little overlap in their domains. The actions of some of these associations suggest that a major function of the system is to protect the member organizations from each other. Jurisdictional disputes and other types of alleged domain incursion are frequent foci of attention. Firms providing professional services are not supposed to steal each other's clients. On the other hand, the association may be little more than an articulated system for the collection and exchange of information about the activities of member organizations. For other multiorganizational systems, the principal focus is outward. Image building, lobbying, protecting the rights of system members, bulk buying and selling, and monitoring of events in the environment are common activities. It is little wonder, then, that the decision-making and coordination devices within these supraorganizations are highly varied and therefore difficult to describe in any summary fashion.[35]

One interesting way to compare the various multiorganizational

[35] For a discussion of types of coordinating units among health service organizations see Basil J. F. Mott, "Coordination and Inter-Organizational Relations in Health," in *Inter-Organizational Research in Health: Conference Proceedings*, Paul E. White and George J. Vlasak, eds. (Baltimore, Md.: The Johns Hopkins University, Department of Behavioral Sciences, School of Hygiene and Public Health, 1970), pp. 55–69.

systems is to consider the extent to which a typical member organization is able to retain control over the activities of the larger system. In its simplest form we may speak of a *simple exchange system.* Here, a limited number of organizations mutually agree on some set of activities that they want carried out. There is specific agreement on the type of activities to be carried out and the intensity or level of activity in each case. Some identifiable unit is established for these purposes. The unit carries out the activities following what can be called programmed instructions. It is analogous to programming a computer to receive information from various organizations, process it in certain standardized ways, and return the output to all member organizations. The Crop Hail Insurance Actuarial Association provides such a function for the major insurance companies. The unit carrying out the activities makes no decisions for the system. It only applies simple, detailed instructions. Thus, once the initial agreement is reached regarding the standard operating procedures, each member organization retains an identical degree of control over what the newly formed system will do (unless, of course, the programmed instructions have been secretly altered in violation of the agreement). Any proposed changes in the performance of the system will require a new round of negotiation among member organizations.

A second point along this continuum may be termed a *mediated system.* Here, member organizations reach agreement on the policies to be used by the new system unit in carrying out the desired activities. Although there may be some programmed instruction, there is also some discretion given to the system administrative personnel to interpret the policies that have been formulated. Once this system has been set in motion, however, the amount of control by any member may begin to vary. The new system administrators are in fact making some decisions for the operation of the system. They are interpreting policy and acting or instructing their subordinates in the control unit to act on the basis of their interpretations. Now the system members who consistently have the greatest interaction with the central staff will retain a higher level of control than will those who fail to keep up such monitoring. Member organizations located in the same community as the central staff have an advantage in this regard. Physical proximity is an aid in surveillance. Those who, looking over the shoulders of the central staff, help interpret policy are also helping to shape policy. Members on an advisory body or a council, if they meet with any regularity also have an advantage. It is unlikely that all member organizations will retain the same degree of control over the performance of a mediated system.

Farm organizations such as the Farm Bureau, Farmers Union, and the National Farmers Organization illustrate this process. A major activity at the state and especially the national level is lobbying for favorable farm legislation. The typical pattern is for national and state staffs to send to the various county organizations a list of the issues on which they anticipate the need to lobby in the forthcoming legislative sessions. The issues are discussed within the county organizations, and through a complex process, policy positions are arrived at. The staff at the national level, for example, then attempts to plan and conduct lobbying activity based on policy it has been given. But these policy statements are usually worded in *general* terms and often phrased in terms of *objectives* to be achieved. Thus the staff must interpret the policies in their day-to-day lobbying activities. They must decide when to compromise on one issue in the hope of gaining a more favorable outcome on another issue. The staff clearly is in a position to do more than carry out programmed instructions.

The next type on the continuum is the *delegated system*. Here the member organizations agree to delegate to some central unit of the system the right and responsibility to formulate policy. The participants in this policy-making unit of the system may be full-time system staff members, or they may be part-time system policy makers whose principal organization tie is with a member organization or some combination of the two. Here, the possibility that some member organizations will gain greater control over the system than others is significantly increased. New policies may be formulated and old policies altered without the specific informed consent of each organizational member, for that is the meaning of the term *delegation*. Whereas system policies may be reviewed for approval or disapproval by all member organizations, once the general concept of delegation has been accepted it becomes impossible to keep a continuous tight rein on the body to which policy making has been delegated. Now the process of system control becomes essentially a political one. It is hard to imagine a situation where each member organization is equally successful in maintaining its fair share of control over the policy-making unit of the system. That seldom happens even within a single organization.[36]

The athletic conferences (e.g., the "Big 10" and the "Big 8") of universities illustrate the delegated system. The governing board of such a system as a part of the agreement to establish the system has been specifically delegated the authority to establish and enforce policy. It sets up policy for coordinating the scheduling of athletic events and for standardizing the benefits that may be offered to prospective athletes. Furthermore, the board is empowered to discipline individual athletes and even member university athletic departments when the board determines that its policies have been violated. Because some member organizations (the more "successful" ones) contribute more financial

---

[36] Baldridge, op. cit. See especially Chapter 6, "The Politics of Coordination," and Chapter 9, "The Legislative Process."

support to the system than do others, it would be surprising if they did not also wield greater influence in the decision-making process within the governing board. Thinly veiled threats of withdrawing from the system gives the successful members added leverage.

On the extreme end of the continuum is the *hierarchical* system. Here member organizations cannot withdraw from the system, but they can maneuver to keep the central unit as impotent as possible. Within a city, the activities of the police, fire, health, and public works departments may be subjected to the coordination efforts of the civil defense unit during times of community-wide emergency, because the mayor and city council have so ordered. If, for purposes of analysis, we view each of these organizations as relatively autonomous units, then civil defense is an imposed coordinating unit that, at least in the official normative structure, has the authority to demand that the activities of the various departments be coordinated during emergency operations. In recent years there is a pattern wherein a state legislature establishes a body usually called a commission on higher education. Although the specific powers of each such commission may vary, the basic idea seems to be that such a body should oversee the development and expansion of both physical facilities and programs of the state-supported colleges and universities. This overseeing function usually entails the authority to approve or disapprove proposed budget requests from the various universities to the state legislature. The commission, it is said, should coordinate the background information and requests that go to the legislature.[37] Thus, from the point of view of the legislature, the universities, colleges, and the commission, taken together, form a multiorganizational system in which the commission is the information processing and coordinating unit. From the perspective of the individual university, it is an imposed multiorganizational arrangement in which the commission stands in a hierarchical position between the university and the legislature. For any university, the commission now becomes a primary target for manipulation attempts. Getting the "right" persons appointed to membership on the commission becomes critical, as survival, autonomy, and prestige rest in large measure on the decisions of that unit. Some members of the system will almost certainly gain greater control over the decisions of the central unit than others. But even under the most favorable circumstances the typical member organization will have less control over key issues in the hierarchical multiorganizational system than in simple exchange, mediated, or delegated systems.

We have suggested that multiorganizational systems may be estab-

---

[37] Although most universities may fight a legislative proposal to establish such a commission, a university that has consistently scored poorly with its proposals before the legislature may welcome the imposition of such a commission in the belief that it couldn't make things worse and might make them better.

lished and operated for a variety of reasons. Member control over the actions of the central unit of such a system is greatest in the simple exchange system and decreases progressively in the mediated and delegated system. The typical member organization has least control in the hierarchical system. Indeed, it is in the extreme form of this type of multiorganizational system that the issue of boundaries may become puzzling.

We have argued consistently that boundary specification must be made by the researcher, based on the problem at hand. For example, one may study a single grocery store within a nationwide chain. Regional and national offices would be viewed as critical environmental sectors that severely limit the autonomy of this individual store. Although in this instance the restriction on system autonomy would usually be greater than that imposed by city council and the mayor's office on fire and police departments, these systems too are linked into a larger multiorganizational system of a hierarchical nature, i.e., the city government system. Thus, specifying boundaries so that we can differentiate the interaction systems we wish to study can become rather complicated. Even more complex is the mapping out of networks of normative ideas held by organizational participants in such multiorganizational systems. But it is precisely these types of overlapping and at times highly ambiguous expectation sets that define a critical aspect of the organizational environment, and are defined with varying degrees of accuracy by participants. As such, these limits on organizational freedom are observed, tested, and manipulated.

The Approach–Avoidance Dilemma

We have seen that many organizations do participate in multiorganizational systems. But such participation presents risks to the organization as well as offering opportunities. On the opportunity side, the multiorganizational system can often provide to a member increased intelligence through mechanisms for monitoring the environment in general. Furthermore, participation in the system sometimes provides clues to what competitors are up to even when such sharing of information is not an officially sponsored activity of the system. As in wartime, a "slip of the lip" (of a competitor) can sometimes be of great advantage to the listener. It is just this potential for inadvertently revealing valuable inside information that has led many business firms and governmental agencies to adopt a policy that requires even their experienced executives to have all of their speeches written and cleared in advance of presentation. Thus, it is sometimes said that at conferences nothing new can be learned by attending the formal sessions, but much can be learned at the social gatherings, i.e., the cocktail hour.

New, small, and little-known organizations may gain increased visibility through membership. Prestige enhancement is a possible benefit as is certification that may be important to clients and customers. Some multiorganizational systems offer financial aid and specialized legal and other services to needy members. And if the system is one that has real leverage at the local, state, or national level, there is the possibility, however small, that a member organization may be able to have significant impact on the major trends in the relevant occupation, profession, industry, or sector of society, and perhaps even on the basic political structure itself. Although much system talk of this kind is mere whistling in the dark, it can and occasionally does happen at the local and state level.

However, consorting with competitors in a system context has its potential drawbacks, and thus there is a dilemma about joining. Quite apart from the direct financial costs, which always seem to be increasing, there are potential hazards to be considered. An organization may inadvertently "give away" more intelligence than it gains from participation. What is more, top executives will seldom know how many important nuggets have slipped away.

If the system falls in general repute, especially with significant sectors of the environment, the prestige of the member organization may be hurt. If the system spokesmen take a radical position on a controversial issue, a member organization can suffer severe losses of more than temporary nature.[38] Unless organizational leaders are especially alert to the possibility, the more the member organization becomes integrated into the larger system, the greater the likelihood that its "precarious values" as Selznick calls them, may be eroded.[39] The initial commitment to participate in the system may be short-term and limited in scope. But once having made the commitment, the relationship is likely to continue unless and until some major point of dissatisfaction becomes the focus of attention. Because the tendency is for one *apparently* insignificant commitment to lead to another, the gradually increasing impact of participation in the system may go unnoticed.

We have pointed out that the joining of a multiorganizational system is not always a completely voluntary matter. Voluntarism is a matter of degree. We will illustrate the point by considering the dilemma confronting agencies in the executive branch of the federal government. During periods of budget tightening, it is common for the Office of Management and Budget to "suggest" to the several federal agencies with similar or identical programs (major activities) that they form an interagency committee or council so as better to coordinate their programs and especially their budget requests, which will go to Congress.

[38] Wood, "Unanticipated Consequences of Organizational Coalitions: Ecumenical Cooperation and Civil Rights Policy," op. cit.
[39] Selznick, *Leadership in Administration* op. cit., pp. 119–33.

Such a suggestion is seldom taken lightly, as the Office of Management and Budget has what is akin to veto power over all budget requests going to Congress. Any experienced agency head knows that participation in such an interagency committee represents certain hazards for his organization. He may be forced by the turn of events within the committee to reveal agency plans ahead of schedule. He may be questioned about details of current programs that he prefers to keep secret. Failure to respond openly to the queries of the other agency heads will arouse additional suspicion, but answering the questions may tip his hand and produce a counterstrategy in another agency. And if his agency already has a good working relation with key officials in the Office of Management and Budget, his organization would seem to have little to gain from joining the interagency enterprise. But he has little choice in the matter if he cares about his agency's survival and growth, to say nothing of his own career in government.

Upon joining this interagency system, which is ostensibly limited to information sharing and coordination, the first task is to try to get agreement that all deliberations and especially conclusions reached will be off the record. This may work for a time, but once such a committee or council is formed it becomes increasingly visible to other agencies and bureaus, with a concomitant increase in requests or demands for the views of the committee on various subjects. Such reports, of course, must be in written form, for only in that way can each agency member of the committee check to see that its perspective and pet programs are not being short-changed in the reports that go out. Now the intrasystem bargaining and horse trading comes to the fore. "My agency won't sabotage your proposed program if your agency will give positive support to my critically needed program." Such an orientation is a typical lead approach in the early bargaining. As each member agency has in effect a semiveto over any expansion or new program proposal of any other member, the process most typically results in the interagency system supporting all of the programs of each member. This works so long as any particular agency does not get too greedy. The focus of attention of the system becomes increasingly oriented to the Office of Management and Budget and key congressional committees, and the mutual back scratching becomes the dominant pattern. Reports that are in effect advertising brochures are issued. Each agency's program is said to be positively critical for the good of the nation.[40] Although experienced senators and congressmen

---

[40] In one case, the agencies cleverly agreed to label each existing or proposed program of each member agency a "National Project" and the entire package a "National Program." Interdepartmental Committee for Atmospheric Sciences, *A National Program for Accelerating Progress in Weather Modification*, Federal Council for Science and Technology, ICAS Report No. 15a, June 1971.

undoubtedly recognize what is going on, the "united front" approach is probably an acceptable outcome for each agency compared to the alternative of refusing to join the interagency system after it was suggested by the Office of Management and Budget.

To review the themes presented in this chapter, we have suggested that any attempt to develop more adequate theory dealing with organization–environment interaction is hampered by the lack of careful research into the various processes of such interaction. Although there is no shortage of speculative treatises on what organizations "must" do in relation to their environments, there is a dearth of studies that document what organizations actually do. There is an inadequate data base to which conceptual frameworks and tentative hypotheses may be compared. Obtaining data on the external performance structure, for example, is a difficult task, but it must be done if we are to move from speculation to knowledge.

Useful concepts that capture the essence of significant organization–environment issues are still in the early development stage. We have suggested several such relational concepts and have tried to indicate their potential utility. Focusing on the external performance structure, we have tried to illustrate the relevance of the external normative, interpersonal, and resource structures as explanatory schemes. We have examined a portion of the patterned interaction of organizations with their environmental sectors through consideration of control configurations in multiorganizational systems.

Only brief consideration was given to the range of consequences for the organization of various types and levels of intensity of organization–environment interaction. The theoretical perspective introduced in earlier chapters suggests that organizations as open systems are subject to varying demands from environmental sectors. The short- and long-term potential consequences of those demands must be understood in light of the strains internal to the organization. We turn next to a detailed consideration of the concepts of stress and strain.

Chapter 7

ORGANIZATIONAL STRAIN AND STRESS

We have emphasized that organizations, like other social systems, are in a constant state of flux. And we have alluded to the idea that, in contrast to some idealized models of organizations, those that we find empirically appear to be characterized by structures that contain many inconsistencies and contradictions. An understanding of these can be most helpful in predicting and explaining system behavior. But structural inconsistencies are varied and highly complex. Using the concepts of strain and stress, let us explore a series of distinctions that will help a great deal in trying to conceptualize such phenomena.[1]

Organizational Strain

Concepts labeled system *strain* have been used by several sociologists. Merton,[2] for example, conceived of strain as the key concept with which to avoid static functional analysis.

The key concept bridging the gap between statics and dynamics in functional

[1] This chapter draws heavily from a paper by Thomas E. Drabek, "A Theoretical Framework for the Analysis of Organizational Stress," presented at the annual meeting of the American Sociological Association in Denver, Colorado, August 31, 1971. In much briefer form the ideas appeared in Thomas E. Drabek, *Laboratory Simulation of a Police Communication System Under Stress* (Columbus, Ohio: College of Administrative Science, Ohio State University, 1969), pp. 14–23.

[2] Robert K. Merton, *Social Theory and Social Structure*, rev. ed. (New York: The Free Press, 1957).

theory is that of strain, tension, contradiction, or discrepancy between the component elements of social and cultural structure. Such strains may be dysfunctional for the social system in its then existing forms; they may also be instrumental in leading to changes in that system. In any case, they exert pressure for change. When social mechanisms for controlling them are operating effectively, these strains are kept within such bounds as to limit change of the social structure.[3]

> In a similar, but more complex sense, Parsons defined strain as ". . . a condition in the *relation* between two or more structured units (i.e. sub-systems of the system) that constitutes a tendency or pressure toward changing that relation to one compatible with the equilibrium of the relevant part of the system." [4]

Recognizing the difficulties inherent in an "equilibrium" model, Moore[5] suggests that we conceptualize social systems as "tension-management units" wherein *both* order and change are viewed as problematical and normal. "Tensions or inconsistencies and strains, if the word 'tensions' is too subjective or has too psychological a connotation are intrinsic to social systems, not simply accidental accompaniments or the product of changes that impinge on the system from external sources. Once the tensions characteristic of all or of particular types of social systems are identified, they are predicted to be the probable sites of change." [6]

This "tension-management" model departs from an equilibrium model in several important ways. Moore emphasizes four differences.

1. To the degree that at least some tensions are really intrinsic, and not simply organizational problems that can be readily resolved, the predicted change will neither restore an equilibrium or static state nor create a new one.

2. The consequences of change will almost certainly be tension-producing as well as possibly tension-reducing.

3. The use of the term "tension" does not imply that change will initially reduce tension. For some sequential analyses it may be appropriate to identify or predict tension-producing changes rather than change-producing tensions, not to evade the postulate of intrinsic tensions, but rather take into account the necessity for a starting point and the frequent desirability of "getting particular," of making rather specific predictions rather than highly general ones. For example, there is an intrinsic tension between any social system that endures beyond the life-time of its members or the age limits of membership, and the system's mode of recruiting new members. Here, then, is a likely place to look for a change. The analysis may begin, however, by

---

[3] Ibid., p. 122.

[4] Talcott Parsons, "An Outline of the Social System," in Talcott Parsons et al., eds., *Theories of Society* (New York: The Free Press, 1961), p. 71.

[5] Wilbert E. Moore, *Social Change* (Englewood Cliffs, N.J.: Prentice-Hall, Inc., 1963).

[6] Ibid., pp. 10–11.

identifying a change in the number or qualities of recruits and then predicting the tensions that change can be expected to produce.

4. The conception of society (or any special structure) as a tension-management system involves no presumption at all that the management is "successful," or that the system as identified in fact persists, or even that it will last long enough to permit us to speak of "transitions" from one system to another. The probability of any of those things happening can be determined only by identifying the system and the variables that will determine the course of its change. One possible course may be destruction.[7]

In contrast to these macrotheorists, others have used somewhat similar ideas at a micro level. Numerous studies have focused on role conflict. Although defined in numerous ways, this concept usually refers to some type of inconsistency or disagreement about normative standards. Thus, Gross, Mason, and McEachern analyzed the expectations held by school superintendents and their respective school boards.[8] Haas[9] assessed the role expectations held among staff in hospital nursing stations and found that the degree of consensus was an effective predictor of friction. Preiss and Ehrlich[10] used role conflict as the central variable in their analysis of a state police organization. Similarly, a long-term research program at the University of Michigan headed by Robert Kahn supports the conceptual and methodological utility of role conflict study.[11]

But role conflict, like system strain, is a complex notion. We have found it useful to merge these two ideas and specify several types of strain. Each type of strain may be found at different structural levels; thus, we may shift our referent unit from a single dyad to a group or department, or to an entire organization. And when this view is taken, we gain both the methodological insights from empirical research at the micro level and the more general hypotheses proposed by the theorists working at the macro level. Let us look now at some necessary clarifications.

Organizational strain is defined as *inconsistencies or discrepancies among structural elements of an organization.* There are three basic types of strain, which may occur at varying levels: (1) normative incompatability; (2) interpersonal incompatability; and (3) resource incompatability. Within each of these types, however, several differences in content require specification.

[7] Ibid., p. 11.

[8] Neal Gross et al., *Explorations in Role Analysis: Studies of the School Superintendency Role* (New York: John Wiley and Sons, Inc., 1958).

[9] J. Eugene Haas, *Role Conception and Group Consensus* (Columbus, Ohio: Bureau of Business Research, Ohio State University, 1964).

[10] Jack J. Preiss and Howard Ehrlich, *An Examination of Role Theory: The Case of the State Police* (Lincoln, Nebr.: University of Nebraska Press, 1966).

[11] Robert L. Kahn et al., *Organizational Stress: Studies in Role Conflict and Ambiguity* (New York: John Wiley and Sons, Inc., 1964).

Normative Incompatability

Eight types of normative incompatability must be differentiated to permit more rigorous measurement than has yet occurred. Basically, the eight types reflect two types of distinctions. First, as Gross, Mason, and McEachern suggest, it is one thing to ask "consensus on what?" and quite another to ask "consensus among whom?" [12] That is, we should distinguish between the object to be defined and the subject definer. Second, inconsistencies may exist within or among referent systems. Thus, distinctions between "intra" and "inter" systems must be kept clearly in mind. [13]

Normative inconsistency is often included in discussions of role conflict. But, as we just suggested, role conflict refers to several different notions. To begin our efforts at clarification, let us first recognize that norms associated with any single position may be inconsistent. If one follows prescription *A*, he violates prescription *B*. And there are two separate structural levels at which strain may be found.

1. *Intrasystem inconsistency* is currently illustrated by the position of a university student. The norms that define that position are inconsistent. For example, the single role-relationship of professor–student contains many discrepancies. "Students ought to become self-motivated and directed" versus "the examination for this course will be objective and will require you to know all the definitions that I presented in lectures throughout the quarter." Persons enacting the student position confront this strain and must cope with it. [14] At times, coping efforts may be directed at system change to reduce the inconsistencies.

2. *Intersystem inconsistency* results because position incumbents enact several positions simultaneously. And normative expectations from other systems do affect behaviors by organizational members. For example, according to organizational norms, police are expected to be on duty twenty-four hours a day. Of course, families and other nonoccupational groups present a different expectation. Preiss and Ehrlich, in their study of state police found that 68 per cent "experienced this as a conflict situation." [15] Another empirical illustration is Killian's[16] analysis

[12] Gross et al., op. cit., pp. 95–96.

[13] Among the many discussions helpful in deriving this formulation were Frederick L. Bates et al., *The Social and Psychological Consequences of a Natural Disaster: A Longitudinal Study of Hurricane Audrey* (Washington, D.C.: National Academy of Sciences–National Research Council, 1963), pp. 53–60; and Preiss and Ehrlich, op. cit., pp. 94–121.

[14] Preiss and Ehrlich reported that "90 percent of the men [state police] interviewed pictured themselves as being confronted with contradictory role expectations," op. cit., p. 98.

[15] Ibid., p. 100.

[16] Lewis M. Killian, "The Significance of Multiple Group Membership in Disaster," *American Journal of Sociology*, 57: 309–14 (January 1952).

of the dilemmas presented by community disasters for local officials when their families' safety was unknown. Their organizational position required that they remain at their post, but their family position demanded that they locate and assist family members. Thus, position incumbents may confront normative inconsistency at either the intra- or inter-system level.

Normative dissensus refers to the extent to which there is disagreement among position incumbents as to the norms that define their relationships. This refers to the amount of disagreement among incumbents about the norms, rather than inconsistencies among the norms per se. Strain exists when there is dissensus about norms; but this again can be at two structural levels, vary in degrees of intensity, and differ in pattern—e.g., polarized into two distinct identified groups or diffuse and rather nonspecific.

3. *Intrasystem dissensus* is the degree to which there is disagreement by incumbents of any specific system as to the norms that define various positions. For example, to what degree is there consensus among university students as to the norms that define that position? It appears that currently the level of dissensus is very high. But then this may be pervasive throughout much of society. In one of the few empirical studies directed at this issue, Kahn's national survey indicated that nearly half of the male wage and salary workers were confronted with this type of strain.[17] Unfortunately, a much larger volume of data of this type will be required before we can even begin to speculate as to the degrees of dissensus that might characterize organizations of different types.[18]

4. *Intersystem dissensus* may be the most significant source of strain in many organizations. Membership in a multiplicity of systems increases the likelihood that persons will be caught in this type of structural trap. Normative dissensus generated by memberships in occupational, family, recreational, service, and religious systems creates expectation networks within which coping is all but impossible. And persons in "boundary positions" will even more frequently confront this type of strain. Kahn's national survey, for example, demonstrated a

[17] Kahn et al., op. cit., pp. 55–56.

[18] In contrast to measuring dissensus among holders of a single position—e.g., students, patrolmen, and so on—Haas developed techniques for measuring the dissensus between incumbents of different positions. Thus, doctors and nurses were compared as *dyads* so as to measure the normative dissensus among the particular actors in a specific interaction system. Haas, op. cit.

In Gross's "language," this would be "interpositional consensus," where the "subject definers" occupy the "object defined." This strategy may prove more productive for studies of strain, since the focus is more narrowly limited to role conceptions confined to actual interaction systems in which incumbents currently are involved, rather than hypothetical cases.

clear relationship between frequency of contact beyond organizational boundaries and incidence of normative dissensus.[19]

Normative ambiguity frequently confronts organizational members. Expectations are unclear. If ambiguous, norms related to authority, status, tasks, sanctions, or affect will provide minimal assistance in structuring behavior.

5. *Intrasystem ambiguity* refers to strain resulting from normative incompatability where norms are highly unclear. Persons simply are not sure what is expected of them. Data from Kahn's national survey indicated that 35 per cent of the male wage and salary workers were "disturbed by lack of clarity about the scope and responsibilities of their jobs." [20] And "29 percent are bothered by ambiguity about what their co-workers expect of them." [21]

6. *Intersystem ambiguity* characterizes much of the normative structure in which persons find themselves. Because of their multiple system memberships, actors simultaneously confront norms in these different systems that are quite unclear. Lacking clarity, these norms must be regarded as a source of strain for the organization under study.

Normative overload characterizes many positions in our society. Demands are so excessive that no individual could meet all of them. Thus, they violate certain norms by default, simply because it is impossible to satisfy all of them. As Goode has emphasized, because this is so typical, priorities are established as a means of coping.[22] And certainly dissensus often emerges about these priorities.

7. *Intrasystem overload* is frequently found in university settings when several professors each assign a hundred or so pages to be read over a weekend. Similarly, students retaliate by requesting individual discussions outside the classroom which eat up the professor's research time. In contrast to such quantitative overloads, Victor Thompson's analysis of the increasing strain due to specialization illustrates how such overload may be of a qualitative nature.[23] He has documented how increasing specialization and expertise make it almost impossible for a supervisor to advise his subordinates. As a dean or department chairman, for example, he simply cannot have expert knowledge in all of the specialties represented among his subordinates. Janowitz reports similar findings for military organizations confronted with the

[19] Kahn, et al., op. cit. pp. 102–14. The same pattern held true for boundary positions within the organization, i.e., interdepartmental contact (pp. 114–23).

[20] Ibid., p. 74.

[21] Ibid.

[22] William J. Goode, "A Theory of Role Strain," *American Sociological Review*, 25: 483–96 (August 1960).

[23] Victor Thompson, *Modern Organization* (New York: Alfred A. Knopf, Inc., 1961).

emergence of highly sophisticated technologies and "skill structures." [24] Similarly, Taub concluded that this was a major source of strain confronted by many administrators in India's civil service system, who were responsible for supervision of engineers and other technically trained personnel.[25] Thus, strain in the form of excessive demands of both a quantitative and qualitative nature is increasingly built into many organizational structures.

8. *Intersystem overload* is undoubtedly experienced by large numbers of adult Americans today. Multiple system memberships accumulate demand loads so that single individuals are frequently confronted with continual priority decisions. Family events may often create demand loads that preclude employee effectiveness. As a significant environmental factor, intersystem strain of this type not only represents a difficult structure with which to cope personally, but also represents a structure subject to changes.

In brief, normative incompatibility may result from inconsistency, dissensus, ambiguity, or overload. And for any focal system selected for analysis, strain may be at intra- and inter-system levels. But there are at least two other major sources of strain—interpersonal and resource incompatability.

Interpersonal Incompatability

Some conflicts arise among persons aside from any normative disagreements. Recalling our discussion of the interpersonal structure (IPS) presented in Chapter 4, how might we conceptualize this type of strain? We proposed that interpersonal relationships could be characterized through five dimensions: (1) dominance–submission; (2) like–dislike; (3) trust–distrust; (4) extensive–limited; and (5) respect–disrespect. The degree of interpersonal incompatability can be assessed by measuring the degree of balance found in the network of relationships. And, like the normative structure, both intra- and inter-system networks must be included.

1. *Intrasystem interpersonal imbalances* could take many forms. In the extreme, however, we would expect the network of relationships to be characterized by ratings emphasizing dislike, distrust, disrespect, and to be highly segmental, i.e., limited to the narrowest aspects of the work environment. One is not inclined to discuss family concerns or to reveal much of oneself when the interpersonal structure is highly strained.

[24] Morris Janowitz, *Sociology and the Military Establishment* (New York: Russell Sage Foundation, 1959), pp. 31–34.

[25] Richard P. Taub, *Bureaucrats Under Stress* (Berkeley and Los Angeles: University of California Press, 1969), pp. 89–105.

2. *Intersystem interpersonal imbalances* would be similar to those within a system except that the term would refer to interpersonal relationships among persons located in different systems. Transactions across system boundaries may be affected by this type of strain. Interpersonal hostilities among department heads, for example, may have repercussions within each of their respective units and among others as well. Certain units may be by-passed in consultation on policy matters despite the official normative structure. As analysts, we should be sensitive to this type of strain as a possible lead in trying to understand such behavior.

Resource Incompatability

Resource incompatability is a common type of strain, but remains little analyzed by sociologists in this context. However, for many years varieties of social scientists have researched factors related to employee fatigue and morale. Although most have increasingly focused on social factors of the type included within normative and interpersonal strain, physical factors and other aspects of the resource structure, such as information, are not to be overlooked. Excessive noise levels and temperatures are obvious annoyances which require some type of coping efforts. Less obvious, however, are building structures whose very walls and halls create physical settings that may isolate work units so as to reduce interaction. A common device used on many university campuses confronted with space problems is to use rented facilities (often older homes) adjacent to the campus for faculty research projects. Department members and graduate students thus find their colleagues scattered about in a maze which effectively isolates each unit. Reduced interaction may gradually lead to total disintegration of the unit at worst—and at best, necessitates frequent use of departmental meetings to "call the troops together." The recent popularity of clusters of smaller residential colleges is in part a response to this same type of strain. Clearly, the consequences of resource strain are important and deserve our future attention.

Although much future work must be directed at further specification of each type of strain and corresponding measurement devices, these three general types (normative, interpersonal, and resource) and their respective subtypes provide us with a foundation. Certainly, we can now at least recognize the complexity of the highly abstract concept— organizational strain.

However, two further points remain. First, we indicated at the outset that strain could occur at different structural levels and in various patterns. Thus, we can vary our referent system depending upon the specific research question of interest. For example, we may wish to focus on a single type of dyad within several different organizations. Here our referent system would be the particular dyad, and the environment would be other facets of the organization as well as external groups and organizations. We might wish to focus on intra- and inter-system normative consistency, dissensus, ambiguity, and overload for such systems. Similarly, we might wish to focus on the total organization. In such an instance, intersystem normative dissensus would refer to the expectational dissensus between organizational members and environmental sectors. Correspondingly, intrasystem normative dissensus would refer to the intensities and patterns of dissensus within the organization. Thus, these various types of strain can be used with several different referent systems. Note Figure 7–1, in which we have designated these two examples.

Second, strain may result from the relationships *among* the normative, interpersonal, or resource structures. For example, Homans[26] and Haas[27] have emphasized the linkage between interpersonal conflicts and normative dissensus. Thus, persons who define their role relationships differently will probably develop interpersonal strains. As explicated in Chapter 4, because such persons cannot interact in mutually satisfying ways, frequent "friction events" tend to occur.

We have proposed that organizational incumbents are one aspect of the resource structure. Strain may emerge between this structure and the normative structure when position incumbents lack the personal ability to fulfill the expectations associated with their positions. Obviously, where the line is drawn between normative overload, which implies some objective standard, and personal inadequacy is most difficult to state. From the subjective view of most incumbents, strain usually is seen as stemming from some source other than their personal inability to meet position requirements. Yet, among Americans, there is a strong tradition to assign blame to defective individuals rather than defective structures even if the latter appears far more appropriate.[28] And lowered self-esteem, negative self-concepts or inferiority complexes may often be accounted for by defective structures wherein actors frequently experience failure regardless of their actions.

The equipment component of the resource structure may require incumbent actions that are not prescribed by the normative structure or ones that are even prohibited. For example, in an analysis of police communication team performance, officers receiving telephone calls from the public frequently violated a norm that prohibited interaction

[26] George C. Homans, *The Human Group* (New York: Harcourt, Brace, Jovanovich, Inc., 1950), pp. 133–35.

[27] Haas, op. cit.

[28] Thomas E. Drabek and E. L. Quarantelli, "Scapegoats, Villains, and Disasters," *Trans-action*, 4: 12–17 (March 1967).

FIGURE 7–1   Typology of Organizational Strain*

| | | Referent System | |
Type of Strain	Dyad	Group or Department	Organization
Normative Incompatability			
1. Intrasystem inconsistency	X		
2. Intersystem inconsistency	X		
3. Intrasystem dissensus	X		X
4. Intersystem dissensus	X		X
5. Intrasystem ambiguity	X		
6. Intersystem ambiguity	X		
7. Intrasystem overload	X		
8. Intersystem overload	X		
Interpersonal Incompatability			
1. Person-to-person			
2. Person-to-position			
Resource Incompatability			

* X Refers to examples discussed in preceding pages.

with the cruiser dispatcher.[29] While normatively prohibited, such inter-action was frequently required given the nature of the resource structure within which they worked. And knowledge of this strain was useful in interpreting how the team's performance structure changed when subjected to a sudden increase in demand load. Thus, we propose that such strains can be used to predict many types of changes in organizations. We will pursue this idea in the next chapter, but now let us see how we might construct an equally useful concept—organizational stress.

In contrast to this very general concept of strain is the more narrowly focused concept of stress. We first emerged with the concept of stress in an effort to conceptualize types of organizational responses to large-scale community disasters. Here we have sudden and intense environmental disruptions. But, in some instances the disruptions seem to have a greater impact. If some organizations seemed better prepared for certain types of disasters, did this mean that there was less stress? In short, was stress to be measured by the degree of environmental disruption (stimulus) or by the type of system response? In trying to come to terms with this question, we found it necessary to construct three additional concepts. Thus, we need first to review the concepts of demand, capability, and capacity so as to derive the concept of stress.

[29] Thomas E. Drabek and J. Eugene Haas, "Laboratory Simulation of Organizational Stress," *American Sociological Review*, 34: 223–38 (April 1969).

An Abstract Look at the Performance Structure

Although we have emphasized the utility of viewing organizations as sets of interrelated processes, for certain types of analyses it also appears necessary to formulate some more abstract concepts with which to construct the concept of organizational stress. Three constructs will be posited and illustrated. All three are abstractions of a "higher" level than any of the processes that comprise the performance structure, and they permit us to view the interrelationships between organizations and their environments in a meaningful way. Let us now discuss organizational demands, capability, and capacity.[30]

Organizational demands are defined as external requests or commands for action either received directly by any member of the organization or resulting from knowledge of demand-relevant cues. Thus, we think of organizational demand as a rather abstract concept that includes a great variety of behaviors. For example, client orders received by a manufacturing firm, customers in restaurants, theaters, or airports, and requests for assistance directed to police departments by frightened or assaulted citizens, all represent specific behaviors that we would classify as organizational demands. Obviously implied in such variations is a most difficult problem of operationally specifying this concept, but let us temporarily assume that this can be overcome.

In addition to these types of demands, which assume the form of requests or orders, demands may be self-imposed by organizational members, who, after receiving certain cues from the environment, proceed to act without waiting for anything resembling a specific request. A telephone or electric company, for example, may immediately dispatch crews to sections of a city struck by a tornado before any specific requests from the community are received. Hence, the normative structure includes a series of "if–then" propositions; "if" a certain external event occurs, "then" a certain set of prescribed actions should take place.

Demands on all organizations vary from day to day. In some organizations they vary considerably from season to season. Such variation may be quantitative and/or qualitative. For example, with the first snow of each year, local police are usually confronted with a marked increase in accident reports. This quantitative change in demands usually lasts only a few days as motorists become accustomed to changed driving conditions. Similarly, highway departments experience a qualitative change in demands as they have snow removal responsibilities and have had no such demands since the previous winter.

In addition to quantitative and qualitative fluctuations, demands vary

---

[30] This section and the next are revisions of material the authors included in "Community Disaster and System Stress: A Sociological Perspective," pp. 264–86 in *Social and Psychological Factors in Stress*, Joseph E. McGrath, ed. (New York: Holt, Rinehart & Winston, Inc., 1970).

in priority. Certain demands have more serious consequences if not fulfilled. That is, some are more important than others, either for the welfare of the organization or the total community. High priority values of the organization are threatened by some demands. Hence, a decision required by the mayor's office to order (or not order) evacuation of a city because of an approaching hurricane may be among the most important decisions the mayor will make during his term of office. Closely related to the degree of seriousness attached to the demand is the variable of time—i.e., how much time is available before organizational action is required. And the priority assessment attached to any single demand is subject to change under varying conditions. Thus, organizational demands may change along three separate axes: quantity of demands, actual qualitative changes in demands, and changes in priorities attached to demands.

However, the measurement of demand level has proved to be complicated. Look at a hospital as an example. We may wish to count the number of patients entering the hospital as a crude indicator of demand level. However, some entering by way of the emergency room are treated and released; others are held for observation, from a few hours to several days; some are critical cases requiring immediate and intensive care; some require many hours of surgery, whereas others need only minor medical treatment. Clearly, each patient does not represent an "equal demand unit." The same may be said for patients entering by way of the regular admiting office.

Quite apart from the time involved for diagnosis and treatment, different patients may represent a different kind of demand. Given the norms of the hospital, ten cases of food poisoning represent a different demand load from ten patients with multiple fractures and massive hemorrhaging. This suggests the necessity for classifying the various types of demand and their concomitant organizational requirements. For example, a thirty-quart supply of whole blood may be more than an adequate resource for accident victims, but it is largely irrelevant for patients with food poisoning.

It is also clear that at a given point in time the demand level may vary considerably within different segments of an organization. The maintenance department of an electric company may experience extremely high demand overload following a tornado, whereas there might be no increase at all in the demand for meter reading and billing.

In brief, we would stress the complexity implicit in this concept of organizational demand. But it has proved a useful concept, if only for heuristic purposes. The following generalizations summarize aspects of organizational demands.

1. "Demand units" may vary in the total amount of *effort* required.
2. The total amount of *time* necessary for an acceptable response may also vary.

3. Speed or *urgency* will be critical in some cases but not in others.
4. Demand units will vary as to the *kind of response required.*
5. At any given point in time, the demand level may *vary among segments* of the organization.
6. *Dissensus* may exist within the organization as to demand priority and legitimacy.
7. Organizations vary in their *degree of autonomy* in defining demands—i.e., some have greater autonomy than others in specifying which demands will be accepted.
8. Environmental segments vary as to the *degree of power* that they can exert in defining for different organizations demand priority and legitimacy.
9. Organizations vary in their ability to *monitor changes* in demands.
10. The *stability* of the demand structure varies among organizations.

Organizational capability is defined as the entire range of possible organizational actions that an organization could perform if appropriate decisions to do so were made. On any given day, organizational incumbents engage in a large number of patterned actions, which, when viewed collectively, constitute the performance structure of that organization. These actions might be enumerated so as to be listed *A* through *E*. It is also clear that, in addition to the current performance structure, other behaviors are possible. That is, alternative designs or internal arrangements among the parts of the organization are possible so that a multitude of actions could be performed. Although calculation would prove most complex, let us simply suggest at this point that an organization's capability is represented not only by what is currently observable but also includes a multitude of additional actions. Hence, actions *F* through *Z* are possible, given other design alternatives.

As with demands, organizational capability poses difficult measurement problems. In every organization there is undoubtedly some interchangeability of parts, but in most modern organizations this possibility is relatively limited. Of course, female clerks in an electric company could make modest contributions in repairing downed electrical lines. But a laboratory technician cannot be substituted for a surgeon. For most organizations, then, the total number of personnel is not a useful indicator of capability level. This suggests that a useful measure of capability must include an assessment of the various capabilities of different organizational segments. In short, it requires a profile of capabilities relevant for the kinds of demands that do or could develop.

Organizational capacity is defined as the maximum level of task or subtask performance that can be relatively sustained over time with a specified structural design. That is, capacity refers to the types and level of performance that can be sustained through the use of a particular set of normative, interpersonal, and resource structures.

In contrast to organizational capability, which refers to the various design and action alternatives that are possible given the components of an organization, capacity refers to specific levels of task performance. And organizations have many subtasks to perform, such as communication, decision making, and so forth. Just like individuals, who have differential capacities for different types of tasks, so too, organizations vary as to capacity level depending on the task considered.

Richard Meier has explored similar definitions of this concept as it might be applied to a communication system.

The capacity of the organization for completing transactions will lie somewhere between the peak performance that could not be maintained and the level chosen for "satisficing" (Herbert A. Simon's term for "doing just well enough to get by"). In this framework, the capacity of an institution for completing a flow of transactions is equivalent to the channel capacity of a communications system for coding and decoding messages.[31]

These concepts—demand, capacity, and capability—provide us with a useful way to conceptualize organizational stress.

Organizational Stress

In thinking about the word *stress*, it is important to recognize at the outset that it has been, and currently is still being used in a variety of ways. First, it has referred to various stimuli, responses, and internal states of the unit of analysis. Second, it has been used in research at the biological, psychological, and sociological levels. And too often these distinctions have been blurred, ignored, or uncritically interchanged. In our own theoretical development, Selye's formulation was helpful in reaching conceptual clarity.[32] Although his research was physiological, much of his thinking dealt with problems analogous to those we have confronted. Among the central elements of his position are these:[33] (1) a distinction should be made between stress as a stimulus, condition, or response; (2) the term should refer exclusively to the state or condition of the organism; (3) stress is an abstraction, a construct that possesses no real independent existence; (4) stress should be thought of as a continuous rather than a discrete variable; and (5) stress can be researched through observable changes in body functioning, which can be interpreted as indicators of stress, hence ". . . the important thing is that all these *changes are measurable* manifestations of stress, and,

[31] Richard L. Meier, "Information Input Overload: Features of Growth in Communications-Oriented Industries," in *Mathematical Explorations in Behavioral Sciences*, Fred Massarik and Philborn Ratoosh, eds. (Homewood, Ill.: The Dorsey Press, 1965), p. 267.

[32] See especially Hans Selye, *The Stresses of Life* (New York: McGraw-Hill Book Co., 1956).

[33] Ibid., pp. 25–43.

therefore, suitable indicators." [34] With these ideas in mind, let us explore the concept of stress as it might apply to organizations.

Organizational stress is defined as the *organizational state or condition indicated by the degree of discrepancy between organizational demands and organizational capacity.* Thus, stress is viewed as a condition of the system that is being analyzed. It is a continuous variable. Some mild degree of stress is always present because of flux in demands and capacity. Thus, high and low degrees of stress are referred to, rather than its presence or absence. A high stress state would be produced by a sudden major shift in either variable.[35] Analogous to psychological stress, organizational stress may result from demand overload, demand deprivation, or changes in capacity so as to produce an increased discrepancy between the variables. Similarly, unmet demands over a long period of time might be thought of as chronic stress, as opposed to "acute" stress where there is a sudden and severe change in demands and capacity. The greater the discrepancy between demands and capacity, the greater the degree of stress.

Thompson's formulation is somewhat similar. "Organizations pointed toward emergencies such as fire departments, attempt to level the need for their services by activities designed to prevent emergencies and by emphasis on early detection so that *demand is not allowed to grow to the point that would overtax the capacity of the organization.*" (Emphasis added.)[36]

Although deceptively simple at first glance, the relationship is most complex. To simplify as much as possible, let us examine an extreme case such as might be produced by a large-scale community disaster. The disaster represents an environmental change that precipitates an increase in the discrepancy between demands and capacity of local organizations. A maximum stress state would thus be characterized by:[37]

---

[34] Ibid., p. 51.

[35] March and Simon have also suggested that stress be defined as a continuous rather than a discrete variable; James G. March and Herbert A. Simon, *Organizations* (New York: John Wiley and Sons, Inc., 1958), p. 184.

Argyris defined organizational stress as "a state that exists when the actual giving and receiving loads of the parts are forced to go beyond their 'threshold' so that there is a disequilibrium in the relationship among the parts." Chris Argyris, *Integrating the Individual and the Organization* (New York: John Wiley and Sons, Inc., 1964), p. 128.

Although somewhat similar to our conceptualization, the specific elements that should be measured to determine the presence or degree of stress remain vague. Note that Argyris also refers to "an organizational state" rather than a set of external conditions or stimuli.

[36] Thompson, *Organizations in Action*, op. cit., p. 21.

[37] Of exceptional assistance in these ideas was James A. Robinson, "The Concept of Crisis in Decision-Making," *Series Studies in Social and Economic Sciences, Symposia Studies No. 11* (Washington, D.C.: The National Institute of Social and Behavioral Sciences), June 1962.

1. Change in Demands.
   a. Quantity.
      (1) Sharp increase.
      (2) Increase is unanticipated.
   b. Priority.
      (1) Consequences of organizational action threaten central values of organization or society, i.e., organizational actions are viewed with increased seriousness.
      (2) Immediate organizational action is required.
   c. Qualitative changes.
      (1) Demands previously met, but not currently being met, are made on the organization.
      (2) New demands not previously made on the organization are made and temporarily accepted by the organization.
2. Changes in Organizational Capacity.
   a. Changes in resource structure.
      (1) Absence[38] of personnel, especially key personnel.
      (2) Absence of important equipment, material, or buildings.
      (3) Absence of crucial information or records.
   b. Changes in normative structure—emergent norms are in contradiction to those previously existing.
   c. Change in interpersonal structure—emergent interpersonal relationships which are highly strained.

To continue using natural disaster as an example, Figure 7–2 illustrates the type of relationship that might exist between the variables.

Note three points. First, a high stress state existed in the time between points A and B. Second, usually demands are below capacity. And third, after high stress ends, often capacity does not return to its original level, because the organization learns.[39]

Of special interest is this third point, the increase in capacity. Recalling the concept of organizational capability, we emphasized that many structural alternatives were possible, as were many types of actions other than those in which the organization usually engaged. As stress increases, different alternatives are sought from the numerous structural alternatives available (as defined by the organization's capability). Some of these alternatives may increase capacity. Thus, organizational behavior is analogous to the coping processes that have been analyzed at the psychological level. As different structural arrange-

---

[38] The term *absence* is used in a broad sense here—e.g., a key official may have been killed or injured in the disaster or may have been out of town at the time he was needed; similarly, equipment, material, and information may have been damaged, or have been taken elsewhere before the disaster. At any rate, they were unavailable when needed.

[39] See Robert L. Chapman and John L. Kennedy, "The Background and Implications of the Rand Corporation Systems Research Laboratory Studies," in *Some Theories of Organization*, rev. ed., Albert H. Rubenstein and Chadwick J. Haberstroh, eds. (Homewood, Ill.: The Dorsey Press, 1966), pp. 149–56.

FIGURE 7–2 Organizational Stress As a Function of Demand-Capacity Relationship

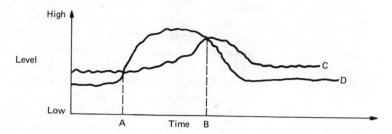

ments are tried, some are found to increase the capacity of the unit, whereas others may result in decreased capacity. And it is clear that most organizations do not have adequate procedures for assessing quickly the effects of their coping efforts.[40]

Let us start with a basic theme. As organizational stress increases, changes in organizational performance structure (i.e., patterned interaction sequences) will occur. Thus, following Selye's analysis, we suggest that organizational stress can be researched by the specification of *observable* changes in performance structure. These changes can be not only observed, but also *measured*. And with future work directed at operationalizing demands, capacity, and capability, these performance structure changes can be directly linked to stress. The eventual goal is that, with prestress data on the performance structure, demands, capability, and capacity levels of an organization, changes in performance structure could effectively be predicted given specified changes in either demands or capacity.

To illustrate, let us assume that a large community disaster has just occurred. Immediately following this event, the demands on emergency organizations will be quickly increased. Certain demands will be viewed by organizational incumbents as legitimate responsibilities. Certain equipment or personnel may have been rendered inoperable by the disaster. Thus, as organizations attempt to cope with the sudden change in demands and capacity precipitated by the event, certain changes in organizational performance structures may be anticipated. For example, following the 1964 Alaskan earthquake, the decision-making pattern in the Anchorage Public Works Department was significantly modified.[41] Many decisions were made at much lower levels

[40] Thompson has suggested that the central problem for complex organizations is "coping with uncertainty," which represents a key element in the "new tradition" of organizational theory. Thompson, op. cit., pp. 9–13.

[41] Daniel Yutzy, *Community Priorities in the Anchorage, Alaska, Earthquake; 1964* (Columbus, Ohio: Disaster Research Center, The Ohio State University, 1969); and David S. Adams, *Emergency Actions and Disaster Reactions: An Analysis of the Anchorage Public Works Department in the 1964 Alaskan Earthquake* (Columbus, Ohio: Disaster Research Center, The Ohio State University, 1969).

than they would have been normally. Organizational members at all levels were faced with many new types of decisions. In general, there was much less consultation; officials often reported, "There just wasn't time to ask anyone else." Similarly, lines of authority were often breached. Upper-echelon officials went directly to specialists or foremen for current information and advice. In addition, many items were purchased without official authorization as ways of "cutting red tape" were sought. In short, as Brouillette and Quarantelli suggest, the organization experienced a "debureaucratization process." [42]

However, future research must be more specific and precise than is possible in descriptive narratives. It is our hope that this stress framework might assist in increased theoretical precision and development. For example, many types of hypotheses can be derived from the framework in a fairly systematic fashion. Recall our initial theme: the greater the degree of stress (as defined by the discrepancy), the greater the change in organizational performance structure. And the degree of stress may be altered by changes in either demands or capacity. Both of these variables have subcomponents of a more specific nature, which can be used in hypothesis statements. Thus, building on the conceptualization presented earlier, we can formulate several hypotheses.

1. The greater the increase in demands, the greater the degree of change in the performance structure.
2. The less anticipated the increase in demands, the greater the degree of change in the performance structure.
3. The more serious the consequences of the demands, the greater the degree of change in the performance structure.
4. The sooner organizational action is required to respond to the demands, the greater the degree of change in the performance structure.
5. The more key personnel are absent, the greater the degree of change in the performance structure.
6. The greater the degree to which emergent norms are in contradiction to previously existing norms, the greater the degree of change in the performance structure.
7. The greater the degree of strain in emergent interpersonal relationships, the greater the degree of change in the performance structure.

These hypotheses are a beginning toward the specification of variables that define a stress situation. But although they flow from the general hypothesis, only one variable is elaborated, i.e., organizational stress. They describe with greater precision *when* stress will increase

[42] John R. Brouillette and E. L. Quarantelli, "Types of Patterned Variation in Bureaucratic Adaptations to Organizational Stress," *Sociological Inquiry*, 41: 40–41 (Winter 1971).

and thereby suggest ideas as to how the degree of stress might be measured. But they do not suggest *what* changes might be anticipated in the performance structure. Following Selye, it is performance structure changes, we have argued, that may also be used as indicators of the intensity of stress.

Note that in this framework the concept of stress is relegated to a position similar to the physician's use of the concept of illness. Illness refers to the state or condition of an organism and is said to exist when certain indicators or symptoms are present. Thus, when changes in normal functioning of the organism occur (as indicated by the presence of a rash, for example), illness is said to be present or the organism is said to be ill. The word *ill* is used as a descriptive adjective, i.e., it describes the state of an organism. However, when used as a noun (e.g., "illness is present"), confusion results, as this implies that a "thing" is present. The connotation of a "thing" is unfortunate, as the concept clearly implies only a description of the state of the organism, which is known only by certain observable indicators, which reflect changes in the normal functioning of the organism.

Similarly, intensification of organizational stress can be identified by certain observable indicators, i.e., changes in performance structure, which occur as organizational members attempt to cope with changed relationships between organizational capacity and demands. More precise measurement of variables of the type just outlined should stipulate not only when the performance structure will change, but also the rate and degree of such change.

Performance structure, however, is also a very abstract concept. What specifically will change? It is toward that question that future empirical work must be directed. For the present, it remains an unanswered question. However, a few leads based on reviews of descriptive narratives provide us with a start. Thus, we can tentatively hypothesize:

1. If the degree of organizational stress consistently increases, the rate of task performance will initially increase, then level off, and finally decrease.
2. As the degree of organizational stress increases, organizational incumbents will increasingly limit their activities to those tasks they define as being of highest priority.
3. As the degree of organizational stress increases, the rate of official and unofficial decision making will increase.
4. As the degree of organizational stress increases, the number of individuals conferred with before a decision is made will decrease.
5. As the degree of organizational stress increases, the lines of authority will shift so as to emphasize special skill and/or knowledge of position incumbents.

6. As the degree of organizational stress increases, the number of organizational incumbents through which directives are transmitted will decrease.
7. As the degree of organizational stress increases, the modes of communication will shift so as increasingly to maximize speed.
8. As the degree of organizational stress increases, there will be an increase in activity directed at environmental surveillance.[43]

As more descriptive data are obtained as to how groups and organizations respond to altered degrees of stress, more hypotheses can be formulated and tested. The next step will be to reformulate multivariate propositions that relate the specific stress level indicators (e.g., degree of increase in demands, degree to which they are unanticipated, and so forth) to specific sets of performance structure changes. After much more insight is attained here, then we will be ready to ask the next question: Why does the organization change the way it does when it is in an acute stress state?

To pursue this question briefly, two variables are of special interest: organizational strain and pre-emergency planning. Organizational strain was defined as inconsistencies or discrepancies between structural elements of an organization. Several hypotheses suggest interrelations between stress and strain. For example, the greater the degree of organizational strain, the less the degree of stress that can be tolerated without complete disintegration. In fact, this hypothesis was used as a mode of definition by Stogdill. He defined group integration "as the extent to which structure and operations are capable of being maintained under stress."[44] But implicit in this approach is a definition of *disintegration*, which may not occur too frequently and is most difficult to define.[45]

An alternative that appears far more productive is to reformulate the hypothesis so that strain is used as a predictive device for performance structure change. Thus, as the degree of organizational stress increases,

---

[43] All of these hypotheses are of one type, however. They deal with the type of stress in which we were most interested, i.e., where demands greatly exceeded capacity. But what of the opposite? Thompson has hypothesized that "organizations with capacity in excess of what the task environment supports will seek to enlarge their domains." Thompson, op. cit., p. 46.

Other than this hypothesis, however, we have not explored performance structure changes that might result from this type of "demand deprivation" stress.

[44] Ralph M. Stogdill, *Individual Behavior and Group Achievement* (New York: Oxford University Press, 1959), p. 198.

[45] Our formulation is somewhat similar to Merton's: "In referring to this as 'capacity' rather than an empirically observed degree of stability, I intend to make explicit the consideration that the observed stability of a group is contingent on the degree of environmental stress and not only on its own internal structure. . . ." Merton, op. cit., p. 323.

performance structure changes will have a greater tendency to occur at those points where strain was most intense. Perhaps aptly labeled a "precracked windshield" hypothesis, it does suggest a relationship between the three variables of stress, strain, and performance structure. The following hypotheses emerge.

1. As the degree of organizational stress increases, performance structure change will vary directly with the intensity of *intersystem normative inconsistency.*
2. As the degree of organizational stress increases, performance structure change will vary directly with the intensity of *intersystem normative dissensus.*
3. As the degree of organizational stress increases, performance structure change will vary directly with the intensity of *intrasystem normative ambiguity.*
4. As the degree of organizational stress increases, performance structure change will vary directly with the intensity of *intersystem normative overload.*
5. As the degree of organizational stress increases, performance structure change will vary directly with the degree of *intrasystem interpersonal imbalance.*
6. As the degree of organizational stress increases, performance structure change will vary directly with the *height of the location of strain* in the structure.

Certainly these hypotheses are only a start toward specification of the intricate interrelationships between stress, strain, and performance structure. But they are a start. Additional hypotheses could be stated using other distinctions that were proposed in the conceptualization of strain, e.g., intersystem normative ambiguity, resource incompatability, and so on. And as additional conceptual refinement emerges for each of these aspects of strain, other hypotheses can be detailed and subjected to empirical testing.

Let us now turn our attention to another type of variable, which may be most important in predicting organizational behavior under acute stress conditions—pre-emergency planning. Following our discussion of organizational capability as alternative actions and structural arrangements, certain organizations may have highly detailed plans that specify such alternatives. Thus shifts into emergency operating procedures may be accomplished quickly with relative ease so that capacity can be increased rapidly to meet demand increases. Hence, the high stress state may be very temporary when adequate predisaster planning has been done. That is, the pre-planning enables the organizational participants to select from among the many possible alternatives (capability), one that may increase capacity so as adequately to meet the

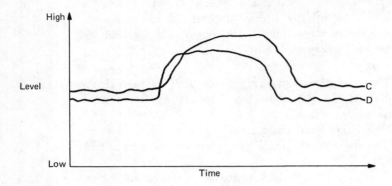

demands. Because both demand and capacity changes are almost simultaneous, there is little or no change in the relationship between them. With adequate monitoring of the environment to detect changes rapidly and predisaster plans to permit rapid reorganization, some emergency units are able to meet drastic demand increases and yet experience little or no stress. See Figure 7–3 for a diagram of this idea.

But what if the predisaster planners misevaluate the demands? In such instances, plans may actually prove to be a handicap to the organization by precipitating coping behavior that is nonproductive. In considering variables that specify relevant factors, the following hypotheses were formulated using the idea of emergency performance structure. This refers to the performance structure as it ought to exist when reorganization is necessary to meet a potential stress situation. As such, it represents a segment of the normative structure that remains dormant until such time as organizational incumbents detect environmental change indicating the appropriateness of this emergency performance structure.

1. The degree to which organizational plans that specify an emergency performance structure *coincide with the actual demands produced* varies directly with the degree to which performance structure change can be predicted by such plans when a potential stress situation is anticipated.
2. The degree to which organizational plans that specify an emergency performance structure are *rehearsed* varies directly with the degree to which performance structure change can be predicted by such plans when a potential stress situation is anticipated.
3. The *proportion* of organizational incumbents *who participate* in rehearsals of organizational plans that specify an emergency performance structure varies directly with the degree to which performance structure change can be predicted by such plans when a potential stress situation is anticipated.

4. The degree to which *rehearsals* of organizational plans that specify an emergency performance structure *coincide with the characteristics of the actual crisis-producing event* varies directly with the degree to which performance structure change can be predicted by such plans when a potential stress situation is anticipated.

These two variables of organizational strain and precrisis plans merit much further research. And as Brouillette and Quarantelli suggest, there are other factors that will have to be incorporated into future analytic work, such as community and societal contexts in which the organization functions.[46] Also related to such predictions are organizational mechanisms for detecting environmental change. How and to what degree are organizational structures equipped to evaluate coping behaviors? It often appears that changes are made with little emphasis on feedback mechanisms to provide evaluation data. The use of feedback so as to cope more effectively under stress is, by itself, a large area in which much more research is needed. And it is clear that too often organizations have no effective mechanisms to provide them with continuous feedback as to how effective, if at all, their coping efforts have been.

The Stress–Strain Relationship: A Dynamic View

Stress and strain are complex concepts. However, they provide us with an important input for the analysis of organizational change. Before we continue our pursuit of that topic, however, let us briefly review the ideas thus far outlined and make sure that the relationship between stress and strain is clear.

In contrast to the imagery that stress and strain are unusual or atypical, we have emerged with a view of organizations wherein stress is always present—only the intensity varies. Strains too, always are present, and consistently are changing both in location and intensity. And there are many types of strains that can be differentiated. Indeed, such differentiation is necessary if better measurement systems are to be developed. Thus, normative incompatabilities may reflect inconsistencies, dissensus, ambiguity, or overload. And these inconsistencies, like those that lie in the interpersonal or resource structures, may reflect intra- or inter-system structural cleavages.

Finally, we have proposed that the referent system we are using can vary. Thus, we may wish to focus on a single structural position and assess the strains found among and within the corresponding role relationships. However, we may shift levels of analysis and focus on a single department, division, or collection of such units. Or again, our focus could be on the total organization and its environment. Here we

[46] Brouillette and Quarantelli, op. cit., p. 44.

might be led to ask about the degree of consensus within the organization about its primary mission, for example. And also, we might investigate the consistency between this image and that held by various environmental sectors. For just as we have learned that much behavior at a dyadic level becomes interpretable when we recognize that role expectations are in the process of negotiation, so also are expectations attached to large collective systems, such as organizations, subject to continual negotiation. Thus, organizational incumbents actively seek to manipulate expectations held by environmental units so as to increase their own autonomy, prestige, and security. And in this process new strains and strain patterns are created, shifted, and dissipated.

Organizational stress was defined as the state or condition indicated by the degree of discrepancy between organizational demands and organizational capacity. Thus, organizations may experience chronic stress, where the discrepancy between demands and capacity is not excessive but continual. In contrast, we used the illustration of emergency organizations confronting community disasters in our discussion of *acute* stress. We emphasized that this permitted a more complex view, but one which was necessarily so. Reactions to any single event are not uniform. And some organizations have designed emergency plans so that they can modify their structure, and thereby alter capacity, so as to keep pace with demand change. By definition, then, they experience less stress because of such adaptive actions. Note that this requires careful environmental surveillance and continual feedback regarding the consequences of coping behaviors. These types of stress patterns are summarized by the diagrams presented in Figure 7–4.

What are the relationships between stress and strain? First, we suspect that information about strain may indicate where performance structure changes are most likely to occur. Using the precracked windshield analogy, structural points of weakness are specified. Thus, when there are sudden shifts in the demand–capacity relationship (acute stress), we have some idea of where the system will break down first, where coping efforts may be directed. Second, in making predictions about the degree of stress that different systems could tolerate, we would hypothesize that in general, systems with greater intensities of strain will evidence more rapid disintegration under acute stress. Strains may prevent or delay rapid modification of capacity so as to cope with increased demands. However, this varies with the pattern and distribution of strain, an idea that we will pursue in the next chapter. Third, some coping behaviors give rise to new strains, which in turn act to lower capacity. Confronted with rapidly increased demands, stress is intensified because this reduction in capacity acts to increase the demand–capacity discrepancy. Thus, the relationships between stress and strain are complex and numerous. However, a final point of clarification remains.

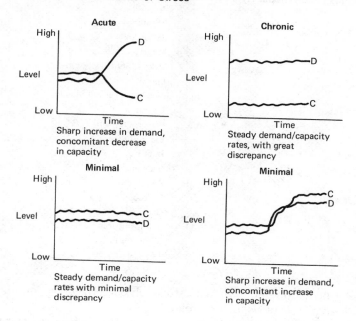

FIGURE 7-4   Patterns of Stress

Acute

High / Level / Low — Time
Sharp increase in demand, concomitant decrease in capacity

Chronic

High / Level / Low — Time
Steady demand/capacity rates, with great discrepancy

Minimal

High / Level / Low — Time
Steady demand/capacity rates with minimal discrepancy

Minimal

High / Level / Low — Time
Sharp increase in demand, concomitant increase in capacity

One type of strain was labeled "normative overload." And the organization can be used as the referent system. Isn't stress, then, just a special type of strain—that is, intersystem normative overload when the organization is used as the referent? The answer is an emphatic no. But in pursuing this question we uncover an important set of distinctions that leads us directly into a discussion of organizational change. Intersystem normative overload, at the organizational level, refers to "excessive" expectations being attached to the system by environmental sectors. Thus, a particular organization confronts *expectations* from numerous sources that are defined by us (the analysts) as "excessive." Isn't that the same thing as stress? No! But let us see why not.

We have consistently made a distinction between role *behavior or performance* and role *expectation or definition*. We propose a similar distinction here. Thus, organizational demands refer to specific behavioral acts initiated externally or resulting from demand-relevant cues (specific behavioral events, actual or anticipated). When we speak of any type of normative strain, we are referring to *norms*, i.e., expectations. We defined *organizational* domain as sets of expectations that are held for an organizational unit. There need not be consensus, within or without, about these expectations, as indicated by the notion of strain. Thus organizational *domain* refers to *expectations* and organizational *demand* refers to *behavior*. Strain, be it exclusively internal or reflecting intersystem inconsistency, refers to a state or condition of

The Stress–Strain Relationship: A Dynamic View   261

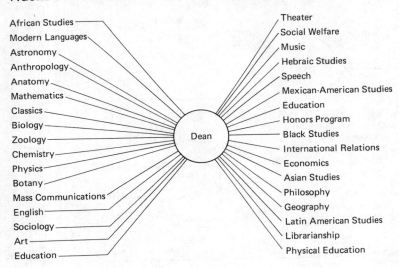

FIGURE 7–5   Normative Overload: Hypothetical University Structure

African Studies
Modern Languages
Astronomy
Anthropology
Anatomy
Mathematics
Classics
Biology
Zoology
Chemistry
Physics
Botany
Mass Communications
English
Sociology
Art
Education

Dean

Theater
Social Welfare
Music
Hebraic Studies
Speech
Mexican-American Studies
Education
Honors Program
Black Studies
International Relations
Economics
Asian Studies
Philosophy
Geography
Latin American Studies
Librarianship
Physical Education

the expectation sets, whereas stress characterizes the organizational state given sets of *behavioral* relationships.

Note Figure 7–5, in which a component of the official normative structure of a hypothetical university is outlined. Here, a large number of departments are to be coordinated by a single administrator. There is no divisional structure provided, so each department head presumably deals directly with the dean. Such a system might function for some time. Only occasionally would things pile up on the dean's desk. And rapid movement "across the desk" might very much reflect the interpersonal structure. However, if all department heads should try to contact this position incumbent simultaneously, the demands could not be met. If their demands were urgent, perhaps stimulated by a student strike or riot, the strain (normative overload) would become apparent quickly. As such, it represents a type of "demand potential" that is judged by the analyst as excessive. Knowledge of such strain provides us with clues of where coping efforts will probably be directed in acute stress situations where demand levels suddenly increase. As many college and university administrators have learned in recent years of student demonstrations and strikes, structures characterized by such strains are highly vulnerable.

Organizational incumbents negotiate expectations continually. And negotiations regarding domain are constantly taking place within organizations, but especially among incumbents and persons representing various sectors of the environment. When confronted with new or atypical demands, incumbents may simply ignore them and use the argument that they are not part of the domain as it has been negotiated at that point. Of course, the domain may be changed so that the new expectations are accepted. Then new demands (behaviorally speaking), when forthcoming, will be viewed as appropriate by the organizational incumbents. If there is no change in capacity, then the demand increase will alter the demand–capacity discrepancy and the organization will be characterized by increased stress. Incumbents may seek to modify capacity so that they can handle the new demands. Alternatively, they may seek to renegotiate the domain expectations so as to have the demands cut off and directed elsewhere. Thus, we have observed that organizations when confronted with acute stress, at times direct their energies toward negotiations of domain so as to modify the demand pattern. For example, police organizations may temporarily abandon their customary task of securing an area following a large-scale disaster; "Such a job is beyond our capacity—we can't be expected to do it." Negotiations result in assignment of the task to the military so that the police can "properly" take care of the demands that are "really police work." This distinction between organizational demand and domain is a critical one and provides us with some very helpful ways of looking at organizational change. With this conceptual apparatus in hand, let us now turn to a more systematic treatment of change.

Chapter 8

ORGANIZATIONAL CHANGE

In many respects, organizational change has been a theme throughout all of the preceding chapters. Such a perspective is inherent in the process view, which we have emphasized. Organizations, conceptualized as patterned interaction systems, are in a constant state of flux. Yet we are also impressed with the stability of many interaction patterns. Thus, the question is not whether organizations change or remain stable, for they do both. But when is change most likely to occur? How do we explain it? And can change be better planned and directed? These are but a few of the questions we will now pursue.

Types of System Change

Three types or intensities of change should be differentiated.[1] They are related, but failure to keep them separate analytically results in numerous pitfalls. Organizations can change in a multitude of ways simultaneously, and this simple threefold distinction is helpful in recognizing some important differences.

Regularized Cycles

First, let us recognize that organizations experience many regularized cycles of change. Seasonal variation occurs in the demand structure for most organizations. For example,

[1] Elaboration on these types of changes and others is presented by Wilbert E. Moore, *Social Change* (Englewood Cliffs, N.J.: Prentice-Hall, Inc., 1963), pp. 12–18.

dry cleaning establishments are confronted with large numbers of winter coats and drapes in the spring, while at the same time highway departments retire snow removal equipment and bring out paint wagons. Students flock to schools during September, which were empty the month before. In accordance with such seasonal demand variation, organizational incumbents have varied their programming so as to adapt easily. Thus, the normative structure, in particular, contains prescriptions as to how departments, divisions, and the like, are to be modified in task and personnel functions at these different times. Demand variation is anticipated, and, following the organizational program, incumbents adapt to such changes.

Less obvious, but somewhat similar, is demand variation of a less predictable nature. We focused on response to natural disaster in the previous chapter. Emergency organizations, like department stores before Christmas, do anticipate demand variation. Of course, when the variation will occur and exactly what its dimensions will be, remain unknown. However, through careful preplanning, sudden demand shifts, such as are precipitated by natural disasters, can be adapted to fairly rapidly. A potentially acute stress situation can thereby be avoided or minimized. Of course, this depends on the degree to which the prescribed adaptations represent coping behaviors that meet the disaster demands.

In some geographical areas many types of disasters are seasonal and similar in type. For example, flooding in some Ohio Valley communities is a common occurrence. As the water rises upstream, local officials in nearby communities know fairly well which streets will be flooded and for how long.[2] The demand change is somewhat predictable, and preplanning permits the organization to adapt so as to avert a stress condition. That is, as demands change so does organizational behavior; thus, marked discrepancy between demand and capacity is averted.

Of course, other disasters present different types of demands. A sudden explosion, a flash flood, or a jet plane crash occur without warning; all represent more difficult coping requirements. Yet, rapid assessment through trained surveillance units can provide information as to the general properties of the event. All sectors of the organization can be alerted that a rapid demand shift is immediately forthcoming. Thus, Thompson hypothesizes: "When the range of task-environment variations is large or unpredictable, the responsible organization component must achieve the necessary adaptation by monitoring that

[2] Communities of this type appear to develop distinct disaster subcultures, i.e., sets of normative guides for both officials and citizens as to appropriate behavior in special types of recurring events, such as floods or hurricanes. See Harry E. Moore, . . . *And the Wind Blew* (Austin, Texas: The Hogg Foundation for Mental Health, 1964), pp. 195–221; and William A. Anderson, "Some Observations on a Disaster Subculture: The Organizational Response in Cincinnati, Ohio, to the 1964 Flood" (Columbus, Ohio: Disaster Research Center, Ohio State University, 1965), unpublished paper.

environment and planning responses, and this calls for localized units."[3]

Adaptation efforts are initiated, but often preplanning does not result in the construction of sufficient feedback mechanisms to permit organizational incumbents to keep track of coping responses and their consequences. Thus, the coping behavior is more sporadic, uneven, and ineffective, as the normative guidelines developed before the event are more general and often lacking in specific direction. And, most importantly, organizations frequently lack means for rapidly assessing the consequences of ongoing coping responses. In such instances, responding emergency organizations will most likely incur increased stress.

What is critical, then, is the predictability and understanding of the event and the degree to which preplanning elicits coping responses that meet the emergent demands. And because there is no warning, events that require immediate responses, like a large explosion, are most likely to precipitate organizational stress.

In short, all organizations confront changing environments. But some types of environmental changes are predictable, well-understood, and recurring. Thus, there is a good deal of time to plan the adaptation and to gain reasonably adequate information as to what might be expected. This represents the most regularized cycles of organizational change. But, as indicated in Figure 8–1, such demand shifts represent only one type of possibility when we look at degree of knowledge and length of warning period. For emergency organizations, cell number three is a common type of occurrence (see Figure 8–1). Automobile accidents, fires, shootings, and the like, have been sufficiently experienced to generate standardized response patterns. Indeed, it was this very type of event that generated the concept of demand-relevant cues, which we discussed as a basic component of the concept of organizational demand. On the basis of knowledge that certain environmental events had occurred (e.g., a fire), organizations respond following standardized patterns. And following our discussion of stress, it is cell number four that most likely precipitates intense acute stress, since the demand–capacity discrepancy can be maximized quickly. And it is, in turn, responses to this type of event that are most likely to precipitate changes of a different kind—that is, changes in the future functioning of the system.

Change in Systems

In contrast to seasonal or regularized cycles in organizational functioning are minor changes, which take place over time. There are many ways to approach this type of change. For example, disaster researchers

---

[3] James D. Thompson, *Organizations in Action* (New York: McGraw-Hill Book Co., 1967), p. 72.

FIGURE 8–1 Knowledge and Warning of Demand Changes

	Degree to Which Members Know What to Expect	
Warning Period	High Knowledge	Low Knowledge
Long (e.g., Seasonal)	1	2
None	3	4

have been interested in short-term responses to large-scale catastrophes. Often, preplanning is inadequate to permit organizational incumbents easily and quickly to modify their behaviors so as to cope in a coordinated fashion. They lack a switching mechanism to convert into a new organizational pattern that deals more effectively with emergent conditions. In addition to focusing on such transitory response patterns, which, usually persist for only several hours, or a few days at most, we have often observed emergent changes that remain after the crisis has ended. For example, a new emphasis on emergency planning might elicit resource allocations designed to produce revised planning and training procedures. Following a large explosion in Indianapolis, the local Red Cross chapter initiated an entire new structure—a radio telephone system that linked the chapter and several local hospitals.[4] Anderson has reported that numerous similar types of changes occurred within organizations in Anchorage as they recovered from the impact of the 1964 earthquake.[5] New patterns of change that were initiated and pre-existing patterns of changes that were accelerated are carefully documented in his analysis of 23 Anchorage organizations. Thus, following acute stress experiences, we often can expect minor changes in organizational functioning. But equally often, the changes are minor and usually reflect an effort to add on new activities rather than change existing operations in any significant manner.

Clearly, some types of organizations appear more likely to adopt innovations than others. Aiken and Hage[6] present a detailed argument in which they conclude that seven key variables differentiate organizational tendencies to adopt new programs or other innovations. Thus,

[4] Thomas E. Drabek, *Disaster in Aisle 13* (Columbus, Ohio: College of Administrative Science, Ohio State University, 1968), pp. 124–27; 132–33.

[5] William A. Anderson, *Disaster and Organizational Change: A Study of the Long-term Consequences in Anchorage of the 1964 Alaskan Earthquake* (Columbus, Ohio: Disaster Research Center, Ohio State University, 1969).

[6] Jerald Hage and Michael Aiken, *Social Change in Complex Organizations* (New York: Random House, 1970).

organizations that are highly complex, in that incumbents have higher educational levels and more professionalized and specialized jobs, are most likely to adopt new programs more rapidly.[7] And organizations characterized by high centralization of authority, formalization of rules, and stratification of reward structures are less likely to adopt innovations.[8] Finally, the higher the volume of production and the greater the emphasis on efficiency, the lower the rate of program change.[9] Research findings from a wide variety of studies lend support for this argument.[10] Thus, we can begin to identify some of the critical variables that allow us to predict and explain varying rates of this type of organizational change.

Noting the scarcity of organizational research on efforts at deliberate change, Corwin reported his assessment of the Teacher Corps—a multi-million-dollar program of the 1960s, which was "designed to promote educational reforms in low income schools through innovative teacher training programs." [11] Would the injection of a large number of ideal-istic, highly motivated teacher apprentices precipitate adoption of ed-ucational innovations? Corwin's research clearly indicated that in this instance the change agents had relatively little overall impact. Why? He suggests that "there will be more technological change in organiza-tional networks in which there is unequal balance of power, but a high degree of interdependence among the organizations, and in which boundary roles are staffed by cosmopolitan, liberal, and professionally competent members." [12] But these variables did not provide an adequate explanation; controlling on the first two factors, "the more liberal the interns in a school, the less innovation that occurred." [13] Thus, Corwin concluded that two additional ingredients, missing in this instance, must be considered: "(a) the change agents must be introduced in sufficiently large numbers, and (b) at more than one echelon in the hierarchy." [14]

In contrast to adoption of new programs or other innovations, which

---

[7] Ibid., pp. 32–38.

[8] Ibid., pp. 38–49.

[9] Ibid., pp. 49–55.

[10] Hage and Aiken argue rather convincingly that their data and interpretations can be viewed as compatible with previous work such as that of Tom Burns and G. M. Stalker, *The Management of Innovation* (London: Tavistock Publications, 1961); Ibid., pp. 69–71.

[11] Ronald G. Corwin, "Strategies for Organizational Innovation: An Empirical Comparison," paper presented at the annual meeting of the American Sociological Association, Denver, Colorado, August 31, 1971, p. 5.

[12] Ibid., p. 11.

[13] Ibid.

[14] Ibid.

may in turn exert new internal pressures for change in system functioning, is the problem of succession. All organizations lose and gain new members. Usually, however, efforts are directed at obtaining replacements who will fit existing niches and so, despite personnel turnover, the pattern of activity remains fairly stable. Moreover, stability is enhanced through a variety of techniques in addition to selection, such as preservice and in-service training programs. Here the normative structure is presented and the "rules of organizational life," at least at the official level, are spelled out. Confronted with high rates of succession in specialized sectors (e.g., military base commanders, or college professors), we see another common device—longevity in key administrative positions.[15] Thus, professors, like students and military personnel, move about from city to city, but the structures they encounter seem almost immune to their coming and going. Why? Because the locals, whose movement is nearly nonexistent, remain at their posts to see that the organization keeps its basic character.[16]

Of course, as new members are added, old ones may remain. Thus, over time many organizations experience growth in just this way. And as they grow, a variety of types of structural adjustments can be anticipated. Some have proposed that growth must be accompanied with decreased efficiency because of excessive administrative costs.[17] That is possible; however, based on empirical evidence gathered to date, such a conclusion appears unwarranted. For example, several researchers have compared the relative size of administrative components in organizations of various sizes.[18] Although results from these cross-sectional analyses have not been totally consistent, four major conclusions can be gleaned.

[15] Oscar Grusky, "The Effects of Succession: A Comparative Study of Military and Business Organization," in The Sociology of Organizations: Basic Studies, Oscar Grusky and George Miller, eds. (New York: The Free Press, 1970), pp. 439–54.

[16] Alvin W. Gouldner, "Cosmopolitans and Locals: Toward an Analysis of Latent Social Roles, I and II," Administrative Science Quarterly, 2: 281–306; 444–80 (1957–1958).

[17] For example, C. Northcote Parkinson, Parkinson's Law (Boston: Houghton Mifflin Company, 1957).

[18] Frederick L. Campbell and Ronald L. Akers, "Organizational Size, Complexity, and the Administrative Component in Occupational Associations," The Sociological Quarterly, 11: 435–51 (Fall, 1970); J. Eugene Haas, Richard H. Hall, and Norman J. Johnson, "The Size of the Supportive Component in Organizations: A Multi-Organizational Analysis," Social Forces, 42: 9–17 (October 1963); Theodore R. Anderson and Seymour Warkov, "Organizational Size and Functional Complexity: A Study of Administration in Hospitals," American Sociological Review, 26: 23–28 (February 1961); and Frederic W. Terrien and Donald L. Mills, "The Effect of Changing Size upon the Internal Structure of Organizations," American Sociological Review, 20: 11–13 (February 1955).

First, bigger organizations tend to have larger numbers of staff involved in administrative activities. However, although administrative staffs increase with greater organizational size, they do so at a decreasing rate.[19] Thus, there appears to be some economy of scale as reflected in the curvilinear relationships (exponential) reported.[20] But note, this is not to say that all large organizations necessarily have larger proportions of administrative staff than any smaller organizations. Clearly, size alone does not determine organizational structure.[21] Thus, second, it is clear that this relationship is affected by technology, proportion of professionals, and the like. As yet, linkages among these various structural features have not been specified adequately.[22]

Organizational size is not equivalent to organizational growth.[23] Thus, the third point of emphasis is that neither size nor growth are the simple, relatively clear-cut variables they appear to be at first. Reviewing the cross-sectional studies just cited makes the point. Organizational size might refer to full-time members, but what of part-time and voluntary personnel? These could be converted into full-time equivalents based on the number of hours actually worked[24] or simply counted as equivalent to full-time members. Obviously, comparison of results based on variations of this type is difficult. But then, who is a member? For example, in schools, prisons, or churches, are paid personnel the only members? If there is increase in the number of students, prisoners, or parishioners, is this a change in size or growth, or neither? Clearly, organizations may add new programs, new products,

---

[19] Campbell and Akers, op. cit., p. 447.

[20] Supplementing Campbell and Akers' (op. cit.) cross-sectional data on 197 national occupational associations are Blau's data on 53 state unemployment insurance agencies (including 1,201 local branches and 354 headquarters divisions). Peter M. Blau, "A Formal Theory of Differentiation in Organizations," *American Sociological Review*, 35: 201–18 (April 1970).

[21] The relative impact of size on structure remains controversial. Blau used it as the initial independent variable in his "Formal Theory of Differentiation," Blau, op. cit.; and Peter M. Blau and Richard A. Schoenherr, *The Structure of Organizations* (New York: Basic Books, Inc., 1971).

In contrast, Hall, Haas, and Johnson, after reviewing data on 75 diverse organizations concluded "that size may be rather irrelevant as a factor in determining organizational structure" (p. 112). Richard H. Hall, J. Eugene Haas, and Norman J. Johnson, "Organizational Size, Complexity, and Formalization," *American Sociological Review*, 32: 903–12 (December 1967).

[22] Hall's review and analysis contains many helpful insights for future research on such matters. See Richard H. Hall, *Organizations: Structure and Process* (Englewood Cliffs, N.J.: Prentice-Hall, Inc., 1972), pp. 109–39.

[23] William H. Starbuck, "Organizational Growth and Development," in *Handbook of Organizations*, James G. March, ed. (Chicago: Rand McNally and Co., 1965), pp. 451–533.

[24] This strategy was followed in Haas, Hall, and Johnson, op. cit.

new services, or new sources of income—are not these also forms of growth?[25]

Fourth, and finally, although a few cross-sectional studies have been completed, there is a real scarcity of *longitudinal* research.[26] We need several types of organizations, with subsamples that are *homogeneous* regarding technology, major activity or output, complexity, formalization, member size, and the like, that can be followed over time.[27] In this way, multiple patterns of growth reflecting variation in both internal and external conditions could be mapped. Until this is achieved, our knowledge base regarding this type of change will remain rather sparse.

Sometimes, however, the types of inputs entering an organization may change dramatically in a short period of time. For example, students enrolling in a university suddenly may be older, with war experience behind them, and an eagerness to gain new occupational skills. Most may be married and eager to complete their families before much more time transpires. Such a shift may be instrumental in precipitating a third type of change, one which will be our focus hereafter—namely, basic change *of* the system itself.[28]

Change of Systems

Sometimes the name of an organization is changed, but little else, other than the letterhead, is altered. More often the name continues,

---

[25] These various types of growth or increase in size may have very different structural consequences. For example, additional programs or products may add to horizontal, but not to vertical complexity. And the relationship between these two types of complexity and administrative ratio may not be the same.

As Akers and Campbell concluded: "Increased *vertical* complexity is accompanied by a stable or declining staff ratio. But greater *horizontal* complexity makes for a larger relative staff size. Thus, horizontal complexity influences the relative staff size somewhat independently of organizational size (recall that relative size is negatively related to organizational size). In fact, the positive association of relative staff size with horizontal complexity becomes stronger when organizational size is controlled." Campbell and Akers, op. cit., 447–48.

[26] An exception, but wherein the implications of this point are emphasized, is the following: Edward A. Holdaway and Thomas A. Blowers, "Administrative Ratios and Organizational Size: A Longitudinal Examination," *American Sociological Review*, 36: 278–86 (April 1971). Also see Gerry E. Hendershott and Thomas F. James, "Size and Growth As Determinants of Administrative-Production Ratios in Organizations," *American Sociological Review*, 37: 149–53 (April 1972).

[27] This point will be pursued in detail when strategies for selecting samples of organizations are discussed in Chap. 9; see pp. 362–74.

[28] As emphasized earlier in discussion of the conflict perspective (see Chap. 2), Coser and others have noted that, although useful to distinguish between change of and change *in* a system, the distinction is always somewhat relative because there is some continuity with the past.

but the structure and some of the processes have changed so markedly that as observers we would conclude that there has been a *qualitative* change of the system. It really has become a different organization.

How can we conceptualize marked changes of system structure, such as the example just cited—major shifts in student characteristics and emergent modifications in university structures?

Using the conceptual tools we have developed so far, we can see that this represents a marked change in one facet of the resource structure. Such a shift creates new strains within the resource structure and sectors of the normative structure. And as these strains become intensified, we may anticipate that efforts will be forthcoming to reduce or redirect them. These changes in the system environment may occur in normative, resource, or interpersonal structures. And such changes will create new sets of conditions with which the organization must cope. Of course, increased strain may also result from changes that are mostly internal to the organization. But the overall process is similar. Changes in structure alter existing patterns of strain, which in turn may precipitate further change. Thus, over time, a series of small unrelated changes may suddenly "collide," creating an intense but localized pattern of strain. Coping behavior is to be expected as incumbents attempt to defuse the crisis.

Instead of or concomitant with shifts in characteristics of student populations, other types of strains would be anticipated, with major shifts in characteristics of faculty. Reviewing data on faculty increases at Vanderbilt and the University of Tennessee, during 1963 and 1969, McNeil and Thompson propose that analysis of such shifts may help in understanding many types of changes in organizational functioning and its basic character. As newcomers arrive, they may have different expectations about how the organization should operate and what its primary mission ought to be. And they may be clustered in a few departments rather than spread throughout. But most importantly: "Such ebb and flow in population of departments and schools may also produce strains or cleavages between departments staffed largely by newcomers and those full of veterans." [29]

Thus, the basic elements of the model are those with which we have been working for some time. As indicated in Figure 8–2 we can posit the organizational and environmental behavior systems (performance structures). Each of these interacts with the three explanatory structures, i.e., normative, interpersonal, and resource. Strains may exist among or within any of these structures. Similarly, changes in any of them may be activated by change in any of the others. For example, a shift in the resource structure of a sector of the environment may alter the corresponding performance structure. The organization now must

[29] Kenneth McNeil and James D. Thompson, "The Regeneration of Social Organizations," *American Sociological Review*, 36: 632 (August 1971).

FIGURE 8–2   The Basic Framework

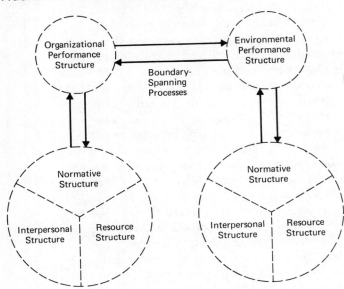

cope with this and may do so by resisting any change and permit the strain created simply to remain. However, organization–environment interaction may gradually intensify the strain so that behavioral changes by organizational incumbents are forthcoming. These coping efforts may then precipitate changes in the normative structure of the organization so that the behavior pattern, which was initially viewed only as a transitory or coping response, becomes institutionalized.

Future empirical research must be directed toward mapping out *sequences* of such changes. For example, a new technological process (resource structure) may be proposed. This may stimulate consideration of changes in the official normative structure so as to increase the likelihood that the performance structure will be modified in the desired manner. Of course, even before the physical machinery arrives, unofficial norms may emerge that may create increased or decreased strain among the structures.

Most system changes appear to reflect coping responses to day-to-day problems whose cumulative effect is to insure that the organization continues to adapt to its changing environment. Of course, organizations experience environments that change at different rates, at different times, and over which they may exert much or little influence. Occasionally, massive and sudden changes take place so as to justify labeling the system modification a "revolution." Like footage of motion-picture film, each instant of organizational life is somewhat different, though slightly so. However, regardless of whether the footage is scanned rapidly or at slow speed, the system continues to change.

And it appears that strain may be a useful concept to help us understand rates and directions of system change.

Confronted with changing patterns of strain, organizational participants have limited alternatives through which they can try to cope. And the consequences—like the alternatives—rarely, if ever, are fully realized by organizational participants. Thus, we must direct our efforts toward analysis of strain patterns and planning of changes with greater realization of consequences for system functioning if we are to assist organizational participants to become involved in the process of self-renewal.[30] For, too often, many modern organizations appear overly resistant to change, and characterized by strains so intense as to threaten their very existence. We must become more skilled at the process of self-renewal as the rate of social change throughout the world increases. And an intense focus on understanding organizational strain appears to be a more important direction. Let us now examine strain and the change process in more detail.

Strain and the Change Process

In analyzing organizational change, it is important to recognize that we can focus on any of several structural levels. However, the processes observed have several important parallels, only the referent systems change. Thus, although we will emphasize different aspects of the theoretical perspective in discussing these different levels, you should think of the implications and applications to the other referent systems. For example, polarization of strain occurs both within and among groups and organizations. However, we will analyze the process using only one referent system—a major division of a single organization. Finally, recognize that we are using a "broad brush" at this point and that more precise statements will be possible only when a larger base of empirical evidence has been obtained. Let us start at the group level and work upward.

Group to Group: Strain and Interdependence

Not all strains are equal. They vary in at least three important ways. First, the *intensity* of the strain can vary greatly, from mild dislikes of an interpersonal nature to intense differences about specific normative

[30] John Gardner's essay is impressive in its precision and perception. The authors found it most helpful in integrating many of the thoughts presented in this chapter. See John W. Gardner, *Self-renewal: The Individual and the Innovative Society* (New York: Harper Colophon Books, Harper & Row, 1965), original publication, 1963.

expectations. Second, the *content* of the strain may vary. Thus, incumbents may disagree intensely about what ought to be the central mission of the organization or the size of desks that are appropriate for persons of different rank. However, if interpersonal ties are close and tasks permit each group of incumbents to work somewhat autonomously from the others, the strain may be tolerated. Indeed, some structures, such as universities, appear to benefit greatly from this type of strain. Diversity in viewpoint is not only tolerated but encouraged. And high levels of professional autonomy, historically labeled "academic freedom," provide the structural requisite so that such differences in views can persist. But note that the differences in view can persist *only if there is consensus at a higher level of abstraction*; that is, the principle of academic freedom must be supported by all. The limits of dissensus are thus specified, and commitment to the more abstract principle is required of most participants, especially those in major power positions. Failure to support the more general principle represents a more intense type of strain.[31] Thus, a third variable is highly important—the *location* of the strain. Intense strain between two units that are highly interdependent is very different from strain of a similar magnitude and content between two units that operate rather autonomously with respect to one another.

Let us think back to Henderson's analogy, which we presented in Chapter 1. We discussed the concept of system interdependence by visualizing a series of differently shaped objects attached to one another with several rubber bands of varying lengths. The rubber-band network defines the proximity of the objects—that is, how close or distant they are from one another. Recall that the rubber-band network represents the degree of interdependence among the objects. Thus, if change occurs in one object (group), it is highly likely to precipitate change in those objects (groups) that are in greatest proximity. Thus, groups that have the highest degree of interdependence with the one experiencing change are most likely also to change in that they most immediately confront the new conditions. However, rather than change, they may simply tolerate the changed condition; that is, tolerate the strain.

The idea is illustrated in Figure 8–3. Note that if the object labeled *E* were pulled in the direction indicated by the arrow, objects *F* and *D* would be the first moved. Indeed, only *F* and *D* might move; relationships among the other units would be only slightly strained. Or, all of the other units could remain stationary and the system would simply absorb the strain caused by the movement of *E*. Relationships between

---

[31] A similar point has been made by Wilbert Moore, who put it thus: "For a competitive system to endure, its participants, or at least the effective makers and enforcers of its rules, must regard the survival of the system as more important than the outcome of particular contests. Failing this criterion, a competitive system is doomed." Moore, op. cit., p. 27.

FIGURE 8–3 Interdependent Groups. Solid objects are attached by rubber bands. And object E is pulled as indicated by the arrow.

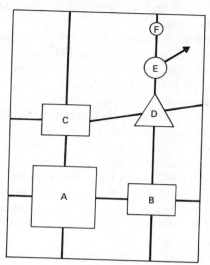

E and F and E and D would be highly strained, with the other relationships left intact.

Thus, in analyzing change among groups we need to look at the quality of the strain, i.e., the intensity, content, and location. But we need further to recognize that the proximity of the units or their degree of interdependence is also critical. Changes in any group represents the greatest threat to those groups that are the most interdependent. Summarizing several research studies, Corwin emphasized this dimension: "The amount of strain, however, varies with the proximity of departments and the relationships between certain key members of each department (Kahn, 1964), and with the consequent need for joint decision making (March and Simon, 1958). White (1961), for example, found that the drive for departmental autonomy was greatest in those areas where the interrelation of tasks was highest; hostility was also highest at these points." [32] At times, such changes may be viewed as

[32] Ronald G. Corwin, *Militant Professionalism* (New York: Appleton-Century-Crofts, 1970), p. 243.

Sources cited in the quote are the following:

Robert L. Kahn, "Field Studies of Power in Organizations," in *Power and Conflict in Organizations*, Robert L. Kahn and Elise Boulding, eds. (New York: Basic Books, Inc., 1964), pp. 52–66.

James March and Herbert Simon, *Organizations* (New York: John Wiley and Sons, Inc., 1958).

Harrison White, "Management Conflict and Sociometric Structure," *American Journal of Sociology*, 69: 195–99 (September 1961).

highly desirable by the incumbents of the affected groups. But often their autonomy, prestige, and security is threatened, which may precipitate a response directed toward trying to prevent the change, redirect it, or to protect their unit in some other way.

Finally, note that if unit E in Figure 8–3 began the designated movement, and at about the same time unit D began only slight movement toward object A, the combination could create sufficient strain to precipitate system breakdown at that point or to require numerous adjustments in other sectors. Thus, at times systems absorb a certain amount of strain only to have a small and apparently insignificant change create the necessary strain to precipitate major changes.

Consequently, we need to be sensitive to the degree of interdependence among units and the quality of particular strains (content, intensity, and location). But we also must be sensitive to the pattern or distribution of strain throughout the entire system. This varies over time, and predicting the consequences of any given change appears to be directly dependent on the strain pattern at the particular point in time. Let us pursue this idea in more detail.

Assume that we are now looking at an organization. We see clusters of patterned interaction that seem somewhat separated from one another. We have identified a series of six groups (interaction clusters). We can identify the normative, resource, and interpersonal structures for each group. Further, we can anticipate that there will be a variety of strains within and among each of these structures at both the intra- and inter-system level. These strains will vary in pattern and intensity. We observe a change in one of the groups. For example, a new department head is appointed. Yet, over the next several weeks the patterns of interaction within and among the groups remain rather stable with only slight modification. Then we note that a new head has arrived in another of the groups. Shortly thereafter, a great deal of time begins to be spent among various clusters of persons so that the boundaries of the six initial groups become blurred. This is followed by a new pattern of interaction, wherein the number of clusters is reduced and the content is modified. Where we had six units initially, we now have three. These three groups persist throughout the remainder of our observation period.

How can we account for the change? Why did it happen shortly after the appointment of the second department head and not after the first? Was it simply because he was a dominant personality? Certainly, our theoretical perspective would lead us toward a different answer. And although we must wait for additional empirical research to trace out the multitude of linkages in such changes, the understanding of three factors appears to be most important—quality of strain, degree of system interdependence, and total strain pattern.

Now, let us fill in some specifics to see how we might use these three ideas to analyze the process of change in this hypothetical organization. When we started our observation (Time One), we had six identifiable units—six social science departments. The heads of each of these departments formed a committee that reported to the dean of a college of arts and sciences. Collectively, the six departments represented a division of social sciences. As indicated in Figure 8–4, these six departments were somewhat autonomous regarding curricular matters. Yet, because of policy at the college level, the interdependence was strong among the departments on this issue. Efforts to change the curriculum by faculty members in all departments were thwarted because of pressure from above that each department make corresponding changes. In an effort to maintain an integrated social science curriculum, official policy granted each department veto power over any major change proposed by another. Several members of the psychology department had proposed experimental courses that reflected a focus on personal counseling and sensitivity training. Although a few faculty members in several of the other departments were eager to participate in such experiments, most were split into two major orientations: (1) commitment to basic research and a pure science perspective about their discipline; and (2) a social action orientation with an emphasis on active involvement in the political process of the local community. Thus, these three types of orientations represented a major strain within and among the departments. Because of the dean's orientation of wanting to view the six units as an integrated division, they were forced into a highly interdependent relationship regarding curricular change. Efforts by psychology department members to modify curricular structure were resisted, as such change would have required further changes that were viewed as highly undesirable by a majority of the members in each of the other departments.

When the first new department head (sociology) arrived, behavior patterns remained unchanged. But the strain was intensified because he added major strength to the group that desired to focus on community action. He proceeded to identify department members within the sociology department and other departments that shared this orientation. He then obtained approval to submit a grant request for interdisciplinary research. This served to intensify further the strain pattern, as those persons with this orientation now begin to identify one another across departments. Gradually, they became aware of their shared interests. Upon the arrival of the new chairman (anthropology), who had a basic science orientation, the final straw had been added. Thus, the fractures had intensified to the point that this small increase in the strain pattern provided the basis for major change. With the awarding of the research grant, the committee of chairmen found the strain so intense that a restructuring proposal was highly acceptable. As receiver of the grant, the sociology chairman appeared to be the great man who had a

FIGURE 8–4 Hypothetical Social Science Division: Time One

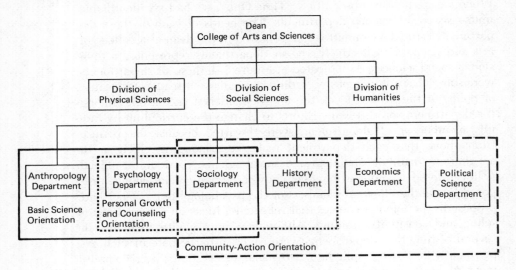

great idea, at the right time.[33] Thus, three new units were created, which reflected the orientations of the various faculty (see Figure 8–5). And the dean accepted the proposal, as he could present it to his superior as a major innovation that reflected upon his leadership ability to promote interdisciplinary work within the college. The three new structures provided students with different types of alternatives than had been present earlier. Of course, this resulted in new strains, and these strains may in turn be instrumental in precipitating additional structural changes.

In looking at the changing pattern of strain in this hypothetical illustration we would find that through interviews or questionnaires we could determine expectations that would vary at different times. Thus, as indicated in Figure 8–6, before Time One we would obtain a rather diffused response pattern reflecting the generally mild commitment to different viewpoints. However, at Time Two, the faculty had become highly polarized on this issue: the proposal for structural change was welcomed.

However, the process is more complex than this. Although our hypothetical university provides us with a simplified example in order to illustrate the idea of how strain patterns may change and thereby precipitate structural changes, we must emphasize that the example *is* highly simplified and that several important qualifications must be noted.

[33] Clark's detailed case studies of Reed, Swarthmore, and Antioch colleges present numerous examples of structural changes where timing, ideological content, and a forceful personality converged. Burton R. Clark, *The Distinctive College: Antioch, Reed and Swarthmore* (Chicago: Aldine Publishing Company, 1970).

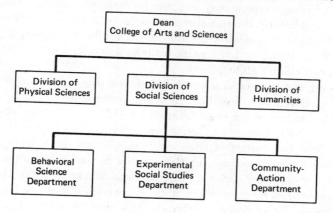

FIGURE 8–5 Hypothetical Social Science Division: Time Two

FIGURE 8–6 Changing Patterns of Strain: The Polarization Process

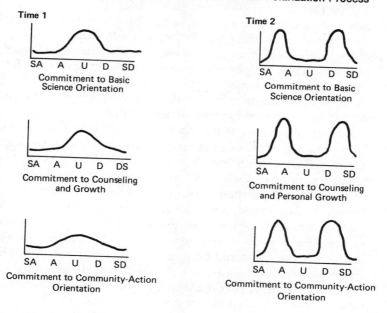

SA = strongly agree; A = agree; U = uncertain; D = disagree; SD = strongly disagree.

First, we assumed a highly visible issue and one that was uncontaminated by other points of disagreement. As polarization on any issue occurs, it is our observation that many issues get brought into the picture. This is a time when many axes are ground. To assume that intelligent and detached discussion of proposal changes could take place under highly polarized conditions may be too idealistic even for university faculty members. Rather, as groups polarize on an issue, many related differences may be dug up. Older scars are reopened, and the points of disagreement may become increasingly diffuse. And specific proposals whereby the initial strain might be resolved become increasingly difficult to evaluate as additional conflicting issues are raised. Thus, it is advisable, that specific proposals germane to the issue be discussed in a calmer atmosphere.

Second, the type of change and strain used in this example was unusual in that there was little inherent interdependence in the task process. That is, one way of arranging faculty and curriculum may be about as effective as any other, given current levels of research knowledge about the impact of such arrangements on the learning process. The interdependence among these units is much less than what is found in most other types of organizations where the core technology is characterized by greater certainty. Even within universities, the payroll process, for example, is a type of task that requires a tighter set of links among the participating units. But some faculty would argue that a departmental structure, organized along disciplinary lines, is absolutely necessary. And we suspect that just as their reasoning is based on personal experiences and limited empirical data, so also are many of the arguments from upper management in most other types of organizations. Thus, despite the exceptionally low degree of interdependence among these units, we suggest that multitudes of alternative structural designs are available for all organizations—alternatives that are rarely considered because of the blinders of tradition.

Finally, let us note that with the new structural design there have been some important cross-cutting cleavages built into the university.[34] Thus, sociology faculty members in our hypothetical example may still interact with other sociologists in the college simply because of disciplinary interests, participation in professional meetings, and the like. However, they might now also interact with persons from other departments because of the new divisional structure. Thus, differences in viewpoint may more likely be communicated *across groups* with differing views. And we would propose that organizations with this type of structural feature, regardless of the content of the cleavage, can better cope with changing environments than those wherein enclaves of noncommunicating groups persist even though the overall level of strain is identical. Thus, the pattern of strain—that is, the degree to which it is segmented and acts to isolate groups with different views—is critical. Organizations with strain patterns distributed throughout the structure will respond to environmental change differently from those in which the fractures are deep and along single lines. We would hypothesize that organizations with cross-cutting strain patterns can change more easily than those in which the cleavages are highly focalized. Thus, as

[34] Lewis A. Coser, *The Functions of Social Conflict* (New York: The Free Press, 1956), p. 157; and Wilbert E. Moore, op. cit., p. 65.

FIGURE 8-7   Patterns of Organizational Strain

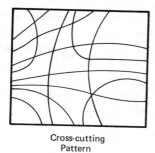

Cross-cutting
Pattern

Focalized Pattern

depicted in Figure 8-7, we must be sensitive to the overall pattern and distribution of strain within the organization.

Levels and patterns of organizational strain can be altered in many ways. In the example of the structural change in the university, we emphasized how changed inputs—new faculty with differing orientations—were critical. Usually, however, as the inputs change, the strain pattern is reinforced through interaction with environmental sectors. Thus, consistent with our open system imagery, we see organizations penetrated at many points. And each point of penetration provides an opening in which new definitions may enter.

Think about public schools for an illustration. Because of changes within many structures, teachers are demanding that they be granted rights enjoyed by other professional groups. They wish to select textbooks and make curriculum decisions. But, as Corwin's research so vividly demonstrates, many other teachers maintain a highly bureaucratic orientation.[35] Thus, some schools may have an even split or an imbalance in either direction.[36] We would expect that as teachers interact with environmental units that reinforce the professional orientation, strain would be intensified unless structural changes in the school are implemented. Thus, principals who strongly encourage their faculty to participate in professional organizations should be aware that such activity may alter existing strain patterns and generate increased pressure for some types of change. If differences in views are to be maintained over time, we would hypothesize that some type of reinforcement is necessary. Thus, the organizational set or reference group system with which units identify can provide important sources for new definitions and reinforcements so as to create new patterns of strain and to intensify existing ones. A clear example is the impact of financial aid to striking teachers provided by union and professional organizations. Here the push for teacher autonomy clearly is reinforced.

[35] Ronald G. Corwin, *A Sociology of Education* (New York: Appleton-Century-Crofts, 1965), pp. 230–47.
[36] Corwin, *Militant Professionalism*, op. cit., pp. 225–34.

Our open systems view sensitizes us to recognize that important environmental interactions take place at many levels in most organizations. The classical perspective, in which the president or the board of directors are the prime contact points with environmental units, is much too simplistic. At times, however, we do wish to focus on organizations as total units. The issue regarding the point of entry is put aside, and we look at organization–environment interaction in more general terms. Let us see how such interaction and corresponding strain patterns might help us to understand change.

Organization–Environment Interaction

Changes in the environment constitute new conditions with which the organization must cope. Major population shifts, alterations in available resources, innovations, and the like, may precipitate major changes within the organization. But there is not a one-to-one correspondence. Organizational change does not automatically follow from given environmental change. There are many reasons for this, but four general factors seem most important.

First, a given environmental change may be highly important for the organization or nearly totally irrelevant. As with our group to group interaction, the degree of interdependence is critical. Thus, changes that greatly affect units which have highly interdependent relationships with the focal organization create new conditions that must be reconciled. But these new conditions may de defined by members of different organizations in many different ways. Thus, second, incumbent definitions of environmental changes are also critical. Third, in addition, the strain pattern of the organization also is important. Existing strain may preclude structural change in one organization, whereas in another, the strain pattern may facilitate rapid adaptation to the new conditions. Fourth, and finally, just as organizations vary in their capacity to monitor the environment, so also do they vary in ability to survey response options. Thus, a given environmental change creates a set of new conditions. Incumbents in one organization may see their options as highly limited, whereas persons in similar organizations, confronting similar conditions, may envision a multitude of appropriate responses.

These four factors appear important in understanding why certain types of environmental changes precipitate organizational change. Surely there are others. But the critical point is that organizations are not to be viewed as identical black boxes. Environmental change is interpreted and assessed by incumbents who find themselves confronting structures with differing patterns and intensities of strain and differing capacities to monitor the environment. At times it appears that options are so limited as to preclude any decision—"one can only respond as one must." At other times, organizations will respond in an effort to act on the environment so as to manipulate the available options. Thus, organizations do not simply respond to environmental change in a general manner; rather, they are highly selective. Thus, as environmental changes constantly take place, organizational incumbents are continually monitoring them and selecting those that appear most important for consideration as the appropriate response. What response is appropriate? As we suggested earlier, that response which, it appears, will increase autonomy, prestige, and security.

Environmental change is filtered. And organizations respond by acting on their environment so as to try and expand their autonomy, prestige, and security. Thus, organizational incumbents are involved in continual renegotiations with the environment. As Thompson has emphasized, they seek to engineer new states of consensus regarding expectation sets.[37] In this way, organizations do not simply respond to environmental change but are actively involved in an interactive process.

We see this bargaining relationship reflected in all aspects of the expectation sets associated with a given organization. For example, following the emergence of public concern about police–community relationships, many police officials have responded with campaigns designed to obtain greater organizational resources: "What do you expect, given our current pay standards?" is their attitude. And by altering the image of the organizational mission, the prestige expectations may also be increased. In short, organizational incumbents continually are involved in negotiations in which they seek to manipulate expectation sets held by environmental sectors. These manipulations are designed to maintain existing levels of autonomy, prestige, and security granted the organization and to expand them whenever possible.

The degree of interdependence that an organization has with environmental units is subject to change. A good illustration of a temporary change of this type is community disaster. Emergency organizations form a very loose organizational network and under normal conditions operate rather autonomously with respect to one another. However, as we have observed in many disasters, emergent demands create a set of conditions in which the interdependence among these units is highly intensified.[38] Thus, here we have sudden environmental change that generates a massive set of demands for the local community. Expectation sets and coordination mechanisms among emergency organizations at the time of the Indianapolis explosion, for example, were vague or nearly nonexistent. Such demands were confronted by an interorganizational structure that was highly strained,

[37] Thompson, op. cit., pp. 28–29.

[38] James D. Thompson and Robert W. Hawkes, "Disaster, Community Organization, and Administrative Process," in *Man and Society in Disaster*, George W. Baker and Dwight W. Chapman, eds. (New York: Basic Books Inc., 1962), pp. 268–300; and James D. Thompson, *Organizations in Action* (New York: McGraw-Hill Book Co., 1967), pp. 52–54.

and under this stress the system gave way at these points of fracture. Coping responses were quick to emerge and were directed at the fractures. Gradually, new mechanisms emerged so that the interorganizational effort could be better coordinated. However, once the demand structure normalized, most units returned to their previous mode of operation in which their individual autonomy was greater.[39] Here the changes were sudden and easier to detect. However, we suspect that the process is common, but usually it takes place at slower rates.

Let us summarize briefly by noting Figure 8–8. We begin with environmental change, which is monitored and interpreted by organizational members. The degree of interdependence between the organization, the sector of the environment that changed, and the organizational strain patterns will constrain the range of options. Coping behaviors are then instigated as the organization acts upon the environment. In doing so, organizational members seek a new consensus with environmental units whereby their security, prestige, and autonomy are expanded or maintained. Any specified environmental change does not automatically result in a single given organizational response. Rather, the change must be viewed within the context of the existing consensus structure between the organization and its environment. The change may create a marked change in that external strain pattern and hence create a condition requiring immediate response. But, as with responses to internal strains, many options are available. Let us now focus on the types of alternative responses to strain.

Responses to Strain

We postulate that strain exists for all organizations at all times—the variation is in terms of intensity, content, location, and general pattern. Although the empirical research is lacking for us to make many predictions as to types of responses given different types of strains, we can identify at least nine possibilities. We suspect that further empirical work will indicate that response patterns are complex so that at any point in time all or most of these processes might be found within an organization reflecting a multiplicity of specific strains. Consideration of these nine types of response may help in designing future empirical work so that the linkages might be better pinpointed between types of strain, coping responses, and emergent structural changes.

Toleration

Confronted with a new area of strain—for example, an emergent viewpoint that a new product or activity should be assumed by the organization—one response is to do nothing. If the conflicts generated are

---

[39] Drabek, op. cit., pp. 170–78.

FIGURE 8–8   Factors in Response to Environmental Change

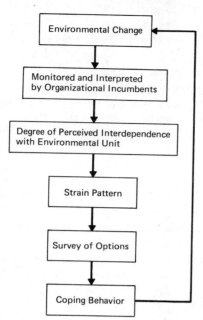

minimal, doing nothing requires nothing. Of course, if those dedicated to the new activity are successful in manipulating the expectations of others, then the strain would become intensified over time. We would expect them to try to convince others that the new activity is appropriate for the organization and that its prestige and security will be enhanced. We suspect that many such new ideas emerge and confront a toleration response. And, almost as often, the advocates may lose interest in their proposal and the prior consensus reappears. Of course, if the proponents of the new activity can sustain themselves, then the possibility of tolerating the conflict becomes lessened, and another type of response would be expected.

Delaying Tactics

When toleration fails or the initial strain appears too intense at the outset, a variety of delaying tactics may emerge. Here, sectors of the organization recognize the strain and seek actively to delay proposed action. By doing so, of course, it is assumed that the proposal backers will lose popularity and interest. Probably the most common device is to assign the proposal to a committee for study. This serves to defuse the proposal backers—something is being done—and by the time a committee report is available new areas of strain may be of greater concern. This is especially effective where time deadlines, set by environmental sectors, are known. Incumbents simply delay the committee report until the time deadline has passed and then reply to the proposal backers: "We like your idea, but it is too late to have it considered this time. Would you be so kind as to resubmit it next year?"

Another commonly used device is to dramatize the severity of external threats: "We like the idea, but right at the moment it is out of the question. We simply may go under if we can't do better in competition with organization X." There are, of course, many variations on the theme. But all of them have the common element of an *active* response in order to delay action.

Smoke Screens

There may be important areas of dissensus. But if groups effectively can keep them diffuse, ambiguous, and low in visibility then they appear less threatening. Again we have an active response. But instead of attempting to delay action, numerous efforts are directed at clouding the issues. At times incumbents seem to sense the structural implications in resolving dissensus, but for many reasons continue to raise tangential issues so as to avoid confronting the specific area of strain. And when the matter is raised, the response is quickly to raise a whole series of other issues so as to redirect attention: "We do wish we had time to pursue that matter, but we have many pressing items on the agenda."

Dismissal

If the strain is largely the product of a few incumbents, the consensus may be restored by simple expulsion. Of course, this has many consequences. One is that some who were only mildly committed to the viewpoint of the deviants may feel threatened and cease to open their mouths. Although dismissal may restore consensus on the particular point of strain in a single instance, we suspect that it may seriously reduce the effectiveness of the organization to resolve future conflicts. As new strains emerge, incumbents may be more frightened to confront them than in the past. If strains are permitted to accumulate over time, the organization begins to resemble a powder keg. And when confronted with even mild environmental disruption, organizational survival may be seriously threatened.

Condemnation

Rather than discrediting or dismissing the proposal backers, at times the ideas may be attacked. Thus, we often hear incumbents speaking of the basic procedures of the organizations, and that the proposed changes "would violate the way we have been doing things for years."

Thus, the response is one of seeking to discredit the content of manipulation efforts. If the proposed ideas can be discredited as inappropriate or self-defeating, then the strain is reduced.

Cooptation

There are many ways to coopt incumbents who emerge with views inconsistent with existing ones.[40] Using again the example of a proposal to engage in new activities, conflict may be resolved by establishing a small program of the type proposed. Incumbents must agree in advance to a series of restrictions and procedures by which they will abide. In this way, the strain is compartmentalized. Over time, the proposal backers may find that the ideas are less workable than they originally thought and the unit may simply be disbanded. Thus, cooptation is less dramatic than confrontation and overt dismissal, but may well have the same effect of resolving the strain without precipitating any type of structural change.

At times, however, cooptation will later lead to change. If the unit survives, its activities have received official sanction. They are viewed as legitimated behaviors. And the organization may confront even more serious threats as the new unit pushes for increased power and size. Once legitimated by official sanction, it is harder to dismantle. And it is clear that many times organizations respond to strain with cooptation approaches only to find that new areas of strain emerge, which become more difficult to reconcile. If resources permit, some organizations have units that are highly contradictory but segregated from one another. This may reflect cooptation responses at different points in time. When resources become more scarce, however, the strains become visible as incumbents from each group seek to insure survival of their unit.

Organizational Birth

In current youth parlance, a person does not leave or walk away from a gathering, rather he "splits." Many an organization was born in an analogous manner. Unresolved or unaccommodated strains may result in a split. Some members withdraw from the organization and form a new one. The multiplicity of Protestant sects and denominations is evidence of the splitting response to strain. Where bringing a new organization into existence does not require huge resources, as for a religious or even a political organization, new organizations are formed from parts of old ones with considerable frequency. In recent decades in the

---

[40] Philip Selznick, *TVA and the Grass Roots* (Berkeley and Los Angeles: University of California Press, 1949), p. 13; and Ruth Leeds, "The Absorption of Protest: A Working Paper," in *The Planning of Change*, 2nd ed., Warren G. Bennis, Kenneth D. Benne, and Robert Chin, eds. (New York: Holt, Rinehart & Winston, Inc., 1969), pp. 194–209.

United States electronics firms have shown a tendency to multiply by splitting. The initial investment required to split and launch may be considerable, but enough of these new organizations have undergone quick, explosive growth so that the high stakes often appear to be worth the risk involved in splitting and going deeply into debt to form a new firm.

The threat of splitting, however veiled, undoubtedly makes some of the protagonists in a strain situation more willing to compromise on the issues around which the strain has developed. As abrasive as the bright rebels may be it is better to have them within the organization where you know what they are thinking and doing than to have them split and form a competitive organization.

Organizational Death

As strains become increasingly intensified, incumbents find less and less ability to use expectation sets to guide their behavior. Interaction among units may decrease, and ambiguities and inconsistencies in expectations further increase. Task performance declines, and the disintegration of the unit simply continues unchecked. No one seems to know what the problems are or what to do about them, but more persons are leaving the organization and replacements are increasingly difficult to locate. Gradually the organization dies, as the patterned interaction becomes less and less stable.

Self-renewal

Finally, organizations may respond to strain and conflict through a self-renewing process.[41] Here the strains are uncovered, separated, and examined. Conflict and change are encouraged. But there are procedures to facilitate the resolution of conflict and the stimulation of change. New integrations of old and new are encouraged. And rather than simply add on a new unit, which will be poorly financed in a co-optative response, major structural reorganization is used. Existing structures are not viewed as permanent, but rather as steppingstones toward different designs whereby the mission of the organization may be more effectively accomplished. Thus, it is assumed that strains will emerge. But the response is to focus on them, rather than to hide from them. And when structural change appears desirable because the conditions confronting the organization have now changed, then such change is encouraged. The underlying assumption is that at any point in time there are many existing structures that fit well with conditions that confronted the organization two, five, ten, or fifty years ago. Strains are

---

[41] Gardner, op. cit.

now apparent. What structural design is needed *now*? The central question becomes, How can the organization maintain a flexible structure so as to insure periodic shifts before strain levels become excessively intense?

All nine of these general response patterns emerge as organizational incumbents attempt to cope with strains. And many are used simultaneously. In future empirical work, we must seek a much better understanding of the links between types of strains and the coping responses. But we need not stop with empirical analyses, for often we wish to intervene as organizational therapists.

What does this theoretical perspective suggest? Most directly, it leads us to recognize the importance of strain as a critical variable in understanding change, both its rate and direction. But it also sensitizes us to the response to strain we have labeled "self-renewal." Let us now examine that process in more detail to see how change might be guided, directed, and planned.

Leadership for Self-renewal

Up to this point we have been concerned primarily with empirical questions. That is, we have asked questions of two types: (1) "How do organizations behave?" and (2) "How can we account for or explain that behavior?" Now we want to use the theoretical perspective to ask a series of normative questions. For example, "How might we go about changing organizations so as to make them more responsive to change?" "How can we better detect the consequences of adopted changes?" "How can we design structures wherein change is more adequately guided and directed so that the system better achieves our purpose?" In short, *how can we build more self-renewing organizations*? Although these opinions are entirely speculative, they may stimulate additional research in order that the stress–strain perspective we have outlined might be extended, modified, and finally replaced with a more powerful paradigm.

Organizational Drift

Throughout the preceding pages we have emphasized the importance of looking closely at the strains in organizations. And we have argued that knowledge of these strains might provide us with important clues for predicting change. As Taub put it: "Strains in an organization are interesting not only for their immediate effects, but also because they may cause the members to act in ways aimed at reducing stress. The stress-reducing activities in turn may be deleterious to the goals of the organization, thus producing, in the long run, more rather than fewer strains in the organization." [42]

Although we have suggested that the official normative structure may be helpful in accounting for some of the patterning in member activity, we have consistently emphasized the great influence of the unofficial normative structure, the interpersonal structure, and the resource structures. Thus, our perspective alerts us to the realization that much of what goes on in organizations and most types of change processes occurs with minimal guidance by members. Empirically, organizations vary in the degree to which they simply drift. However, our suspicion is that, contrary to the excessively rationalistic view of some, most organizations can be best understood if one assumes at the outset that drift, rather than rational planning, is the most characteristic pattern. This is not to say that all organizations are in an equal state of drift. Rather, we merely suggest that organizations appear to vary greatly in this regard and that we suspect that past researchers have mistakenly assumed greater control and rational guidance by participants than actually occurred.

Drift: what does this concept imply? Think of a small wooden board headed toward a distant beach across a lake. As a rainstorm approaches, the board is twisted and torn and heads first in one direction and then in another. It stays afloat, but movement toward the original destination is by accident alone. The board is moved by environmental forces; it quickly changes direction as the water bounces it about.

Perhaps the more appropriate imagery would be that of several boards linked by long bits of twine. And as the waves get higher, each board, responding to a different point in the current, begins to go in a different direction simultaneously. The twine is strained as each exerts pressure to pull the entire collection in a direction that *maximizes its adaptation.* The total network moves in one direction and then in another as each unit is pushed in succession. There is no mechanism for guidance by which the various waves of environmental force can be anticipated, braced against, and used to move the entire system in a desired course. And with a sudden heavy wave the strain at one point may be so intense that the twine is broken.

In short, we have argued that organizations vary in the degree to which they are in a state of drift—a state wherein different units are pulling the entire system in different directions simultaneously; wherein the environment, not the members, determines future change; wherein the organization and its members are unfree. For organizations in extreme drift are not self-determining—they simply stay afloat, at least for a while.

At different points in time organizations vary in the degree of drift.

[42] Richard P. Taub, *Bureaucrats Under Stress* (Berkeley and Los Angeles: University of California Press, 1969), p. 89.

What determines this? We do not have a firm answer. But McNeil and Thompson provide one perceptive lead in their analysis of regeneration rates, i.e., the "rate of change in the ratio of newcomers to veteran members of a social unit." [43] They suggest that drift is most probable when regeneration rates are extreme in either direction. "Drift is perhaps most likely under conditions of slow regeneration, for unless attrition is sudden and dramatic, as in the case of mass resignation, erosion of talent and experience may not be noticed until it has made significant inroads." [44] Similarly, "unless considerable energy is applied to socialization under rapid regeneration, drift seems likely; with many newcomers and few veterans, we would expect the development of new customs and new norms." [45]

Here is the imagery of the stress–strain orientation. But what of self-renewal? How could the boards and twine be linked together into a new structure, a new design where the thrust of the waves would serve to move the entire system toward a predesignated point. And given different weather conditions, might not variation in design be appropriate? Why not? Because in designing human organizations, we have not yet understood the processes and necessity of continuous self-renewal. And we have not appreciated the consequences of system rigidity.

System Rigidity

Crozier concluded: "a bureaucratic system of organization is not only a system that does not correct its behavior in view of its errors; it is also *too rigid to adjust without crisis to the transformations that the accelerated evolution of industrial society makes more and more imperative.*"[46] Organizations do appear to vary over time in their degree of rigidity; but can change occur without crisis or intense stress? Blau, like Crozier, concludes that the answer is no. "New problems and social needs continually arise, but they often persist for long periods of time before the adjustments necessary to meet them occur, since due to these forces of resistance considerable pressure toward change must build up before it is realized." [47] We suspect that future empirical research may lend support to this conclusion wherein structural change appears as an intermittent or dialectical pattern rather than a smooth, continuous process.

[43] McNeil and Thompson, op. cit., p. 625.

[44] Ibid., p. 633.

[45] Ibid., pp. 633–34.

[46] Michel Crozier, *The Bureaucratic Phenomenon* (Chicago: University of Chicago Press, 1964), p. 198.

[47] Peter M. Blau, *Exchange and Power in Social Life* (New York: John Wiley and Sons, Inc., 1964), p. 338.

But *must* such a pattern persist? Must change be resisted until stress is so intense? Clearly, change simply for the sake of change is no great virtue either. We have emphasized a view of organizations in which incumbents in each internal unit exert pressures intended to increase the autonomy, prestige, and security of their particular unit. We suspect that it is the inability to recognize these pressures and conflicts in a more creative manner that intensifies system rigidity. Response to strain and conflict need not be delaying actions, smoke screens, dismissal, condemnation, or the like. Rather, conflict can be viewed as a desired process—a normal phenomenon, a process that is absolutely necessary to the vitality of any system.

However, for conflict to have this consequence, certain structural mechanisms must also be present, for it appears that the typical response to strain and conflict are those other than self-renewal. Why? Partially because conflict and strain tend to be viewed as inherently harmful and undesirable. Frequently, experience bears out this conclusion. But why? Chiefly because there are inadequate procedures for resolution. Lacking mechanisms of conflict resolution, system incumbents seek to hide conflicts, avoid them, and permit strain to intensify until resolution is extremely costly to all parties involved. Early detection and rapid response could allow conflict to provide the necessary pressure to keep the system flexible, adaptive, and vital.

Thus, when we look at extremely rigid systems we see efforts at environmental isolation. Boundary permeability is difficult and carefully controlled. Only those with the proper credentials may enter. New members are carefully selected so as to insure that they will properly fit existing niches. Socialization is intense, and all must toe the mark. Deviation is met with immediate sanction. Expulsion is used as a threat and a reality in order to maintain tight social control. With intense member commitment, such systems may persist even for several generations of membership turnover. (Think of the longevity of such groups as the Amish.) But as environmental change continues, even these groups must modify their structures or face extinction. The limits on what can be accomplished through the use of overpowering system controls, where many participants are confronted with organizational networks that they detest, have been revealed clearly in research on concentration camps[48] and prisons.[49]

New systems emerge with vitality and innovation. But following Michels[50] "iron law of oligarchy" over time they become paralyzed in

[48] Bruno Bettelheim, "Individual and Mass Behavior in Extreme Situations," *Journal of Abnormal and Social Psychology*, 38: 417–52 (October 1943).

[49] Gresham M. Sykes, *The Society of Captives* (Princeton, N.J.: Princeton University Press, 1958).

[50] Robert Michels, *Political Parties*, trans. Eden Paul and Cedar Paul (New York: The Free Press, 1949), first published 1915.

structure and decay with increasing speed. Thus, "Organizations operate conservatively regardless of whether they are viewed as radical or as reactionary by the general population," [51] Hall argues.

> In education, schools in urban areas have seen their constituencies change around them,[38] but there is strong tendency toward maintenance of the educational programs that were appropriate in the past, despite their growing irrelevance—and the same change could be documented in higher education. In private industry, the plight of the railroads in the United States is indicative of the resistance of this organizational form to change. Here the resistance is more than the desire to maximize income; in fact, some suggest that the railroads' persistence in their past practices is in spite of the fact that profits could be increased if practices were altered. Organized religions have similarly resisted change, with apparently damaging results for themselves, both as organizations and as social movements.[52]

The premise of the self-renewal perspective is that this process of paralysis, although empirically a major pattern in the past, need not be the pattern of the future. Armed with even the few insights available at present, and with the promise of systematic research to be conducted in the immediate future, we have the basic knowledge necessary to free ourselves of this past pattern. Much remains to be learned, but several structural components can be identified that characterize self-renewing systems.

Toward Self-renewing Organizations[53]

Organizations that are going to survive must have a capacity for self-renewal. And such organizations must establish structural mechanisms for the renewal of participants. Members must experience continual growth. Mobility, both vertical and horizontal, within the organization is one commonly used device to stimulate such growth. Additionally, members must be helped to understand the central organizational missions and how their activity contributes to them. Meaning beyond the local office is essential. Travel, vacations, training programs of various types, and the like can all provide in small ways the interruptions in activity that are necessary to prevent paralysis.

Participants who are excited, vital, and learning create a type of work atmosphere that is contagious. However, we recall the plight of the rate buster and how group pressures may destroy the overly eager participant. New ideas are welcomed only when member security is high.

---

[51] Hall, *Organizations: Structure and Process*, op. cit., p. 343.

[52] Ibid., p. 345. Footnote 38 in the quote reads: "For a discussion of this point, see Morris Janowitz, *Institution Building In Urban Education*: New York: Russell Sage Foundation, 1969, p. 210."

[53] Several of the ideas discussed here were adapted from Gardner, op. cit.

Thus, it appears that individual growth is maximized under conditions of psychological and physical safety.[54] "If your new ideas are going to cost me my job, you can hardly expect me to greet them with anything except resistance." Thus, at all levels of the self-renewing organization, efforts must be made to insure member security. Frightened men seldom welcome change, conflict, or innovation. If we have learned anything from psychological research of the past decade, it is the stifling effect of fear on innovation and personal growth.[55] We must encourage participants to experiment. And all must recognize ahead of time that they may fail, but failure need not elicit punishment, for with failure must come new motivation to try another route, another approach. Frightened men risk little.

However, the issue is still more complex. Crozier, for example, in his study of white-collar workers in six Parisian insurance companies found "the existence of a considerable mass of employees who are completely disinterested in company activities and systematically adopt attitudes of retreat." [56] Why? The answer is not totally clear, but Crozier suggests that they lack acculturation, that is, "most of the subjects who have not attained, socially and culturally, the minimum level corresponding to the status of office workers have trouble accepting the conditions necessary for participation. They can become integrated into the environment in a passive way, but cannot take any responsibility there." [57]

Clearly, we need a much better understanding of this and other types of barriers to participation. Crozier suggests some important hypotheses if greater participation is to occur: "the freer a man is in relation to the organization on which he depends, the less vulnerable he is and the greater his chances to become involved and to participate consciously and voluntarily, and therefore more effectively, in its activities." [58] Lacking this, apathy and retreatism will flourish. Also, high degrees of stratification may retard participation. "One cannot participate in the activities of a milieu unless social distances within that milieu are not too large, and unless there is no risk of being rejected." [59] But homogeneity within units that encourages participation may be blunted by heterogeneity among units, which may result in exaggeration of differences and rejection of groups labeled inferior. Although these ideas are

[54] Carl R. Rogers, *On Becoming a Person* (Boston: Houghton Mifflin Company, 1961).

[55] Ibid.; Carl R. Rogers, "Toward a Theory of Creativity," in *A Source Book for Creative Thinking*, Sidney J. Parnes and Harold F. Harding, eds. (New York: Charles Scribner's Sons, 1962), pp. 63–72; and John Holt, *How Children Fail* (New York: Pitman Publishing Corporation, 1964).

[56] Michel Crozier, *The World of the Office Worker*, trans. David Landau (Chicago: University of Chicago Press, 1971), p. 153.

[57] Ibid., pp. 155–56.

[58] Ibid., p. 158.

[59] Ibid., p. 160.

only a start, Crozier clearly suggests that organizational loyalty, in the traditional paternalistic sense, is not conducive to participation. "The weaker a person is, the more he is faithful. The better he is armed for the struggle, the less he is loyal to the company; but at the same time the more he is disposed to participate in its activities." [60] These hypotheses, based on research among white-collar workers, recast what appears at first to be contradictory, and suggest the complexity we must be prepared to face when we put aside conceptual perspectives of organizations based on the philosophical assumptions of "hard determinism." [61]

Self-renewing systems must have information mechanisms to enhance self-awareness. Previously, accountants have focused exclusively on economic data: which departments, they were asked, have overspent their projected budgets and by how much? We must now think of social systems accounting, wherein variables of equal or greater importance to system renewal are measured. Likert's[62] proposal gives us important leads as to how this might be accomplished. Among the variables of foremost importance is system strain. What are the contents of the strains? Where are they located? What are the intensities? What patterns have emerged? As it is, we have argued, these strains act as the major impetus for change. But the change remains undirected because system members lack knowledge of them in any complete sense. Armed with greater self-awareness, participants can better make the necessary modifications so as to permit the system to remain on course, and, at times, to decide that the time has come to set sights on a different course. Small and manageable reforms can be made in a coordinated fashion, so as to have considerable impact when carried out. And contradictory consequences can be detected earlier in order to avoid false starts that become self-defeating.

But a note of caution should be inserted here. We are not arguing that awareness of strain should always be followed by attempts at strain resolution. The continuation of certain mild strains such as normative ambiguity regarding the domain of a work group may in fact be better than efforts at resolution. A manager recognizing domain ambiguity, for example, might be able to persuade the group members that they ought to assist in developing detailed written job descriptions comparable to those used in other groups. But if the job descriptions reduce ambiguity they may also stifle the creativity of the group as well as reducing its autonomy. Thus, some strain may be useful.

[60] Ibid., p. 210.

[61] This imagery appears similar to that applied by Matza in his analysis of juvenile delinquency. See David Matza, *Delinquency and Drift* (New York: John Wiley and Sons, Inc., 1964).

See also Sidney Hook (ed.), *Determinism and Freedom in the Age of Modern Science* (New York: Collier, 1961).

[62] Rensis Likert, *The Human Organization* (New York: McGraw-Hill Book Co., 1967), pp. 128–55.

Self-renewing systems must have planning as an integral feature. Knowledge without action is futile, but establishment of a planning unit to produce neatly drawn organizational charts to fill up file cabinets is equally futile. Planning must be viewed as an organizational process. Leadership here implies not the design of an ideal plan, for these, dreamed up at the top, will surely be sabotaged. Rather, members from all levels of the organization must participate in the planning process. The only route to effective planning is simultaneous overlapping planning groups, which are confronted with goal-setting tasks for which they must devise suggested solutions. And these same groups become instrumental feedback mechanisms, in order to provide a base for implementation. Once the plan is implemented, the consequences of the change can then be monitored by the ongoing information system. As data are available, they are fed back to the planning groups who now may make necessary adjustments or start over following some other approach.

Through overlapping group memberships, vertical and horizontal communication flows are implemented. In this way, the strain patterns are more likely to be of a cross-cutting type rather than drifting into highly polarized segments. Should the organization begin to drift toward polarization, the information system, like a periodic temperature reading, should provide an alert.

Mechanisms for conflict resolution are essential. One way to deter participants in self-renewing organizations from hiding from conflicts is to provide protections for dissenters. Disagreement must not mean dismissal. Use of compulsory arbitration procedures, where each party submits his case to an outsider, both agreeing at the outset that he will support the decision of the arbitrator, is but one of many avenues. Thus, basic commitment to the continuation of the system is essential. And such commitment is easier to maintain if members feel that there are procedures whereby their views can result in change. We suspect that self-renewing organizations are characterized by greater degrees of pluralism. For in such pluralism lies the diversity that permits differences in views. And this is in sharp contrast to the apathy and absence of viewpoint that distinguishes participants in organizations in drift.

Lawrence and Lorsch report that one of the distinguishing characteristics of the three most highly effective organizations in their sample was such open confrontation. "The managers involved in settling conflicts were accustomed to open discussion of all related issues and to working through differences until they found what appeared to be an optimal level." [63] These managers, more so than those in less effective firms, confronted conflicts and got them out on the table rather than trying to avoid them. This approach to conflict was assisted by another

[63] Paul R. Lawrence and Jay W. Lorsch, *Organization and Environment* (Homewood, Ill.: Richard D. Irwin, Inc., 1969), p. 149.

differentiating characteristic of the effective firms—trust. For, in order to disagree, one must trust one's colleagues. And in the case of highly centralized structures like the container organization in their study, one must have a strong sense of trust in one's superiors.[64]

There are times when the planned introduction of strain may have merit. Top management or a planning department within an organization may propose a radical alteration in the divisional and departmental structure of the organization. For a month or so arguments and counter arguments are heard regarding the radical proposal. In the process of responding to the proposal, various groups bring forth less radical alternatives which in turn are discussed at length. Finally, there is some resolution of the dispute. The principal consequences of the induced strain, in this instance, is that many groups stopped assuming that the status quo was satisfactory. They examined a range of proposed alternatives because they were dissatisfied with the radical proposal. This serious consideration of alternatives would not have taken place in the absence of induced strain. Usually such a critical examination of alternatives is better than drift.

Self-renewing organizations must monitor their environments and seek to manipulate them so as to maximize autonomy. Organizational freedom, like that of individuals, is a precarious state that must be continually exercised if it is not to be lost. But the interaction is not one way. Increasingly, we find that organizational participants are horrified to learn of the consequences of organizational actions on physical and social aspects of the environment. Commitment in the face of pollution and destruction is difficult. And whether the destruction is of a mountain stream or the self-concept of a black adolescent barred from employment, members of self-renewing organizations are increasingly going to be concerned with the impact and responsibilities of their organization on its environment. The web of interdependence has become too tight for them to do otherwise.

Finally, we must recognize the necessity of an enlarged research base if we are to build organizations with greater capacities for self-renewal. And we suggest that the stress–strain perspective offers an image of organizations that can serve as a productive guide for such research. In contrast to others, this image has a behavioral focus, emphasizes process, and sees strain as a normal condition of organizational life. The imagery rests on assumptions similar to those proposed by Crozier. "The story of the French white collar workers is puzzling in its complexity and fails to make much sense in a revolutionary perspective or one of unilinear progress. To understand the story, one must adopt a more open, flexible view. It is a story in which persons are constantly trying to make the best of shifting circumstances, always wanting to

[64] Ibid., p. 151.

have their cake and eat it too—and curiously enough, more often than not succeeding." [65]

But relative success at the individual or group level may not culminate in success at the organizational or larger system level. Clearly, we need to have a much better understanding of such conflicts and the strains inherent in them. Group conflicts are constrained and channeled by normative ideas that are organizationally based. But we must move beyond the simplistic notion of using only concepts that reflect an image of organizations as "master blueprints" for participant behavior. Participants *use* organizational structures, they are not wholly determined by them. While the structures do constrain their freedom of action, the constraint remains relative—some are more free than others. But all, in varying degrees, seek to alter the expectations held by others, both within and without the organization, so as to maximize their own autonomy, security, and prestige. Thus, the organization—i.e., a system of patterned interaction units—is the outgrowth of these manipulative efforts. And so participants confront strains, contradictions, and inconsistencies that are constantly shifting. As they try to cope with these on a day-to-day basis, too often they lack much self-awareness to see where they are drifting. A better understanding of these types of processes can come only through additional empirical research. Let us now look into a series of strategies whereby we might conduct organizational research.

[65] Crozier, op. cit., p. xiii.

Chapter 9

ORGANIZATIONAL RESEARCH STRATEGIES

Despite much criticism of the methodological excesses in American sociology during the 1940s and 1950s, relatively few sociologists explored research strategies whereby organizations might be analyzed as systems. Review of standard methodology texts still reflects a heavy social psychological bias, in which most issues concerning research strategies are formulated with individuals as the basic units of analysis. Recently, however, many have begun to explore new leads—some of which were proposed earlier, but were never pursued. And innovations have appeared. Sociology of the 1970s clearly appears destined to outgrow an excessive emphasis on the analysis of individual attitudes.[1]

Abraham Kaplan[2] proposes a useful distinction between methods and methodology. *Methodology* refers to general strategies for knowing, whereas *methods* refers to specific techniques or tools. In this chapter we will be concerned with both.

[1] Brown and Gilmartin's review of articles published in the *American Sociological Review* and the *American Journal of Sociology* during 1940–1941 and 1965–1966 support this point. Articles classified as "social psychology" accounted for 29 and 22 percent of the two for the two time periods. In contrast, articles classified as "formal organizations" or "work and occupations" shifted from 4 to 35 percent. Julia S. Brown and Brian G. Gilmartin, "Sociology Today: Lacunae, Emphases and Surfeits," *The American Sociologist*, 4: 283–91 (November 1969).

[2] Abraham Kaplan, *The Conduct of Inquiry: Methodology for Behavioral Sciences* (San Francisco, Calif.: Chandler Publishing Company, 1964).

Sophistication at both levels of abstraction is necessary if organizational research is to be improved. And although our major emphasis thus far has been with substantive theories of organizations, we have occasionally alluded to methodological issues in an effort to emphasize the interrelatedness of research and theory. We do not want to de-emphasize the interrelatedness, but let us change the emphasis through a survey of several research strategies and methods with which organizations can be used as units of analysis. While our referent will be organizations, many of the points discussed could be applied to other types of systems, e.g., groups or communities. We have organized this discussion around the following questions: What do you want to know? Where can you find the phenomena you want to study? What do you do when you get there? How can typologies and taxonomies assist in the development of a science of organizations? And finally, what are some of the design alternatives available for organizational research?

What Do You Want to Know?

Developing the ability to ask the right questions, it has been suggested, is most critical in conducting research. Indeed, some suggest that it is *the* most significant ability. Yet, how does one develop this ability? How do you know when you are asking the right questions? Certainly, in one sense, the answer is clear—you don't! Even a cursory look at the history of science suggests that most research leads to a dead end. And usually, even if the same individual exclusively pursues a well-defined problem for most of his lifetime, which few sociologists seem disposed to do, the assessment as to whether or not the work will terminate in a dead end remains unknown until—and this happens occasionally—it is rescued from its library tomb, dusted off, twisted about, and then pursued within a new context.

Our intent here is not to depress you. It is not to belittle your creative skills, your enthusiasm, or your commitment. Rather, it reflects our personal experiences with a large number of social science students who seem to want very quick answers, and preferably easy ones, to complex questions. And when we begin to dissect their broad questions, so as to recast them into a series of related queries amenable to empirical investigation, they often respond in a dejected and depressed fashion, "Oh well, that's the trouble with you research people, the only questions that interest you are about trivia!"

Research need not be about trivia. However, quick and easy answers are rarely worth much in the long run. Let us then return to our initial question: "How can students develop their ability to ask the right questions?" In answer, we are suggesting that they first come to understand something about the history of science and its implications for individual researchers. After brief discussion of a few such ideas, we will discuss four other topics: (1) some implications of a system perspective for empirical research; (2) variations in the types of questions asked; (3) specifying questions and defining variables; and (4) measurement of variables.

Some Observations from the History of Science

Although several entire books have been written on this topic,[3] six observations are most salient regarding the asking of questions. First, as previously indicated, recognize that much research does lead to a dead end. Yet, in sociology, careful exploration within a particular area or strategy is rarely carried out with sufficient rigor and discipline so as actually to lead to much of a decision regarding the utility of continued work. Like other young disciplines, sociology seems still to reflect what some have called a prima-donna complex. Each researcher feels the need to start from scratch, to begin as if he were the first to look at a particular area. Replications of previous work have yet to gain much status even for master's degree candidates. Until we can begin to define research areas more carefully and follow up original research with numerous replication studies, we will continue to flounder, with expectations of major breakthroughs attached to every study. Although creativity, imagination, and fresh insights are always of critical importance in the development of any discipline, it is time that we began to recognize the need for more replication studies rather than continuing to encourage every researcher to do his own thing in his own language. In this way we can begin more systematically to explore some of the numerous alternatives that have been proposed and to push them as far as possible.

Second, and implicit above, we need to think more seriously about information retrieval systems whereby we can rapidly get at least a crude look at some of the research related to a particular theoretical problem. A few efforts along these lines have been made, e.g., *Current Contents, Sociological Abstracts, Index of the Social Sciences and Humanities*. But these are far from adequate. A few encyclopedic summaries have been written, such as James March's *Handbook of Organizations* (Chicago: Rand McNally, 1964). And some of the efforts to compile inventories of empirical findings are also helpful, e.g., Joseph E. McGrath and Irwin Altman, *Small Group Research: A Synthesis and*

---

[3] Among those we have found most helpful are James B. Conant, *On Understanding Science* (New Haven: Yale University Press, 1947); and Isaac Asimov, *The New Intelligent Man's Guide to Science* (New York: Basic Boooks, Inc., 1965).

Critique of the Field (New York: Holt, Rinehart & Winston, Inc., 1966); James L. Price, *Organizational Effectiveness: An Inventory of Propositions* (Homewood, Illinois: Richard D. Irwin, 1968); and Bernard Berelson and Gary A. Steiner, *Human Behavior: An Inventory of Findings* (New York: Harcourt, Brace, Jovanovich, 1964). This is especially critical in organizational analysis, as scholars in several disciplines are reporting their work in an even wider variety of journals. Hence, the establishment of a rather elaborate information retrieval system is badly needed to help us more systematically and rapidly to review previous research on a given topic.

Third, as social scientists, we should be the first to recognize that scientific work itself is a type of social phenomenon. From scholars like Thomas Kuhn[4] we should be keenly aware of the place of dogma in science—both as a liberating and coercive force. Thus, in contrast to the points made above, at times it is the ability to break out of the blinders that limit the view of one's colleagues that is most important. One should recognize that the emergence of a new dogma in a discipline appears to be very much subject to the same types of social processes as are the adoption of innovations in other sectors of the society. Hence, you should look at your sociological belief system as you have been taught to look at the belief systems of various political or religious groups. Realize that just as their belief systems serve to define reality for them, so too have your socialization experiences in the social sciences given you a set of conceptual blinders.

Fourth, despite the absolute necessity of rigor and discipline in conducting research, studies should not be limited exclusively to testing hypotheses that were formulated before the research was begun.[5] This is not to suggest that such work is undesirable. Rather, in addition to that type of skill, you should acquire the habit of tinkering. Develop skill and spend time enjoying the process of *playing* with ideas. Too often we have seen college classes, thesis advisors, and especially methodology courses, so sterilize students that any curiosity that they had about anything was killed or made to appear sinful. Be curious! And acquire a habit of mind so that you are constantly playing with alternative hypotheses, analogies, metaphors, and the like. And recognize that insights from persons outside the social sciences may be most helpful in this regard.[6]

---

[4] Thomas Kuhn, *The Structure of Scientific Revolutions* (Chicago: The University of Chicago Press, 1962).

[5] For explication of this point, see Barney G. Glaser and Anselm L. Strauss, *The Discovery of Grounded Theory: Strategies for Qualitative Research* (Chicago: Aldine Publishing Company, 1967).

[6] This point is nicely illustrated by Severyn T. Bruyn, *The Human Perspective in Sociology* (Englewood Cliffs, N.J.: Prentice-Hall, Inc., 1966), pp. 84–125.

Fifth, read the experiences of others. For example, William F. Whyte's Appendix to *Street Corner Society*[7] remains a useful document because he presents to us the worries, fears, and problems he encountered while doing his first piece of field research.[8] Hammond's[9] collection of several research "diaries" also is helpful, as are shorter statements by Skinner[10] and Gans.[11] In these writings we go behind the research report and see the scientist as a social creature—one who is puzzled at times, and one who is continually confronted with time pressures, fears, and other types of nonscientific factors that become so important in determining the final product. Occasional reading of such pieces wherein the scientist *as a human being*, and scientific work as daily activity, are described, can be very refreshing. Indeed, such appendixes, autobiographies, and biographies can perform important therapeutic functions at times. Scientific research like other scholarly activity is not only physically fatiguing but is also emotionally draining. One often feels very alone with his work—and reliving similar experiences had by another can be comforting at times.

Sixth, and finally, ask questions about which *you* care. The reasons for your concern will be private. Indeed, you may not even have much understanding of the basis for them. But unless you care, really care, about your research, it can easily become a purely technical matter that gets less and less interesting each day. Ask questions about topics in which *you* see value. For only with these can you become the kind of craftsman that Mills[12] and Rose[13] have challenged us to be. Individuals who have made major contributions have been persons who cared. Do not feel guilty because you care, but constantly remember that more than good intentions are required to solve social problems. In contrast to sterilized technicians, who, like Sisyphus, continue to roll a stone up a mountain only to have it roll back down, you can develop a sense of passion about your work and seek to interpret it into larger theoretical and social contexts.

Although these brief comments don't really even scratch the surface,

[7] William F. Whyte, *Street Corner Society* (Chicago: University of Chicago Press, 1943).

[8] A similar but more recent statement by Elliot Liebow is also helpful: *Talley's Corner* (Boston: Little, Brown and Company, 1967).

[9] Phillip Hammond, *Sociologists at Work* (New York: Basic Books, Inc., 1964).

[10] B. F. Skinner, "A Case History in Scientific Method," *The American Psychologist*, 11: 221–33 (May 1956).

[11] Herbert Gans, *The Levittowners* (New York: Pantheon Books, 1967), pp. 435–51.

[12] C. Wright Mills, *The Sociological Imagination* (New York: Oxford University Press, 1959).

[13] Arnold Rose, "Varieties of Sociological Imagination," *American Sociological Review*, 34: 623–30 (October 1969).

perhaps they make the point. Through such study the ability to ask important questions may be improved. But equally important is the development of skill in understanding the research implications of a particular theoretical perspective. For example, we have used a system concept throughout this book. What are some of the implications of this theoretical perspective for research?

Research Implications of a Systems Perspective

We have argued for the utility of conceptualizing research in systemic terms. This is not to say that social psychological questions are unimportant, but only that there appears to us great utility in asking additional types of questions. But given this, one immediately confronts a rather puzzling situation. Where are systems found? How are they observed? In what sense do they "behave"? After all, don't people, not systems, really do the interacting? Upon thinking about it even for a minute or two, you should realize that we have "opened a can of worms"! The implications raised by the above questions, in a sense, will be dealt with throughout this entire chapter. However, to get us started, let's look briefly at five different issues.

First, some persons charge that a systems perspective necessarily involves reification; that is, treating a conceptual construct as if it were a physical reality. It is important to recognize that one needs to think carefully through the set of assumptions or presuppositions that underlie the theoretical perspective used. These presuppositions remain untested. Thus, frequently, the critic needs to be helped to understand that what he actually is saying is that he would choose to begin with a different theoretical perspective. But remember, his perspective also rests on a set of assumptions even though they may not be explicated. His assumptions, like yours, remain untested. Failure to recognize this may lead each of you to talk past each other.

However, some have found it useful to reify the system so as more easily to think about or write about various research questions. Most organization texts abound with such reified statements as these: "Organizations subject to rationality norms and competing for support seek prestige";[14] "Organizations with sequential interdependence not contained by departmentalization rely on committees to accomplish the remaining coordination." [15]

In contrast, we have always tried to present a viewpoint consistent with our initial definition, i.e., organizations are relatively permanent and relatively complex interaction systems. Thus, we have presented a

[14] James D. Thompson, *Organizations in Action* (New York: McGraw-Hill Book Co., 1967), p. 33.
[15] Ibid, p. 61.

view that emphasizes social process. We have tried to refrain from statements wherein organizations were reified. Our explanations for the patterning in behavior and interaction were built upon normative and interpersonal ideas that incumbents believed.

However, it was frequently desirable to shift levels of abstraction and state propositions wherein the *analytic qualities of a normative structure, rather than its specific content, were considered*. For example, in Chapter 7 we proposed: "As the degree of organizational stress increases, performance structure changes will vary directly with the intensity of intersystem normative dissensus."

Hence, we emphasize the importance of going beyond the actor's definition of his reality on the assumption that the view of any single individual organizational incumbent, like his interaction, is only a small part of the total whole. And it is the consequences of his behaviors that he does not anticipate which most frequently interested us. Thus, treat organizations and such analytic relationships as inferred realities. They do not exist in the same sense that a table does, but they are conceptualized as *coercive constraints* that limit actor behavior.[16]

Second, this system perspective refutes reductionism. Explanations for the patterning of social behavior are not to be found in analysis of the psychological, biological, or chemical make-up of individuals. Although there is a degree of interpenetration among these levels, there also is independence.[17] Thus, we have argued that abstracted characteristics of normative and interpersonal structures could be used as the major explanatory elements. Again, note that shifts in levels of abstraction are critical. We might begin by obtaining a description of the normative structure as defined by various organizational incumbents. But these descriptions are also used as a basis for analytic classification. Hence, from highly descriptive normative statements, we *infer* the intensity of dissensus or other types of strain. Organizational strain is then used as the explanatory variable in our propositions. Thus, we may often begin with actor definitions and behaviors, but will use these as a basis for abstraction.

Third, the focus is on relationships among actors. Thus, both the phenomena of study—i.e., patterned behavior—and the explanation of those phenomena are in a sense invisible. But then how does one collect data on social systems? The question is complex, and many answers have been proposed. Tausky, for example, elicited some important ideas from Aiken and Hage when he questioned "the methodological assump-

---

[16] For a more detailed analysis of this view see Boyd Littrell, "Complex Organizations: Models and Reality," *The Rocky Mountain Social Science Journal*, 6: 155–62 (October 1969).

[17] Marvin E. Olsen, *The Process of Social Organization* (New York: Holt, Rinehart & Winston, 1968), p. 7.

tion that structural properties, e.g., a system property such as organizational centralization, can be measured by computing the average of individual responses to interview items on the relevant dimension." [18] In a forthcoming section, we shall pursue this question and look at some of the many measurement strategies that have been developed. The point here, however, is that a system perspective has many implications regarding measurement and conceptualization of variables. As we indicated earlier, it is the unique *relationships* among the parts that define the whole, and measurement of the size of each part in isolation tells you little about the functioning of any system.

Fourth, clusters of variables are viewed as interacting sets of processes. Single variable analysis and investigation of relationships between any two variables are helpful at times, but such analysis must be related back to the entire cluster of variables. Coleman and others have been especially critical of what might be called the "2 × 2 table mentality," which somehow often emerges as a limiting factor once students begin to use data cards and a countersorter.[19] The systems perspective demands that we look at systems as networks of relationships.

Fifth, and finally, two major assumptions implicit in the above remarks are those of *change* and *interdependence*. Parts or components of systems are assumed to be interdependent so that changes in any subsystem will result in various types of changes in others. We have emphasized this idea many times, but it is essential to recognize that there are *degrees* of *interdependence*. The point here is that our methodological strategies for study must be compatible with this assumption. And similarly, systems are viewed as dynamic, in a constant state of flux. Thus, it is specified ranges of values on variables and rates of change that are interrelated rather than single values. Cycling, recycling, and recycling again, among several clusters of variables becomes the underlying imagery, rather than a set of static relationships among several related pairs of variables.

These are some of the more critical research implications in a systems perspective. But given this, what else can we consider that might assist us to improve our ability to ask and pursue interesting and productive research questions? It is helpful to recognize that there are many variations in the types of questions that one might ask. Let us explore those variations.

[18] Curt Tausky, "On Organizational Alienation," *American Sociological Review*, **32**: 118 (February 1967); Michael Aiken and Jerald Hage, "Reply to Tausky," *American Sociological Review*, **32**: 118-20(February 1967).

[19] James S. Coleman, "Relational Analysis: The Study of Social Organizations with Survey Methods," in *A Sociological Reader on Complex Organizations*, Amitai Etzioni, ed. (New York: Holt, Rinehart, & Winston, Inc., 1969), pp. 517–28.

Variations in the Types of Questions Asked

In listening to numerous seminar discussions among students evaluating organizational research, we have become impressed with the frequency with which they talk past one another. There are many reasons for this, but an important one is an absence of any understanding of the variety of styles that characterize the manner in which persons ask questions. Failure to recognize this variation frequently results in endless digressions and, at times, mounting hostility.

First, let us distinguish between questions that are primarily about values as opposed to questions that can be empirically investigated. Despite elementary and secondary school curricula, which introduce students to distinctions between opinion and fact, many college students seem unable to recognize such distinctions when they emerge in discussion. Thus, a student may ask, "What is the best way to organize a fire department facing a large disaster?" Among the initial responses elicited might be: "That's a dumb question because there obviously is not one best way for anything"; "Yes, and 'best' implies a value judgment and values are just a matter of opinion"; "What's a large disaster?" "Well, why should we be concerned with the fire department anyway? Why not be more concerned with preventing the disaster"; "Yea, that question just shows your political bias—you want to help the establishment put out the fires, rather than get at the real cause of disasters like riots."

Obviously, these are only a few of the responses that might emerge. And they would vary greatly with the level of sophistication and ideological views that characterized the students. In the discussion that followed, however, failure to differentiate between questions that could be investigated empirically and value decisions would prevent much headway.

Thus, we shall start by considering several types of questions:

1. What is good?
2. Given several choices among something designated as good, what are the consequences of each choice?
3. Given my decision about which of these choices is good, how can I go about changing things so that my choice becomes reality?
4. What exists now? Regardless of how people feel about it, what is there (given some set of linguistic categories)?
5. How do people feel about what is there? That is, what do they perceive it to be? How much variation in these conceptions is there? How is the variation distributed among groups of individuals?
6. Given what is there, how can I account for it? That is, how and why did it emerge? How can I explain or understand its emergence?

7. Given what is there now, what predictions can I make about it at some future date?

This set of questions does not exhaust the types of questions we might ask, but with these simple distinctions let us see what we can do.

Thinking back to the question about the best way to organize a fire department, note that this is something like question number 1. It is an important type of question—indeed, it may be the most important among the bunch. But it is a question that immediately directs us to ask, "Okay, but what is best? What criteria are you using to define 'best'?" Some students seldom seem to think in such terms, and others seem to have difficulty in thinking any other way. While some would choose to pursue this question endlessly, we would prefer to rephrase it and make it situational. That is, let us investigate the criteria that might differentiate *effective* fire departments in disaster from *ineffective* ones. But note that in this example, we have a problem where it is easy to assume general consensus about mission. That is, most fire department officials would agree that it is an important question for them. And most citizens would accept the necessity for effective fire departments. Often, there is dissensus about mission. Hence, some continue to ask important value or normative questions—e.g., what is the best pattern of organization for a university? For a city? For a nation? For a family? And even in this instance, once we got into it, we would probably end up with a question like number 2 above.

In contrast with students who are constantly asking normative questions, others ask questions like number 4. They appear content to describe an organization and enjoy reading descriptions written by others. Normative or value questions irritate them, as do questions involving abstractions of the type such as emerge with questions like 6 or 7. Our position is not to diminish the importance of any of these types of questions. And we don't mean to imply anything like a typology of student personalities! Rather, the point is to emphasize this type of variation in question formulation. All types are desired, but it is useful to distinguish which type you are asking and not let someone sidetrack you because *they would prefer* to ask a different type of question.

But there are two other important variations in the style in which questions are asked. First, levels of abstraction can vary greatly. It is difficult for some to work at a rather abstract level using variables like degree of centralization among military organizations in eighty different countries. Others would prefer to work at a more concrete level and look at a single subunit of one military organization in a very descriptive manner. Second, time, or the absence of it, is a critical variable in many questions. Blau elaborates this nicely, and argues that we must construct research which enables us to investigate both "synchronic organizing principles, which comprise the connections between different elements in a social structure at one point in time, and diachronic ones, which consist of the historical connections between structural elements existing at different periods." [20] Thus, once again, we emphasize that there is value in asking many different types of questions. And understanding this may help you in both asking and pursuing a question. Pursuing a question? That's what it's all about! Let's look at a strategy that many of us have found helpful in that regard.

Specifying Questions and Defining Variables

One of the most useful aids we have found to assist us and our students to think through research questions is what we have come to call the "open box technique." You may not find it at all helpful; some haven't. But many students have indicated that it is one of the most effective devices they have discovered to help them develop complex networks of relationships through which they could explore a particular question.

Basically, the method is rather simple. Remember the children's set of puzzle boxes? You open a large box and discover another one inside. Take it out, open it up, and there is another box. Box after box is removed, opened, and found to contain another box. In a rather simple way, this collection of boxes, all stored within the large one, represents a system of relationships. And the system is dissected by opening box after box and seeing the relationship of each to the other.

Following this analogy, we start by specifying the particular phenomena we wish to explain. Designate a label or name for the phenomena. Write it down and draw a box around what you wrote. Then ask, "What factors might be related to this?" Draw a box around each factor as you think of it. Examine the position of the boxes. Do some belong above others in the way in which they relate to the initial box? Are there relationships among the various boxes? Are the different factors listed single variables, or might they be better reconceptualized as three or four separate variables? And what of the phenomena with which you began? Should it be reconceptualized? Was this the variable in which you were really interested?

The diagram in Figure 9–1 is illustrative of the technique in general terms. Note that many factors are related to the focal variable in an indirect manner. Note also that several of the relationships are in one direction only, while others are two-way in influence. And finally, note how the boxes are arranged spatially, so as more easily to reveal their position relative to one another. Sometimes a simple numbering scheme is helpful in discussion.

In a sense, this technique combines the visual imagery of a sociogram with the system concept of feedback. And pedagogically we have found

---

[20] Peter Blau, "Objectives of Sociology," in *A Design for Sociology: Scope, Objectives and Methods*, Robert Bierstedt, ed. (Philadelphia, Pa.: The American Academy of Political and Social Science, April 1969), p. 70.

FIGURE 9–1   The Open-Box Technique

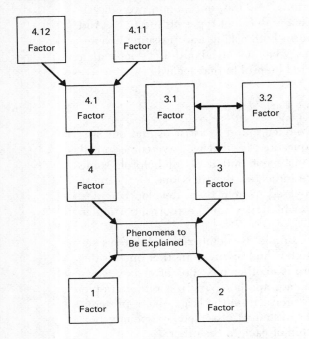

it most helpful as a device with which crude theoretical models—networks of interrelations among variables—could be constructed and refined.[21] Let us be more specific now and think through a question using this technique.

Returning to our earlier example, why are some fire departments more effective in dealing with community disasters than others? It seems reasonable to assume that they are. But what kinds of variables might explain the differences in effectiveness? The variable we wish to explain then might be labeled "Variation in Effectiveness of Disaster Response Among Fire Departments." We would undoubtedly wish to think about this variable in measurement terms; that is, how could we measure effectiveness among fire departments? But let's assume for the moment that we could devise an adequate measurement instrument and proceed.

After drawing a box around the label, we can ask: "What might explain the variation?" Some departments probably have better disaster

[21] This highly simplified discussion could be pursued through books on theory construction, e.g., Arthur L. Stinchcombe, *Constructing Social Theories* (New York: Harcourt, Brace, Jovanovich, Inc., 1968); Robert Dubin, *Theory Building* (New York: The Free Press, 1969); Scott Greer, *The Logic of Social Inquiry* (Chicago: Aldine Publishing Company, 1969); and Paul Davidson Reynolds, *A Primer in Theory Construction* (Indianapolis, Ind.: Bobbs-Merrill, 1971).

FIGURE 9–2   Stage 1: Fire Department Effectiveness

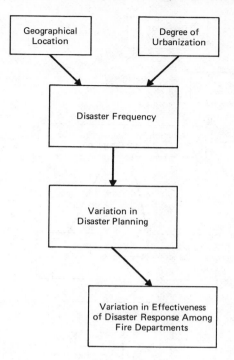

plans than others. Prior planning might improve response effectiveness. Some literature suggests that organizations located where disasters occur frequently are more likely to have emergency plans. Where are disasters most likely to occur? Two variables are obviously important. First, geographical location. The Gulf Coast has frequent hurricanes, parts of the Midwest have nearly seasonal flooding, and the West Coast has large forest fires and mudslides. Second, highly urbanized areas with greater population densities, larger building complexes, and airports are more liable to natural disasters such as explosions and plane crashes. Okay, that's a start. Now let's put this into boxes.

Reviewing Figure 9–2, note that we can clearly see the linkages among the variables. With some thought, at least a crude measurement device could be designed for each of these. But let's continue with this for a moment. Fire departments do not respond as isolated units to community disaster. And the effectiveness of any single fire department may be greatly enhanced or hindered depending upon the ease with which it can activate assistance from other organizations, e.g., police, hospitals, Red Cross, Civil Defense, and the like. Thus, interorganizational communications, which will largely reflect prior planning at this level, is a critical variable. Similarly, the internal communication system and decision-making pattern will also partially determine the

FIGURE 9–3   Stage 2: Fire Department Effectiveness

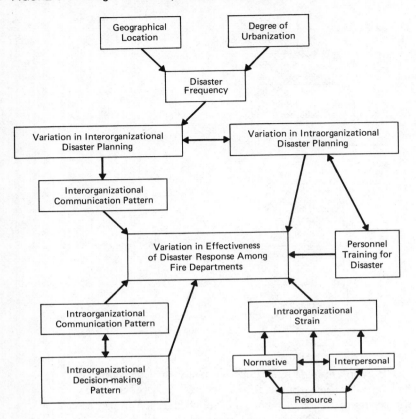

effectiveness level. What of personnel training for disaster? This interacts with planning in that training exercises frequently stimulate new
plans and planning efforts often precipitate training exercises. Finally,
internal strains predating the event provide important clues as to where
difficulties will be encountered. Although these strains may be of a
variety of types, they do affect the response effectiveness. Now let us
see what our system of boxes looks like.

The variables we mentioned are diagramed in Figure 9–3. Clearly,
this is only a start in pursuing our initial question; but it is a start. And
as the diagram becomes increasingly complex, we begin to see the possibility of actually collecting empirical data of a variety of types with
which to test our open-box relationships. In essence, what we are
moving toward is a crude theoretical model composed of a large number of interrelations among variables. And such model construction can
lead directly into empirical research. Thus, we can begin with a question and continue with it until we have actually empirically tested, re-
formulated, and retested a theoretical model that relates to the initial
question.

FIGURE 9–4 Determinants of Communication About Collective Deprivation

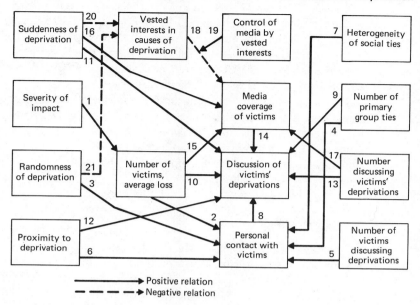

FIGURE 9–4 Determinants of Communication About Collective Deprivation

SOURCE: Adapted from Allen H. Barton, *Communities in Disaster: A Sociological Analysis of Collective Stress Situations* (Garden City, New York: Doubleday and Company, Inc., 1969), p. 217.

This technique has many other strengths. For example, often you may start with a question and, upon spending a rather short amount of time working with it in this manner, decide that it is a "bad" question. It may be that the initial variable is too vague, or maybe too inclusive. Second, you may decide that you started in the wrong spot. Other relationships may turn up that are far more interesting. Third, complex networks of relationships can be dealt with much more easily. And subcircuits can be singled out, scrutinized, elaborated, and then placed back into the larger system. Fourth, literature reviews can be greatly enhanced if formulated in this format. For example, Allen Barton nicely illustrated the power of this technique in his review of disaster literature.[22] Using numerous empirical studies composed of hundreds of pages, he emerged with seventy-one different sets of relationships. These relationships comprise a complex theoretical model composed of several submechanisms of the type diagramed in Figure 9–4.

Fifth, and finally, this technique directs empirical research so as greatly to enhance its cumulative effects. For example, with Barton's theoretical reconceptualization, we have much more than just a series of scattered studies dealing with rather esoteric topics. Rather, we

[22] Allen H. Barton, *Communities in Disaster: A Sociological Analysis of Collective Stress Situations* (Garden City, N.Y.: Doubleday & Company Inc., 1969).

emerge with a theoretical system with a great deal of explanatory power. And we can see which links in the system require further testing and/or reformulation. In short, the technique's greatest advantage is that it may stimulate empirical research that is guided by theory. And in so doing, theoretical models may emerge much more rapidly. The overall consequence of this could be a sharp acceleration in the rate of cumulation of social science knowledge.

We hope that you will find this device of some help in pursuing questions. Along with the other matters with which we have been concerned so far, it may improve your ability to ask the right questions. Another topic that may also help in this regard is measurement. If relationships are to be tested empirically, then the variables must be measured in some fashion.

Measurement of Variables

We have argued consistently for the advantages of conceptualizing research in system terms. But how does one collect data on social systems? We raised this question earlier and cited Tausky's criticism of a study by Aiken and Hage wherein they interviewed a cross-sectional panel of organizational participants. Recall Tausky's basic point: "I question the methodological assumption that structural properties, e.g., a system property such as organizational centralization, can be validly measured by computing the average of individual responses to interview items on the relevant dimension." [23] But if one is not to interview organizational incumbents, then how are data to be collected?

In response to Tausky, Aiken and Hage make an important distinction, which is a helpful starting point in thinking about measurement of *system* properties: one may interview individuals, they argue, or observe them. What matters is what is done next. These data are used *to derive* measurements of system properties.[24]

As Aiken and Hage put it: "Are reports of occupational activity psychological merely because they have been obtained by interviews? We think not. It is our belief that it is the nature of the phenomenon studied that differentiates psychological and sociological variables. In our case, we have aggregated these individual reports about organizational behavior to infer social structure." [25]

Thus, two points about measurement are to be noted. First, we are interested in *system properties*. We *infer* the reality of the system and its properties. These inferences have to do with inferred relationships rather than concrete physical objects. Second, what we use as a base for

[23] Tausky, op. cit., p. 118.
[24] Aiken and Hage, op. cit.
[25] Ibid., p. 119.

data, or from where we get it, matters little. What is critical is how it is *treated*. Organizational reports are not necessarily better than answers to interview items; what is critical are the inferences we make about any data regardless of their source. Of course, some sources may be more reliable than others, but the general point remains. Thus, we suspect that payroll records are a better source to establish "wages paid" than aggregation of responses to questionnaires or interviews. However, if respondents were asked how they *felt* about wages paid or how much they *thought* others were paid, then the issue is not *reliability* but different phenomena.

To develop this idea further, the typology developed by Lazarsfeld and Menzel is especially helpful.[26] They distinguish between properties of collectives and members. Members are the parts that comprise collectives. Members may be individuals, departments, divisions, or any other unit one might wish to select given the problem at hand. Thus, in a study of university decision-making patterns, departments might serve as the members and a university could be the collective. But similarly, in another study, universities could be the members and the American higher educational system could represent the collective. Or, to elaborate further, one might pursue a variety of research problems wherein the higher educational systems of numerous nation states serve as members of an international education system.

They suggest that properties of collectives may be of three different types: (1) analytical; (2) structural; and (3) global. Each type of property is different in that alternative kinds of inferences are being made.

Analytical properties of collectives are based on measurements of members. For example, one might compute the average age of the individuals attending several different churches over a six-month period. These averages would represent an analytical property of each collective (church). Such averages might be an important independent control variable in analysis of a variety of problems. Note, however, that such a measurement would not represent the age of the collective per se. A particular church organization might have developed recently and yet could have a membership of mostly older persons. Failure to recognize this type of distinction can result in endless difficulties.

Structural properties of collectives are based on measurements of the relationships among the members. Patterns of interaction frequency among church members, cohesion of the memberships, and friendship patterns among the members are all structural properties. Note that such data may at times be collected through interviews, questionnaires,

---

[26] Paul F. Lazarsfeld and Herbert Menzel, "On the Relation Between Individual and Collective Properties," in *A Sociological Reader on Complex Organizations,* Amitai Etzioni, ed. (New York: Holt, Rinehart & Winston, Inc., 1969), pp. 499–516.

or observations of individuals. However, inferences are made regarding relationships among members.

The level of abstraction at which one may work can vary greatly. Thus, at a very concrete level, one could record and diagram the major communication patterns within a church organization. Or at a more abstract level, one might wish to measure the degree of centralization in communication among several churches.

Global properties are not based on measurements of members. Following our example of churches, what types of collective properties might be global? The most obvious is the yearly budget. The size of the church, type of ideology, economic assets, or age are all collective properties that are in a sense independent of characteristics of individual members. Most global properties characterize the collective because it is a part of other larger structures. For example, geographic location or parent affiliation, e.g., Methodist, Lutheran, Roman Catholic, Jewish, and so on, are global properties of a collective derived directly from superstructure relationships.

To summarize: think how we might describe an automobile. We could tell you the average tire pressure (analytic) derived from measurements of the four tires (whether or not to include the spare could lead to some arguments!). Or, a relationship among the parts could be described, e.g., the sequence of activities involved in braking action (structural). But you might be more interested in the length, color, weight, manufacturer, or model (global) than any of these other characteristics.

Thus, analytical, structural, and global properties of collectives can be differentiated. But note that within any of these types, the level of abstraction at which variables are conceptualized can vary greatly. Also, variables may reflect process or structure. For example, in the case of the automobile a global property could reflect process (e.g., time required to reach a speed of sixty miles per hour from a stationary position) or structure (e.g., weight or color). Finally, variables may reflect actual behavior *or* some aspect of the normative structure. Thus, it is one thing to try and establish who *ought* to make certain kinds of decisions or how centralized decision making is using such data (i.e., information on how decisions *ought* to be made), and something else to look at decision making behaviorally. There may be high correspondence between the behavior and the normative structure, or there may not. Here again, it is *not* a question of which measurement strategy is best but rather a matter of what one wishes to measure.

Collectives are composed of members. What is a member in one study may serve as a collective in another. It is helpful to distinguish among three types of properties of collectives. But what of members? Lazarsfeld and Menzel propose four types: (1) absolute; (2) relational; (3) comparative; and (4) contextual. Let's look at each of these briefly.

Absolute properties of members are based solely on information derived from the member without reference to the particular collective. If a single church were the collective under study, the sex of an individual being interviewed would be an absolute property. The sex distribution of the entire membership, e.g., 70 per cent female, 30 per cent male, would be an analytic property of the church (collective). If an entire conference of churches were the focal collective, the sex distribution of each particular church would be an absolute property of each church, since each individual church would be defined as a member of the conference (collective).

Relational properties of members refer to the relationships among them. Persons A, B, and C within a church membership would each make separate sociometric choices as to whom they would like to have on a particular committee. The *pattern* of such choices within the entire church or subunits of it would be a structural property of the church (collective).

Comparative properties of members are very similar to absolute ones. Basically, the difference is that the value of the measurement from the individual members is interpreted by referring to the distribution found throughout the entire collective. For example, the relative length of membership for a particular individual might be assessed by reviewing the entire range found in each unit. Individuals might be classified as long-, medium- or short-term members depending on how they ranked on the entire continuum. Thus, in one church anyone who had been a member over five years might be designated as "long-term," whereas in another church, anyone whose membership was less than ten years might be designated as "short-term." The actual number of years (absolute property) remains important for comparison among churches where a standard scale would be needed. But such comparative properties are frequently useful. However, care must be taken in analysis to keep them distinct. If comparing two churches of very different histories, it would be possible to classify some members as younger in each church as both collectives would have some "long-term" members relative to the other participating individuals.

Finally, *contextual properties* are characteristics of members derived from characteristics of other systems in which they are members. Thus, the political party of a church member is an absolute property. But the proportion of Democrats in his neighborhood is a contextual property. This information tells us something about the social context within which he finds himself. Similarly, if a single church was our member, as part of a conference of churches, the political party composition of its membership would be an absolute property, in contrast to the neighborhood or community political party composition, which would be a contextual property.

These distinctions may be useful in helping you to think with more precision about any variable you wish to measure. But they are also of great value in exploring system–subsystem and system–supersystem interactions. Relationships between collective and member properties can be especially exciting. For example, Scott cites the research by Lipset, Trow, and Coleman on the International Typographical Union. They "found that a higher proportion of men in small shops marked by high political consensus were active in union politics than was the case in small shops marked by low consensus. Here an analytical property of a collective (degree of consensus) is shown to have an influence on an absolute property of its members (political activity)." [27]

However, in working with relationships of this type, care must be taken to avoid several types of errors. Two most common ones are the "fallacy of aggregation" and the "ecological fallacy."

The fallacy of aggregation is committed when one assumes that relationships on the individual (member) level also apply on the collective level. Barton illustrates this idea nicely:

Consider the effect of a high casualty rate on collective behavior in a community. On the individual level, being a victim is related to feeling deprived, asking for help, and being incapable of helping others. By simple aggregation, we would conclude that the more victims a community has, the more people will have feelings of deprivation and demand help, and the fewer people will help others.

But this ignores the contextual effects on individuals. A person in a community with a high casualty rate is surrounded by other people who are suffering; this makes the non-victims feel relatively advantaged and even the victims feel less deprived, so that they are more motivated to help others. The individual who is in the vicinity of many victims also has many more opportunities to actually help, at any given level of motivation. [28]

The ecological fallacy is committed when one assumes characteristics of members based on data from collectives. For example, Robinson has shown that the percentage of blacks correlates very highly with the percentage of illiterates in regions of the United States, $r = 0.95$. But the correlation between race and illiteracy *when individuals* are used as a basis for the correlation is rather slight, $r = 0.20$. "The inflation of the ecological correlation between race and literacy is due largely to the fact that the more Negroes there are in a region the higher is the proportion of illiterate *whites* in the same region." [29]

With these cautions in mind, the typology proposed by Lazarsfeld

[27] W. Richard Scott, "Field Methods in the Study of Organizations," *Handbook of Organizations*, James G. March, ed. (Chicago: Rand McNally & Co., 1965), p. 297.

[28] Barton, op. cit., pp. 214–15.

[29] Theodore R. Anderson and Morris Zelditch, Jr., *A Basic Course in Statistics* (New York: Holt, Rinehart & Winston, Inc., 1968), p. 132. Primary source is W. S. Robinson, "Ecological Correlations and the Behavior of Individuals," *American Sociological Review*, 27: 351–57 (June 1950).

and Menzel can be helpful in conceptualizing variables and designing measurement indexes.

Equally helpful are measurement inventories that list various indexes which have been used by previous researchers. James Price has assembled the most detailed presentation of measurement indexes for variables most frequently used in organizational research.[30] He thoroughly discusses one or more measurement procedures for twenty-two critical variables, e.g., complexity, formalization, centralization, effectiveness, size, autonomy, and the like. Data concerning reliability and validity of each measure are included. Certainly, this and future such summaries will prove most helpful. More general inventories developed by Barton,[31] Miller,[32] Bonjean, Hill, and McLemore,[33] and Shaw and Wright[34] are especially useful also. A quick review of the measurement techniques developed for a particular variable can often provide you with some excellent starting points, or, in a few cases, an instrument you can use with little or no modification.

Role conception inventories and the methodological steps for developing them have been included in the appendixes of books by several authors, e.g., Gross et al.,[35] Haas,[36] and Kahn et al.[37] Lengthy discussions summarize the strategies used in determining the norms for particular role relationships and how these normative statements were then transferred into questionnaires or interview schedules for data collection. Reliability and validity tests of the measurement inventories are also discussed.

Working at the organizational level, Hall[38] developed six measurement scales to assess organizational structure. Using Weber's ideal type formulation of bureaucracy as a base, Hall's scales provide a basis for empirically determining the degree to which actual behaviour fits the bureaucratic model. Each scale is comprised of about ten items, which

[30] James L. Price, *Handbook of Organizational Measurement* (Lexington, Mass.: D. C. Heath, 1972).

[31] Allen H. Barton, *Organizational Measurement and Its Bearing on the Study of College Environments* (New York: College Entrance Examination Board, 1961).

[32] Delbert C. Miller, *Handbook of Research Design and Social Measurement* (New York: David McKay Co., Inc., 1964).

[33] Charles M. Bonjean et al., *Sociological Measurement: An Inventory of Scales and Indices* (San Francisco, Calif.: Chandler Publishing Company, 1967).

[34] Marvin E. Shaw and Jack M. Wright, *Scales for the Measurement of Attitudes* (New York: McGraw-Hill Book Co., 1967).

[35] Neal Gross et al., *Explorations in Role Analysis* (New York: John Wiley and Sons, Inc., 1968).

[36] J. Eugene Haas, *Role Conception and Group Consensus* (Columbus, Ohio: Bureau of Business Research, Ohio State University, 1964), pp. 105–36.

[37] Robert Kahn et al., *Organizational Stress: Studies in Role Conflict and Ambiguity* (New York: John Wiley and Sons, Inc., 1964).

[38] Richard H. Hall, "The Concept of Bureaucracy: An Empirical Assessment," *American Journal of Sociology*, **69**: 32–40 (July 1963).

are administered to samples of organizational respondents and then summarized into average scores for comparison across organizations. Respondents are asked to agree strongly, agree, be uncertain, disagree, or disagree strongly with each item. Following the traditional Likert technique, scores of 1–5 are assigned. The six dimensions and sample items are as follows:

1. Hierarchy of authority scale: "A person can make his own decisions without checking with anyone else."
2. Division of labor scale: "One thing people like around here is the variety of work."
3. System of rules scale: "The time for coffee breaks is strictly regulated."
4. System of procedures scale: "We are to follow strict operating procedures at all times."
5. Impersonality scale: "We are expected to be courteous, but reserved at all times."
6. Technical competence scale: "Employees are periodically evaluated to see how well they are doing." [39]

Hall's scales or variants of them have been used by several researchers.[40] They are an excellent illustration of deriving measures of organizational characteristics from data supplied by individual members. Thus, by modifying traditional measurement strategies such as the Likert technique, more complex, and presumably more useful, measures can be constructed.[41]

Measurement of organizational effectiveness was explored by Georgopoulos and Tannenbaum,[42] who used several different types of data. Effectiveness was conceptualized as reflecting three criteria: "(1) organizational productivity; (2) organizational flexibility in the form of successful adjustment to internal organizational changes and successful adaptation to externally induced change; and (3) absence

[39] Ibid., p. 35. Complete copies of the scales and much additional methodological discussion are contained in Richard H. Hall, "An Empirical Study of Bureaucratic Dimensions and their Relation to Other Organizational Characteristics" (unpublished Ph.D. dissertation, Columbus, Ohio State University, 1961).

[40] For example, Jerald Hage and Michael Aiken, "Routine Technology, Social Structure and Organizational Goals," *Administrative Science Quarterly*, 14: 366–76 (September 1969).

[41] For a critique of Hall's strategy see David Gold, "A Criticism of an Empirical Assessment of the Concept of Bureaucracy on Conceptual Interdependence and Empirical Independence," *American Journal of Sociology*, 70: 225–26 (September 1964).

[42] Basil S. Georgopoulos and Arnold S. Tannenbaum, "A Study of Organizational Effectiveness," *American Sociological Review*, 22: 534–40 (October 1957).

For another application and further discussion, see Basil S. Georgopoulos and Floyd Mann, *The Community General Hospital* (New York: The Macmillan Company, 1962).

of intraorganizational strain, or tension, and of conflict between organizational subgroups." [43] Using an organization that specialized in delivery of retail merchandise, effectiveness of thirty-two subunits (stations) was assessed. *Station productivity* was measured by using the average productivity of all drivers within each station during the preceding month. Driver productivity was determined by company performance records which indicated "units of time consumed by the worker below or above what is 'allowed' according to the standard." [44] Numeric values ranged from 0.81 (highest productivity) to 2.93 for the thirty-two stations. *Intraorganizational strain* was assessed by asking nonsupervisory station personnel to check one of five alternatives (ranging from there is "a great deal of tension" to "no tension at all") in response to the following question: "On the whole, would you say that in your station there is any tension or conflict between employees and supervisors?" [45] Finally, *organizational flexibility* was measured by two indicators that were later combined into one score. Nonsupervisory personnel were asked two questions:

(1) "From time-to-time changes in methods, equipment, procedures, practices, and layout are introduced by the management. In general, do you think these changes lead to better ways of doing things?" (Five response alternatives were used which ranged from, "They are always an improvement" to "They never improve things".)

(2) "In general, how well do you think your station handles sharp changes in volume during peak periods?" Five response alternatives were used which ranged from "excellent" to "poor." [46]

These three indexes were then transformed into a consistent five-point scale and averaged to obtain a single measure. Correlation analysis clearly indicated that the three separate measures were tapping different aspects of effectiveness in that they were not highly intercorrelated. However, each dimension correlated rather highly with an independent validation measure of station effectiveness. The validation measure was based on cumulated rating data provided by a group of experts who had firsthand knowledge of the stations but were not directly involved in the stations that they were rating. "Included among the raters were the plant manager, the assistant plant manager, some division managers, and other key plant personnel, comprising a total of six to nine experts in each of the five company plants." [47] Using performance over the previous six months, data forms instructed raters "to cross out those stations he was not able to evaluate, and to judge the remaining stations by placing them into five categories of overall

[43] Ibid., p. 536.
[44] Ibid., p. 537.
[45] Ibid., p. 538.
[46] Ibid.
[47] Ibid., p. 536.

effectiveness, ranging from 'best' to 'poorest.' "[48] The combined effectiveness measure based on the three dimensions was highly correlated with the validation measure; r = .77. And the three measures yielded high statistical reliability when considered in combination.

Thus, using combinations of several types of data, Georgopoulos and Tannenbaum emerged with a general measurement strategy that appears applicable to many types of organizations. And their data suggested that this strategy was tapping organizational rather than individual phenomena. This was true even for the productivity measure, which was based exclusively on station averages of individual worker performance records (an analytic property of each collectivity, i.e., station). Analysis of variance indicated that the between-station variance in productivity was far greater than the within-station variance, hence supporting the interpretation that station (collectivity) rather than individual (member) differences were reflected in the measure.

Confronted with managers who would not provide data on such indicators of organizational performance as "return on investment" or "profits as a percentage of sales," Lawrence and Lorsch devised an alternative. Organizational performance is a global characteristic that they crudely assessed using three different measures: "change in profits over the past five years; change in sales volume over the past five years; and new products introduced in the past five years as a percent of current sales."[49] Managers were given a form on which to record their responses and instructed as follows:

In the table below we would like you to indicate the percentage *change on a year-to-year basis* of three performance indicators: sales; before tax profits; and return on investment before taxes. Considering the base year 1960 (or the year five years before the study) as 100, would you please indicate, in the space provided below, the level for each indicator for each year. For example, if sales in 1961 were 5% above 1960, you would put 105 in the 1961 column. If sales were 5% below the 1960 level in 1962, you would put 95 in the 1962 column, and so forth.

	1960	1961	1962	1963	1964
Sales	100				
Before Tax Profits	100				
Return on Investment Before Tax	100				50

48 Ibid.

49 Paul R. Lawrence and Jay W. Lorsch, *Organization and Environment* (Homewood, Ill.: Richard D. Irwin, Inc., 1969), p. 39. Measures for other variables (e.g., differentiation, integration, mode of conflict resolution, etc.) used in this study are described in detail in a helpful appendix.

50 Ibid., pp. 261–62.

FIGURE 9–5   Illustrative Measurement of Organizational Performance

Organization	Change in Profits Over 5 years	Change in Sales Volume Over 5 years	New Products Developed in Last 5 Years As Per Cent of Current Sales	Total Ranking[a]	Managers' Subjective Appraisals[a]	Performance Rating
High A	2	3	1	6(2)	2 1/2	High
High B	1	1	3	5(1)	2 1/2	High
Medium A	3[b]	2	4	9(3)	1	Medium
Medium B	6	4	2	12(4)	4	Medium
Low A	4	6	6	16(6)	6	Low
Low B	5	5	5[c]	15(5)	5	Low

[a] Spearman's rank-order correlation between the ranking of index totals (in parentheses) and the ranking of managers' subjective appraisal was significant at .05 (corrected for ties).

[b] Organization medium A had been operating at or near the break-even point during this period. A small increase in profit made this index rise unrealistically in relation to the other organizations, so the average of the other two indices was used.

[c] Organization low B, which has been in existence only five years, could report only that all products had been introduced in the past five years, so the average for the rankings of the other two indices was used.

SOURCE: Adapted from Paul R. Lawrence and Jay W. Lorsch, *Organization and Environment* (Homewood, Ill.: Richard D. Irwin, Inc, 1969, p. 40.

These data were then reviewed collectively, and each firm was placed in a rank order on each of the three measures. High, medium, and low designations were made by combining the ranks across all three indexes (see Figure 9–5).

Neither this crude index of organizational performance nor any of the measures cited here should be viewed as the ultimate, but they do illustrate some of the variations in strategies developed by organizational researchers. Certainly here is an area where much future work will, and must, be allocated.

With these ideas regarding the history of science, research implications of a systems perspective, variations in question formulation, the open box technique, and measurement, you should be able to think through what it is you want to know with much greater precision and rigor.

Let us turn to our next question: Where can you find the phenomena you want to study?

Where Can You Find the Phenomena You Want to Study?

Basically, you have two choices. Either you locate a functioning social system in the field that will meet your research needs, or you construct one. Either choice has both advantages and disadvantages. Traditionally, most organizational research has been conducted in field settings. Researchers have located an organization or a collection of them and proceeded to collect data by a variety of means.

Traditionally, laboratory research has been highly social-psychological. Gatherings—e.g., students meeting for an hour or so, rather than real groups—have often been used as subjects in highly artificial settings. Recently, however, these issues have been explored more carefully, and several useful distinctions have appeared.[51] Our own view is that increasingly researchers will find it useful to shuttle back and forth between the field and the laboratory. No longer is it useful to argue that one type of setting is inherently superior to the other. Rather, the advantages of each must be recognized, and both can be utilized to maximize flexibility in designing research that tests theory.

Some researchers have designed laboratory studies to test relationships between specified variables. This research is conceptualized in abstract terms and is sometimes charged with being artificial: "What relevance do findings based on college students playing card games have to the real world?" it may be asked. The question is a serious one, which will continue to bother many. However, it seems to us that three

[51] Thomas E. Drabek and J. Eugene Haas, "Realism in Laboratory Simulation: Myth or Method?" *Social Forces*, **45**: 337–46 (March 1967).

points can be made which don't eliminate the question but recast it considerably.

First, the quality of laboratory research is not to be judged using the degree of similarity between the laboratory and the real world as the criterion. This research is designed to test theory. The theory is then transferred to the real world. As Morris Zelditch has put it, "Experiments are relevant to theory, and *theory* is applied to natural settings." [52] Implicit in this view, however, is the assumption that social processes and variables can be identified and controlled so as to be studied in isolation. Thus, Zelditch argues, you would never want to bring an army into a laboratory, as you can use less complex systems to test relationships among variables and then test these relationships in a natural setting.

Second, rather than argue that laboratory settings are artificial, it is more useful to ask, "What is it that makes an experimental setting realistic?" Dimensions identified can be used as a basis for establishing sets of *experimental conditions*. Results obtained within the same or similar sets of experimental conditions can then be compared. In this way we can begin to ascertain what the consequence of various experimental conditions are.

For example, after reviewing the literature, we found that the term *realism* was used in a variety of ways. Groups of students participating in an experiment for thirty minutes are a different type of system from a work group that has persisted over several years. But it doesn't help much to call one real and the other unreal. Also, work groups that are asked to play scrabble, chess, or what have you, may not respond as they do when tasks similar to those they usually confront are given to them. A game is fine, but usually it should be viewed as a novel task for the group. In short, we identified five critical dimensions that serve as a start toward classifying experimental conditions: (1) life of group, i.e., is it a transitory system or one with more permanence and culture? (2) task, activity, or demand; (3) physical setting; (4) environmental interaction; and (5) subject awareness that they are in an experiment and are being observed.[53] These five dimensions are a crude specification of sets of experimental conditions, which may vary when hypotheses are tested. What we need to know, then, are the consequences of such on tests of hypotheses relating substantive variables.

Third, laboratory settings have greatest utility for theory construction. When you bring systems into the laboratory, you quickly realize that you have great power of control. You are in charge, but what is it

---

[52] Morris Zelditch, Jr., "Can You Really Study an Army in the Laboratory?" in Amitai Etzioni, ed., *A Sociological Reader on Complex Organizations* (New York: Holt, Rinehart & Winston, Inc., 1969), p. 539.

[53] Elaboration of this discussion is presented in Thomas E. Drabek and J. Eugene Haas, "Realism in Laboratory Simulation: Myth or Method?" op. cit.

you want in the experimental setting? You are forced to confront the question head on. In the field, participants behave regardless of your presence. In the lab, you must decide who will be there, what they will be instructed to do, how they will be instructed to do it, and, most important of all, why?[54] The laboratory is an excellent setting in which to sharpen up concepts and measurement techniques. These can then be taken into the field and tested on natural systems.

In contrast to studying social processes or single relationships in isolation, others have elected to *simulate systems* in the laboratory. The difference is not just in choice of words. Rather, the simulators are committed to the assumption that *the entire system or subsystem is the natural unit of study.* Attempts to study relationships between two variables under highly controlled conditions may destroy the system—the very unit of study.

Three approaches have been used in system simulations. First, some investigators have constructed systems specifically for the research problem. For example, Wager and Palola[55] hired persons through normal channels to develop ideas for advertising the 1962 World's Fair in Seattle. They actually created an organization to meet their research needs. But it was one they could manipulate to test the theoretical relationships in which they were interested. Second, others have brought parts of systems into the laboratory and then have replicated the system environment. For example, we placed teams of police officers who manned the communications room of a metropolitan police department into a laboratory.[56] Most aspects of the system environment were replicated so that this work group could function as it did normally. We manipulated the environment in accordance with our design in order to investigate how this system would respond to drastic demand changes. Third, and finally, others have simulated systems on the computer. Here, complex networks of relationships comprising a theoretical model are programmed. And when values on one or two variables are manipulated, the consequences throughout the entire system can be estimated.

Although we will explore examples of all of these strategies in a future section, let us now review the answer to our initial question. Social systems can be found in natural settings, but little control is possible and manipulation is difficult at best—both for practical and ethical

---

[54] The systemic interdependence of subjects, laboratory, and experimenters, and its consequences are explored in Theodore Mills, *The Sociology of Small Groups* (Englewood Cliffs, N.J.: Prentice-Hall, Inc., 1967), pp. 49–56.

[55] L. Wesley Wager and Ernest Palola, "The Miniature Replica Model and Its Use in Laboratory Experiments of Complex Organizations," *Social Forces*, 42: 418–29 (May 1964).

[56] Thomas E. Drabek and J. Eugene Haas, "Laboratory Simulation of Organizational Stress," *American Sociological Review*, 34: 223–38 (April 1969).

reasons. One can construct experimental systems and/or settings in which to test theoretical relationships. These relationships may be tested in highly controlled situations in which central variables are isolated and separately manipulated. Or one may choose to simulate a system that is constructed specifically for the experiment, bring an ongoing system into a simulated setting, or simulate the system by means of the computer. Thus there are many possibilities. And there appear to be distinct advantages in shuttling among these settings so as to utilize the advantages that each of them offers. Begin in the field, then take your theoretical model into the laboratory to sharpen it up. Simulate in the laboratory and then on the computer. Take this model back into the field to see where it needs modification.[57] Of course, what you actually do in each of these settings obviously varies a great deal. Let us briefly look at each of them from an operational viewpoint.

What Do You Do When You Get There?

We will briefly discuss working in both field and laboratory settings. However, four introductory comments are necessary at the outset. First, sets of ethical questions confront researchers at every stage of the research process. We will not concern ourselves with these beyond this point, except to emphasize that changes in system and individual functioning can be a direct result of participation in your research. You may, at times, judge change to be desirable. More likely, however, you won't even know it has occurred until after it has happened. Despite the scientific necessity of certain manipulations and occasional deception, we would urge you carefully to consider the impact of your research on the subjects and your ethical responsibilities to them.[58]

Second, lack of cooperation may force you to reconsider a particular research question. In fact, it may prevent you from doing the research at all.[59] However, other design strategies may be available. Lack of cooperation, like ethical responsibilities that prevent you from subjecting random samples of emergency organizations to natural disasters, may weaken your design. But it is far better, in our opinion, to sacrifice design elegance than grossly to violate individual dignity or privacy.[60]

[57] A somewhat similar view is discussed in more detail by William M. Evan, ed., *Organizational Experiments: Laboratory and Field Research* (New York: Harper & Row, 1971), p. 4.

[58] Herman Kelman, "Human Use of Human Subjects: The Problem of Deception in Social Psychological Experiments," *Psychological Bulletin*, 67: 1–11 (January 1967).

[59] See Harwin L. Voss, "Pitfalls in Social Research: A Case Study," *The American Sociologist*, 1: 136–40 (May 1966).

[60] Oscar M. Ruebhausen and Orville G. Brim, "Privacy and Behavioral Research," *American Psychologist*, 21: 423–37 (May 1966).

Third, unusual circumstances may occur, which offer you a unique opportunity to investigate a particular type of rare phenomenon. If it appears that you can pursue some theoretically important questions, don't be afraid to change your design and take advantage of the situation. It may not come along for a long time in the future.

Fourth, although many of the issues discussed are germane, we will not explore, except in passing, problems and strategies for organizational analysis in crosscultural settings. Certainly such analyses are desired. But, as Holt and Turner indicate, "In principle, there is no difference between comparative crosscultural research and research conducted within a single society. The differences lie, rather, in the magnitude of certain types of problems that have to be faced." [61] Thus, we allude to the need to recognize differences in social class and educational levels when using questionnaires across levels of an organization. Questions posed in a vocabulary appropriate for upper management may not do for men on an assembly line. But the problem of equivalence of meaning is mild here, compared to what is encountered when crossing cultures.[62] Thus, this and other such problems are outside the scope of this chapter.[63] With these thoughts in mind, let us go to the field and then look into the laboratory.

Field Research

A great many volumes have been written on field research and on specialized topics such as interviewing techniques. Extremely useful summaries are Scott's chapter in the *Handbook of Organizations* entitled "Field Methods in the Study of Organizations" [64] and the collection of articles assembled by Adams and Preiss.[65] We will limit our discussion to three topics: (1) problems of entrée and rapport; (2) data

[61] Robert T. Holt and John E. Turner, "The Methodology of Comparative Research," in *The Methodology of Comparative Research,* Robert T. Holt and John E. Turner, eds. (New York: The Free Press, 1970), p. 6.

[62] For elaboration of this issue see:

Ibid., pp. 13–18.

Frederick W. Frey, "Cross-cultural Research in Political Science," in Holt and Turner, op. cit., pp. 240–48.

Robert M. Marsh, *Comparative Sociology* (New York: Harcourt, Brace, Jovanovich, Inc., 1967), pp. 271–80.

[63] Udy's work is especially helpful for beginning students. See Stanley H. Udy, Jr., *Organization of Work: A Comparative Analysis of Production Among Nonindustrial Peoples* (New Haven, Conn.: Human Relations Area Files Press, 1959); and Stanley H. Udy, Jr., "Cross-cultural Analysis: A Case Study," in Hammond, op. cit., pp. 161–83.

[64] W. Richard Scott, "Field Methods in the Study of Organizations," op. cit.

[65] Richard N. Adams and Jack J. Preiss, eds., *Human Organization Research: Field Relations and Techniques* (Homewood, Ill.: Dorsey Press, 1960).

collection; and (3) sampling. Careful reading of a more lengthy statement such as Scott's is encouraged.

Problems of Entrée and Rapport. Strategies concerning entrée and rapport depend to a large measure upon decisions about data collection. That is, it is one thing to solicit permission to distribute a short questionnaire to three men on an assembly line and quite another to request two-hour interviews with a 70 per cent sample of all personnel. Similarly, the level of cooperation may force re-evaluation of the data collection techniques. Three specific issues are most important in this area.

First, you immediately confront a decision of identity. How will you present yourself to organizational members? Scott has elaborated the advantages and disadvantages of the disguised and "open" researcher. After class discussions with numerous students, it is our impression that many would prefer the disguised strategy. "After all, isn't that the best way to keep people from lying to you? How better to study a prison than to be committed as a prisoner?" Although many arguments can be advanced to support this position, it is far from a panacea. Among the numerous objections, aside from ethical ones, are the limitations imposed by the role selected, e.g., researchers posing as prisoners will have much of the organization closed to them. Second, role playing demands so much attention that limited energy is left for observation. And third, as a role player the researcher contaminates the research setting by his presence. Our bias is towards the open researcher unless the circumstances and research question are most atypical. We have seen too many instances where deception was used for the sake of deception rather than because the study design actually required it. Hence, we would argue that you should present yourself in an honest and straightforward manner unless you have an extremely good case for doing otherwise.

Second, having made a decision as to how to present yourself, whom do you approach? Most researchers have begun near or at the top. Of course, this varies depending upon the data required. And upper-level permission may leave many doors locked and severely bias responses. For example, Gusfield[66] experienced particular difficulty with a local office despite endorsement from above. "The Secretary of the Illinois WCTU was quite critical of the national leaders and the 'large salaries' they received. Apparently, working from the top level had been a mistake, as it gave me a role within the organization that made me an unwilling ally of one side in an organizational dispute." [67] Obviously, such problems may have their counterpart in any study. However, apart from demanding much additional effort on the part of the researcher to

[66] Joseph R. Gusfield, "Field Work Reciprocities in Studying a Social Movement," in Adams and Preiss, op. cit., pp. 99–108.

[67] Ibid., p. 101.

What Do You Do When You Get There?

be as tactful as possible, the problem is often one that can be tolerated. We have experienced such problems as minimal except where intense hostility is a reflection of an idiosyncratic attitude of a particular person; e.g., "Universities are corrupting this country—and I'll be damned if I am going to help you." Social science research is increasingly familiar to and accepted by Americans. In a recent crossnational study involving persons from forty different nations, Miles indicates that the level of understanding of social science research was the most important factor he could detect in predicting cooperation.[68]

In short, formulate a pitch in which you describe your research objectives and the specific requests you wish to make. Also, indicate that other organizations have already participated, that information received will not be presented by naming an individual person or organization, and that some broader social goal may result from your work. The major problem remaining, which can be disastrous, is one of feedback. Be very careful regarding any trade-off to reveal information obtained in an interview. This issue is of extreme importance. Let's explore it briefly.

In trying to obtain access to organizational data, be very careful about any promises you might make regarding using such data. Among the pitfalls of which you should be aware are first to realize that you may be thrust into a communication role. For example, an interviewer may reply, "Boy, would I ever like to hear Sam's answer to that one." If rapport has been difficult and you still feel that improvement is required, it is very tempting to reveal data obtained. However, if you do, realize that this interviewee is now likely to be highly guarded in his responses in that he wonders to whom you will be passing his responses. Similarly, he may distort many responses knowing that you have yet to interview another official. He may assume that you will communicate his responses to that official.

Second, beware of promising confidentiality in a broad and sweeping fashion. Unless you can assume one of the trusted positions in American society, i.e., doctor, lawyer, or minister, you legally cannot meet your promise. Thus, although you usually will treat all information as confidential, don't be afraid to stop an interviewee if you find yourself being used as a confessional.

Third, you may be invited into a group or organization where feedback is desired. Before you begin, clarify when such feedback will be given, to whom, and in what form. Argyris has emphasized that it is usually undesirable to provide any feedback until all data have been collected.[69] Feedback before that time may greatly affect responses by

[68] Edward Miles, "The Logistics of Interviewing in International Organizations," *International Organization,* **24:** 361–70 (Spring 1970).

[69] Chris Argyris, "Creating Effective Relationships in Organizations," in Adams and Preiss, op. cit., pp. 109–33.

those interviewed later. Also, conclusions based on partial data may result in administrative actions that may change the system under study. And such changes may not even be warranted when later viewed within the context of all data. Finally, administrative limitations as to distribution of the conclusions should be carefully evaluated. As Argyris notes:

> In most cases, the administrator asks for feedback to himself and a few of his co-workers. A smaller number request feedback at all levels. If the latter request is not made of the researcher, it may be helpful to inquire why the administrator does not desire feedback to his employees. The researcher tries to help the administrator become aware that if he maintains his position he may be interpreted as using research to control the employees, or to keep them in the dark because he finds the results disturbing or because he has no intention of doing anything about the implications of the findings.[70]

From these comments, it should be clear that there are no simple answers regarding entrée and rapport. However, being sensitized to these questions should help in mapping out the many decisions one must make. Interrelated with these are decisions regarding data collection. Let's briefly look at some of the major strategies currently in use.

Data Collection. Four major types of data collection strategies have been used by field researchers: (1) questionnaires; (2) interviews; (3) observation; and (4) use of primary source materials. Although we will discuss each strategy separately, our bias is that researchers should, whenever possible, use all of these jointly. Each has its advantages and disadvantages. But findings can be greatly strengthened when data collected by different means can be shown to reinforce a particular conclusion. Thus, findings based on interviews may be supported with questionnaire or observational data. Our treatment of each of these strategies will be extremely brief, but we will indicate a few of the lengthy summarizing statements that we have found to be especially helpful.

Questionnaires have long been a highly popular mode of data collection, and little wonder. A short questionnaire can be quickly prepared, cheaply printed and mailed, and returned without the researcher even leaving his office. Many specific procedures have been tested sufficiently for high returns to be obtained frequently. It is recommended, for example, that a letter be sent announcing that the questionnaire will be arriving soon; that hand-pasted stamps be affixed to return envelopes; that the printed layout be carefully considered so as to make the questionnaire easy to read with an uncrowded appearance. Before trying to construct a questionnaire, consult a good guide book,

[70] Ibid., p. 116.

such as Oppenheim's,[71] and review the appendixes of published reports that present sample questionaires.[72]

Three important observations should be made about questionnaires, however. First, return rates usually will be much higher if the questions are specific and response categories are provided. The specificity of the question is far more important in determining the time required to answer than the number of questions asked. While a few open-ended type questions may yield high response, persons tend to make each answer shorter. And after more than half-a-dozen or so open-ended questions, many will tend to drop the paper into the nearest trash can. Thus, broad questions about vague issues are to be minimized or avoided.

Second, carefully pretest the schedule with persons similar to those who will be receiving it. Ask them to fill it out and then interview them regarding suggestions for change. Among the most important factors to be determined in the pretest is the availability of data. We have found this to be more critical than any other factor in organizational studies. For example, a student once confronted us with a two-page questionnaire that she had sent to nearly two hundred ministers. Her report that only three or four had responded seemed impossible. The questionnaire had been printed and was nicely spaced, giving it an attractive appearance. Review of the content, however, indicated that she had badly assessed the type of information to which ministers would have easy access, for example: "How many in your congregation are currently receiving welfare payments from the city?" "How many in your congregation have quit and formally joined another church in the last five years?" Although it might appear that ministers should have such information, most do not. And even responses obtained would have to be carefully analyzed as they would most likely reflect the minister's perception, which may or may not correspond to the objective situation. Therefore, in pretesting a questionnaire, be especially careful to ascertain the availability of data to the respondent. Failure to do so may prevent high returns or, just as worthless, responses that are crude guesses (unless, of course, you are interested in the pattern of perception).

Finally, recognize that many phenomena cannot be studied through responses to fixed choice questions. Cicourel's critique is excellent in this regard.[73] Response choices created by the researcher force subjects to use the linguistic structure of the researcher. This may result in great

---

[71] A. N. Oppenheim, *Questionnaire Design and Attitude Measurement* (New York: Basic Books, Inc., 1966). Problems in cross-cultural surveys are summarized by Frey, op. cit.

[72] For example, Kahn et al., *Organizational Stress*, op. cit.

[73] Aaron V. Cicourel, *Method and Measurement in Sociology* (New York: The Free Press, 1964).

distortion, especially when the responses are aggregated. Frequency tables listing responses to standardized questions have a cut and dried quality to them that implicitly indicate clarity and structure in each respondent's perceptual world which matches that of the researcher and all other respondents. As Cicourel cautions:

> Throughout the literature for and against survey and questionnaire methods, there are frequent references to the possibility that data are the product of vague or loosely structured thinking on the part of respondents. Why not assume that the actor's thoughts about social objects are loosely structured but are perceived as concrete until we begin to probe them with specific questions that put him on the spot about matters which he takes for granted and to which he seldom gives much time? Survey research procedures do not assign variable status to ignorance, much less acknowledge it as a critical factor in the structure of social action.[74]

Thus, questionnaires can be useful data collection devices for some types of data, especially that which is highly objective and readily available to the respondent. However, there are many shortcomings, and validation of data obtained through questionnaires by another strategy is desirable wherever possible.

Interviewing has been the most widely used data collection technique by organizational researchers. Its wide use among persons in all areas of the social sciences and related fields such as personnel and administration has generated numerous studies and reports. Let us briefly look at four of the many lessons that have emerged from these studies.

First, interviewer–interviewee interactions must be viewed as any other role relationship. And therefore researchers must be sensitive to ways in which role expectations will distort data obtained. Interviewers will be socially defined and acted toward accordingly. For example, Gusfield[75] suggests that he was defined in his WCTU study by some interviewees as a member of the public. And when so defined, informants tried to convince him of the rightness of the movement. But others defined him as an "informed stranger" with whom they could talk safely. As a consequence, Gusfield discovered he was "at her mercy," because he had "no relation to the WCTU which would give consequence to her answers. Because of this she can 'let off steam' in a harmless manner. But the interviewer has another therapeutic function. He becomes the bearer of the justification and sympathy of the respondent. By presenting her grievances, the respondent may seek to gain the sympathetic alliance of the impartial person."[76] Others have

---

[74] Ibid., p. 115.
[75] Gusfield, op. cit.
[76] Ibid., p. 105.

illustrated many additional expectation sets associated with the interviewer–interviewee role. Consequently, remember that an interview is a social situation and, because of this, position incumbents are going to bring expectations into the situation that will greatly affect the quality of data received.

Second, there are great variations in the mode of participation in interviews among groups of persons. Thus, following from the above point, whites interviewing blacks will be received differently from blacks interviewing blacks. But equally important are ethnic, religious, and social class differences in interview participation. For example, upon reviewing tape recordings of interviews conducted with natural disaster victims, Strauss and Schtazman[77] concluded that there were major social class differences. Lower-class persons responded with vague accounts of what had happened to them with little chronology. They frequently had to be probed on even the most obvious details, e.g., "Well, who was there besides you?" In contrast, middle-class victims were much more verbal and generally gave complete descriptions of their behaviors and thoughts with little probing. "Middle-class persons, on the whole, are amazingly sensitive to the requirements of various kinds of queries: when asked to list, they list; when invited to describe, they describe; when asked for an illustration, they supply one." [78] Often, organizational research is designed so that data are collected from respondents at varying hierarchical levels. Thus, interview schedules need to be prepared and pretested with an understanding of such response variations.

Third, interviews can vary widely in the degree to which they are structured. The degree of structure should reflect the research objectives. And a single interview session may vary greatly in this regard with some very loosely structured questions followed by highly structured ones. Interview questions may be so highly structured that the schedule actually resembles a fixed-choice questionnaire. Other schedules may be highly unstructured so that the interviewee is permitted more adequately to reveal his perceptions rather than being forced into the linguistic structure of the researcher. Highly nondirected interviews can be extremely useful in obtaining many kinds of data. Tape recorders that are inexpensive, reliable, and easy to use greatly increase the power of this technique.[79] General questions are asked, and the interviewee is permitted to tell his story with only minimal comment by the interviewer.

[77] Anselm Strauss and Leonard Schatzman, "Cross-class Interviewing: An Analysis of Interaction and Communicative Styles," in Adams and Preiss, op. cit., pp. 205–13.

[78] Ibid., p. 208.

[79] Rue Bucher, Charles E. Fritz, and E. L. Quarantelli, "Tape Recorded Interviews in Social Research," *American Sociological Review*, 21: 359–64 (June 1956).

However, in less structured settings, the interviewers use a variety of techniques to push interviewees to reveal relevant data.[80] For example, at a pause he may reply with an "uh-huh," a nod of the head, or "that's interesting." In this way he indicates that he is following the interviewee, who is encouraged to add more details if he has any. We have been most impressed with the importance of training interviewers who are using this style so as to increase their tolerance for silence. The typical novice will quickly jump in with another question and often severely curtail data obtained. Often, an interviewee will pause for a minute, two, or even three, and then continue with additional information, if he is not confronted with a different question. But such pauses can seem like an eternity to the beginning interviewer. Other techniques are simply to repeat the last few words offered by the interviewee, which encourages him to continue. Or, you may respond with a question, e.g., "How's that?" or "In what way do you mean that?" Thus, in considering use of interviews as a data collection device, recognize that the degree of structure or directedness can vary greatly. And there may be many instances where less structured interviews will serve best.

Fourth, validity of data obtained through interviews may be corrupted in numerous ways.[81] Misinformation may be subtly given when respondents slant information so as to make themselves, their department, organization, or community look good. Or information may be overdramatized to make the informant or his organization appear special or unusually important. Informal desires to stimulate reform or curb it may elicit overinformation or blockage of information. Interviewers may confront stylized and stereotype answers to questions caused by rumors about the research study. Finally, purposeful misinformation may take the form of "rationalizations of publicly unacceptable behavior ('you don't find people doing much drinking in this town') and pseudo-definitions of the character and inter-workings of the community ('One thing about this town, if you try to throw your weight around—I can't care who you are—you soon get cut down to size.')." [82]

Equally important are less obvious error sources, to which the researcher must be alert. Involuntary errors do occur, but can be minimized by careful cross-checking. More subtle, however, are errors that occur because the respondent is trying to be overly helpful. He has his view of the organization, the community, and social science research. He may feel that the questions being asked are not really germane to

---

[80] Whyte's discussion of this point is extremely helpful; see William F. Whyte, "Interviewing in Field Research," in Adams and Preiss, op. cit., pp. 352–74.

[81] The following points were adapted from Arthur Vidich and Joseph Bensman, "The Validity of Field Data," in Adams and Preiss, op. cit., pp. 188–204.

[82] Ibid., p. 191.

the research problem as he understands it. And so he seeks to redirect the interview toward information that he views as important. Of course, this is related to the earlier point made by Cicourel that the symbolic meanings of the interviewee may differ significantly from those of the researcher, who often proceeds simply to interpret responses into his own linguistic set without realizing the consequences or implications. Cicourel has presented detailed analysis of this issue and many specific examples that merit close review.[83]

Thus, interviews like questionnaires are far from a panacea for data collection. Numerous error sources must be more widely recognized than they have been in the past. And some critics have suggested that use of both techniques should be severely curtailed in view of these arguments. Instead of or as a cross-check, observational procedures are often recommended. Let us look briefly at this technique.

Observation as a data collection technique has a long history of a cyclical nature in sociology. Reaching a peak in the 1930s with numerous publications that originated or were brought into print by the University of Chicago, the technique enjoyed a new popularity in the 1960s, perhaps as a response to criticisms to the excessive popularity of questionnaire and interview studies during the 1940s and 1950s. But there is more to it than the single interchange of data collection devices. Led by sociologists such as Howard S. Becker, Everett Hughes, Herbert Blumer, Anselm Strauss, Erving Goffman, and Harold Garfinkel, many began to question the basic methodological assumptions on which researchers using questionnaires and interviews had proceeded.[84] And emerging from this symbolic interactionist perspective has come a variety of statements in which different sets of methodological assumptions are proposed.

Whereas some researchers may elect to proceed in a highly detached manner and systematically record their observations by counting the frequency with which A initiates interaction with B,[85] others attempt to ascertain the subjective meanings of the interaction for the participants. Thus, the researchers must begin with minimal preconceptions of the subject's reality and surrender himself to the situation. "He should have some control over his perspective, but he cannot control the perspective of his subjects or remain uninfluenced by them, and still understand them. It is through this encounter between observer and participants—wherein the viewpoint of the observer is modified by

---

[83] Cicourel, op. cit., pp. 73–104. See also Aaron V. Cicourel and John I. Kitsuse, *The Educational Decision-Makers* (Indianapolis, Ind.: Bobbs-Merrill, 1963), pp. 149–73.

[84] A brief but thorough overview of this literature is contained in Norman K. Denzin, "Symbolic Interactionism and Ethnomethodology: A Proposed Synthesis," *American Sociological Review*, 34: 922–34 (December 1969).

[85] For example, Robert F. Bales, *Interaction Process Analysis* (Reading, Mass.: Addison-Wesley Publishing Co., 1950).

contact with the reality of the subjects—that the observer discovers a greater truth about the nature of himself and his subjects." [86] More specifically, "By taking the role of his subjects he re-creates in his own imagination and experience the thoughts and feelings which are in the minds of those he studies." [87] Thus, *the researcher himself* is the central tool in participant observation.

In discussing the participant observation procedures used in their study of medical students, Becker and Geer indicate that they followed the student's daily routine.[88] "We went to lectures with students taking their first two years of basic science and frequented the laboratories in which they spent most of their time; watching them and engaging in casual conversation as they dissected cadavers or examined pathology specimens." [89] And they thereby attempted to formulate a perspective, i.e., "a set of ideas and actions used by a group in solving collective problems." [90] Once the content of a perspective was formulated, they proceeded to check its frequency and range. In this way they were able to segment and validate the perspectives represented among different sectors of the medical school.

But how can the researcher be sure that he has captured the perspective of a group? How can his readers? Obviously, there is no simple answer. However, Bruyn summarizes a lengthy discussion of this question through the following propositions, reflecting six different indexes of subjective adequacy: (1) "the more time an individual spends with a group, the more likely it is that he will obtain an accurate interpretation of the social meanings its members live by";[91] (2) "the closer the observer works geographically to the people he studies, the more accurate should be his interpretations";[92] (3) "the more varied the status opportunities within which the observer can relate to his subjects, and the more varied the activities he witnesses, the more likely the observer's interpretations will be true";[93] (4) "the more familiar the observer is with the language of his subjects, the more accurate should be his interpretations";[94] (5) "the greater the degree of intimacy the observer achieves with his subjects, the more accurate his interpretations";[95] and (6) "the more the observer confirms the expressive meanings of the

---

[86] Bruyn, op. cit., p. 253.

[87] Ibid., p. 12.

[88] Howard S. Becker et al., *Boys in White* (Chicago: University of Chicago Press, 1961).

[89] Howard S. Becker and Blanche Geer, "Participant Observation: The Analysis of Qualitative Field Data," in Adams and Preiss, op. cit., p. 269.

[90] Ibid., p. 280.

[91] Bruyn, op. cit., p. 181.

[92] Ibid.

[93] Ibid., p. 182.

[94] Ibid.

[95] Ibid.

community, either directly or indirectly, the more accurate will be his interpretations of them." [96] Although these propositions clearly do not answer the question, they are a helpful beginning.

Finally, in using this method, how does one go about it? Bruyn has elaborated on an earlier statement by Spiegelberg and suggests several steps or stages of knowing. First, investigating the particular phenomena. This involves: (1) "an intuitive grasp of the phenomena, (2) their analytic examination, and (3) their description." [97] During this stage the investigator "must have no hypotheses to direct him as to what he should find in his investigation." [98] Second, "investigating general essences," i.e., "can a phenomenon remain the same phenomenon without the elements deemed essential by the observer? For example, Spiegelberg states, can a triangle still remain a triangle without three sides and three angles?" [99] Third, "apprehending essential relationships among essences." Fourth, "watching modes of appearing," i.e., recognition that as an observer he can make many different distinctions and conceptual elaborations so as to detect where the linguistic structures of subjects begin to "shade off" because categories are lacking. For example, "when a member of the upper class socially observes the classes at his extreme opposite, they become indistinct and shade into a general group." [100] The sociologist presumably has a more total view of class structure and differences because of his training, but he must seek to ascertain such shading by those under observation. Fifth, "exploring the 'constitution' of phenomena in the consciousness of the observer." For example, "Spiegelberg illustrates this process by describing how one obtains a 'picture' of a new city which is visited for the first time." [101] Such mental imagery gradually comes into form and the final image and the process by which the image was built up would be very different for a migrant worker than for an urban sociologist. Sixth, "suspending belief in existence," i.e., detaching "the phenomena of our everyday experience from the context of our naive or natural living, while preserving their content as fully and as purely as possible." [102] Finally, the seventh step involves the interpretation of "concealed meanings"—that is, "moving to the theoretical level of interpreting data, and what Spiegelberg calls moving to ontological formulations of essences which illuminate phenomena for the observer. Ontological formulations have been made by Martin Heidegger and Jean-Paul Sartre and function, we

[96] Ibid., p. 183.
[97] Ibid., p. 272.
[98] Ibid.
[99] Ibid., p. 274.
[100] Ibid., p. 215.
[101] Ibid., p. 276.
[102] Loc. cit.

would say, at a comparable level with 'theory' in relationship to the 'data' of social research." [103]

Many argue that this approach or phenomenology precedes or underlies empiricism, i.e., "that there is something in the nature of human experience other than sheer reason or sensory observation, which can produce knowledge." [104] Of course, other researchers have used observation as a data collection technique without accepting the method or assumptions outlined here. Unlike disciples of either camp, we would argue that both strategies are useful, depending upon the questions one is asking. But we would especially emphasize the value and utility of the phenomenological approach when one is interested in descriptive or in-depth analysis of the normative structure of an organization.

Primary source materials can be used exclusively to supplement or to crossvalidate data or conclusions based on other techniques. It is our bias that too much energy from the sociological enterprise is being expended by asking people questions. Many analyses could be done entirely, or at least greatly strengthened, with primary source materials. Too often students assume that this refers only to frequently used collections such as the United States Census. But as Webb, Campbell, Schwartz, and Sechrest[105] dramatically demonstrate, many kinds of primary source materials are available. Let's briefly look at a few.

First, a multitude of materials are available from nearly all organizations, policy manuals, and the like. Also, many organizations publish newsletters, newspapers, and even periodicals. Personnel files, departmental budget breakdowns, criteria for hiring, promotion, and termination, or minutes of divisional meetings frequently can be obtained. All of these types of materials can be used descriptively. But more importantly, with a little imagination they can be transformed into data sets that provide the basis for indexes of analytic variables. For example, Evan hypothesized that students would quit less frequently if they were in work settings where high levels of interaction with other students were possible.[106] He used personnel records, and was able to support the hypothesis that job turnover was directly correlated with the number of peers with whom a student worker could interact.

As emphasized earlier, such materials can also be used to validate information obtained through interviews or questionnaires. For example, perceptions of the degree of attention given to patients may be

[103] Ibid.

[104] Ibid., p. 277.

[105] Eugene J. Webb et al., *Unobtrusive Measures: Non-Reactive Research in the Social Sciences* (Chicago: Rand McNally and Co., 1966).

[106] William M. Evan, "Peer-Group Interaction and Organizational Socialization: A Study of Employee Turnover," *American Sociological Review*, 28: 436–40 (June 1963).

contaminated by a variety of factors, e.g., degree and type of illness. An objective measure could be derived using the technique of Rashkis and Wallace, based on the frequency of notes made on the patient's bedside record.[107] Thus, in addition to validation possibilities, important discrepancies between perceptions by various members of subunits and the objective record can be useful clues for investigation of conflict.

Less obvious organizational resources are such items as tape recordings and telephone directories, which can be used for many research purposes. Audio recordings are made routinely of telephone conversation and radio exchanges by many emergency organizations such as police and fire departments, ambulance services, and hospitals. Conduct of organizational behavior is in fact captured in action. Recordings of this type proved invaluable in Drabek's analysis of organizational response to the 1963 explosion in Indianapolis.[108] Hence, routine organizational instruments can provide abundant data.

Even less obvious are such items as in-house telephone directories. For example, McNeil and Thompson[109] used this source to calculate "regeneration rates" (i.e., "the rate of change in the ratio of newcomers to veteran members of a social unit")[110] at Vanderbilt and the University of Tennessee. Consequences of such rates could be explored, for example, by comparing changing proportions of administrative positions, which could also be secured from telephone directories. As higher rates of newcomers arrive, are more administrative posts created because of increased socialization and coordination difficulties? Of course, such data could be combined with other types of institutional records to expand the basis for analysis.

Similarly, promotion practices could be ascertained by analysis of directories from several time periods. Inexpensively available, such a data source might permit analysis of several hundred organizations with differing structural characteristics. Data on specific variables, hypothesized as being related, could be gathered through other techniques, such as a mailed questionnaire. In some geographical areas, relative presence or absence of types of names (e.g., Spanish-American or female) could be ascertained by such directories. When compared to city-wide directories, the long-term hiring and promotion practices of many organizations could be estimated. And the impact of community and agency employment programs could be crudely evaluated over a long time span with relatively little expense.

[107] Cited in Webb et al., op. cit., p. 81.

[108] Thomas E. Drabek, *Disaster in Aisle 13* (Columbus, Ohio: College of Administrative Science, Ohio State University, 1968).

[109] Kenneth McNeil and James D. Thompson, "The Regeneration of Social Organizations," *American Sociological Review*, 36: 624–37 (August 1971).

[110] Ibid., p. 625.

In contrast to materials available directly from organizations, a second broad category of primary source data are those compiled by governmental agencies. Mountains of such materials are available from the United States federal government. An exceptional aid for organizational researchers has been prepared by James Price,[111] wherein he catalogs data most related to organizational phenomena. For example, Price lists 144 separate sources of data dealing with agricultural, transportation, communication, power-generating, and military organizations, and others. Starting with Price's book, you probably will be startled with the assistance that a good government documents librarian can give you. For example, summaries of on-going Defense Department research projects and findings are listed in an index issued by the Defense Documentation Center, which appears regularly. Varieties of data from all branches and levels of the federal government are stored away in regional depository libraries. As such, they are gold mines for organizational researchers.

Shifting governmental levels, United Nations reports provide a basis for many types of comparative studies. Similarly, state and local records and reports also can be used. Historical libraries and archive collections contain masses of institutional data. Traditionally confined to endless piles of budgetary records, many libraries are expanding the variety of data stored. Perhaps most exciting for sociology students are the growing oral history collections containing tape recorded speeches and interviews. Although currently confined to a few political figures such as former President Lyndon Johnson (Johnson Library at the University of Texas) collections of this type will undoubtedly become more common in the future.

Supplementing these types of data are a wide variety of miscellaneous materials. While you are in the library reviewing the government documents section, review some of the standard reference books such as *Who's Who* and *American Men of Science*. It takes only a bit of imagination to think about research projects using such data. For example, Oscar Grusky[112] used baseball record books as the data base for his analysis of managerial recruitment. He discovered that a higher proportion of players who had been in-fielders and catchers (high-interaction personnel) later became managers, compared to pitchers and out-fielders (low-interaction personnel).

The Encyclopedia of Associations[113] contains a variety of types of

---

[111] James L. Price, *Annotated Bibliography of Federal Government Publications Presenting Data about Organizations* (Iowa City: Center for Labor and Management, College of Business Administration, University of Iowa, 1967).

[112] Oscar Grusky, "The Effects of Formal Structure on Managerial Recruitment: A Study of Baseball Organization," *Sociometry*, **26**: 345–53 (March 1963).

[113] Frederick G. Ruffer, ed., *Encyclopedia of Associations* (Detroit, Mich.: Gale Research, 1964).

data on voluntary organizations. Using this source exclusively, Campbell and Akers[114] were able to explore the relationships among organizational size, complexity, and administrative components in 197 occupational associations. Thus, they were able to provide empirical support for such theoretically important hypotheses as: "The larger the organization, the more vertically and horizontally complex it is and the greater the total size of its staff component." [115] And "while the staff increases with greater organizational size, it does so at a decreasing rate." [116]

Stepping outside the library, most telephone companies have large collections of phone books. These documentary records list organization after organization in the Yellow Pages. Comparative community studies could be done using such sources exclusively. What kinds of organizations appear once a large manufacturing plant is built in a small town, or perhaps a military base or Atomic Energy Commission facility? The Yellow Pages contain a physical record of organizational birth and death. They are available for different time periods and for communities of all sizes and locales. Several of our students have demonstrated that some exciting research questions can be pursued through this data source when approached in an imaginative manner.

Following the tradition of Thomas and Znaniecki[117] in their classic study of Polish immigrants to the United States, many types of personal documents can be used. Appointment books, letters, diaries, and the like can provide many types of data. For example, Janowitz[118] used letters and diaries captured from German soldiers to try and assess the impact of propaganda on them. Letters from various environmental sectors may provide an important basis for organizational definitions of outsiders' expectations.

Relative impact of environmental changes can often be ascertained through combining several types of primary source materials. For example, many variations could be made on the design used by Parker.[119] He tried to ascertain the differential impact of television on reading habits through a time series design using library records. By comparing book withdrawal rates before and after the introduction of television in several Illinois cities, he determined that nonfiction books remained unaffected in contrast to a significant drop in the check-out rate for fiction titles.

---

[114] Frederick L. Campbell and Ronald L. Akers, "Organizational Size, Complexity, and the Administrative Component in Occupational Associations," *The Sociological Quarterly,* II: 435–51 (Fall 1970).

[115] Ibid., p. 447.

[116] Ibid.

[117] W. I. Thomas and Florian Znaniecki, *The Polish Peasant in Europe and America* (Chicago: University of Chicago Press, 1918).

[118] Cited in Webb, et al., op. cit., p. 106.

[119] Cited in ibid., p. 81.

It is clear that in addition to the usual skills developed in research methods courses, students of organizations would benefit from exposure to research librarians and historians, who have developed many useful techniques that have heretofore remained relatively unused by most sociologists.

Thus, these four different modes of data collection—questionnaires, interviews, observation, and primary sources—provide enormous variety for researchers. But we again emphasize two critical points. First, it appears highly undesirable to become exclusively attached to a single data collection technique. Let your problem determine which technique will be used, rather than selecting or avoiding problems simply because they do not lend themselves to your favorite field style. Second, wherever possible try to use several techniques simultaneously. Cross-validate data and conclusions based on one technique with data from another collection strategy. Armed with these varied data collection techniques and some sensitivity regarding problems of entrée and rapport, we need to now consider one final topic regarding field research—sampling.

Sampling. There are two levels on which sampling occurs—among and within the units of analysis. Recall our earlier discussion regarding measurement and the typology proposed by Lazarsfeld and Menzel regarding properties of members and of collectivities. We will focus here on a few points regarding *internal* sampling, i.e., sampling members so as to infer characteristics of the collectivity. Thus, discussion of selecting a sample of organizations will be delayed until a later section. Let us now assume that we have selected one or more organizations for study. What alternatives might we consider regarding sampling in field research? Unfortunately, the simple technique of drawing a random sample from a membership list has little relevance. Imagine trying to understand university functioning by interviewing a random sample that contained one dean, one faculty member, one janitor, one cook, and 296 students!

Four major points deserve emphasis. First, many studies, especially case studies, descriptive analysis, or exploratory work, use organizational incumbents as informants. Thus, following the traditions of social anthropologists, organizational researchers may select for interviewing a wide variety of participants on the basis of their presumed knowledge of organizational functioning as it relates to the particular problem under study. For example, if the researcher is interested in comparative turnover rates among several organizations with varying structural characteristics, personnel officers might be interviewed. In this way sampling of interviewees is determined by presumed knowledge of organizational functioning, and a global characteristic of the collectivity is thereby ascertained. Examples of data that might be obtained through selected informants are these; total operating budget; divisional budgets; presence or absence of orientation, insurance, or retirement programs; types of entry requirements such as education or past experience; and degree to which job descriptions, promotion practices, and disciplinary procedures are written or formalized. As indicated, sampling of such informants is determined by the data required and their presumed relationship and familiarity with it.

Second, sampling plans can be devised where many of the assumptions made above are viewed as problematic. For example, assume that you had contacted personnel managers in fifty large organizations and had obtained from them information regarding the division of labor. Using their comments and drawings depicting tables of organization, you might seek to construct an index of horizontal and vertical complexity. After you have all fifty organizations classified, you might proceed to relate your measures of structural complexity to other organizational characteristics. Certainly, many have followed this procedure. But others would choose to make the issue problematic. What *really* do you have as a basis for your measure of complexity? Only the report of one incumbent, whose knowledge of the *actual* behavior pattern may be very slight. Thus, others would select a sampling plan in which they would actually trace out the lines of authority by including in interviews such questions as, "If you were to be fired, who has the most immediate power to do so?" "Who decides what work or tasks you will be assigned to over a one-month period?" "Who evaluates the quality of your work?" This interview is used as a basis for determining who will be interviewed in the next one, which in turn is used for the one following. This *circuitry sampling* permits one to trace out the actual or operating authority structure of an organization. Such data could then be used as a basis for specifying structural complexity for comparative analysis. Rather than using any single informant, or trying to average the figures given by three or four organizational representatives, the researcher may find that this strategy, although time consuming, ought to yield a far more valid measure for many types of variables, especially structural ones, i.e., those specifying relationships among parts. And note, one could compare the degree of correspondence between measures with a behavioral base to those depicting some aspect of the normative structure.

A variant of this technique has been found to be highly useful in studies of transitory groups.[120] For example, emergent rescue groups formed after a disaster persist for maybe a day or, more likely, only a few hours. Researchers have located such groups using a *snowball sampling* technique, in which each person interviewed is asked the names of all others involved. Often, each participant knows only a few others by name, but gradually the entire snowball can be reconstructed.

---

[120] Daniel Yutzy, *Community Priorities in the Anchorage Alaska Earthquake, 1964* (Columbus, Ohio: Disaster Research Center, Ohio State University, 1969).

Third, *dense* or *saturation*[121] samples may be used. For example, assume that you are studying faculty–student relationships on a campus. You might select interviewees or questionnaire respondents by using all faculty—no deans, janitors, or cooks. This saturation sample of faculty (i.e., all members of a given social unit or social category) could be compared with a dense sample of students, say 50 per cent. In this way you narrow your focus on those structural units most related to the particular problem and then sample all or a large number of incumbents who occupy the designated structures.

Fourth, and finally, *multistage sampling* techniques are frequently desirable. Thus, in contrast to the above plan for the faculty–student relationship study, let us assume you are investigating a large university where limited resources prohibited interviews with all faculty and half, or even a tenth, of the student body. You might first consider whether or not the needed data could be collected nearly as well by a mailed questionnaire. Let us assume that it could not; then a multistage sampling strategy would be your best alternative. For example, you might first list all colleges and schools, their respective departments, and the number of faculty in each department. The college (e.g., College of Arts and Sciences, College of Law) is your first level. All units could be included at this level. Then a 75 per cent random sample might be selected among the departments in each college. You then might select a 50 per cent random sample within each of three faculty ranks (full, associate, and assistant professor) for all selected departments with fewer members. A one-third stratified random sample could be used for larger departments. Similarly, students might be randomly sampled from each selected department using year in school (freshman, sophomore, junior, senior, graduate) as a basis for stratification. Of course, the variables selected for criteria at each sampling stage greatly determine your data collection sources and hence should be carefully considered given available theory and the problem at hand. Unfortunately, existing theory is of limited help; so recognize that your best hunch regarding variables for each sampling stage should reflect whatever empirical evidence you can relate.

It should be clear that field research on organizations involves many varied considerations. We have briefly reviewed some critical points regarding entrée and rapport. Four types of data collection strategies, their advantages, and disadvantages were compared. And we emphasized the desirability of combining observational, questionnaire interview, and primary source techniques to supplement and/or cross-validate data and conclusions. Finally, we looked at several alternative strategies for sampling within organizations. But as we suggested at the

[121] Coleman, op. cit.

outset of this section, you need not work only in the field; there are unique advantages in taking many types of problems at certain states of theoretical development into a laboratory. Let us review some of the strategies for studying organizations under laboratory conditions.

Laboratory Research

As indicated earlier, most organizational research has been conducted in field settings. Increasingly, however, many advantages of the laboratory are being realized.[122] The laboratory does afford the possibility of control and experimental manipulation. It is an excellent place to sharpen up concepts and measurement techniques. Hypothesis generation also is stimulated by laboratory work. Of course, as emphasized earlier, it appears highly desirable to take theories derived and tested in the laboratory back into field settings. And emergent ideas obtained there can be returned to the laboratory for further refinement.

But how is the laboratory used? Four major alternatives are available: (1) study organizational characteristics and processes in isolation at varying levels of abstraction; (2) build your own laboratory organization with specified characteristics; (3) bring an organization or segment into the laboratory, simulate system environment, and then manipulate it, or other variables of interest; and (4) simulate abstracted system relationships on an electronic computer. Let us look at research examples of each of these alternatives and then some generic problems in laboratory research.

Studies of Isolated Organizational Processes. Excellent lengthy summaries of efforts to use the laboratory for organizational research have been prepared by Karl Weick.[123] He emphasizes that laboratory replicas can vary greatly in level of abstraction. He illustrates this point neatly by briefly describing ten different studies that are rank ordered from highly concrete to highly abstract.[124] More concrete replicas are highly realistic and generally reflect a *systemic* focus on a network of variables. But a systemic focus need not be at a low abstraction level. Computer simulations are highly abstract, but usually retain the system imagery by focusing on the interrelations among numerous clusters of variables. Thus, although abstraction level can vary, so also can the

---

[122] Typical of this trend is a recent journal issue edited by Karl Weick entitled, "Laboratory Studies of Experimental Organizations," which includes several empirical studies, descriptions of newly constructed laboratories, and some perceptive concluding remarks regarding problems and potentials of this strategy. See *Administrative Science Quarterly*, **14** (June 1969), entire issue.

[123] Karl E. Weick, "Laboratory Experimentation with Organizations," in March, op. cit., pp. 194–260; and "Organizations in the Laboratory," in *Methods of Organizational Research*, Victor H. Vroom, ed. (Pittsburgh, Pa.: University of Pittsburgh Press, 1967), pp. 1–49.

[124] Weick, "Organizations in the Laboratory," op. cit., pp. 22–33.

number of variables under study. In contrast, some investigators have found it useful to focus on a few relationships, or a single organizational process under highly isolated conditions. In this way they seek to control extraneous influences. Often the variables or processes are conceptualized at a high level of abstraction, but this need not be so. It is the assumption that relationships among variables or processes can be studied in isolation that demarks this approach. Although much research designed under this assumption is social-psychological in focus, many researchers have attempted to study variables or processes germane to organizational theory.

An excellent example is the study by Hackman and Vidmar regarding the effects of group size and task type on group performance and member reactions.[125] By designing laboratory groups that varied from two through seven participants, they carefully manipulated group size. Also, thirty-six different tasks were used; that is, twelve for each of these three general task types: (1) *production tasks* required groups to produce ideas, images, and arrangements, e.g., "Write a story about this inkblot"; (2) *discussion tasks* called for evaluation of issues and usually required group consensus, e.g., "Should birth control pills be made available without prescription?"; and (3) *problem-solving tasks* necessitated spelling out a specific course of action to be followed to resolve some problem, e.g., "How could you safely change a tire on a busy expressway at night?" Volunteer subjects were assigned randomly to the six different-sized groups. Six groups of each size were used, and the experiment was conducted simultaneously at two institutions yielding a total of seventy-two different groups in all.

Member reactions were assessed by a post-experiment questionnaire containing such items as "This group was too small (in number of members) for best results on the task it was trying to do." Subjects responded by checking one of five choices, ranging from "Not true at all" to "Very true." The other dependent variable, "group products," was measured through analysis of the materials written by the groups while in the laboratory setting.

Among the numerous findings presented were that size directly affected member reaction, e.g., expressions of dissatisfaction increased directly with group size. Group performance measures, however, appeared unrelated to size. Concerning optimal size—estimated on member satisfaction—their data supported earlier research that four or five members are best under these conditions. Task type was significantly related to all dimensions used in the group product analysis and to half of the items used to assess member reactions. For example, "Products from production tasks were very original, tended to be lengthy, had

[125] J. Richard Hackman and Neil Vidmar, "Effects of Size and Task Type on Group Performance and Member Reactions," *Sociometry*, 33: 37–54 (March 1970).

high literary quality, and were generally pessimistic or negative in tone. . . . Products from discussion tasks were characterized by high issue involvement, and also tended to have high literary quality. Products from problem solving tasks were especially high on action orientation and were the most optimistic or positive in tone. Problem solving products tended to be low in quality of presentation." [126]

One additional finding merits special note. As indicated, laboratory effects were assessed by running the experiment simultaneously at two different universities, Yale and the University of Illinois, Urbana. Male undergraduates were obtained at the University of Illinois from an introductory psychology subject pool in which they were required to participate. Yale subjects were recruited from the student body at large and paid $1.25 per hour. Did the school make any difference? Hackman and Vidmar clearly indicate that it did. "For the seven measures of performance characteristics, there was one significant main effect involving experimental. laboratory, two interactions between group size and laboratory, and four interactions between task type and laboratory. For the 20 member reaction items, there were seven significant main effects involving experimental laboratory and eight interactions between task type and laboratory." [127] Among some of the more interesting dimensions that characterised the differences between subjects at the two universities were: "Groups run at Yale tended to have more severe difficulties with interpersonal processes than did Illinois groups. Yale subjects more often reported that their groups were too large to be effective, that there was too much competition and disagreement among members, and that there was too little time to complete the task. Members of Illinois groups indicated that they felt their solutions were of higher quality and more creative than did Yale subjects, but on the objective performance measures at Yale solutions tended to be superior." [128]

Of course, which of these differences are due to student body characteristics and which reflect procedural differences (e.g., one set of groups was paid and the other was not) remains unknown. Thus, even in such a tightly designed experiment as this one, extraneous variables may greatly affect findings. As Hackman and Vidmar conclude, "The generalizability of much small group research would appear . . . to be very much a live issue." [129] Clearly, the laboratory is no research panacea. And we should always be sensitive to ways in which the validity of the experiment may be underminded despite our best efforts at control. We shall explore some of the more common pitfalls in this regard later, but let us now focus our attention on a different approach to the laboratory—constructing a simulated organization.

---

[126] Ibid., p. 44.
[127] Ibid., p. 46.
[128] Ibid., p. 52.
[129] Ibid., p. 53.

Building Laboratory Organizations. In an effort to manipulate an entire system, or at least one with greater complexity, some researchers have constructed laboratory organizations of many different types. For example, Chapman, Kennedy, Newell, and Biel[130] designed an air defense command center in which air force personnel attempted to keep track of air traffic. They were interested in emergent shifts in organizational structure precipitated by increases in demand loads. Evan and Zelditch[131] hired college students to work for a fictitious survey research organization in an effort to test the consequences of differing types of bureaucratic structures. After receiving instructions for coding questionnaires, all students were supervised for forty-five minutes by persons with superior technical knowledge. Then a second set of supervisors were assigned so as to create three possible outcomes: (1) supervisor displayed inferior knowledge; (2) supervisor was about equal to coder; and (3) supervisor displayed superior knowledge. Thus, authority of position was held constant, but level of technical expertise (knowledge of coding procedures) was varied.

Even more realistic and concrete was the organization constructed by Wager and Palola.[132] Persons were hired to work four hours a day for a month to develop ideas whereby community interest might be stimulated in an "important community event," i.e., the Seattle World's Fair. Two separate work units composed of ten persons each were constructed and monitored for eight days. Then one unit was manipulated so that the consequences of a "taller" structure with higher task specialization, rule orientation, and the like could be compared to a "flatter" organizational structure.

All of these experimental settings closely approximate the conditions of a realistic simulation; that is, persons interacted in groups over time. The task they performed reflected the basic goal ideas of the group. Interaction took place in a physical setting appropriate for the organization. System environment interaction was simulated, e.g., memos from external organization and headquarters units were provided. And finally, the participants were not informed that they were in an experiment. Presumably, such highly concrete replicas not only resemble organizations of similar types, but more importantly, also function in a comparable manner.

[130] Robert L. Chapman et al., "The Systems Research Laboratory's Air Defense Experiments," in *Simulation in Social Science: Readings*, Harold Guetzkow, ed. (Englewood Cliffs, N.J.: Prentice-Hall, Inc., 1962), pp. 172–88; and Robert L. Chapman and John L. Kennedy, "The Background and Implications of the Rand Corporation Systems Research Laboratory Studies," in *Some Theories of Organization*, in Albert H. Rubenstein and Chadwick J. Haberstroh, eds. (Homewood, Ill.: Richard D. Irwin, Inc., and Dorsey Press, 1966), pp. 149–56.

[131] Morris Zelditch, Jr. and William M. Evan, "Simulated Bureaucracies: A Methodological Analysis," in Guetzkow, op. cit., pp. 48–60; and William M. Evan and Morris Zelditch, Jr., "A Laboratory Experiment on Bureaucratic Authority," *American Sociological Review*, 26: 883–93 (December 1961).

[132] Wager and Palola, op. cit.

One can, however, build an organization of a more abstract nature so as to comply with specified design characteristics. An excellent example is the complex experiment conducted by Rodolfo Alvarez.[133] Starting with leads from Homans, Hollander, Merton, and others, Alvarez attempted to explore how informal reactions to deviance might vary under three different structural conditions: (1) the hierarchical status occupied by the deviant; (2) the success or failure of the group; and (3) the impositions of formal sanctions upon the deviant. A fictitious parent organization (National Card Company) served as the system environment for the simulated units, which had three hierarchical levels and ten participants. Sixteen separate simulated organizations functioned for one-hour sessions on four different days. "The task was to generate creative ideas for the manufacture of greeting cards. A division of labor was established by dividing the task into three elements of a greeting card; pictorial, prose (message content), and style of print used to convey the message." [134] Experimental manipulation was in accordance with the $2 \times 2 \times 2$ factorial design pictured in Figure 9–6. Thus, for each of the eight cells, two organizational units were assigned.

Research accomplices performed the deviant role in each organization by making "40 percent of the task-relevant behavior which he initiated during the first session violate specific task instructions as well as general standards of social intercourse, and to direct his deviant acts mostly toward the chairman. During the second work session he was to increase this to 60 percent and to include department coordinators as objects of his aggression. For the third and fourth work sessions he was to increase it to 80 percent and direct his aggressions toward workers as well as toward persons in supervisory positions." [135] Organizational success or failure was operationalized by feedback from the parent organization at the end of the second, third, and fourth work periods. Imposition of formal sanctions was manipulated by either promoting or demoting the deviant, who, following the design, appeared at middle-level or low-level structural positions in different organizations. Reactions to the deviant were assessed by measurement of esteem as rated by the nine other participants at the end of each of the work periods.

This complex design permitted testing of numerous hypotheses. Thus, as expected, "continued acts of deviance perpetrated by the research accomplice did reduce the esteem which naive organizational participants were willing to allocate him." [136] But what effect does the social

[133] Rodolfo Alvarez, "Informal Reactions to Deviance in Simulated Work Organizations: A Laboratory Experiment," *American Sociological Review*, 33: 895–912 (December 1968).
[134] Ibid., p. 905.
[135] Ibid.
[136] Ibid. p. 907.

FIGURE 9–6   Design of Alvarez Experiment

	Successful Organizations		Unsuccessful Organizations	
	Positive Sanctions	Negative Sanctions	Positive Sanctions	Negative Sanctions
Middle Rank in Hierarchy	Deviant remains in same position for four sessions.	Deviant demoted after second session.	Deviant remains in same position for four sessions.	Deviant demoted after second session.
Low Rank in Hierarchy	Deviant promoted after second session.	Deviant remains in same position for four sessions.	Deviant promoted after second session.	Deviant remains in same position for four sessions.

SOURCE: Adapted from Rodolfo Alvarez, "Informal Reactions to Deviance in Simulated Work Organizations: A Laboratory Experiment," *American Sociological Review,* 33 (December 1968), p. 903.

rank of the deviant have, if any, on this process? Although empirical support has been presented that the higher the rank of a deviant the less the loss in esteem, Alvarez's design permitted an important specification of when this relationship is actually reversed. Thus, "in unsuccessful organizations it is the high status members who may be held most accountable for system failure." [137] Continuing with the more complex analyses possible with this design, Alvarez carefully traced through numerous interrelations among this cluster of variables. For example:

> For those simulated organizations in which the deviant was demoted, the expected sizeable drop in esteem appears in both successful and unsuccessful organizations. Similarly, for organizations in which the deviant was promoted, the expected rise in esteem between the second and third work sessions occurs regardless of organizational success. It is interesting to note, however, that the overall drop in esteem between the first and the fourth work sessions is greater for both the demoted and the promoted deviant within unsuccessful organizations than it is within successful ones. . . . Thus, whether the deviant is placed high or low, if his behavior hurts the entire system by placing a negative evaluation on all participants, the informal reaction against him is stronger, i.e., he loses a greater degree of esteem. Following the frustration–aggression theorists, the aggression generated by the failure to achieve collective objects is "displaced" onto the most salient and likely target, the deviant presumed responsible for the failure of the organization. But what about the deviant in a successful organization?

[137] Ibid.

Presumably his deviant actions generate threat of future organizational failure but, since the organization continues to be successful despite his deviance, the threat may not generate frustration and thus the amount of esteem withdrawn may be less.[138]

Thus, integrating some rather abstract and sophisticated theoretical concepts, Alvarez was able to use the laboratory to test numerous important hypotheses. Clearly, construction of a series of simulated organizations with specified structural characteristics is a viable research strategy.

Bringing Organizations into the Laboratory. In contrast to building an organization for the purposes of the experiment, you can move one into a laboratory. Environmental conditions can be manipulated so as to comply with design requirements. Again, the level of abstraction at which this is done can vary considerably. Thus you might bring a series of ongoing work groups into a lab and confront them with a set of novel tasks such as a series of games, or you might have them perform their usual tasks. Many different strategies may be used, which reflect different degrees of realism or, more accurately, different sets of experimental conditions under which hypotheses are tested.

Working from field studies of organizational response to natural disasters, we simulated the communication system of a metropolitan police department.[139] The laboratory system was designed so that when a team of officers activated their positions, an exact replica of the system was created. Simulators provided input so that officers in the lab received complaint calls, processed them, and dispatched cruisers, following procedures identical to those normally used. Thus, the constructed simulate *functioned* in a manner identical to the system after which it was modeled.

Figure 9–7 presents a summary of the various elements involved in the simulation. Complaints were telephoned into the lab by several simulators who had been trained to place each in accordance with specified criteria, e.g., black bartender confronting three drunks who will not leave. Police department statistical data were used to construct the sets of phone calls so as to match normal system demand input regarding geographical location, type of event, sex of caller, and time of day. Telephone caller simulators, like cruiser officer simulators, listened .to audio recordings of actual police telephone and radio interaction and rehearsed their roles so as to be able to play their parts appropriately during the simulation. Data were collected through the use of a twenty-four track audio recorder and two television cameras.

---

[138] Ibid., pp. 910–11.
[139] Thomas E. Drabek and J. Eugene Haas, "Laboratory Simulation of Organizational Stress," op. cit.; and Thomas E. Drabek, *Laboratory Simulation of a Police Communication System Under Stress* (Columbus, Ohio: College of Administrative Science, Ohio State University, 1969).

FIGURE 9-7 Laboratory Design for Police Simulation

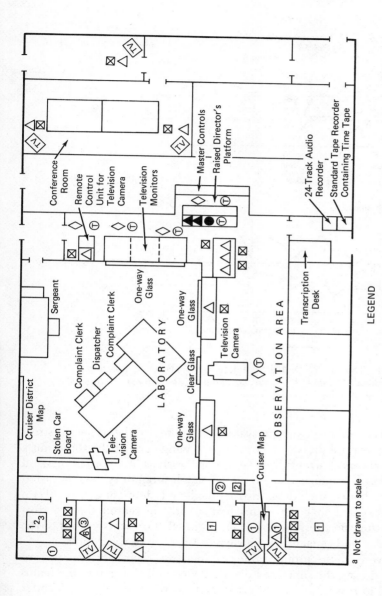

LEGEND

△ Phone, number given for "outside" line
◀ Phone, standard (line to video tape room)
△ Phone, closed circuit
① Microphone, Radio Channel 1
② Microphone, Radio Channel 2
③ Microphone, Radio Channel 3

Ⓣ Microphone, Inter-organizational monitor
▣ Speaker, Radio Channel 1
▨ Speaker, Radio Channel 2
▨ Speaker, Radio Channel 3
◇ Engineer

⊠ Simulator
Ⓣ Television Communications System, microphone and headset
● Microphone, master (broadcast over all speakers)
TV Television Receivers

a Not drawn to scale

SOURCE: Adapted from Thomas E. Drabek and J. Eugene Haas, "Laboratory Simulation of Organizational Stress," *American Sociological Review* **34** (April 1969), p. 228.

FIGURE 9–8 Police Communication System Demands and Capacity

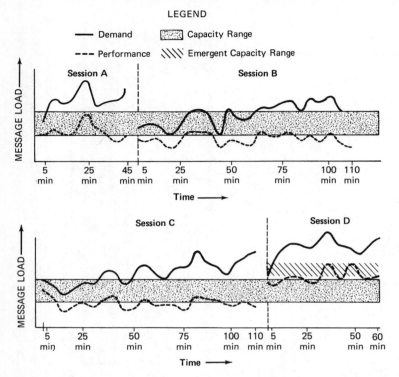

SOURCE: Adapted from Thomas E. Drabek and J. Eugene Haas, "Laboratory Simulation of Organizational Stress," *American Sociological Review* 34 (April 1969), p. 231.

Our basic interest was in system response to the type of stress created by natural disasters. Thus, after having each of the three shifts of police officers confront three laboratory sessions of a normal demand load, an airplane crash was simulated. Each laboratory session lasted about two hours, including instructional and debriefing time. Data analysis revealed that the teams had greatly increased their performance during the stress session (D). Figure 9–8 presents graphs of the demand load and capacity (performance) for one of the groups.

How were these groups able to increase their performance so markedly during the simulated disaster? Generally speaking, the teams continued to function in a pattern similar to what we observed under normal conditions. However, there were several interrelated changes in performance structure. Most dramatic was the marked increase in interaction among the officers in the laboratory, especially for the sergeants. As the disaster unfolded, officers discovered that they needed information from one another far more frequently than was the usual case. And gradually the team sergeants began to function as a display mechanism for the system so that information could be more rapidly shared. Furthermore, officers reduced the average length of time for telephone conversations and increasingly limited their activity to follow up calls of highest priority.

Such highly concrete simulations may provide an important tool for future researchers, especially during exploratory stages of work. The very act of creating a replica that functions identically to an existing system is of much value in locating critical variables. Similarly, manipulation of system environment can permit tests of existing theories as well as act as a major stimulus to the development of new ones. But once a series of such simulations are completed, every effort should be made to shift abstraction levels and formulate analytic relationships. Once a network of such relationships are formulated, then new research settings can be sought. For example, the network of relationships might be simulated on a computer. Although still in its infancy, this technique appears to offer an enormous potential for organizational research.

Computer Simulation. In the past ten years, numerous social scientists have explored simulation of various types of social systems using electronic computers. Several excellent summaries outline the state of the art in a general manner; see especially Borko[140] and chapters by Coleman,[141] Roby [142] and by Cohen and Cyert.[143] More technical statements have been prepared for researchers interested in actually preparing computer simulation programs.[144] The primary advantage of this technique is that it permits researchers to deal with large numbers of variables in an orderly manner. Thus, highly complex systems of variables can be constructed, and then one, or several, can be modified. Consequences throughout the entire system can be traced out and identified. Results obtained can then be compared to field data. Inconsistencies can be used as a basis for modification of the simulation model until results generated closely approximate "real-world" phenomena. As a consequence, the technique may prove to be highly useful in theory construction. And similar to the realistic simulation of the police communication system we just discussed, merely the construction of the initial simulation model forces one to be highly precise in

[140] Harold Borko, ed., *Computer Applications in the Behavioral Sciences* (Englewood Cliffs, N.J.: Prentice-Hall, Inc., 1962).

[141] James S. Coleman, "Analysis of Social Structures and Simulation of Social Processes with Electronic Computers," in Guetzkow, op. cit., pp. 61–69.

[142] Thornton B. Roby, "Computer Simulation Models for Organization Theory," in Vroom, op. cit., pp. 171–211.

[143] Kalman J. Cohen and Richard M. Cyert, "Simulation of Organizational Behavior," in March, op. cit., pp. 305–34.

[144] Jay W. Forrester, *Industrial Dynamics* (New York: John Wiley and Sons, Inc., 1961).

specifying theoretical relationships. Of course, such "forced specification" usually results in gross oversimplification, but if the technique is
used after adequate research has been done using other strategies, both
field and laboratory, then it appears especially powerful.

Many variations are possible; an entire system may be simulated or
only a small segment. For example, using field data on role conflict
resolution among labor union leaders, John and Jeanne Gullahorn[145]
developed a computer simulation program from which results obtained
could then be compared with questionnaire findings.

A more descriptive study of an existing organizational segment is the
program constructed by Cyert, March, and Moore, which simulates the
decision-making processes of department store buyers.[146] Again, they
used data collected from employees of an actual department store to
develop and refine the model. Others have elected to develop more
general models that do not simulate existing systems but that have wide
applicability when specifics are supplied. For example, Cohen, Cyert,
March, and Soelberg[147] developed a model of price and output determination in oligopoly firms. "This model is not a direct attempt to
simulate the behavior of any specific business firm, but rather an attempt to illustrate in specific quantitative form some general hypotheses about oligopoly behavior and to derive some of the implications of
these hypotheses." [148] Training simulations also have been constructed
wherein personnel are required to make decisions based on input supplied and manipulated by means of a computer. For example, we
alluded previously to the Air Defense Command Center constructed by
Chapman, Kennedy, Newell, and Biel. Air force personnel were track-
ing simulated aircraft with the demand load controlled by a computer
program. Finally, many initial efforts have been made to use this technique for organizational planning and design. Among the more complex
models which have been developed for design purposes is Forrester's
Industrial Dynamics, wherein six major networks of variables are interrelated: (1) materials; (2) orders; (3) money; (4) personnel; (5) capital equipment; and (6) information.[149] Let us look briefly at a more
simple model of this type.

Using a basic model developed by the Midwest Research Institute,[150]
Adrian has constructed a computer simulation for use in institutional

[145] John T. Gullahorn and Jeanne E. Gullahorn, "Some Computer Applications in
Social Science," *American Sociological Review*, 30: 353–65 (June 1965).

[146] Cited in Cohen and Cyert, op. cit., p. 308.

[147] Ibid., p. 315.

[148] Ibid.

[149] Forrester, op. cit.

[150] Economics and Management Science Division, Midwest Research Institute,
*Plantran Planning Translator: A Simulation Modeling System for Long Range
Planning* (Kansas City, Mo.: Midwest Research Institute), undated.

planning at the University of Denver.[151] Basically, one starts with a set of assumptions and then uses the computer model to trace out consequences over time. Variables are of four types: (1) *system state*, initial baseline data, such as student body size, faculty salaries, income from various sources, and the like; (2) *environment*, variables not totally under the control of university decision makers, but which may have great affect, e.g., contract research income and expenses, athletic income and expenses; (3) *decision variables*, projections that can be controlled directly by decision makers, e.g., tuition; average class size; average faculty salaries; and (4) *effect variables*, e.g., instructional cost per student credit hour, surplus or deficit yearly balance, as well as any of the above variables if they are used as dependent. An earlier model included 125 such variables, which were plotted over ten-year time projections. Adrian currently is using an expanded program that permits use of three hundred variables.

To illustrate the type of question that can be pursued with this technique, let us take a simple example. Assume that we wish to raise faculty salaries an average of 6 per cent each year over a ten-year period. We also wish to increase tuition one hundred dollars a year for five years and hold it constant for the next five. We further wish to expand the graduate programs in five social science departments with a 5 percent increase in teaching assistant funds and faculty members each of the ten years. Assuming that major environmental variables remain constant, what consequence would these changes have on such variables as average class size at the undergraduate level if we must increase enrollment each year so as to meet expenditures?

Such questions can be explored with this model.[152] Of course, critical variables having to do with such allusive factors as "the quality of the educational experience," or faculty "research productivity" have yet to be explored in this manner. All of the variables included in the Adrian model were easily quantified and largely reflect economic concerns. However, the strategy, like most areas of laboratory research, has yet to be more than mildly scratched by organizational reseachers. Clearly, all of these laboratory approaches have enormous potential. But there are many problems. Let us review a few, some of which may have occurred to you during this brief survey.

Basic Problems in Laboratory Research. Although a multitude

[151] Based on personal communication and memos from Dr. William Adrian, Special Assistant to the Chancellor, University of Denver, Denver, Colorado, 1971.

[152] Among the more popular simulation models for university organizations are "Campus" (information available from Systems Research Group, 2522 Bloor Street West, Toronto 5, Canada) and "RRPM" (information available from Western Interstate Commission on Higher Education, Planning and Management System Division, Drawer P, Boulder, Colorado).

of fundamental problems confront researchers who seek to use laboratory settings, three general types appear most important: (1) internal validity; (2) external validity; and (3) ethical dilemmas. Each of these has its counterpart in field research, and many illustrations were integrated into our discussion of that topic. As we look at a few examples within each of these categories, you might think about the parallels in field settings.

Internal validity refers to a general question: Were changes in the dependent variable actually caused by manipulation of the independent variable?[153] In short, has the experiment been designed adequately so as to insure that reported changes in the dependent variables are caused by what the investigator attributes them to? Weick has discussed many ways in which efforts to manipulate selected variables may be undermined. For example, experimenters may unintentionally threaten the status or esteem of subjects, and subject response may be more affected by this than the manipulations of other variables. Among the several specific illustrations cited by Weick is Pepitone's criticism of experiments on aggression, consistency, and conformity.[154] Subjects may feel uncertain, incompetent, or belittled in laboratory settings where they are asked to act inconsistently, e.g., by writing strong arguments opposed to their basic beliefs. And Weick argues: "The existence of these feelings constitutes an alternative explanation for the obtained results." [155]

Of course, this is only one of a multitude of ways in which internal validity may be threatened. Experimenters attempting realistic simulation, like the police communications study, confront different types of problems. For example, to maintain the realism of the setting, input into the laboratory varied greatly among the groups, as certain telephone calls could not be placed because of team response to earlier ones. Also, this experiment was defined by some participants as having possible effect on future promotions, whereas others did not think of this. Thus, efforts to introduce realism into the laboratory is no panacea. In short, even under what appears to be highly controlled conditions, investigators must be concerned with ways in which internal validity may be destroyed.

External validity refers to a different set of issues: To what can I generalize? Weick suggests that: "It is possible that experiments tell us more about how a person will act on his first day at work than on his 400th day. A person who is in an experiment, like the newcomer on a job, often has low confidence in his judgments, is easily influenced,

---

[153] Many of the ideas briefly presented here are developed in much greater detail in Weick, "Organizations in the Laboratory," op. cit.

[154] Weick, "Organizations in the Laboratory," op. cit., p. 37.

[155] Ibid.

misunderstands instructions, is uninformed, finds the job novel and interesting, is cautious, and tolerates many demands that would anger him in more familiar settings." [156] Thus, generalization from the laboratory to field settings must be made cautiously. But then, so must generalization from one field setting to another.

However, laboratory research presents some intriguing questions regarding external validity. The factor of time has several subtle implications. In addition to Weick's point above, for example, is a general question regarding qualitative variation in systems. Following Goffman, we have referred to a distinction between gatherings, i.e., highly transitory systems and groups.[157] Like the "first day at work syndrome," it appears that most laboratory research on groups is actually applicable to gatherings rather than groups per se. Of course, some of the findings may be applicable to both types of systems, but until further work is completed the generalizability of these findings remains highly constrained. We are reminded of the comment by one of the police officers who participated in the simulated disaster study. His sergeant had been assigned only recently to the radio room at the time of the study. During the simulated disaster, the sergeant's lack of knowledge became increasingly clear. During a private interview shortly afterward, the patrolman was asked why he didn't assume more leadership for the team as he had commented on the sergeant's incompetence. With a slight smile he replied, "Simply because he'll still be sergeant come Monday morning."

Another common problem for much laboratory research results from efforts to control extraneous influences. Events in field settings are highly complex and are affected by complex networks of interacting variables. As Weick acknowledges: "The problem is essentially one of how to handle these additional variables in the laboratory so that control and external validity are retained." [158] Doing this is not easy. However, efforts to integrate and contrast findings from field and laboratory settings, using realistic simulations and shuttling back and forth between the field and lab within the same research program, appear to offer promising solutions. Each of these alternatives has its own unique problems. Certainly, realistic simulation does not lend itself to wide applicability. Equally important, few organizational officials would be willing to permit staff participation, thus raising serious biases as an outgrowth of recruitment patterns.

Ethical dilemmas are numerous in all social research, but several issues become highlighted once laboratory experimental manipulation

---

[156] Ibid., p. 47.

[157] This point and several related ones are developed at length in Drabek and Haas, "Realism in Laboratory Simulation: Myth or Method?" op. cit.

[158] Weick, "Organizations in the Laboratory," op. cit., p. 47.

is considered. For example, should one use only volunteers? But if persons volunteer to participate in an experiment, what about generalization to those who do not? How does knowing that you are participating in an experiment affect behavior? Even using volunteers, many questions remain; e.g., what do you tell them about the experimental objectives? What efforts will they make to modify behavior given what they understand to be your research objectives? In organizational research especially, a question arises as to *who volunteers?* For example, in our police simulation, permission was granted by the top officials. Of course, individual officers could have refused, but they knew that permission had come from above. Was this undue coercion?

Assume, however, that you answer adequately all of these questions and find yourself observing work groups in a laboratory. Do you have any responsibility for long-term consequences on group or individual functioning that might result from your manipulations? What constitutes invasion of privacy under these circumstances? Will you permit superiors to observe the sessions, realizing that future promotion decisions may be affected?

These are only a few of the many problems encountered in laboratory research. But as emphasized at the outset, these ethical problems, like those of internal and external validity, have their counterparts in field research. Neither setting is a panacea, and there appears to be utility in using each at different points in the research process.

We have now reviewed problems of entrée and rapport, field data collection techniques (including interviews, questionnaires, observations, and primary source materials), and internal sampling strategies, as well as various approaches to laboratory research. We hope that this brief survey has helped you to begin to appreciate the range of research styles possible, and, more importantly, that you see the utility of combining several of these strategies to crossvalidate your data and conclusions. Remember, let your selection of methods be determined by the theoretical questions you find interesting, rather than vice versa.

One final area requires exploration. Although we briefly considered internal sampling we have not addressed ourselves to the question of sampling organizations per se. How do you select a random sample of organizations?

Toward a Science of Organizations

How do you design research in which organizations per se are the units of analysis? How can typologies and taxonomies be helpful in future organizational research? Now that we have explored the other questions posited at the outset of this chapter, we will conclude with these two questions. We see them as related because of a point of view we would like to propose. The argument will be elaborated throughout this section, but in essence the idea is expressed by Willer's term *conditional universals*, i.e., empirically tested relationships with the universe to which they apply specified.[159] Thus, we propose that a major strategy that ought to be explored is the specification of *types of systems*, defined in analytical terms, wherein various propositions would hold. *Samples of systems* with specified characteristics could then be used for research purposes, and generalization would be appropriate to systems with similar characteristics. This view, we suggest, lays a foundation for a science of organizations. With this idea in mind, let us see how we might use organizational typologies and taxonomies, and then we shall survey some design alternatives.

Organizational Typologies

Typologies and taxonomies are important for organizational research because they provide a basis for classification. But then, why classify in the first place? Basically, because that is a way to reduce data. Organizations, like any other phenomena, can be viewed as unique products of idiosyncratic sets of historical events. However, as scientists, it is our aim to shift abstraction levels and begin looking for similarities. Thus, each organization is different from any other in certain respects and similar to all others in some other ways. As scientists, we seek to reduce our data—knowledge of the particulars about several organizations— so as to blot out differences and focus on similarities. But although it is possible to seek generalizations that hold for all organizations at all points in time, it is our view that it will be more productive to seek conditional universals, i.e., propositions that hold for a particular *type* of organization. Why? Mainly because propositions that might hold for all types of organizations will be at such a high level of abstraction that they are nearly impossible to operationalize and may tell us very little.

Our aim, then, is to classify organizations into types. And typologies and taxonomies are useful because they specify sets of criteria that might be used in defining what we mean by *type* in a particular study. But what specific criteria have been proposed? Let us review four.

First, based on the reasoning of Weber and Parsons, many persons have classified organizations on the basis of their goals. Some have followed the Parsonian scheme and view organizations as reflections of AGIL;[160] that is, the primary goal or output of the organization for the supersystem is of four types: (1) adaptation (e.g., a business firm); (2) goal attainment (e.g., military); (3) integration (e.g., a hospital);

---

[159] David Willer, *Scientific Sociology* (Englewood Cliffs, N.J.: Prentice-Hall, Inc., 1967), pp. 97–115.

[160] For development and application of such a typology, see R. Jean Hills, *Toward a Science of Organization* (Eugene, Oreg.: Center for the Advanced Study of Educational Administration, 1968), pp. 70–76.

and (4) latency (e.g., churches, which seek to perpetuate basic value patterns). Thus we emerge with four types of organizations.

Second, Blau and Scott propose a somewhat similar idea when they classify on the basis of *cui bono*, i.e., who benefits? [161] Thus, they propose four basic organizational types: "(1) 'Mutual-benefit associations,' where the prime beneficiary is the membership; (2) 'Business concerns,' where the owners are prime beneficiary; (3) 'Service organizations,' where the client group is the prime beneficiary; and (4) 'Commonweal organizations,' where the prime beneficiary is the public-at-large." [162] Of course, some organizations will be of a mixed type, and therein lies one of the initial difficulties in using the system.

Third, Van Riper proposes six types of organizations based on the degree of power or control exercised from the top.[163] *Control* organizations presumably reflect the familiar pyramid where control is centralized at the top. *Production* organizations are somewhat similar, but a staff unit intercedes between the centralized top and the line of production component. *Bargaining* organizations are like a cluster of pyramids that somewhat overlap, with a constitution or contract that specifies rights and obligations of each unit. *Representative* organizations are illustrated by the idealized version of American political parties, trade unions, and many other voluntary groups. Of course, as Michels pointed out long ago, it is easy for units of this type to shift to the control type. *Research* organizations are primarily committed to innovation, creativity, and discovery of the unknown. They are rather "flat" in structure, and the participants dart about like fish in an aquarium, continually grouping and regrouping depending upon the task at hand. *Communal* organizations are informal and rather spontaneous. Some types of family and neighborhood gatherings illustrate the idea.

In contrast, a fourth alternative is offered by Etzioni.[164] He suggests that two structural variables are critical in understanding compliance: "the power applied by the organization *to* lower participants and the involvement in the organization developed *by* lower participants." [165] He proposes three kinds of power: (1) coercive; (2) remunerative; and (3) normative. Also, three kinds of involvement are proposed: (1) alienative; (2) calculative; and (3) moral. Using these in a contingency table (see Figure 9-9), we get nine alternative combinations.

[161] Peter M. Blau and W. Richard Scott, *Formal Organizations* (San Francisco, Calif.: Chandler Publishing Company, 1962), pp. 42-58.

[162] Ibid., p. 43.

[163] Paul P. Van Riper, "Organizations: Basic Issues and a Proposed Typology," in *Studies on Behavior in Organizations*, Raymond V. Bowers, ed. (Athens, Ga.: University of Georgia Press, 1966), pp. 1-12.

[164] Amitai Etzioni, *A Comparative Analysis of Complex Organizations* (New York: The Free Press, 1961), pp. 3-67.

[165] Ibid., p. 12.

FIGURE 9–9   Etzioni's Typology of Compliance Relations

Kinds of Power	Kinds of Involvement		
	Alienative	Calculative	Moral
Coercive	1	2	3
Remunerative	4	5	6
Normative	7	8	9

SOURCE: Adapted from Amitai Etzioni, *A Comparative Analysis of Complex Organizations* (New York: The Free Press, 1961), p. 12.

Those three cells located on the diagonal—i.e., 1, 5, and 9—are defined as congruent types. These three types occur empirically more frequently than the other six because they provide a basis for compliance that is consistent. "For instance, inmates are highly alienated from prisons; coercive power tends to alienate, hence this is a case of congruent compliance relationship." [166] Thus, many prisons would be of Type 1, which Etzioni labels "coercive organizations." Type 5 are "utilitarian," e.g., blue-collar and white-collar industries. Type 9 are "normative," e.g., most voluntary organizations like religious, fraternal, or fund-raising.

But what of the incongruent types? Etzioni proposes that there are some organizations that appear to have dual structures. For example, combat units appear to rely heavily on both normative and coercive power. Similarly, most labor unions are both utilitarian and normative, and some farms and company towns are both utilitarian and coercive. But most organizations are located on the diagonal, i.e., in Types 1, 5, or 9. And empirically, those that are not will evidence tendencies of movement so as to reach a state characterized by one of the congruent types. As Etzioni puts it: "organizations tend to shift their compliance structure from incongruent to congruent types and organizations which have congruent compliance structures tend to resist factors pushing them toward incongruent compliance structures." [167]

Following this hypothesis, we might speculate that efforts at slow reform within a prison to shift from a custodial- to a treatment-centered ideology will be especially difficult, as this would require a change in classification. Once entirely reformed, the prison would be a different type of organization. And gradual reform will be difficult because of contradictions precipitated. Indeed, Etzioni has proposed that it might be far more humane to gather all available prison psychologists and other treatment-oriented personnel, and place them in a few prisons and let the others remain entirely custodial in orientation.[168]

[166] Ibid.

[167] Ibid., p. 14.

[168] Amitai Etzioni, "Dual Leadership in Complex Organizations," *American Sociological Review*, 30: 688–98 (October 1965).

As it is, we have a few such personnel in most prisons, but not enough to do much more than slightly push the structure toward an incongruent type. And, as with all incongruent types, the structure evidences instability as it seeks to move toward one of the congruent types.

Julian's[169] research applied Etzioni's typology. He investigated five hospitals, and using patients' perceptions of the frequency with which coercive, normative, and utilitarian sanctions were applied, he ranked the hospitals on a normative to normative–coercive continuum. The ranking of these hospitals was then compared with data on patients' reports regarding their ease of communication with hospital staff members. The results are not clear-cut but there is a suggestion in the findings that the more normative hospitals show somewhat fewer communication blocks.

Shortly after the Julian study, Hall, Haas, and Johnson[170] published a critique of both the Blau-Scott and the Etzioni typologies. They presented data from a heterogeneous sample of 75 organizations, which were categorized according to each of the typologies. The basic question was, If you know where any particular organization is placed in one of these typologies, what else do you know about that organization? Data were presented on a long list of indicators of organization complexity, formalization, goal specificity, organizational activities, internal interdependency, prestige, and power, and external relations and organizational change.

Taken as a whole, their findings indicate that the two typologies have only a limited application for organizational analysis in general. Their limited applicability may be owing to their simplicity; only one or two variables are used as a basis for classifying what appears to be a very heterogeneous set of phenomena—organizations.

A possible alternative to the intuitively based typology is to try to construct empirically a *taxonomy* of organizations after the manner of the life sciences.

Embryonic Organizational Taxonomies

In 1961, Haas, Hall, and Johnson[171] began collecting data on seventy-five organizations, including government agencies, labor unions, mass

---

[169] Joseph Julian, "Compliance Patterns and Communication Blocs in Complex Organizations," *American Sociological Review*, 31: 382–89 (June 1966).

[170] Richard H. Hall, J. Eugene Haas, and Norman J. Johnson, "An Examination of the Blau-Scott and Etzioni Typologies," *Administrative Science Quarterly*, 12: 118–39 (June 1967).

[171] J. Eugene Haas, Richard H. Hall, and Norman J. Johnson, "Toward an Empirically Derived Taxonomy of Organizations," in Bowers, op. cit., pp. 157–80.

FIGURE 9–10   Illustration of Levels in Tentative Taxonomy of Organizations

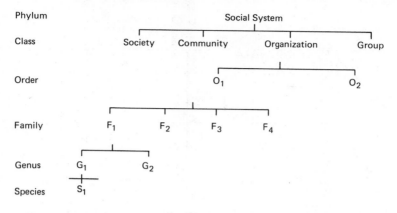

SOURCE: J. Eugene Haas, Richard H. Hall, and Norman J. Johnson, "Toward an Empirically Derived Taxonomy of Organizations," pp. 157–86 in *Studies on Behavior in Organizations*, Raymond V. Bowers (ed.) (Athens, Ga.: University of Georgia Press, 1966), p. 173.

communication organizations, religious organizations, educational institutions, and the like. Data were collected on ninety-nine variables, including major goals and activities, interdependency of departments, centralization of authority, formalization of authority structure, penalties for rule violation, restrictions on membership, primary sources of income, and so on. These data were then processed so as to locate general clusters of variables that might be interrelated. This represented the first major effort to develop a taxonomy of organizations empirically.

Note the contrast in logic when compared to the typologies presented above. The strategy of the taxonomist is to locate a large sample of phenomena and then to look for "critical" structural features that can serve as a basis for classification. Picture yourself as pre-Linnaeus; would it have occurred to you to put a bat, a whale, and a man into a similar taxonomical niche and call them mammals? Probably not.

Yet they have several common structural features that are deemed critical. And note the complexity of the biological taxonomy, which includes, in descending order of similarity, species, genera, family, order, class, and phyla. Why not a similarly complex strategy for social systems, which could be infinitely elaborated as further research warranted. For example, Haas, Hall, and Johnson suggested the imagery portrayed in Figure 9–10 as a model. S_1 would represent a clearly defined taxonomical niche that would contain those social units meeting the specific analytic criteria.

After collecting and coding their data, they began analysis. Using a methodology similar to personality profiles, wherein an individual

FIGURE 9–11   Illustrative Organizational Profiles

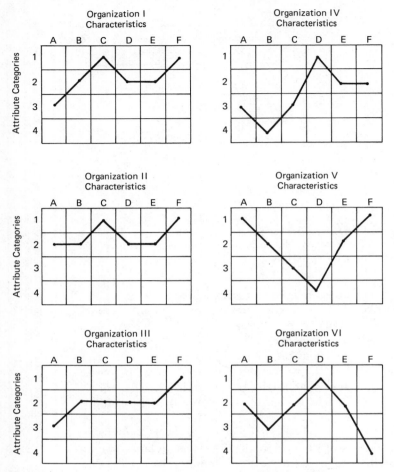

SOURCE: J. Eugene Haas, Richard H. Hall, and Norman J. Johnson, "Toward an Empirically Derived Taxonomy of Organizations," pp. 157–86 in *Studies on Behavior in Organizations,* Raymond V. Bowers (ed.) (Athens, Ga.: University of Georgia Press, 1966), p. 166.

is presented as a pattern or profile across several separate scores, they emerged with charts like those presented in Figure 9–11. Note the similarity in Organizations I, II, and III. However, as is obvious in reviewing these illustrations, the task of locating clusters of similarities with seventy-five organizations and ninety-nine variables was not a simple matter. They next turned to a taxonomy computer program used by botanists and four distinct levels emerged. A summary of the number of organizations and shared attributes for each level is presented in Figure 9–12. Unfortunately, further analysis of the data has been

Class	First Level No. of Organizations	First Level No. of Attributes	Second Level No. of Organizations	Second Level No. of Attributes	Third Level No. of Organizations	Third Level No. of Attributes	Fourth Level No. of Organizations	Fourth Level No. of Attributes
I	9	7	2	30	—	—	—	—
			2	36	—	—	—	—
			2	40	—	—	—	—
			2	48	—	—	—	—
					3	34	2	51
					3	27	2	50
			11	14	2	49	—	—
					2	39	—	—
II	30	4			2	46	—	—
			5	10	2	39	—	—
					3	15	2	41
			6	5	2	43	—	—
					3	16	2	37
			6	3	2	42	—	—
III	3	34	2	32	—	—	—	—
			2	45	—	—	—	—
IV	3	29	2	43	—	—	—	—
			3	22	2	40	—	—
V	8	4	2	33	—	—	—	—
			2	42	—	—	—	—
VI	2	40	—	—	—	—	—	—
VII	2	33	—	—	—	—	—	—
			3	30	2	44	—	—
			4	14	3	24	2	40
VIII	14	3			2	32	—	—
			4	13	2	27	—	—
			2	33	—	—	—	—
IX	2	34	—	—	—	—	—	—
X	2	27	—	—	—	—	—	—

SOURCE: J. Eugene Haas, Richard H. Hall, and Norman J. Johnson, "Toward an Empirically Derived Taxonomy of Organizations," pp. 156–86, in *Studies on Behavior in Organizations*, Raymond V. Bowers, ed. (Athens, Ga.: University of Georgia Press, 1966), p. 171.

directed at specific relationships, e.g., size and formalization,[172] rather than crystallization of a taxonomy with specified sets of analytic criteria. No additional effort has been made to expand the volume of data collected so as to provide a larger sample of computer input. And so a critical challenge remains unmet.

Using data from fifty-two work organizations in the English Midlands, Pugh, Hickson, and Hinings[173] also have begun initial work on an empirically based taxonomy. They factored analyzed data from sixty-four scales used to operationalize five structural variables. Three of the four emergent factors were used as a basis for taxonomical exploration: (1) *Structuring of activities,* "the degree to which the behavior of employees was overtly defined, incorporating the degree of role specialization in task allocation, the degree of standardization of organizational routines, and the degree of formalization of written procedures";[174] (2) *Concentration of authority,* "the degree to which authority for decisions rested in controlling units outside the organization and was centralized at the higher hierarchial levels within it";[175] (3) *Line control of workflow,* "the degree to which control was exercised by line personnel as against its exercise through impersonal procedures." [176]

The fifty-two organizations were reviewed in terms of these three dimensions and empirically were found to cluster into seven cells. Thus, when conceptualized as a three-dimensional figure, the seven types are registered as indicated in Figure 9–13. The actual types of organizations that were found to cluster into these seven taxonomic niches are listed in Figure 9–14.

Of course, neither the Haas nor Pugh groups claim that they have developed anything more than a start toward an organizational taxonomy. However, the methodology and work thus far completed is most promising for the future.

Returning to our initial point: how do such taxonomies assist in research? Mainly in two ways. First, they ought to help in synthesizing previous research. Using the Pugh group's model to illustrate, studies completed on organizations fitting criteria of a workflow bureaucracy,

[172] Richard H. Hall, J. Eugene Haas, and Norman J. Johnson, "Organizational Size, Complexity, and Formalization," *American Sociological Review,* **32**: 903–12 (December 1967).

For elaboration of this argument and a critique of this particular taxonomic effort, see Richard H. Hall, *Organizations: Structure and Process* (Englewood Cliffs, N.J.: Prentice-Hall, Inc., 1972), pp. 39–78.

[173] Derek S. Pugh, David J. Hickson, and C. Robin Hinings, "An Empirical Taxonomy of Structures of Work Organizations," *Administrative Science Quarterly,* **14**: 115–25 (March 1969).

[174] Ibid., p. 116.

[175] Ibid.

[176] Ibid.

FIGURE 9–13   Three-Dimensional Taxonomic Model

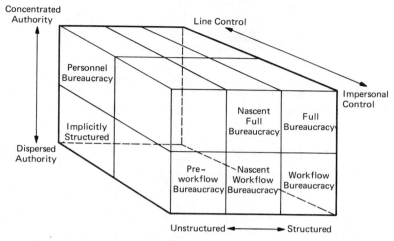

SOURCE: Adapted from Derek S. Pugh, David J. Hickson, and C. Robin Hinings, "An Empirical Taxonomy of Structures of Work Organizations," *Administrative Science Quarterly,* **14** (March 1969), p. 123.

FIGURE 9–14   Organizational Taxonomy: Produce or Service (N = 52)

Full Bureaucracy (*N* = 1)
  Repairs for government department
Nascent Full Bureaucracy (*N* = 4)
  Civil engineering firm
  Abrasives manufacturer
  Local authority transport department
  Paper manufacturer
Workflow Bureaucracy (*N* = 15)
  Vehicle manufacturer
  Food manufacturer
  Confectionery manufacturer
  Tire manufacturer
  Nonferrous metal manufacturer
  Printer
  Three motor components manufacturers
  Commercial vehicle manufacturer
  Omnibus company
  Glass manufacturer
  Metal motor components manufacturer
  Heavy electrical engineering equipment
    manufacturer
  Aircraft components manufacturer
Nascent Workflow Bureaucracy (*N* = 5)
  Metal goods manufacturer
  Components manufacturer
  Brewery
  Engineering component manufacturer
  Domestic appliances manufacturer

Preworkflow Bureaucracy (*N* = 11)
  Four metal component manufacturers
  Motor component manufacturer
  Two metal goods manufacturers
  Carriage manufacturer
  Engineering tool manufacturer
  Food manufacturer
Personnel Bureaucracy (*N* = 8)
  Government inspection department
  Local authority baths department
  Cooperative chain of retail stores
  Local authority education department
  Savings bank
  Local authority civil engineering department
  Food manufacturer
  Local authority water department
Implicity Structured Organizations (*N* = 8)
  Component manufacturer
  Chain of retail stores
  Department store
  Insurance company
  Research division
  Chain of shoe repair shops
  Building firm
  Toy manufacturer

SOURCE: Adapted from Derek S. Pugh, David J. Hickson, and C. Robin Hinings," "An Empirical Taxonomy of Structures of Work Organizations," *Administrative Science Quarterly,* **14** (March 1969), p. 120.

for example, could be assembled. Propositions pertaining to organizations of this type might be more readily synthesized. Thus, we begin to stipulate the analytic criteria that define the types of social systems to which certain propositions are applicable.

Second, taxonomic models provide a basis for sampling. Thus, in defining future research, larger samples of organizations might be selected on the basis of analytic criteria rather than sheer happenstance or more simplistic typologies like goals. Generalization presumably could be made to units with similar analytic characteristics—that is, that occupy a common taxonomical niche. Thus, a framework for selecting *samples of organizations* is provided.[177]

Let us use a simple example to illustrate the idea. Assuming that we are interested in responses to internal organizational strain, we might suspect that organizations characterized by certain analytic criteria might respond differently to similar strains when compared to organizations with differing qualities. Note that the "same" organization, defined by the continuity of specific persons, might respond differently at a later point in time if the analytic criteria that characterize it at this later point in time had now changed. Thus, we predict our response and specific relationships among sets of other variables on the basis of the analytic criteria that place it in a particular analytic niche. *We are assuming that persons participating in structures characterized by a given set of criteria will have a higher probability of responding within a particular range of options, than persons participating in structures with different characteristics.*

How could we use this idea to select a sample of organizations? Let us assume that on the basis of existing research and our own best hunch we decided that three variables appeared critical: (1) complexity; (2) permanence; and (3) certainty in major technology. By dichotomizing each of these variables, we build a sampling cube with eight cells, i.e., $2 \times 2 \times 2$. Rather than select organizations just because they are available, or fifty organizations that share the same analytic characteristics, we could select a purposive sample. We might choose five organizations to represent each cell of the sampling space and thus seek forty organizations for the study: i.e., eight cells by five organizations for each cell (note Figure 9–15).

What might this tell us? If the three variables selected at the outset are critical to the problem at hand, we might find that the five organizations located in cell one—i.e., *H, H, H*—respond to areas of strain very

---

[177] A somewhat similar view, but without the focus on taxonomies, is presented by Barney G. Glaser and Anselm L. Strauss, *The Discovery of Grounded Theory* (Chicago: Aldine Publishing Company, 1967), in their chapter entitled "Theoretical Sampling," pp. 45–77.

See also David Mechanic, "Some Considerations in the Methodology of Organizational Studies," in *The Social Science of Organizations: Four Perspectives*, Harold J. Leavitt, ed. (Englewood Cliffs, N.J.: Prentice-Hall, Inc., 1963), pp. 158–66.

FIGURE 9–15   Illustrative Sampling Scheme

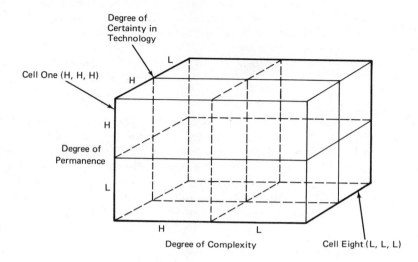

differently from those in cell eight (*L, L, L*). Those with high complexity, high permanence, and high certainty in the major technological process might respond with efforts to create new rules and otherwise expand the bureaucratic quality of the structure by gaining standardization and conformity. In contrast, those in cell eight might opt for a policy that protects the differences among the units and thereby increases the autonomy of each unit. Other variations would be suspected from organizations located elsewhere. Think about how those that are characterized by low permanence, high complexity, and low technological certainty might respond.

Of course, it is possible that no differences in response would be found at all. We might then conclude that for this type of problem these variables are not critical. But at least we have a systematic way to proceed in hypothesis testing wherein we can specify the kinds of units to which our findings do or do not apply. It provides us with a method whereby we might begin to cumulate our research findings so as to have a basis for generalization. In addition, "The scope of a substantive theory can be carefully increased and controlled by such conscious choices of groups." [178]

However, in discussing a similar idea, which he labels "dimensional sampling," Arnold[179] cautions us of the major pitfall:

> Clearly the dimensional sampling approach provides no assurance that the most effective dimensions will be used. When dealing with conceptual frameworks the question is not whether the concepts used are in some absolute

[178] Glaser and Strauss, op. cit., p. 52.

[179] David O. Arnold, "Dimensional Sampling: An Approach for Studying a Small Number of Cases," *The American Sociologist*, **5**: 147–50 (May 1970).

sense "correct," but whether they pay off, whether they are useful. The framework of classical mechanics, which focuses on the dimensions length, mass, and time, is widely used not because it is "right," but because it is a useful tool for understanding aspects of the physical world. In sociology we have yet to reach a consensus regarding the most useful dimensions for our research. So dimensional sampling is no cure-all; the sampling can be no better than the dimensions selected, and there is no automatic procedure for this selection.[180]

Despite this caution, it is clear that the strategy has much utility. Indeed, it is our belief that it provides the necessary breakthrough whereby organizational research can become cumulative—both in the design of new research and in the synthesis of old. Thus, future taxonomic work is an essential ingredient in the enterprise of a science of organizations. With this view in mind, let us now turn to consideration of several design alternatives.

Designing Organizational Research

Research design, like many of the other areas discussed in this chapter, is a complex topic about which many volumes have been written. For general coverage, statements by Campbell[181] have proved especially helpful with our students. In addition, discussions by Barnes,[182] Burns,[183] Price,[184] Starbuck,[185] and Udy,[186] present many ideas and problems dealing specifically with designing organizational research. From the numerous designs possible, let us consider three general types: (1) nonexperimental; (2) quasi-experimental; and (3) experimental. Before starting, however, one point should be emphasized. Any of these design strategies could be used in either field or laboratory settings. Although the past trend generally has been to use nonexperimental designs in field settings and experimental or quasi-experimental

[180] Ibid., p. 148.
[181] Donald T. Campbell and Julian C. Stanley, *Experimental and Quasi-Experimental Designs for Research* (Chicago: Rand McNally and Company, 1966); and Donald T. Campbell, "Factors Relevant to the Validity of Experiments in Social Settings," *Psychological Bulletin,* 54: 297–312 (1957).
[182] Louis B. Barnes, "Organizational Change and Field Experiment Methods," in Vroom, op. cit., pp. 57–112.
[183] Tom Burns, "The Comparative Study of Organizations," in Vroom, op. cit., pp. 113–72.
[184] James L. Price, "Design of Proof in Organizational Research," *Administrative Science Quarterly,* 13: 121–34 (June 1968).
[185] William H. Starbuck, "Some Comments, Observations and Objections Stimulated by 'Design of Proof in Organizational Research,'" *Administrative Science Quarterly,* 13: 135–61 (June 1968).
[186] Stanley H. Udy, Jr., "The Comparative Analysis of Organizations," in March, op. cit., pp. 678–709.

designs in the laboratory, increasingly we should look toward usage of experimental or quasi-experimental designs in the field. The major barrier in designing experimental research has been the lack of theory that must guide such designs regarding selection of variables for both manipulation and control. Increased efforts to use, test, and modify taxonomic schemes can be of great significance in this regard, as we move with greater precision toward specifying sets of analytic criteria that serve as a basis for defining different types of systems. However, designs of all three types discussed below have utility. Each permits separate types of contributions to theory construction.

Nonexperimental Designs. Clearly, most organizational research to date has been nonexperimental. Detailed case studies have been completed on numerous types of organizations. Some investigators have focused on a single organization for intensive descriptive analysis.[187] Others have completed longitudinal analysis of one organization over several years.[188] And many have selected several organizations, say four or five, and then have tried to make some general comparisons as to the consequences of different structures or have focused on the interorganizational transactions among them.[189] Still others, interested less in details regarding any one organization, have surveyed larger numbers of units, gathering only highly selective data. Recall that the Haas and Pugh taxonomic research groups just discussed initially surveyed seventy-five and fifty-two organizations respectively. With what appears to be a similarly refined focus, Blau[190] has reported initial findings based on his survey of 1,500 component organizations in fifty-three state governmental units (all fifty states, plus the District of Columbia, Puerto Rico, and the Virgin Islands).

If we think about the variety of study designs represented in the above paragraph, three critical dimensions quickly emerge that characterize much of the variability: (1) *level of abstraction,* i.e., analysis and data collected vary from highly descriptive and concrete to very abstract conceptualization; (2) presence or absence of *time,* (some studies reflect only one point in time, others are longitudinal); and (3) the *number of units* selected for study. Note that these three dimensions are clearly related. Thus, as one increases the number of units selected for study, there is of necessity an increase in the level of

---

[187] For example, Gresham M. Sykes, *The Society of Captives* (Princeton, N.J.: Princeton University Press, 1958).

[188] For example, William A. Anderson, *Disaster and Organizational Change: A Study of the Long Term Consequences in Anchorage of the 1964 Alaskan Earthquake* (Columbus, Ohio: Disaster Research Center, Ohio State University, 1969).

[189] For example, Julian's hospital study using Etzioni's typology or Drabek's analysis of the response of twelve organizations to the 1963 Indianapolis Coliseum explosion, *Disaster in Aisle 13,* op. cit.

[190] Peter M. Blau, "A Formal Theory of Differentiation in Organizations," *American Sociological Review,* 35: 20–118 (April 1970).

FIGURE 9–16 Variations in Organizational Research Designs

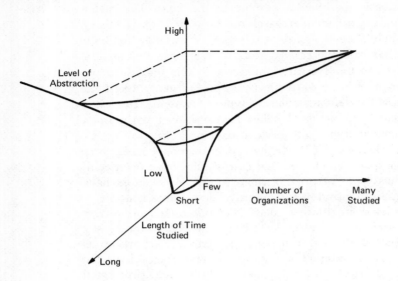

abstraction at which the analysis will be conducted. This shift in abstraction levels usually is reflected even at the point of data collection. Diagramatically, these relationships resemble those presented in Figure 9–16; that is, most studies would be placed on the surface of a solid object shaped like the one pictured.

Three important observations should be emphasized. First, given the relative void in organizational theory and only initial taxonomic work even started, future research should continue to reflect this type of methodological variability. Some persons are highly adept at organizing mountains of descriptive data into perceptive analyses. Others enjoy shifting to high abstraction levels and completing elaborate statistical calculations. All ought to be encouraged, and none should feel intimidated or self-righteous simply because a particular style of methodology suits him. Of course, we would argue, as we have throughout this chapter, that the method selected should depend on the problem of interest rather than the reverse. But it is on the dimensions diagramed in Figures 9–16 that many appear most rigid. Note that in a sense this is not unlike the implicit distinction between the styles of clinicians and more statistically oriented psychologists.

Second, even simple organizational case studies, completed at a low level of abstraction, can be integrated with others. In this way, they may serve as a basis for comparative analysis. Price's[191] inventory of

[191] James L. Price, *Organizational Effectiveness: An Inventory of Propositions* (Homewood, Ill.: Richard D. Irwin, Inc., 1968).

propositions regarding organizational effectiveness is an excellent illustration. Using fifty studies, he was able to ferret out fifty-one propositions at a more abstract level dealing with a topic that was of only peripheral focus in the original studies.

Third, no simple dicta are to be accepted regarding improvement of such research. For example, as Starbuck[192] suggests regarding two of Price's recent suggestions, it is undesirable to belittle researchers for not including standardized sets of variables. Of course, for some persons this may provide an important data base for comparative analysis. But as Starbuck emphasizes, consensus may be difficult regarding which variables ought to be selected and how they ought to be made operational. Further, simply to encourage research wherein larger numbers of organizations are sampled is not appropriate. As indicated in Figure 9–16, descriptive studies conducted at lower abstraction levels preclude large numbers. The value of such studies lies primarily in the new conceptual insights and the hypotheses they generate. Including more organizations in the study design almost always reduces the richness of the data available on any single organization, and that might severely retard development of new theory. Thus, such simple dicta must be criticized and the questions recast. *Including additional organizations in a design, like collecting more data, does not necessarily produce a better study.* Improved theory, which in turn permits use of quasi-experimental and experimental designs, is the important consideration, which greatly complicates any suggestions made about an ordering of priorities that might accelerate the progress toward a science of organizations.

Quasi-Experimental Designs. Campbell and several colleagues have used a collection of designs that are quasi-experimental.[193] That is, some control and manipulation are possible, but total control is lacking. Let us look at three such designs that appear especially appropriate for organizational research.

First, in a *time-series experiment* we gather data at several points in time both before and after a particular manipulation has occurred. In this way we can see if the imposition of a particular variable has coincided with a departure from the previous trend line or pattern. Of course, changes in the dependent variables may or may not be due to the assumed independent variable, but several such patterned

---

[192] Starbuck, op. cit., pp. 153–61.

[193] This discussion was adopted largely from Campbell and Stanley, op. cit., pp. 34–64.

For an excellent discussion and application of one quasi-experimental design— time series experiment—see H. Laurence Ross and Donald T. Campbell, "The Connecticut Crackdown on Speeding: Time Series Data in Quasi-Experimental Analysis," *Law and Society Review*, 3: 33–53 (August 1968).

fluctuations collected with *different* organizations with *similar* taxonomic characteristics clearly provides support. Following Campbell and Stanley,[194] such experiments can be diagramed as follows where O represents observation or measurement and X represents manipulation of an independent variable:

$$O_1 \quad O_2 \quad O_3 \quad O_4 \quad X \quad O_5 \quad O_6 \quad O_7 \quad O_8$$

Thus, following four observations made prior to the stimulus (manipulation of independent variable), we complete four more observations to ascertain the consequence.

Use of *nonequivalent control groups* with before and after measurements may be a frequent way to strengthen a design. Indeed, given Campbell's bias, the only way to obtain equivalence is through random assignment. And rarely will organizational analysts have the luxury of randomly assigning matched pairs of organizations to experimental and control groups for treatment purposes. However, by specifying a series of analytic criteria in advance, researchers would have available a pool of organizations which meet those criteria. Some organizations may experience naturally (e.g., community is struck by a natural disaster) or may self-select (e.g., adoption of a merit day program by a school system) to experience a particular exposure. In either instance, random assignment by the investigator is not possible. However, this design is far superior to a single group design, despite nonequivalence, as the relative impact of the experimental manipulation can be compared to the control group. Of course, where self-selection occurs, the design is weakened. Pre- and post-testing of both experimental and control groups is the major advantage, which assists in interpretation of results. Diagramatically, the design is as follows, with the dotted line indicating non-equivalence:[195]

$$
\begin{array}{ccc}
O & X & O \\
\hline
O & & O
\end{array}
$$

The above type of design ought to enjoy widespread future usage because of the difficulties in random assignment in organizational research. Where random assignment is possible with comparable groups, a *separate-sample, pretest-posttest control group* design may be used. Here it is assumed that the units to receive experimental manipulation can be randomly assigned by the investigator (indicated by the R in the diagram below). Separate experimental and control groups are used for the time one and time two measurements. Distortion due to

[194] Campbell and Stanley, op. cit., p. 37.
[195] Ibid., p. 47.

the measurement process is thereby avoided. However, the equivalence of the experimental and control groups with their counterpart in the design remains in question, despite randomization. This design would be excellent, but Campbell and Stanley indicate that its actual use remains unknown, undoubtedly because of its expense.[196]

$$
\begin{array}{lll}
RO & (X) & \\
R & X & O \\
\hline
RO & & \\
R & & O
\end{array}
$$

Although none of these three alternatives is a pure experiment, each represents an important direction in which organizational research must move. And, these are but three of several such quasi-experimental designs. More data and more organizations, if sampled *to comply with these types of design strategies* will be required before even basic taxonomic work can be pushed much further. But note that more data and/or more organizations in any sample do not result necessarily in improved research.

Experimental Designs. Let us look at three types of pure experimental designs so as to contrast those presented above. A primary requirement of all such designs that most often will be difficult to meet is that of randomization. The investigator must, in each instance, randomly assign units to the experimental and control groups. Matching pairs of organizations on several variables may be done initially, but only *as an adjunct* to later random assignment.[197]

The most classic and commonly used experimental design is the familiar *pretest–posttest control group* design. Note that equivalence between experimental and control groups is achieved through randomization.[198]

$$
\begin{array}{lll}
R & O_1 & X \quad O_2 \\
R & O_3 & \quad O_4
\end{array}
$$

The *Solomon four-group* design is an important modification as it permits analysis of the possible effects of measurement. That is, by having an additional experimental and control group that are tested only at time two, the impact of measurement at time one can be assessed.[199]

[196] Ibid., p. 55.
[197] Ibid., p. 15.
[198] Ibid., p. 13.
[199] Ibid., p. 24.

$$R \quad O_1 \qquad X \quad O_2$$
$$R \quad O_3 \qquad \quad O_4$$
$$R \qquad \qquad X \quad O_5$$
$$R \qquad \qquad \quad O_6$$

Finally, the *posttest-only control group* design reflects the power of randomization. Thus, Campbell and Stanley propose "within the limits of confidence stated by the tests of significance, randomization can suffice without the pretest." [200] Thus, where random assignment is possible, this design may at times be preferable over the classical pre-posttest design as time one measures are not involved.[201]

$$R \qquad X \quad O_1$$
$$R \qquad \qquad O_2$$

In order to summarize the advantages and limitations of these various design alternatives, let us look briefly at the factors that affect internal and external validity. As indicated in our discussion of laboratory problems, *internal validity* asks: "Did in fact the experimental treatments make a difference in this specific experimental instance? *External validity* asks the question of *generalizability*: To what populations, settings, treatment variables, and measurement variables can this effect be generalized?" [202] Campbell and Stanley list the following twelve factors.

Internal Validity

1. *History,* the specific events occurring between the first and second measurement in addition to the experimental variable.
2. *Maturation,* processes within the respondents operating as a function of the passage of time per se (not specific to the particular events), including growing older, growing hungrier, growing more tired, and the like.
3. *Testing,* the effects of taking a test upon the scores of a second testing.
4. *Instrumentation,* in which changes in the calibration of a measuring instrument or changes in the observers or scorers used may produce changes in the obtained measurements.
5. *Statistical regression,* operating where groups have been selected on the basis of their extreme scores.
6. Biases resulting in differential *selection* of respondents for the comparison groups.
7. *Experimental mortality,* or differential loss of respondents from the comparison groups.
8. *Selection-maturation interaction,* etc., which in certain of the multiple-group quasi-experimental designs . . . is confounded with, i.e., might be mistaken for, the effect of the experimental variable. . . .

[200] Ibid., p. 25.
[201] Ibid.
[202] Ibid., p. 5.

FIGURE 9–17   Sources of Validity

	Internal								External			
	History	Maturation	Testing	Instrumentation	Regression	Selection	Mortality	Interaction of Selection and Maturation, etc.	Interaction of Testing and X	Interaction of Selection and X	Reactive Arrangements	Multiple-X Interference
Nonexperimental Designs:												
One-shot Case Study X 0	–	–				–	–				–	
One-Group Pretest–Posttest Design 0 X 0	–	–	–	–	?	+	+	–	–	–	?	
Static-Group Comparison X _0_ / 0	+	?	+	+	+	–	–			–		
Quasi-experimental Designs:												
Time Series 0 0 0 0X0 0 0 0	–	+	+	?	+	+	+	+	–	?	?	
Non-equivalent Control Group Design 0 X 0 / 0 0	+	+	+	+	?	+	+	–	–	?	?	
Separate-Sample Pretest–Posttest Design R 0 (X) / R X 0	–	–	+	?	+	+	–	–	+	+	+	
True Experimental Designs												
Pretest–Posttest Control Group Design R 0 X 0 / R 0 0	+	+	+	+	+	+	+	+	–	?	?	
Solomon Four-Group Design R 0 X 0 / R 0 0 / R X 0 / R 0	+	+	+	+	+	+	+	+	+	?	?	
Posttest-Only Control Group Design R X 0 / R 0	+	+	+	+	+	+	+	+	+	?	?	

NOTE: "In the tables, a minus indicates a definite weakness, a plus indicates that the factor is controlled, a question mark indicates a possible source of concern, and a blank indicates that the factor is not relevant.

"It is with extreme reluctance that these summary tables are presented because they are apt to be 'too helpful,' and to be depended upon in place of the more complex and qualified presentation in the text. No + or − indicator should be respected unless the reader comprehends why it is placed there. In particular, it is against the spirit of this presentation to create uncomprehended fears of, or confidence in, specific designs." (Campbell and Stanley, p. 8.)

SOURCE: Adapted with permission from Donald J. Campbell and Julian C. Stanley, *Experimental and Quasi-experimental Designs for Research* (Chicago: Rand McNally & Co., 1966), pp. 8 and 40.

9. The *reactive* or *interaction* effect of *testing*, in which a pretest might increase or decrease the respondent's sensitivity or responsiveness to the experimental variable and thus make the results obtained for a pretested population unrepresentative of the effects of the experimental variable for the unpretested universe from which the experimental respondents were selected.
10. The *interaction* effects of *selection* biases and the *experimental variable*.
11. *Reactive effects of experimental arrangements*, which would preclude generalization about the effect of the experimental variable upon persons being exposed to it in nonexperimental settings.
12. *Multiple-treatment interference*, likely to occur whenever multiple treatments are applied to the same respondents, because the effects of prior treatments are not usually erasable.[203]

A summary of each of the designs discussed, nonexperimental, quasi-experimental, and experimental, are presented in Figure 9–17 with the corresponding defects in internal or external validity designated. It is hoped that this discussion of design alternatives, along with the multitude of other topics we have surveyed in this chapter, will assist you in your efforts to conduct better research. For it will only be through the disciplined rigor and creative innovations of persons like you that a science of organizations will emerge.

[203] Ibid., pp. 5–6.

BIBLIOGRAPHY

ADAMS, DAVID S. *Emergency Actions and Disaster Reactions: An Analysis of the Anchorage Public Works Department in the 1964 Alaskan Earthquake.* Columbus, Ohio: Disaster Research Center, Ohio State University, 1969.

ADAMS, RICHARD N., and JACK J. PREISS (eds.). *Human Organization Research: Field Relations and Techniques.* Homewood, Ill.: Dorsey Press, 1960.

AIFFA, HOWARD R. *Decision Analysis.* Reading, Mass.: Addison-Wesley Publishing Co., Inc., 1968.

AIKEN, MICHAEL, and JERALD HAGE. "Reply to Tausky." *American Sociological Review,* **32** (February 1967), 118–20.

AITKEN, HUGH G. J. *Taylorism at Watertown Arsenal.* Cambridge, Mass.: Harvard University Press, 1960.

ALDRICH, HOWARD E. "Organizational Boundaries and Interorganizational Conflict." *Human Relations,* **24** (August 1971), 279–82.

————. "The Sociable Organization: A Case Study of Mensa and Some Propositions." *Sociology and Social Research,* **55** (July 1971), 429–41.

————, and ALBERT J. REISS, JR. "Police Officers As Boundary Personnel: Attitude Congruence Between Policemen and Small Businessmen in Urban Areas." Pp. 193–208 in *Police in Urban Society.* Ed. by Harlan Hahn. Beverly Hills, Calif.: Sage Publications, Inc., 1971.

ALLPORT, FLOYD H. *Theories of Perception and the Concept of Structure.* New York: John Wiley & Sons, Inc., 1955.

ALVAREZ, RODOLFO. "Informal Reactions to Deviance in Simulated Work Organizations: A Laboratory Experiment." *American Sociological Review,* **33** (December 1968), 895–912.

ANDERSON, THEODORE R., and SEYMOUR WARKOV. "Organizational Size and

Functional Complexity: A Study of Administration in Hospitals." *American Sociological Review,* **26** (February 1961), 23–28.

ANDERSON, WILLIAM A. *Disaster and Organizational Change: A Study of the Long Term Consequences in Anchorage of the 1964 Alaskan Earthquake.* Columbus, Ohio: Disaster Research Center, Ohio State University, 1969.

———. "Some Observations on a Disaster Subculture: The Organizational Response in Cincinnati, Ohio, to the 1964 Flood." Columbus, Ohio: Disaster Research Center, Ohio State University, 1965 (unpublished paper).

ARGYRIS, CHRIS. "Creating Effective Relationships in Organizations." Pp. 109–33 in *Human Organization Research: Field Relations and Techniques.* Ed. by Richard N. Adams and Jack J. Preiss. Homewood, Ill.: Dorsey Press, 1960.

———. *The Impact of Budgets on People.* Ithaca, N.Y.: School of Business and Public Administration, Cornell University, 1952.

———. *Integrating the Individual and the Organization.* New York: John Wiley & Sons, Inc., 1964.

———. *Organization of a Bank.* New Haven, Conn.: Labor and Management Center, Yale University, 1954.

———. *Understanding Organizational Behavior.* Homewood, Ill.: Dorsey Press, 1960.

ARNOLD, DAVID O. "Dimensional Sampling: An Approach for Studying a Small Number of Cases." *The American Sociologist,* **5** (May 1970), 147–150.

BAKKE, E. WRIGHT. "Concept of the Social Organization." Pp. 16–75 in *Modern Organization Theory.* Ed. by Mason Haire, New York: John Wiley & Sons, Inc., 1959.

BALDRIDGE, J. VICTOR. *Power and Conflict in the University.* New York: John Wiley & Sons, Inc., 1971.

BALES, ROBERT F. "The Equilibrium Problem in Small Groups." Pp. 424–56 in *Small Groups.* Ed. by A. Paul Hare et al. New York: Alfred A. Knopf, Inc., 1961.

———. *Interaction Process Analysis.* Cambridge, Mass.: Addison-Wesley Publishing Co. Inc. 1950.

———. *Personality and Interpersonal Behavior.* New York: Holt, Rinehart & Winston, Inc., 1970.

———, and FRED L. STRODTBECK. "Phases in Group Problem Solving." Pp. 624–40 in *Group Dynamics: Research and Theory.* Ed. by Dorwin Cartwright and Alvin Zander. Evanston, Ill.: Row, Peterson & Co., 1960.

BARNARD, CHESTER I. *The Functions of the Executive.* Cambridge, Mass.: Harvard University Press, 1938.

BARNES, LOUIS B. "Organizational Change and Field Experiment Methods." Pp. 57–112 in *Methods of Organizational Research.* Ed. by Victor H. Vroom, Pittsburgh Pa.: University of Pittsburgh Press, 1967.

BARTON, ALLEN H. *Communities in Disaster: A Sociological Analysis of Collective Stress Situations.* Garden City, N.Y.: Doubleday & Co., Inc., 1969.

————. *Organizational Measurement and Its Bearing on the Study of College Environments*. New York: College Entrance Examination Board, 1961.

BATES, FREDERICK L., et al. *The Social and Psychological Consequences of a Natural Disaster: A Longitudinal Study of Hurricane Audrey*. Washington, D.C.: National Academy of Sciences–National Research Council, 1963.

BAVELAS, ALEX. "Communication Patterns in Task-oriented Groups." *Journal of the Acoustical Society of America*, **22** (1950), 725–30.

BECKER, HOWARD. "Four Types of Religious Organizations." Pp. 252–55 in *Complex Organizations: A Sociological Reader*. Ed. by Amitai Etzioni. New York: Holt, Rinehart & Winston, Inc., 1961.

BECKER, HOWARD S., and BLANCHE GEER. "Participant Observation: The Analysis of Qualitative Field Data." Pp. 267–89 in *Human Organization Research: Field Relations and Techniques*. Ed. by Richard N. Adams and Jack J. Preiss. Homewood, Ill.: Dorsey Press, 1960.

————, et al. *Boys in White*. Chicago: University of Chicago Press, 1961.

BECKER, SELWYN W., and DAVID GREEN, JR. "Budgeting and Employee Behavior." *Journal of Business*, **4** (1962), 392–402.

BELL, GERALD D. "Formality versus Flexibility in Complex Organizations." Pp. 97–106 in *Organizations and Human Behavior*. Ed. by Gerald D. Bell. Englewood Cliffs, N.J.: Prentice-Hall, Inc., 1967.

BERELSON, BERNARD, and GARY A. STEINER. *Human Behavior, an Inventory of Scientific Findings*. New York: Harcourt Brace Jovanovich, Inc., 1964.

BERRIEN, F. KENNETH. *General and Social Systems*. New Brunswick, N.J.: Rutgers University Press, 1968.

BERTALANFFY, LUDWIG VON. *General System Theory*. New York: George Braziller, Inc. 1968.

BETTELHEIM, BRUNO. "Individual and Mass Behavior in Extreme Situations." *Journal of Abnormal and Social Psychology*, **38** (October 1943), 417–52.

BEYER, ROBERT. *Profitability Accounting for Planning and Control*. New York: Ronald Press Co., 1963.

BIBLE, BOND L., and JAMES D. McCOMAS. "Role Consensus and Teacher Effectiveness." *Social Forces*, **42** (December 1963), 225–32.

BIDDLE, BRUCE J., and EDWIN J. THOMAS (eds.). *Role Theory: Concepts and Research*. New York: John Wiley & Sons, Inc., 1966.

BLACK, MAX. "Models and Archetypes." Pp. 219–43 in *Models and Metaphors*. Ed. by Max Black. Ithaca, N.Y.: Cornell University Press, 1962.

———— (ed.). *Social Theories of Talcott Parsons*. Englewood Cliffs, N.J.: Prentice-Hall, Inc., 1961.

BLAU, PETER M. *Exchange and Power in Social Life*. New York: John Wiley & Sons, Inc., 1964.

————. "A Formal Theory of Differentiation in Organizations." *American Sociological Review*, **35** (April 1970), 201–18.

————. "Objectives of Sociology." Pp. 43–71 in *A Design for Sociology: Scope, Objectives and Methods*. Ed. by Robert Bierstedt. Philadelphia: The American Academy of Political and Social Science, April 1969.

————, and MARSHALL W. MEYER. *Bureaucracy in Modern Society*. 2nd ed. New York: Random House, Inc., 1971.

————, and RICHARD A. SCHOENHERR. *The Structure of Organizations.* New York: Basic Books, Inc., 1971.

————, and W. RICHARD SCOTT. *Formal Organizations.* San Francisco, Calif.: Chandler Publishing Co., 1962.

BLAUNER, ROBERT. *Alienation and Freedom.* Chicago: University of Chicago Press, 1964.

BLUM, MILTON C. *Industrial Psychology and Its Social Foundations.* New York: Harper & Row, Publishers, 1956.

BONJEAN, CHARLES M., et al. *Sociological Measurement: An Inventory of Scales and Indices.* San Francisco, Calif.: Chandler Publishing Co., 1967.

BORKO, HAROLD, (ed.). *Computer Applications in the Behavioral Sciences.* Englewood Cliffs, N.J.: Prentice-Hall, Inc., 1962.

BOULDING, KENNETH E. *The Organizational Revolution.* Chicago: Quadrangle Books, Inc., 1968. (Original publication, 1953.)

————. "A Pure Theory of Conflict Applied to Organizations." Pp. 136–45 in *Power and Conflict in Organizations.* Ed. by Robert L. Kahn and Elise Boulding. New York: Basic Books, Inc., 1964.

BROUILLETTE, JOHN R., and E. L. QUARANTELLI. "Types of Patterned Variation in Bureaucratic Adaptations to Organizational Stress." *Sociological Inquiry,* **41** (Winter, 1971), 36–46.

BROWN, JULIA S., and BRIAN G. GILMARTIN. "Sociology Today: Lacunae, Emphases and Surfeits." *The American Sociologist,* **4** (November 1969), 283–91.

BRUYN, SEVERYN T. *The Human Perspective in Sociology.* Englewood Cliffs, N.J.: Prentice-Hall, Inc., 1966.

BUCHER, RUE, CHARLES E. FRITZ, and E. L. QUARANTELLI. "Tape Recorded Interviews in Social Research." *American Sociological Review,* **21** (June 1956), 359–64.

BUCKLEY, WALTER. *Modern Systems Research for the Behavioral Scientist.* Chicago: Aldine Publishing Company, 1968.

————. *Sociology and Modern Systems Theory.* Englewood Cliffs, N.J.: Prentice-Hall, Inc., 1967.

BURNS, TOM. "The Comparative Study of Organizations." Pp. 113–72 in *Methods of Organizational Research.* Ed. by Victor H. Vroom. Pittsburgh, Pa.: University of Pittsburgh Press, 1967.

————, and G. M. STALKER. *The Management of Innovation.* London: Tavistock Publications, 1961.

CAMPBELL, DONALD T. "Factors Relevant to the Validity of Experiments in Social Settings." *Psychological Bulletin,* **54** (1957), 297–312.

————, and JULIAN C. STANLEY. *Experimental and Quasi-Experimental Designs for Research.* Chicago: Rand McNally & Co., 1966.

CAMPBELL, FREDERICK L., and RONALD L. AKERS. "Organizational Size, Complexity, and the Administrative Component in Occupational Associations." *The Sociological Quarterly,* **11** (Fall, 1970), 435–51.

CAPLOW, THEODORE. *Principles of Organization.* New York: Harcourt Brace Jovanovich, Inc., 1964.

CAREY, ALEX. "The Hawthorne Studies: A Radical Criticism." *American Sociological Review,* **32** (June 1967), 403–16.

CARZO, ROCCO, JR., and JOHN N. YANOUZAS. *Formal Organization: A Systems Approach.* Homewood, Ill.: Richard D. Irwin, Inc. and Dorsey Press, 1967.

CHAPMAN, ROBERT L., and JOHN L. KENNEDY. "The Background and Implications of the RAND Corporation Systems Research Laboratory Studies." Pp. 149–56 in *Some Theories of Organization.* Ed. by Albert H. Rubenstein and Chadwick J. Haberstroh. Homewood, Ill.: Richard D. Irwin, Inc., and Dorsey Press, 1966.

————, et al. "The Systems Research Laboratory's Air Defense Experiments." Pp. 172–88 in *Simulation in Social Science: Readings.* Ed. by Harold Guetzkow. Englewood Cliffs, N.J.: Prentice-Hall, Inc., 1962.

CHAPPLE, ELIOT D. "Measuring Human Relations: An Introduction to the Study of the Interaction of Individuals." *Genetic Psychology Monographs,* **22** (1940), 3–147.

CICOUREL, AARON V. *Method and Measurement in Sociology.* New York: The Free Press, 1964.

————, and JOHN I. KITSUSE. *The Educational Decision-Makers.* Indianapolis, Ind.: The Bobbs-Merrill Co., Inc., 1963.

CLARK, BURTON. *The Distinctive College: Antioch, Reed and Swarthmore.* Chicago: Aldine Publishing Company, 1970.

COHEN, HARRY. "Bureaucratic Flexibility: Some Comments on Robert Merton's 'Bureaucratic Structure and Personality.'" *British Journal of Sociology,* **21** (1970), 390–99.

COHEN, KALMAN J., and RICHARD M. CYERT. "Simulation of Organizational Behavior." Pp. 305–34 in *Handbook of Organizations.* Ed. by James G. March. Chicago: Rand McNally & Co., 1965.

COLEMAN, JAMES S. "Analysis of Social Structures and Simulation of Social Processes with Electronic Computers." Pp. 61–69 in *Simulation in Social Science: Readings.* Ed. by Harold Guetzkow. Englewood Cliffs, N.J.: Prentice-Hall, Inc., 1962.

————. "Relational Analysis: The Study of Social Organizations with Survey Methods." Pp. 517–28 in *A Sociological Reader on Complex Organizations.* Ed. by Amitai Etzioni. New York: Holt, Rinehart & Winston, Inc., 1969.

CORWIN, RONALD G. *Militant Professionalism.* New York: Appleton-Century-Crofts, 1970.

————. "The Professional Employee: A Study of Conflict in Nursing Roles." *The American Journal of Sociology,* **66** (May 1961), 604–15.

————. *A Sociology of Education.* New York: Appleton-Century-Crofts, 1965.

————. "Strategies for Organizational Innovation: An Empirical Comparison." Paper presented at the annual meeting of the American Sociological Association, Denver, Colorado, August 31, 1971.

COSER, LEWIS A. *Continuities in the Study of Social Conflict.* New York: The Free Press, 1967.

————. *The Functions of Social Conflict.* New York: The Free Press, 1956.

COSER, ROSE L. "Insulation from Observability and Types of Social Conformity." *American Sociological Review,* **26** (February 1961), 28–39.

CRAIG, JOHN G., and EDWARD GROSS. "The Forum Theory of Organizational

Democracy: Structural Guarantees as Time-Related Variables." *American Sociological Review,* **35** (February 1970), 19–33.

CROZIER, MICHEL. *The Bureaucratic Phenomenon.* Chicago: University of Chicago Press, 1964.

———. *The World of the Office Worker.* Trans. by David Landau. Chicago: University of Chicago Press, 1971.

CURRY, TIMOTHY J., and RICHARD M. EMERSON. "Balance Theory: A Theory of Interpersonal Attraction." *Sociometry,* **33** (June 1970), 216–38.

DAHRENDORF, RALF. *Class and Class Conflict in Industrial Society.* Stanford, Calif.: Stanford University Press, 1959.

———. *Essays in the Theory of Society.* Stanford, Calif.: Stanford University Press, 1968.

———. "Out of Utopia: Toward a Reorientation of Sociological Analysis." *American Journal of Sociology,* **64** (September 1958), 115–27.

DALTON, MELVILLE. *Men Who Manage.* New York: John Wiley & Sons, Inc., 1959.

DAVID, JAMES W., and KENNETH M. DOLBEARE. *Little Groups of Neighbors: The Selective Service System.* Chicago: Markham Publishing Co., 1968.

DAVIS, KINGSLEY, and WILBERT MOORE. "Some Principles of Stratification." *American Sociological Review,* **10** (April 1945), 242–49.

DENZIN, NORMAN K. "Symbolic Interactionism and Ethnomethodology: A Proposed Synthesis." *American Sociological Review,* **34** (December 1969), 922–34.

DILL, WILLIAM R. "Environment as an Influence on Managerial Autonomy." *Administrative Science Quarterly,* **2** (March 1958), 409–43.

DRABEK, THOMAS E. *Disaster in Aisle 13.* Columbus, Ohio: College of Administrative Science, Ohio State University, 1968.

———. *Laboratory Simulation of a Police Communication System Under Stress.* Columbus, Ohio: College of Administrative Science, Ohio State University, 1969.

———. "A Theoretical Framework for the Analysis of Organizational Stress." Paper presented at the annual meeting of the American Sociological Association in Denver, Colorado, August 31, 1971.

———, and E. L. QUARANTELLI. "Scapegoats, Villains, and Disasters," *Trans-action,* **4** (March 1967), 12–17.

———, and J. EUGENE HAAS. "Laboratory Simulation of Organizational Stress." *American Sociological Review,* **34** (April 1969), 223–38.

———. "Realism in Laboratory Simulation: Myth or Method?" *Social Forces,* **45** (March 1967), 337–46.

DUBIN, ROBERT. *Theory Building.* New York: The Free Press, 1969.

———. *The World of Work.* Englewood Cliffs, N.J.: Prentice-Hall, Inc., 1958.

DUNCOMBE, MARGARET. "A Theoretical Model of the Interaction Between Total Institutions and Their Inmates." Paper presented at the annual meeting of the Rocky Mountain Social Science Association, in Ft. Collins, Colorado, May 7, 1971.

DURKHEIM, ÉMILE, *Rules of the Sociological Method.* Trans. by Sarah A.

Solovay and John Mueller. New York: The Free Press, 1964. (Original publication, 1895.)

Economics and Management Science Division, Midwest Research Institute. *Plantran Planning Translator: A Simulation Modeling System for Long Range Planning.* Kansas City, Kans.: Midwest Research Institute (undated).

Emerson, Richard M. "Power-Dependence Relations." *American Sociological Review,* 27 (February 1962), 31–40.

Emery, F. E., and E. L. Trist. "Causal Texture of Organizational Environments." *Human Relations,* 18 (February 1965), 21–32.

Etzioni, Amitai. *A Comparative Analysis of Complex Organizations.* New York: The Free Press, 1961.

———. "Dual Leadership in Complex Organizations." *American Sociological Review,* 30 (October 1965), 688–98.

———. *Modern Organizations.* Englewood Cliffs, N.J.: Prentice-Hall, Inc., 1964.

———. "Two Approaches to Organizational Analysis: A Critique and a Suggestion." *Administrative Science Quarterly,* 5 (September 1960), 257–78.

Evan, William M. "The Organization Set: Toward a Theory of Interorganizational Relations." Pp. 173–88 in *Approaches to Organizational Design.* Ed. by James D. Thompson. Pittsburgh, Pa.: University of Pittsburgh Press, 1966.

——— (ed.). *Organizational Experiments: Laboratory and Field Research.* New York: Harper & Row, Publishers, 1971.

———. "Peer-Group Interaction and Organizational Socialization: A Study of Employee Turnover." *American Sociological Review,* 28 (June 1963), 436–40.

———, and Morris Zelditch, Jr. "A Laboratory Experiment on Bureaucratic Authority." *American Sociological Review,* 26 (December 1961), 883–93.

Forrester, Jay W. *Industrial Dynamics.* New York: John Wiley & Sons, Inc., 1961.

Freund, Julian. *The Sociology of Max Weber.* Trans. Mary Ilford. New York: Pantheon Books, 1968.

Frey, Frederick W. "Cross-Cultural Research in Political Science." Pp. 173–294 in *The Methodology of Comparative Research.* Ed. by Robert T. Holt and John E. Turner. New York: The Free Press, 1970.

Fullan, Michael. "Industrial Technology and Worker Integration in the Organization." *American Sociological Review,* 35 (December 1970), 1028–1039.

Gans, Herbert. *The Levittowners.* New York: Pantheon Books, 1967.

Gardner, John W. *Self-Renewal: The Individual and the Innovative Society.* New York: Harper Colophon Books, Harper & Row, Publishers, 1965. (Original publication, 1963.)

GEORGOPOULOS, BASIL S., and ARNOLD S. TANNENBAUM. "A Study of Organizational Effectiveness." *American Sociological Review*, **22** (October 1957), 534–40.

———, and FLOYD MANN. *The Community General Hospital*. New York: The Macmillan Company, 1962.

GERTH, HANS, and C. WRIGHT MILLS (eds.). *From Max Weber: Essays in Sociology*. New York: Oxford University Press, 1946.

GLANZER, MURRAY, and ROBERT GLASER. "Techniques for the Study of Group Structure and Behavior: II Empirical Studies of the Effects of Structure in Small Groups." *Psychological Bulletin*, **58** (January 1961), 1–27.

GLASER, BARNEY G., and ANSELM L. STRAUSS. *The Discovery of Grounded Theory: Strategies for Qualitative Research*. Chicago: Aldine Publishing Company, 1967.

GOFFMAN, ERVING. *Encounters*. Indianapolis, Ind.: The Bobbs-Merrill Co. Inc., 1961.

———. *The Presentation of Self in Everyday Life*. Garden City, N.Y.: Doubleday-Anchor, 1959.

GOLD, DAVID. "A Criticism of an Empirical Assessment of the Concept of Bureaucracy on Conceptual Interdependence and Empirical Independence." *American Journal of Sociology*, **70** (September 1964), 225–26.

GOODE, WILLIAM J. "A Theory of Role Strain." *American Sociological Review*, **25** (August 1960), 483–96.

GOODMAN, PAUL. *People or Personnel*. New York: Random House, Inc., 1965.

GOULDNER, ALVIN W. "Cosmopolitans and Locals: Toward an Analysis of Latent Social Roles, I and II." *Administrative Science Quarterly*, **2** (1957–1958), 281–306; 444–80.

———. "The Norm of Reciprocity: A Preliminary Statement." *American Sociological Review*, **25** (April 1960), 161–78.

———. "Organizational Analysis." Pp. 400–28 in *Sociology Today*. Ed. by Robert K. Merton et al. New York: Basic Books, Inc., 1959.

———. *Wildcat Strike*. New York: Harper & Row, Publishers, 1965.

GREER, SCOTT. *The Logic of Social Inquiry*. Chicago: Aldine Publishing Company, 1969.

———. *Social Organization*. New York: Random House, 1955.

GROSS, EDWARD. "Universities as Organizations: A Research Approach." *American Sociological Review*, **33** (August, 1968), 518–44.

———. "The Definition of Organizational Goals," *British Journal of Sociology*, **20** (September 1969), 277–94.

GROSS, NEAL, et al. *Explorations in Role Analysis: Studies of the School Superintendency Role*. New York: John Wiley & Sons, Inc., 1958.

GRUSKY, OSCAR. "The Effects of Formal Structure on Managerial Recruitment: A Study of Baseball Organization." *Sociometry*, **26** (March 1963), 345–53.

———. "The Effects of Succession: A Comparative Study of Military and Business Organization." Pp. 439_54 in *The Sociology of Organizations: Basic Studies*. Ed. by Oscar Grusky and George Miller. New York: The Free Press, 1970.

GUETZKOW, HAROLD. "Communications in Organizations." Pp. 534–73 in *Handbook of Organizations*. Ed. by James D. March. Chicago: Rand McNally & Co., 1965.

———. "Relations Among Organizations." Pp. 13–44 in *Studies on Behavior in Organizations*. Ed. by Raymond V. Bowers. Athens, Ga.: University of Georgia Press, 1966.

GULICK, LUTHER. "Notes on the Theory of Organizations." Pp. 1–46 in *Papers on the Science of Administration*. Ed. by Luther Gulick and Lyndall F. Urwick. New York: Institute of Public Administration, Columbia University, 1937.

———, and LYNDALL F. URWICK (eds.). *Papers on the Science of Administration*. New York: Institute of Public Administration, Columbia University, 1937.

GULLAHORN, JOHN T., and JEANNE E. GULLAHORN. "Some Computer Applications in Social Sciences." *American Sociological Review*, 30 (June 1965), 353–65.

GUSFIELD, JOSEPH R. "Field Work Reciprocities in Studying a Social Movement." Pp. 99–108 in *Human Organization Research: Field Relations and Techniques*. Ed. by Richard N. Adams and Jack J. Preiss. Homewood, Ill.: Dorsey Press, 1960.

HAAS, J. EUGENE. *Role Conception and Group Consensus*. Columbus, Ohio: Bureau of Business Research, Ohio State University, 1964.

———. "Role, Position, and Social Organization: A Conceptual Formulation." *Midwest Sociologist*, 19 (December 1956), 33–37.

———, and THOMAS E. DRABEK, "Community Disaster and System Stress: A Sociological Perspective." Pp. 264–86 in *Social and Psychological Factors in Stress*. Ed. by Joseph E. McGrath. New York: Holt, Rinehart & Winston, Inc., 1970.

———, RICHARD H. HALL, and NORMAN J. JOHNSON, "The Size of the Supportive Component in Organizations: A Multi-Organizational Analysis." *Social Forces*, 42 (October 1963), 9–17.

———. "Toward an Empirically Derived Taxonomy of Organizations." Pp. 157–80 in *Studies on Behavior in Organizations*. Ed. by Raymond V. Bowers. Athens, Ga.: University of Georgia Press, 1966.

HACKMAN, J. RICHARD, and NEIL VIDMAR. "Effects of Size and Task Type on Group Performance and Member Reactions." *Sociometry*, 33 (March 1970), 37–54.

HAGE, JERALD, and MICHAEL AIKEN. "Routine Technology, Social Structure and Organizational Goals." *Administrative Science Quarterly*, 14 (September 1969), 366–76.

———. *Social Change in Complex Organizations*. New York: Random House, Inc., 1970.

HALL, A. D., and R. E. FAGEN. "Definition of System." Pp. 81–92 in *Modern Systems Research for the Behavioral Scientist*. Ed. by Walter Buckley. Chicago: Aldine Publishing Company, 1968.

HALL, RICHARD H. "The Concept of Bureaucracy: An Empirical Assessment." *American Journal of Sociology*, 69 (July 1963), 32–40.

————. *Organizations: Structure and Process.* Englewood Cliffs, N.J.: Prentice-Hall, Inc., 1972.

————, J. EUGENE HAAS, and NORMAN J. JOHNSON. "An Examination of the Blau-Scott and Etzioni Typologies." *Administrative Science Quarterly,* **12** (June 1967), 118–39.

———— "Organizational Size, Complexity, and Formalization." *American Sociological Review,* **32** (December 1967), 903–12.

HAMMOND, PETER B., et al. "On the Study of Administration." Pp. 3–15 in *Comparative Studies in Administration.* Ed. by James D. Thompson et al. Pittsburgh, Pa.: University of Pittsburgh Press, 1959.

HAMMOND PHILLIP E. (ed.). *Sociologists at Work.* New York: Basic Books, Inc., 1964.

HARE, A. PAUL. *Handbook of Small Group Research.* New York: The Free Press, 1962.

————, and ROBERT F. BALES. "Seating Position and Small Group Interaction." *Sociometry,* **26** (December 1963), 480–86.

HARVEY, EDWARD. "Technology and the Structure of Organizations." *American Sociological Review,* **33** (April 1968), 247–59.

HELD, VIRGINIA. "PPBS Comes to Washington." *The Public Interest,* **4** (Summer, 1966), 102–15.

HENDERSHOTT, GERRY E., and THOMAS F. JAMES. "Size and Growth as Determinants of Administrative Production Ratios in Organizations," *American Sociological Review,* **37** (April 1972), 149–53.

HENDERSON, LAWRENCE J., T. N. WHITEHEAD, and ELTON MAYO. "The Effects of Social Environment." Pp. 144–58 in *Papers on the Science of Administration.* Ed. by Luther Gulick and Lyndall F. Urwick. New York: Institute of Public Administration, Columbia University, 1937.

HICKSON, DAVID J., DEREK S. PUGH, and DIANA C. PHEYSEY. "Operations Technology and Organization Structure: An Empirical Reappraisal." *Administrative Science Quarterly,* **14** (September 1969), 378–97.

HILLS, R. JEAN. *Toward a Science of Organization.* Eugene, Oregon: Center for the Advanced Study of Educational Administration, 1968.

HITCH, CHARLES J. *Decision-Making for Defense.* Berkeley and Los Angeles: University of California Press, 1965.

HOFSTEDE, G. H. *The Game of Budget Control.* Assen, The Netherlands: Van Gorcum and Co., 1967.

HOLDAWAY, EDWARD A., and THOMAS A. BLOWERS. "Administrative Ratios and Organizational Size: A Longitudinal Examination." *American Sociological Review,* **36** (April 1971), 278–86.

HOLT, ROBERT T., and JOHN E. TURNER. "The Methodology of Comparative Research." Pp. 1–20 in *The Methodology of Comparative Research.* Ed. by Robert T. Holt and John E. Turner. New York: The Free Press, 1970.

HOMANS, GEORGE C. "Bringing Men Back In." *American Sociological Review,* **29** (December 1964), 809–18.

————. *The Human Group.* New York: Harcourt Brace Jovanovich, Inc., 1950.

————. *The Nature of Social Science.* New York: Harcourt Brace Jovanovich, Inc., 1967.

————. "Social Behavior as Exchange." *American Journal of Sociology,* **62** (May 1958), 597–606.

————. *Social Behavior: Its Elementary Forms.* New York: Harcourt Brace Jovanovich, Inc., 1961.

————. "The Western Electric Researches." Pp. 210–41 in *Human Factors in Management.* Ed. by Schuyler Dean Hoslett. New York: Harper & Row, Publishers, 1951.

HOOK, SIDNEY (ed.). *Determinism and Freedom in the Age of Modern Science.* New York: Collier, 1961.

HOPKINS, TERRENCE K. "Bureaucratic Authority: The Convergence of Weber and Barnard." Pp. 82–98 in *Complex Organizations: A Sociological Reader.* Ed. by Amitai Etzioni. New York: Holt, Rinehart & Winston, Inc., 1961.

HORSFALL, ALEXANDER B., and CONRAD M. ARENSBERG. "Teamwork and Productivity in a Shoe Factory." *Human Organization,* 8 (Winter, 1949), 13–25.

JACOBSON, EUGENE, W. W. CHARTER, JR., and S. LIEBERMAN. "The Use of the Role Concept in the Study of Complex Organizations." *Journal of Social Issues,* 7 (1951), 18–27.

JANOWITZ, MORRIS. *Sociology and the Military Establishment.* New York: Russell Sage Foundation, 1959.

JULIAN, JOSEPH. "Compliance Patterns and Communication Blocks in Complex Organizations." *American Sociological Review,* 31 (June 1966), 382–89.

KAHN, ROBERT L. "Field Studies of Power in Organizations." Pp. 52–66 in *Power and Conflict in Organizations.* Ed. by Robert L. Kahn and Elise Boulding. New York: Basic Books, Inc., 1964.

————, et al. *Organizational Stress: Studies in Role Conflict and Ambiguity.* New York: John Wiley & Sons, Inc., 1964.

KAKAR, SUDHIR. *Frederick Taylor: A Study in Personality and Innovation.* Cambridge, Mass.: M.I.T. Press, 1970.

KAPLAN, ABRAHAM. *The Conduct of Inquiry: Methodology for Behavioral Sciences.* San Francisco: Chandler Publishing Company, 1964.

KATZ, DANIEL, and ROBERT L. KAHN. *The Social Psychology of Organizations.* New York: John Wiley & Sons, Inc., 1966.

KELMAN, HERMAN. "Human Use of Human Subjects: The Problem of Deception in Social Psychological Experiments." *Psychological Bulletin,* 67 (January 1967), 1–11.

KEMENY, JOHN G., et al. *Introduction to Finite Mathematics.* Englewood Cliffs, N.J.: Prentice-Hall, Inc., 1956.

KERLINGER, FRED N. *Foundations of Behavioral Research.* New York: Holt, Rinehart & Winston, Inc., 1964.

KILLIAN, LEWIS M. "The Significance of Multiple Group Membership in Disaster." *American Journal of Sociology,* 57 (January 1952), 309–14.

KNUDSEN, DEAN D., and TED R. VAUGHN. "Quality in Graduate Education: A Reevaluation of the Rankings of Sociology Departments in the Cartter Report." *The American Sociologist,* 4 (February 1969), 12–19.

KRUPP, SHERMAN. *Pattern in Organizational Analysis.* New York: Holt, Rinehart & Winston, Inc., 1961.

KUHN, THOMAS. *The Structure of Scientific Revolutions*. Chicago: The University of Chicago Press, 1962.

LANDSBERGER, HENRY A. *Hawthorne Revisited*. Ithaca, N.Y.: Cornell Universtiy Press, 1958.

LANGWORTHY, RUSSELL L. "Process." Pp. 538–40 in *A Dictionary of the Social Sciences*. Ed. by Julius Gould and William Kolb. New York: The Free Press, 1964.

LAWRENCE, PAUL R., and JAY W. LORSCH. *Organization and Environment*. Homewood, Ill.: Richard D. Irwin, Inc., 1969.

LAZARSFELD, PAUL F., and HERBERT MENZEL. "On the Relation Between Individual and Collective Properties." Pp. 499–516 in *A Sociological Reader on Complex Organizations*. Ed. by Amitai Etzioni. New York: Holt, Rinehart & Winston, Inc., 1969.

LEEDS, RUTH. "The Absorption of Protest: A Working Paper." Pp. 194–209 in *The Planning of Change*. Warren G. Bennis, Kenneth D. Benne, and Robert Chin. 2nd ed. New York: Holt, Rinehart & Winston, Inc., 1969.

LELLA, JOSEPH W. Review of *The Social Psychology of Organizations*. *American Journal of Sociology*, **72** (May 1967), 677.

LENSKI, GERHARD. *Human Societies*. New York: McGraw-Hill Book Company, 1970.

———. *Power and Privilege*. New York: McGraw-Hill Book Company, 1966.

LERNER, MAX. "Social Process." Pp. 148–51 in *Encyclopedia of the Social Sciences*. Vol. 14. Ed. by Edwin Seligman and Alvin Johnson. New York: The Macmillan Company, 1934.

LEVIN, RICHARD I., and CHARLES A. KIRKPATRICK. *Planning and Control with PERT/CPM*. New York: McGraw-Hill Book Company, 1966.

LEVINE, SOL, and PAUL E. WHITE. "Exchange as a Conceptual Framework for the Study of Interorganizational Relationships." *Administrative Science Quarterly*, **5** (March 1961), 583–601.

LIEBOW, ELLIOT. *Talley's Corner*. Boston: Little, Brown and Company, 1967.

LIKERT, RENSIS. *The Human Organization*. New York: McGraw-Hill Book Company, 1967.

———. *New Patterns of Management*. New York: McGraw-Hill Book Company, 1961.

LINDESMITH, ALFRED R., and ANSELM L. STRAUSS. *Social Psychology*. 3rd ed., New York: Holt, Rinehart & Winston, Inc., 1968.

LIPSET, SEYMOUR M., et al. *Union Democracy*. New York: The Free Press, 1956.

LITTLE, RODGER W. "Buddy Relations and Combat Performance." Pp. 195–219 in *The New Military*. Ed. by Morris Janowitz. New York: Russell Sage Foundation, 1964.

LITTRELL, BOYD. "Complex Organizations: Models and Reality." *The Rocky Mountain Social Science Journal*, **6** (October 1969), 155–62.

LITWAK, EUGENE. "Models of Bureaucracy Which Permit Conflict." *American Journal of Sociology*, **67** (September 1961), 177–84.

LOMBARD, GEORGE F. *Behavior in a Selling Group.* Boston: Harvard Business School, 1955.

McGRATH, JOSEPH E., and IRWIN ALTMAN. *Small Group Research: A Synthesis and Critique of the Field.* New York: Holt, Rinehart & Winston, Inc., 1966.

McGREGOR, CAROLINE, and WARREN G. BENNIS (eds.). *The Professional Manager.* New York: McGraw-Hill Book Company, 1967.

McGREGOR, DOUGLAS. *The Human Side of Enterprise.* New York: McGraw-Hill Book Company, 1960.

MACK, RAYMOND W., and RICHARD C. SNYDER. "The Analysis of Social Conflict—Toward an Overview and Synthesis." *Journal of Conflict Resolution,* 1 (June 1957), 212–48.

McNEIL, KENNETH, and JAMES D. THOMPSON. "The Regeneration of Social Organizations." *American Sociological Review,* 36 (August 1971), 624–37.

MADGE, JOHN. *The Origins of Scientific Sociology.* New York: The Free Press, 1962.

MANIS, JEROME G., and BERNARD N. MELTZER. *Symbolic Interaction: A Reader in Social Psychology.* Boston: Allyn & Bacon, Inc. 1967.

MARCH, JAMES G., (ed.). *Handbook of Organizations.* Chicago: Rand McNally & Co., 1965.

———, and HERBERT A. SIMON. *Organizations.* New York: John Wiley & Sons, Inc., 1958.

MARSH, ROBERT M. *Comparative Sociology.* New York: Harcourt Brace Jovanovich, Inc., 1967.

MARTINDALE, DON. *The Nature and Types of Sociological Theory.* Cambridge, Mass.: Riverside Press, 1960.

MARWELL, GERALD, and JERALD HAGE. "The Organization of Role-Relationships: A Systematic Description." *American Sociological Rveiew,* 35 (October 1970), 884–98.

MASLOW, ABRAHAM H. *Motivation and Personality.* New York: Harper & Row, Publishers, 1954.

MATZA, DAVID. *Delinquency and Drift,* New York: John Wiley & Sons, Inc., 1964.

MAYER, KURT, and SIDNEY GOLDSTEIN. *The First Two Years: Problems of Firm Growth and Survival.* Washington, D.C.: Small Business Administration, 1961.

MAYO, ELTON. *The Human Problems of an Industrial Civilization.* New York: The Macmillan Company, 1933.

MECHANIC, DAVID. "Some Considerations in the Methodology of Organizational Studies." Pp. 139–82 in *The Social Science of Organizations: Four Perspectives.* Ed. by Harold J. Leavitt. Englewood Cliffs, N.J.: Prentice-Hall, Inc., 1963.

MEEHAN, EUGENE J. *Explanation in Social Science: A System Paradigm.* Homewood, Ill.: Dorsey Press, 1968.

MEIER, RICHARD L. "Information Input Overload: Features of Growth in

Communications-Oriented Industries." Pp. 233–73 in *Mathematical Explorations in Behavioral Sciences*. Ed. by Fred Massarik and Philborn Ratoosh. Homewood, Ill.: Richard D. Irwin, Inc. and Dorsey Press, 1965.

MERTON, ROBERT K. "The Role-Set: Problems in Sociological Theory." *British Journal of Sociology*, 8 (June 1957), 106–20.

———. *Social Theory and Social Structure*, Rev. ed. New York: The Free Press, 1957.

MESSINGER, SHELDON L. "Organizational Transformation: A Case Study of a Declining Social Movement." *American Sociological Review*, 20 (February 1955), 3–10.

MICHELS, ROBERT. *Political Parties*. Trans. Eden Paul and Cedar Paul. New York: The Free Press, 1949. Original publication, 1915.

MILES, EDWARD. "The Logistics of Interviewing in International Organizations." *International Organization*, 24 (Spring, 1970), 361–70.

MILLER, DAVID W., and MARTIN K. STARR. *The Structure of Human Decisions*. Englewood Cliffs, N.J.: Prentice-Hall, Inc., 1967.

MILLER, DELBERT C. *Handbook of Research Design and Social Measurement*. New York: David McKay Co., Inc., 1964.

———, and WILLIAM H. FORM. *Industrial Sociology*. New York: Harper & Row, Publishers, 1951.

MILLER, JAMES G. "Living Systems: Basic Concepts." *Behavioral Science*, 10 (July 1965), 193–237.

———. "Toward a General Theory for the Behavioral Sciences." *American Psychologist*, 10 (September 1955), 513–31.

MILLS, C. WRIGHT. *The Sociological Imagination*. New York: Oxford University Press, 1959.

MILLS, THEODORE M. *Group Transformation*. Englewood Cliffs, N.J.: Prentice-Hall, Inc., 1964.

———. *The Sociology of Small Groups*. Englewood Cliffs, N.J.: Prentice-Hall, Inc., 1967.

MOORE, HARRY E. . . . *And the Wind Blew*. Austin, Texas: The Hogg Foundation for Mental Health, 1964.

MOORE, WILBERT E. *The Conduct of the Corporation*. New York: Random House, Inc., 1962.

———. *Social Change*. Englewood Cliffs, N.J.: Prentice-Hall, Inc., 1963.

MORENO, JACOB L. *Who Shall Survive?* Boston, Mass.: Beacon Press, 1953.

MORRIS, RICHARD T. "A Typology of Norms." *American Sociological Review*, 21 (October 1956), 610–13.

MOTT, BASIL J. F. "Coordination and Inter-Organizational Relations in Health." Pp. 55–69 in *Inter-Organizational Research in Health: Conference Proceedings*. Ed. by Paul E. White and George J. Vlasak. Baltimore, Md.: The Johns Hopkins University, Department of Behavioral Sciences, School of Hygiene and Public Health, 1970.

MURPHY, ROBERT F., and JULIAN H. STEWARD. "Tappers and Trappers: Parallel Process in Acculturation." *Economic Development and Cultural Change*, 4 (July 1956), 335–55.

NEWCOMB, THEODORE M. *The Acquaintance Process*. New York: Holt, Rinehart & Winston, Inc., 1961.

OBERSCHALL, ANTHONY. *Empirical Social Research in Germany, 1848-1914.* Paris: Monton and Company, 1965.

OLSEN, MARVIN E. *The Process of Social Organization.* New York: Holt, Rinehart & Winston, Inc., 1968.

OPPENHEIM, A. N. *Questionnaire Design and Attitude Measurement.* New York: Basic Books, Inc., 1966.

PALISI, BARTOLOMEO J. "Some Suggestions About the Transitory–Permanence Dimension of Organizations." *The British Journal of Sociology,* **21** (June 1970), 200–206.

PARKINSON, C. NORTHCOTE. *Parkinson's Law.* Boston, Mass.: Houghton Mifflin Company, 1957.

PARSONS, TALCOTT. "An Outline of the Social System." Pp. 30–76 in *Theories of Society.* Ed. by Talcott Parsons et al. New York: The Free Press, 1961.

———. *The Social System.* New York: The Free Press, 1951.

———. "Suggestions for a Sociological Approach to Theory of Organizations." *Administrative Science Quarterly,* **1** (June 1956), 63–85.

PERLSTADT, HARRY. "Comments on 'Power, Visibility and Conformity in Formal Organizations,'" *American Sociological Review,* **34** (December 1969), 937–41.

———. "Goal Implementation and Outcome in Medical Schools," *American Sociological Review,* **37** (February 1972), 73–82.

PERROW, CHARLES. "The Analysis of Goals in Complex Organizations." *American Sociological Review,* **26** (December 1961), 854–66.

———. *Complex Organizations: A Critical Essay.* New York: Scott, Foresman & Company, 1972.

———. "A Framework for the Comparative Analysis of Organizations." *American Sociological Review,* **32** (April 1967), 194–208.

———. "Hospitals: Technology, Structure, and Goals." Pp. 910–71 in *Handbook of Organizations.* Ed. by James G. March. Chicago: Rand McNally & Co., 1965.

———. *Organizational Analysis: A Sociological View.* Belmont, California: Brooks/Cole Publishing Company, 1970.

———. "Organizational Goals," pp. 305–311 in *International Encyclopedia of the Social Sciences, Vol. 11.* Ed. by David L. Sills. New York: The Macmillan Company and The Free Press, 1968.

———. "Organizational Prestige: Some Functions and Dysfunctions." *American Journal of Sociology,* **66** (January 1961), 335–41.

PERRUCCI, ROBERT, and MARC PILISUK. "Leaders and Ruling Elites: The Interorganizational Bases of Community Power." *American Sociological Review,* **35** (December 1970), 1040–1057.

PREISS, JACK J., and HOWARD EHRLICH. *An Examination of Role Theory: The Case of the State Police.* Lincoln, Nebr.: University of Nebraska Press, 1966.

PRESTHUS, ROBERT. *The Organizational Society.* New York: Vintage Books, 1962.

PRICE, JAMES L. *Annotated Bibliography of Federal Government Publications Presenting Data About Organizations.* Iowa City, Iowa: Center for

Labor and Management, College of Business Administration, University of Iowa, 1967.

————. "Continuity in Social Research: TVA and the Grass Roots." *Pacific Sociological Review*, **1** (Fall, 1958), 63–68.

————. "Design of Proof in Organizational Research." *Administrative Science Quarterly*, **13** (June 1968), 121–34.

————. *Handbook of Organizational Measurement*. Lexington, Mass.: D. C. Heath & Company, 1972.

————. *Organizational Effectiveness: An Inventory of Propositions*. Homewood, Ill.: Richard D. Irwin, Inc., 1968.

————. "The Study of Organizational Effectiveness." *The Sociological Quarterly*, **13** (Winter 1972), 3–15.

PUGH, DEREK S., DAVID J. HICKSON, and C. ROBIN HININGS. "An Empirical Taxonomy of Structures of Work Organizations." *Administrative Science Quarterly*, **14** (March 1969), 115–25.

RAZAK, W. NEVELL. "Razak on Homans." *American Sociological Review*, **31** (August 1966), 542–44.

REYNOLDS, PAUL DAVIDSON. *A Primer in Theory Construction*. Indianapolis and New York: The Bobbs-Merrill Co., Inc., 1971.

RIECKEN, HENRY W., and GEORGE C. HOMANS. "Psychological Aspects of Social Structure." Pp. 786–832 in *Handbook of Social Psychology*. Ed. by Gardner Lindzey. Cambridge, Mass.: Addison-Wesley Publishing Co. Inc., 1954.

RILEY, MATILDA WHITE. *Sociological Research*. New York: Harcourt Brace Jovanovich, Inc., 1963.

ROBINSON, JAMES A. "The Concept of Crisis in Decision-Making." *Series Studies in Social and Economic Sciences, Symposia Studies No. 11*. Washington, D.C.: The National Institute of Social and Behavioral Sciences (June 1962).

ROBY, THORNTON B. "Computer Simulation Models for Organization Theory." Pp. 171–211 in *Methods of Organizational Research*. Ed. by Victor H. Vroom, Pittsburgh, Pa.: University of Pittsburgh Press, 1967.

ROE, BETTY B., and JAMES R. WOOD. "Adaptive Innovation and Organizational Security in Solidary Organizations." N.d., mimeo.

ROETHLISBERGER, FRITZ J., and WILLIAM J. DICKSON. *Management and the Worker*. Cambridge, Mass.: Harvard University Press, 1939.

ROGERS, CARL R. *Client-Centered Therapy*. Boston: Houghton Mifflin Company, 1951.

————. *On Becoming a Person*. Boston: Houghton Mifflin Company, 1961.

————. "Toward a Theory of Creativity." Pp. 63–72 in *A Source Book for Creative Thinking*. Ed. by Sidney J. Parnes and Harold F. Harding. New York: Charles Scribner's Sons, 1962.

ROSE, ARNOLD. *Human Behavior and Social Processes*. Boston: Houghton Mifflin Company, 1962.

————. "Varieties of Sociological Imagination." *American Sociological Review*, **34** (October 1969), 623–30.

ROSS, H. LAURENCE, and DONALD T. CAMPBELL. "The Connecticut Crackdown on Speeding: Time Series Data in Quasi-Experimental Analysis." *Law and Society Review*, **3** (August 1968), 33–53.

ROTH, GUENTHER, and CLAUS WITTICH (eds.). *Economy and Society.* Trans. by Ephraim Fishchoff et al. Totowa, N.J.: The Bedminster Press, Inc., 1968.

RUEBHAUSEN, OSCAR M., and ORVILLE G. BRIM. "Privacy and Behavioral Research." *American Psychologist,* **21** (May 1966), 423–37.

RUFFER, FREDERICK G., (ed.). *Encyclopedia of Associations.* Detroit: Gale Research, 1964.

SCHEIN, EDGAR H. *Organizational Psychology.* Englewood Cliffs, N.J.: Prentice-Hall, Inc., 1965.

SCOTT, W. RICHARD. "Field Methods in the Study of Organizations." Pp. 261–304 in *Handbook of Organizations.* Ed. by James G. March. Chicago: Rand McNally & Co., 1965.

——. *Social Processes and Social Structure.* New York: Holt, Rinehart & Winston, Inc., 1970.

——. "Theory of Organizations." Pp. 485–520 in *Handbook of Modern Sociology.* Ed. by Robert E. L. Faris. Chicago: Rand McNally & Co., 1964.

——, et al. "Organizational Evaluation and Authority." Pp. 392–98 in *Social Processes and Social Structures.* W. Richard Scott. New York: Holt, Rinehart & Winston, Inc., 1970.

SCOTT, WILLIAM G. *The Management of Conflict*: *Appeal Systems in Organizations.* Homewood, Ill.: Richard D. Irwin, Inc., 1965.

SELYE, HANS. *The Stresses of Life.* New York: McGraw-Hill Book Company, 1956.

SELZNICK, PHILIP. *Leadership in Administration.* Evanston, Ill.: Row, Peterson and Company, 1957.

——. *The Organizational Weapon*: *A Study of Bolshevik Strategy and Tactics.* New York: McGraw-Hill Book Company, 1952.

——. *TVA and the Grass Roots.* Berkeley and Los Angeles: University of California Press, 1949.

SHAMBLIN, DON H. "Prestige and the Sociology Establishment." *The American Sociologist,* **5** (May 1970), 154–56.

SHAW, MARVIN E., and JACK M. WRIGHT. *Scales for the Measurement of Attitudes.* New York: McGraw-Hill Book Company, 1967.

SHERIF, MUZAFER, and CAROLYN W. SHERIF. *Reference Groups: Exploration into Conformity and Deviation of Adolescents.* New York: Harper & Row, Publishers, 1964.

SHILLINGLAW, GORDON. "Divisional Performance Review: An Extension of Budgetary Control." Pp. 149–63 in *Management Controls.* Ed. by Charles P. Bonini et al. New York: McGraw-Hill Book Company, 1964.

SIMMEL, GEORG. *Conflict.* Trans. by Kurt H. Wolff. New York: The Free Press, 1955.

SIMON, HERBERT A. *Administrative Behavior.* 2nd ed. New York: The Macmillan Company, 1957.

——. "On the Concept of Organizational Goal." *Administrative Science Quarterly,* **9** (June 1964), 1–22.

SIMPSON, RICHARD L. "Vertical and Horizontal Communication in Formal Organizations." *Administrative Science Quarterly,* **4** (September 1959), 188–96.

SKINNER, B. F. "A Case History in Scientific Method." *The American Psychologist*, 11 (May 1956), 221–33.

SORENSEN, JAMES E. "Professional and Bureaucratic Organization in the Public Accounting Firm." *The Accounting Review*, 42 (July 1967), 553–65.

———. "Professional and Organizational Profiles of the Migrating and Non-Migrating Large Public Accounting Firm CPA." *Decision Sciences*, 1 (July–October 1970), 489–512.

STARBUCK, WILLIAM H. "Organizational Growth and Development." Pp. 451–533 in *Handbook of Organizations*. Ed. by James G. March. Chicago: Rand McNally & Co., 1965.

———. "Some Comments, Observations and Objections Stimulated by 'Design of Proof in Organizational Research,'" *Administrative Science Quarterly*, 13 (June 1968), 135–61.

STEDRY, ANDREW C. *Budgetary Control: A Behavioral Approach.* Publication No. 43 of the School of Industrial Management, Cambridge, Mass.: M.I.T., 1964.

STEWARD, JULIAN H. *Theory of Culture Change.* Urbana, Ill.: University of Illinois Press, 1955.

STIEGLITZ, HAROLD. "Optimizing Span of Control." *Management Record*, 24 (September 1962), 25–29.

STINCHCOMBE, ARTHUR L. *Constructing Social Theories.* New York: Harcourt Brace Jovanovich, Inc., 1968.

———. "Social Structure and Organizations." Pp. 142–93 in *Handbook of Organizations*. Ed. by James G. March. Chicago: Rand McNally & Co., 1965.

STOGDILL, RALPH M. *Individual Behavior and Group Achievement.* New York: Oxford University Press, 1959.

STRAUSS, ANSELM, and LEONARD SCHATZMAN. "Cross-class Interviewing: An Analysis of Interaction and Communicative Styles." Pp. 205–13 in *Human Organization Research: Field Relations and Techniques*. Ed. by Richard N. Adams and Jack J. Preiss. Homewood, Ill.: Dorsey Press, 1960.

STRODTBECK, FRED L., and L. HARMON HOOK. "The Social Dimensions of a Twelve-Man Jury Table." *Sociometry*, 24 (December 1961), 397–415.

SWANSON, GUY E. "On Explanations of Social Interaction." *Sociometry*, 28 (June 1965), 101–23.

SYKES, GRESHAM M. "The Corruption of Authority and Rehabilitation." *Social Forces*, 34 (March 1956), 257–62.

———. *The Society of Captives.* Princeton, N.J.: Princeton University Press, 1958.

TANNENBAUM, ARNOLD S. *Control in Organizations.* New York: McGraw-Hill Book Company, 1968.

TAUB, RICHARD P. *Bureaucrats Under Stress.* Berkeley and Los Angeles: University of California Press, 1969.

TAUSKY, CURT. "On Organizational Alienation." *American Sociological Review*, 32 (February 1967), 118.

————. *Work Organizations: Major Theoretical Perspectives.* Itasca, Ill.: F. E. Peacock Publishers, Inc., 1970.

TAYLOR, FREDERICK WINSLOW. *Scientific Management.* New York: Harper & Row, Publishers, 1947.

TAYLOR, JAMES B., LOUIS A. ZURCHER, and WILLIAM H. KEY. *Tornado.* Seattle, Wash.: University of Washington Press, 1970.

TERRIEN, FREDERIC W., and DONALD L. MILLS. "The Effect of Changing Size upon the Internal Structure of Organizations." *American Sociological Review,* **20** (February 1955), 11–13.

THOMAS, W. I., and FLORIAN ZNANIECKI. *The Polish Peasant in Europe and America.* Chicago: University of Chicago Press, 1918.

THOMPSON, JAMES D. "Organizations and Output Transactions." *American Journal of Sociology,* **68** (November 1962), 309–24.

————. *Organizations in Action.* New York: McGraw-Hill Book Company, 1967.

————, and ROBERT W. HAWKES. "Disaster, Community Organization and Administrative Process." Pp. 268–300 in *Man and Society in Disaster.* Ed. by George W. Baker and Dwight Chapman. New York: Basic Books, Inc., 1962.

THOMPSON, VICTOR A. "How Scientific Management Thwarts Innovation." Pp. 121–33 in *American Bureaucracy.* Ed. by Warren G. Bennis. New York: Aldine Publishing Co., 1970.

————. *Modern Organization.* New York: Alfred A. Knopf, Inc., 1961.

TURK, HERMAN. "Interorganizational Networks in Urban Society: Initial Perspectives and Comparative Research." *American Sociological Review,* **35** (February 1970), 1–19.

UDY, STANLEY H., JR. "The Comparative Analysis of Organizations." Pp. 678–709 in *Handbook of Organizations.* Ed. by James G. March. Chicago: Rand McNally & Co., 1965.

————. "Cross-Cultural Analysis: A Case Study." Pp. 161–83 in *Sociologists at Work.* Ed. by Phillip Hammond. New York: Basic Books, Inc., 1964.

————. *Organization of Work: A Comparative Analysis of Production Among Non-industrial Peoples.* New Haven, Conn.: Human Relations Area Files Press, 1959.

VAN RIPER, PAUL P. "Organizations: Basic Issues and a Proposed Typology." Pp. 1–12 in *Studies on Behavior in Organizations.* Ed. by Raymond V. Bowers. Athens, Ga.: University of Georgia Press, 1966.

VEBLEN, THORSTEIN. *Theory of Business Enterprise.* New York: Charles Scribner's Sons, 1904.

VIDICH, ARTHUR, and JOSEPH BENSMAN. "The Validity of Field Data." Pp. 188–204 in *Human Organization Research: Field Relations and Techniques.* Ed. by Richard N. Adams and Jack J. Preiss. Homewood, Ill.: Dorsey Press, 1960.

VOLD, GEORGE B. *Theoretical Criminology.* New York: Oxford University Press, 1958.

Voss, Harwin L. "Pitfalls in Social Research: A Case Study." *The American Sociologist*, 1 (May 1966), 136–40.

Wager, L. Wesley, and Ernest Palola. "The Miniature Replica Model and Its Use in Laboratory Experiments of Complex Organizations." *Social Forces*, 42 (May 1964), 418–29.

Walker, Charles R., and Robert H. Guest. *The Man on the Assembly Line.* Cambridge, Mass.: Harvard University Press, 1952.

Wamsley, Gary L. *Selective Service and a Changing America.* Columbus, Ohio: The Charles E. Merrill Publishing Company, 1969.

Warren, Donald I. "Power, Visibility, and Conformity in Formal Organizations." *American Sociological Review*, 33 (December 1968), 951–70.

———. "Reply to Perlstadt." *American Sociological Review*, 34 (December 1969), 941–43.

Warren, Roland L. "The Interorganizational Field as a Focus for Investigation." *Administrative Science Quarterly*, 12 (December 1967), 396–419.

Warriner, Charles K. "Groups Are Real: A Reaffirmation." *American Sociological Review*, 21 (October 1956), 549–54.

———. "The Problem of Organizational Purpose." *The Sociological Quarterly*, 6 (Spring, 1965), 139–46.

Webb, Eugene J., et al. *Unobtrusive Measures: Non-Reactive Research in the Social Sciences.* Chicago: Rand McNally & Co., 1966.

Weber, Max. *Basic Concepts in Sociology.* Trans. by H. P. Secher. New York: The Citadel Press, 1962.

———. *The Theory of Social and Economic Organization.* Trans. by Alexander M. Henderson and Talcott Parsons. New York: The Free Press, 1947.

Weick, Karl E. "Laboratory Experimentation with Organizations." Pp. 194–260 in *Handbook of Organizations.* Ed. by James G. March. Chicago: Rand McNally & Co., 1965.

——— (ed.). "Laboratory Studies of Experimental Organizations." *Administrative Science Quarterly*, 14 (June 1969), entire issue.

———. "Organizations in the Laboratory." Pp. 1–49 in *Methods of Organizational Research.* Ed. by Victor H. Vroom. Pittsburgh, Pa.: University of Pittsburgh Press, 1967.

———. *The Social Psychology of Organizing.* Reading, Mass.: Addison-Wesley Publishing Co., Inc., 1969.

White, Harrison. "Management Conflict and Sociometric Structure." *American Journal of Sociology*, 67 (September 1961), 185–99.

Whyte, William F. *Human Relations in the Restaurant Industry.* New York: McGraw-Hill Book Company, 1948.

———. "Interviewing in Field Research." Pp. 352–74 in *Human Organization Research: Field Relations and Techniques.* Ed. by Richard N. Adams and Jack J. Preiss. Homewood, Ill.: Dorsey Press, 1960.

———. *Men at Work.* Homewood, Ill.: Richard D. Irwin, Inc. and Dorsey Press, 1961.

———. *Organizational Behavior: Theory and Application.* Homewood, Ill.: Richard D. Irwin, Inc. and Dorsey Press, 1969.

———. "Parsons' Theory Applied to Organizations." Pp. 250–67 in *The*

Social Theories of Talcott Parsons. Ed. by Max Black. Englewood Cliffs, N.J.: Prentice-Hall, Inc., 1961.

———. "The Social Structure of the Restaurant." *American Journal of Sociology,* **54** (January 1949), 302–10.

———. *Street Corner Society.* Chicago: University of Chicago Press, 1943.

WILLER, DAVID. *Scientific Sociology: Theory and Method.* Englewood Cliffs, N.J.: Prentice-Hall, Inc., 1967.

WILLIAMS, ROBIN, JR. "Some Further Comments on Chronic Controversies." *American Journal of Sociology,* **71** (May 1966), 717–21.

WOLFF, KURT. *The Sociology of* GEORG SIMMEL. New York: The Free Press, 1950.

WOOD, JAMES R. "Authority and Controversial Policy: The Churches and Civil Rights." *American Sociological Review,* **35** (December 1970), 1057–1069.

———. "Unanticipated Consequences of Organizational Coalitions: Ecumenical Cooperation and Civil Rights Policy." *Social Forces,* **50** (June 1972), 512–21.

WOODWARD, JOAN, (ed.). *Industrial Organizations: Behavior and Control.* London: Oxford University Press, 1970.

———. *Industrial Organization: Theory and Practice.* London: Oxford University Press, 1965.

YUCHTMAN, EPHRAIM, and STANLEY E. SEASHORE. "A System Resource Approach to Organizational Effectiveness." *American Sociological Review,* **32** (December 1967), 891–903.

YUTZY, DANIEL. *Authority, Jurisdiction and Technical Competence: Interorganizational Relationships at Great Falls, Montana, During the Flood of June 8–10, 1964.* Columbus, Ohio: Disaster Research Center, Ohio State University, 1964.

———. *Community Priorities in the Anchorage Alaska Earthquake, 1964.* Columbus, Ohio: Disaster Research Center, Ohio State University, 1969.

———, and J. Eugene Haas. "Chronology of Events in Anchorage Following the Earthquake." Pp. 403–24 in National Academy of Sciences, Committee on the Alaska Earthquake. *The Great Alaska Earthquake of 1964: Human Ecology.* Vol. 7. Washington, D.C.: National Academy of Sciences and National Research Council, 1970.

ZALD, MAYER N. "Comparative Analysis and Measurement of Organizational Goals: The Case of Correctional Institutions for Delinquents." *The Sociological Quarterly,* **4** (Spring, 1963), 206–30.

———. *Organizational Change: The Political Economy of the YMCA.* Chicago: University of Chicago Press, 1970.

———, and ROBERTA ASH. "Social Movements of Organizations: Growth, Decay, and Change." *Social Forces,* **44** (March 1966), 327–39.

ZELDITCH, MORRIS, JR. "Can You Really Study an Army in the Laboratory?" Pp. 528–39 in *A Sociological Reader on Complex Organizations.* Ed. by Amitai Etzioni. New York: Holt, Rinehart & Winston, Inc., 1969.

———, and WILLIAM M. EVAN. "Simulated Bureaucracies: A Methodological Analysis." Pp. 48–60 in *Simulation in Social Science: Readings.*

Ed. by Harold Guetzkow. Englewood Cliffs, N.J.: Prentice-Hall, Inc., 1962.

ZETTERBERG, HANS L. *On Theory and Verification in Sociology.* 3rd ed. Totowa, N.J.: The Bedminster Press, Inc., 1965.

ZWERMAN, WILLIAM L. *New Perspectives on Organization Theory.* Westport, Conn.: Greenwood Press, Inc., 1970.

AUTHOR INDEX

Corwin, Ronald G., 40, 55–57, 59, 269, 277, 283
Coser, Lewis A., 54–59, 272, 282
Coser, Rose L., 144
Craig, John G., 210
Crozier, Michel, 85, 87–88, 91, 178, 181, 293, 296–97, 299–300
Curry, Timothy J., 161
Cyert, Richard M., 357–58

Dahrendorf, Ralf, 55–56, 58
Dalton, Melville, 139
David, James W., 208
Davis, Kingsley, 190
Denzin, Norman K., 338
Dewey, John, 102
Dickson, William J., 42, 110
Dill, William R., 100–101
Dolbeare, Kenneth M., 208
Drabek, Thomas E., 6, 8, 116, 210, 237, 245, 268, 286, 326–28, 342, 354–56, 361
Dubin, Robert, 139, 312
Duncombe, Margaret, 108
Durkheim, Emile, 8

Ehrlich, Howard, 110, 239–40
Emerson, Richard M., 161, 193
Emery, F. E., 207
Etzioni, Amitai, 9, 13, 30, 48, 108, 132, 144, 183, 188, 308, 317, 327, 364–66
Evan, William M., 208, 329, 341, 351

Fagen, R. E., 89
Faris, Robert E. L., 2
Form, William H., 43
Forrester, Jay W., 357–58
Freund, Julian, 26
Frey, Frederick W., 330, 334
Fritz, Charles E., 336
Fullan, Michael, 73

Gans, Herbert, 305
Gantt, H. L., 33–34
Gardner, John W., 121, 275, 290, 295

Geer, Blanche, 339
Georgopoulos, Basil S., 322–24
Gerard, Ralph, 84
Gerth, Hans, 25
Gilmartin, Brian G., 301
Glanzer, Murray, 102
Glaser, Barney G., 304, 372
Glaser, Robert, 102
Goffman, Erving, 5, 6, 110, 161, 197
Gold, David, 322
Goldstein, Sidney, 214
Goode, William J., 242
Goodman, Paul, 40
Gould, Julius, 98
Gouldner, Alvin W., 24, 27, 50, 63, 141, 270
Green, David, Jr., 200
Greer, Scott, 4, 312
Gross, Edward, 29, 210
Gross, Neal, 110–11, 149, 239–41, 321
Grusky, Oscar, 270, 343
Guetzkow, Harold, 10, 75, 102, 208, 351, 357
Gulick, Luther, 32, 36–39, 42
Gullahorn, Jeanne E., 358
Gullahorn, John T., 358
Gusfield, Joseph R., 331, 335
Gynther, Reginald S., 200

Haas, J. Eugene, 6, 10, 111, 148–49, 151, 163, 225, 239, 241, 245–46, 270–71, 321, 326–28, 354–56, 361, 366–70
Haberstroh, Chadwick J., 252, 351
Hackman, J. Richard, 349–50
Hage, Jerald, 82, 180, 268–69, 308, 316, 322
Hahn, Harlan, 216
Haire, Mason, 116
Hall, A. D., 89
Hall, Richard H., 10, 183, 270–71, 295, 321–22, 366–70
Hammond, Peter B., 99
Hammond, Phillip, 305
Harding, Harold F., 43, 296

Hare, A. Paul, 5, 129, 150–51, 167
Harvey, Edward, 80–83
Hawkes, Robert W., 7, 285
Held, Virginia, 32
Hendershott, Gerry E., 272
Henderson, Lawrence J., 12, 42
Hickson, David J., 82, 370–71
Hill, Richard J., 321
Hills, R. Jean, 363
Hinings, C. Robin, 370–71
Hitch, Charles J., 32
Hofstede, G. H., 200
Holdaway, Edward A., 272
Holt, John, 296
Holt, Robert T., 330
Homans, George C., 3, 13, 42, 53, 61–65, 67, 70–72, 109–110, 150, 245
Hook, L. Harmon, 116, 129
Hook, Sidney, 297
Hopkins, Terrence K., 132
Horsfall, Alexander B., 61
Hoslett, Schuyler Dean, 42

Jacobson, Eugene, 148
James, Thomas F., 272
Janowitz, Morris, 172, 243, 295, 344
Johnson, Alvin, 98
Johnson, Norman J., 10, 270–71, 366–70
Julian, Joseph, 366

Kahn, Robert L., 12, 18, 85, 88, 90, 98, 102, 107, 110, 131, 139, 239, 241–42, 277, 321, 334
Kakar, Sudhir, 31
Kaplan, Abraham, 2, 301
Katz, Donald, 12, 18, 85, 88, 90, 98, 102, 139
Kelman, Herman, 329
Kemeny, John G., 115,
Kennedy, John L., 252, 351, 358
Kerlinger, Fred N., 2
Key, William H., 6
Killian, Lewis M., 13, 240
Kirkpatrick, Charles A., 32–34

SUBJECT INDEX

Evaluation of performance
  related to role consensus, 148–50
  related to sociometric preference, 152
Exchange perspective
  critique, 71–72
  general image, 60–70
  illustrative propositions, 70–71
Exchange transactions
  defined, 66
  types of, 66
Experimental designs, 379–80
Explanatory structures, interdependence
    among, 118–19, 170–73
  See also Normative, Interpersonal, and Re-
    source structures
External interpersonal structure, 222–24
External normative structure, 217–20
  dimensions of, 217–18
  official vs. unofficial, 219–20
External performance structure
  constrained by domain, 215–16
  constrained by external interpersonal struc-
    ture, 223–24
  constrained by resource structure, 224–28
  defined, 215
External validity, assessment of, 382

Fallacy of aggregation, 320
Feedback
  problem in field research, 332–33
  system, 87–89
Field research, 330–48
  contrasted to laboratory, 326–29
  cross validation, 345
  design alternatives, 374–82
  feedback as a problem, 332–33
  interviewing, 335–38
  observation, 338–41
  open vs. disguised entrée, 331
  primary source materials, 341–45
  problems of entrée and rapport, 331–33
  questionnaires, 333–35
  sampling, 345–47
Formal organizations, defined, 21–22
Functionalism, 49–53
  critique, 205–207

Gathering, 5–6
General system theory, 83–84
Georgopoulas–Tannenbaum measurement of
    effectiveness, 322–24
Goals. See Organizational goals

Group cohesion, 60
  outgroup conflict, 57
  supervisory style, 44
Group domain, 133–34
  analysis of, 180–81
  dimensions of, 178–82
  See also Domain
Group emergence, 5–6, 68–69
Group norms, 68–69
  official vs. unofficial, 139–40
  sources of, 134–38
  type of social constraint, 44–45
Groups
  analysis of, 123–30
  defined, 8

Hall bureaucracy scale, 321–22
Hawthorne studies, 42–43
Hierarchical system, type of multiorganiza-
    tional system, 232–33
Human relations perspective
  critique, 47–48
  general image, 42–47
  illustrative propositions, 47

Ideal type, defined, 26
Indulgency pattern, 140–41
Interaction process analysis, 155
Interaction systems, basic typology, 5–8
Interdependence
  alteration of, 285–86
  degrees of, 308
Internal validity, assessment of, 380
Interorganizational relations, 227–33
Interpenetration, system, 3
Interpersonal incompatibility, 243–44
Interpersonal relationships
  defined, 128, 156
  degree of balance, 159–61
  dimensions of, 158–59
Interpersonal structure, 114–16
  analysis of, 153–63
  consequences for normative structure, 173
  consequences for resource structure, 172
  consequences of degree of balance, 161–62
  defined, 114, 128, 157
  degree of balance, 159–61
  dimensions of, 115, 158–59
  external, 222–24
Interviewing, 335–38
  difficulties in, 337
  variation in response, 336
  variation in structure, 336–37

Intrusive roles, 134
Iron Law of Oligarchy, 9, 49, 294

Laboratory research, 348–62
  computer simulation, 357–59
  constructing organizations, 351–54
  contrasted to field research, 326–29
  ethical dilemmas, 361–62
  experimental conditions, 327
  external validity, 360–61
  internal validity, 360
  isolated organizational processes, 348–50
  theory construction, 327–28
  using existing organizations, 354–57
Lawrence–Lorsch measurement of organizational performance, 324–26
Lazarsfeld–Menzel typology of variables, 317–19
Legitimacy, 25–26, 143
Likert typology of management systems, 46–47
Linking pin principle, 45–46

Maintenance processes, 101
Management systems, types of, 46–47, 104
Measurement, 316–26
  bureaucracy, 321–22
  effectiveness, 322–24
  general inventories, 321
  organizational performance, 324–26
Mediated system, type of multiorganizational system, 230–31
Members vs. collectives, 318–19
Membership
  criteria for establishment, 14
  definitions of, 13–14
Methodology vs. methods, 301–302
Models, theoretical, 311–16
Multilineal evolution, 74, 86
Multiorganizational systems
  risks and opportunities, 233–36
  types of, 228–33

Natural disaster. See Disaster
Natural system perspective
  critique, 52–53
  general image, 49–52
  illustrative proposition, 52
Negative entropy, 86
Negotiation. See Domain negotiation
Neo-classical theory, 32–34
Nonexperimental designs, 375–77
Normative ambiguity, 242

extent of, 242
Normative boundaries, 20–21
Normative dissensus, 241–42
  extent of, 241
Normative incompatibility, 239–43
Normative inconsistency, 240–41
Normative overload, 242–43, 261–62
  types of, 242–43
Normative structure, 110–14, 131–53
  consequences for interpersonal structure, 172
  consequences for resource structure, 171–72
  defined, 110
  external, 217–20
Norms, 44–45, 63, 68–69, 110–11, 131–53
  affect, 112, 133, 179
  authority, 112, 132–33, 142–43, 179
  defined, 110, 127
  enforcement of, 140–41
  indulgency pattern, 140–41
  norm of reciprocity, 63
  official vs. unofficial, 139–40
  sanctions, 44–45, 133, 179
  sources of, 134–38
  status, 133, 179
  task, 132, 179
  types of, 113, 132–33, 179

Observability, factor in compliance, 144
Observation, used in field research, 338–41
Official external normative structure, 219–20
Official norms, 139
Open-box technique, 311–16
Open-system perspective
  critique, 92–93
  general image, 83–92
  illustrative propositions, 92
Open vs. disguised entrée in field research, 331–32
Opportunism, characteristic of organization–environment relation, 212–13
Organization–environment relations
  degree of activism, 211–12
  degree of opportunism, 212–13
  degree of power, 208–210
  degree of responsiveness, 210–11
  degree of security, 213–14
  patterns of strain, 284–86
  propositions, 214
  See also Organizational environments
Organizational birth, 185
  affected by technology, 75
  response to strain, 289–90